EVOLVING GRASSROOTS DEMOCRACY

By the same Author

* Building Skills and Capability Among Gram Panchayat Presidents: An Experience Report from the Field
* Capacity Building for Local Leaders
* Dynamics of New Panchayatiraj System in India (10 Volumes)
* Emerging Dimensions in Decentralisation
* Ethnic Identity and National Loyalty of Ethnic Group: A Case Study of Tamil Nadu
* Functional Efficiency of Gram Sabha in Tamil Nadu
* Grassroot Democracy in Indian Society
* Handbook for Panchayati Raj Administration (Tamil Nadu)
* New Panchayati Raj in Tamil Nadu (with Act in Original)
* New Panchayati Raj System At Work : An Evaluation
* New Public Mangement: A Case Analysis of District Administration
* Process and Performance of Gram Panchayat Women and Dalit Presidents (With 38 Case Studies of Tamil Nadu)
* Rural Transformation and Peoples Entitlements

About the Author

Prof. Ganapathi Palanithurai, Chairperson, Rajiv Gandhi Chair, Chairperson, The Hunger Project of Tamil Nadu Council, Gandhigram Rural Institute is an academic activist working with the people in rural areas for building the capacity of the leaders and people to reinvent and strength grassroots democracy and to achieve sustainable Rural Development. He is heading the Department of Political Science and Development Administration, in Gandhigram Rural University, Tamil Nadu. His policy advocacy role at the governmental level is increasingly felt at present in all the three levels, namely, sub-regional, regional and national as he does more filed work than theorisation. He has been associating himself with Central Planning Commission, State Planning Commission of Tamil Nadu, State Finance Commission of Tamil Nadu and he carried out several research studies in decentralization for both governments. His activities are supported by Population Foundation of India, the Ford Foundation, UNICEF, Rajiv Gandhi Foundation, CAPART, Ministry of Rural Development and DANIDA (Danish-Indo Development Agency) in specific areas of activities in connection with empowerment of people. He is in the network of the Non-Governmental Organisations for Panchayat activities. He involves himself in capacity building exercise for local body leaders. He has evolved training module and manual for local body leaders. He has to his credit thirty nine books, seventy nine articles in reputed journals, twelve working papers, seven monographs and seven review articles on three major areas, namely, Legislative Behaviour, Ethnicity and Panchayati Raj System. He was a recipient of Fellowship from Sastri Indo-Canadian Institute, New Delhi and World Academy of Art and Science, USA. He has visited the US and Canada, on academic assignments. He was a visiting fellow in the MiGill University, Canada in 1989. He is a life member of Indian Institute of Public Administration, Indian Association of Public Administration, Indian Association of Political Science, Indian Association of American Studies and Indian Association of Canadian Studies. He is a member of the expert committee constituted by the Government of Tamil Nadu, to monitor the training programme for local body leaders.

EVOLVING GRASSROOTS DEMOCRACY

G. PALANITHURAI

CONCEPT PUBLISHING COMPANY, NEW DELHI-110059

Cataloging in Publication Data—DK
Courtesy: D.K. Agencies (P) Ltd. <docinfo@dkagencies.com>

Palanithurai, G. (Ganapathy), 1953-
Evolving grassroots democracy / G. Palanithurai.
p. cm.
Analyses the raminifications and dimensions of decentralization of powers in Tamil Nadu, in the light of the 73rd Constitutional Amendment Act.
Includes bibliographical references (p.)
Includes index.
ISBN 13: 9788181694851
ISBN 10: 8180694852

1. Panchayat—India—Tamil Nadu. 2. Decentralization in government—India—Tamil Nadu. 3. Women in politics—India—Tamil Nadu. I. Title.

DDC 320.809 548 2 22

ISBN-13: 978-81-8169-485-1
ISBN-10: 81-8069-485-2

First Published 2007

Published and Printed by
Ashok Kumar Mittal
Concept Publishing Company
A/15-16, Commercial Block, Mohan Garden
NEW DELHI-110059 (India)

Phones : 25351460, 25351794
Fax : 091-11-25357103
E-mail : publishing@conceptpub.com

To

The Divine Mother

Preface

India is known for many paradoxes and in India Tamil Nadu is known for many paradoxes. Tamil Nadu is known for its struggle for state autonomy. In any book on Centre-State relationship, Tamil Nadu figures maximum in analysis and explanation. It was in the trick of politics for three full decades. Where has it gone now? Nobody knows. But the question now is the autonomy of Panchayats. As Central Government is firm in centralizing powers, the State Government follows the same pattern and behaviour with Panchayat institutions.

A realistic analysis of state-local body relations will reveal the design of the State Government in creating the local body institutions. There is no difference of opinion between the DMK and the AIADMK towards devolving powers to local bodies. These two political parties concur on two tier system. They strongly believe that bureaucracy can deliver better at district level.

For them local bodies are no institutions of governance but they are only implementing agencies. For about a decade is over after the establishment of the New Panchayati Raj System in Tamil Nadu. If an analysis is made on the devolution of powers, there is no difference between day one and to-day. But officials claim that Panchayats are performing well. How without powers, functions, functionaries and finance can the Panchayats perform is a question to be answered.

No doubt the Panchayats are performing very well as Panchayat leaders acquired skill and capacity and assumed responsibilities and carried out activities. Many of the Panchayats have emerged as models in social development activities. They are the pathfinders and models to be emulated by others. The paradox is, despite poor devolution of functions, functionaries and finances, Panchayats are able to achieve results, deliver services and govern the institutions. The Rajiv Gandhi Chair for Panchayati Raj Studies have taken series of steps to strengthen the Panchayati Raj System through its partnership with civil society organization and media. It builds the capacity of the leaders of the grassroots institutions and the media in governance at grassroots.

It is interesting to analyse the evolution of New Panchayati Raj System in Tamil Nadu after the enactment of the 73rd Amendment to the Constitution of India. The Tamil Nadu devolution scenario provides a new hypothesis that lesser the power devolution, higher the efficient governance at grassroots provided the leaders are capacitated and conscientised on governance and social development.

This book brings to the readers the paradoxes from the articles and reports. Many of the articles and reports are drawn from the action projects carried out by the Rajiv Gandhi Chair for Panchayati Raj Studies with the support of various agencies.

The reports and articles are written based on the input given by project staffs and for which I express my deep sense of appreciation to all of them. In our team there are twenty-four staff working on different projects. They are committed staff, working round the clock in the field along with the Panchayat leaders. Panchayat leaders who spare their time for discussion and take initiatives as per our suggestion and for which I owe a great deal to them. I express my thanks to my colleagues who have been with me for the past one decade in Panchayati Raj activities.

Last but not the least my family. My wife Mrs. Mala deserves my appreciation for her dedicated service to me by keeping our family intact and progressing without giving any disturbance to my academic and extension work.

Gandhigram **G. PALANITHURAI**

Contents

CHARTER FOR THE PANCHAYATS

PROLOGUE

- Searching for an institutional frame for a caring, humane and responsive administration at the local level;
- Recognizing the strength and the weakness of the present district administration;
- Noticing that administration was not adequately accountable to those whom it was designed to serve, in spite of the administration and political wings being generally efficient and enlightened;
- Recalling numerous instances and complaints of callous, negligent even cruel responses of the district administration to the individual and/or small group/community causes;
- Finding that the lack of responsiveness of the administration was due to non-accountability;
- Affirming that administration can be made responsive only if it is made representative;
- Rajiv Gandhi conceived of a third tier of representative governance at the district level and below thereby in a basic change in the architecture of Indian polity; and
- Developing aforesaid idea, parliament enacted the Seventy-third and Seventy-fourth Amendments to the Constitution of India with the explicit purpose of transferring power to the people.

ARTICLES

- It is noticed with grave concern that the basic ideology behind the Seventy-third Amendment of making Panchayat institutions of self-governance has been largely ignored in the recent state legislation. It is urged that all sections in such legislation which militate against these overarching objectives should be deleted or appropriately further amended to make panchayats genuine institutions of participatory self-government.

- Panchayats cannot develop as genuine units of self-governance without corresponding and restructuring of the powers and administrative set up of Central and State Governments at least in respect of items included in Eleventh Schedule of the Constitution. Stifling overhang of enormous Central and State administrative structures is a serious impediment to development of autonomous panchayat administrative structure. To ensure this reduction of functions and structural readjustment of Central and State Governments, a National Commission should be constituted.
- There should be a single Ministry of Panchayats and Nagarpalikas.
- The demonstration of our pluralistic society cannot be ensured merely through legislative and administrative actions of the State. These enabling provisions would require massive mobilisational support. NGOs, academic and professional bodies, trade unions, political parties and other groups and individuals should involve themselves in exerting pressure, to restore power to where it belongs.
- In the preparation and implementation of plans for economic development and social justice, NGOs and cooperatives should be functionally associated with panchayats.
- There are numerous Central and State Acts, regulations, manuals, government orders which go against appropriate devolution of powers and functions to panchayats. All these items require to be identified for appropriate remedial, legislative and executive action by the Central and State Governments. Either the Law Commission or any other expert body should immediately be entrusted with this job so that it may make recommendations within six months. The Central and State

Governments should then initiate action on both sets of recommendations, for amending the laws and regulations and restructuring the administrative set up by redeployment/ reduction of excess manpower.

- Elected panchayats should not be subordinate to government officials. Elected representatives should be enable superintendence and control over government officials to be placed under panchayats along with devolution of functions.
- The power of dissolution as well as of accountability of lower level panchayats units must rest with the next higher levels of panchayats and not with government officials so that peer group accountability is established.
- Requirements of financial accountability should be designed and supervised by the Comptroller and Auditor General.
- The artificial divide between development and general administration should be done away with. Since Eleventh Schedule only provides the floor, there is no legal authority to empower panchayats with necessary judicial and police powers to settle petty cases both of civil and criminal nature and to defuse any potential conflict-situation both among individuals and groups.
- The basic principles of allocations of powers and functions should be that what can be done at the lower level must necessarily be done at that level and not on a higher level. Functions and powers should be given by the legislature. There should not be any scope for executive fiat in this respect.
- Inter-Zilla Parishad or Panchayat Council should be constituted in every State with the Chief Minister as the Chairperson, all the Zilla Parishad elected Chiefs, Leader of Opposition and Ministers of concerned Departments as members to discuss and thrash out matters relating to Panchayats in general and Zilla Parishad in particular, and the State Governments in respect of legislative, financial, administrative and other relevant issues.
- Panchayats should not merely be implementing agencies of preconceived schemes passed on to them with the funds as

centrally or state sponsored schemes. To become self-governing institutions there should be true decentralised planning so that district level schemes should be either sponsored by the village or intermediate or district panchayats but not handed over to them from above. Panchayats at three levels should have reasonable percentages of the funds of the State Plan and other financial resources with should be totally united so that they can use these funds on the basis of their own priorities and choices. These together with other sectoral outlays should constitute a district plan budget reflecting the sum total of allocations under the district sector plan. This should be clearly and transparently shown in the State budget to be voted upon by the State Legislature. The District Planning Committee should be headed by the elected Chairperson of the Zilla Parishad.

- Panchayats should be constituted for every part of the country including the areas covered under the Fifth and Sixth Schedules of the Constitution. In these areas the basic principles of the Seventy-third Amendment should be harmonised with local ethos, traditions and institutions so as to have democracy with continuity. The central law contemplated in Article 243M of the Constitution should be enacted early.
- A Constitutional Amendment should be brought for ensuring cooperatives for the successful functioning of the cooperative system is crucial to attainment of the objectives of Panchayati Raj.

EPILOGUE

"*We trust the people. We have faith in the people. It is the people who must determine their own destinies and the destiny of the nation. To the people of India, let us ensure maximum democracy and maximum devolution. Let the people be empowered.*"

— ***Rajiv Gandhi***

Introduction

New Panchayati Raj system in India came into being as an institution of governance for the past twelve years. It is not a concept alone but a constitutional provision which has got its own sanctity as any other provision in the Constitution. In India, this new dispensation has been perceived differently by different individuals, and groups. The new institutions are struggling to emerge as institutions of governance with an objective of achieving economic development and social justice through the planning at micro and multi-levels with the participation of people. As the 73rd and 74th Amendments to the Constitution of India possess rich potentials to alter the power structure and development paradigm at grassroots, barriers and obstacles are created by the forces and class which enjoy power at present. People who are going to be empowered are not aware of the significance of the 73rd Amendment to the Constitution of India. But people those who are going to loose power by this new dispensation are fully aware of the potentials.

Seventy-third and Seventy-fourth Amendments are not instant phenomena. They are the outcome of the conscious exercises done in India and the result of the worldwide movement towards empowering people. Arguments are projected from different quarters that the process of decentralization is moving in a snails' pace. As it is a state subject, the State Governments will decentralize powers at their will and discretion. No doubt, it was a state subject in the Constitution till the enactment of the 73rd Amendment. After passing the 73rd and 74th Constitutional Amendments, the logic of state subject do not hold good as the State Governments have given their concurrence to the proposal of enacting such amendments to the Constitution of India. Having agreed to the new dispensation, any violation in implementing the provisions of the 73rd and 74th

Amendments will be construed as violation of the provisions of the Constitution of India. Thus the argument brought forward by a group as it is a centralized drive to devolve powers to the grassroots institutions without having any demand from the society or people as false and do not stand test of logic. When a survey was undertaken in a massive way in the whole country with different stakeholders on the failure of institutions to deliver services and goods to the people, it was found that the failure is due to the absence of responsive, responsible and representative institutions down below the district. All our failures are attributed towards the absence of the above. There are other problems due to absence of the representative institutions. One such problem is that people are perceived as dole receivers or beneficiaries or petitioners. As a result people are made powerless and voiceless. There is a perceptible gap between the people and the government. All the development activities are supply driven and not demand driven. The expenditure incurred on activities are not based on the needs of the people but on the activities planned by the government officials. People have aspiration, demands and visions but they are not met. To meet the needs and basic demands of the people, governments need not borrow money from the World Bank, but by making a small change in carrying out activities on the supply to carrying out activities on demands many of the problems will be solved. It is nothing but listening to people before doing any activity in the society. All the ills we found out so far in development paradigm is due to the absence of decentralized governance.

Seventy-third Amendment to the Constitution of India was enacted with a set of goals. 73rd Amendment will be translated into action only if there is political will on the part of the State Government. A state conformity act has to confirm the spirit of the 73rd Amendment. The state act has to be translated into action by preparing proper rules, procedures and guidelines through government orders. For proper devolution and its percolation, the mindset of the officials have to be changed. For this purpose a constant drive has to come from the above. In the same way, the elected local body leaders have to be sensitized and trained properly to build their skill, capacity and capability to manage the Panchayat institutions. Further the people who are to be empowered to use the potentials of the panchayats and for which media has to be used to create awareness among the people to make use of the Panchayati Raj to achieve development. Moreover support structure has to be created for the women and Dalit Leaders to function independently in Panchayats as leaders.

The above mentioned activities have to be carried out in a movement mode, not in a programme or scheme mode. When all these activities are initiated, they are to be carried out with a deep sense of commitment. In reality very few states have shown interest in Panchayati Raj. But all the states want to have Panchayati Raj to implement their state programmes and schemes. Bureaucracy wants a subordinate local body system as they are the officials of the State Government and hence they want to make the local body leaders as subordinates. Now, a picture has been created that the local body system has been set in motion but how they are positioned is a major question. In order to escape from the Constitution, the State Governments have created a representative local body system. But the new system is not in conformity with the spirit of the 73rd Amendment to the Constitution of India. Tamil Nadu is known for its paradox. 64th Amendment Bill was defeated because of two of the representatives from Tamil Nadu abstained from voting. Had they supported, the story of new Panchayati Raj System would have been a different one. Tamil Nadu Panchayati Act of 1994 is one of the most backward acts in India.

The process of implementing the New Panchayati Raj as indicated the half-heartedness of the State Government. The present Panchayati Raj System in Tamil Nadu is tottering because they are created with severe conditional disabilities. To overcome the barriers the Panchayat leaders have to struggle. Many of the panchayat leaders have been subsumed by the corrupt administrative system. As a result panchayats are struggling to come out from the yoke of bureaucracy. Yet there are a number of Panchayats emerged as powerful models to be emulated by others. Despite all constraints Panchayat have evolved as institutions of governance. To retain the power of the Panchayat, leaders fight against bureaucracy, fight against State Government, and struggle against traditional panchayat.

They go to the court to retain the power of the panchayat. On the one hand, they have to work for delivery of services to satisfy the people on the other hand, they have to wage relentless war against bureaucracy. But these successes are attributed that the panchayat are continuously getting the support of the structure from the civil society organizations. For the past one decade devolution process is static. But Panchayats are dynamic. The higher level officials have no concern for Panchayat system. This book is a collection of articles written on different periods about the on going activities in the panchayat. The first article entitled "The Framework for Devolution of Powers" gives the detailed account of the context in which devolution of powers was thought of in India has been explained. Still officials look at rural development schemes not the Panchayats. They concentrate their attention on achieving the target of the programmes and schemes. They never bother about the problems in governance at grassroots. Panchayats are evaluated from the perspective of implementation of schemes and programmes and not from the perspective of governance. Officials want the Panchayati Raj System under their control.

This article gives the direction for creating Panchayati Raj structure in the states. Based on the framework a structure was created in Tamil Nadu through the conformity legislation. To the extent the power functions and functionaries have been devolved to the panchayat in Tamil Nadu have been analysed in detail. Some of the potentials of the Panchayat have been explained through case studies in the second article entitled "New Panchayati Raj System in Tamil Nadu".

Third article brings to light the poor devolution of finance and power to Panchayats in Tamil Nadu. It gives a critical account of the devolution process in Tamil Nadu. Fourth article is a report on the experiments conducted in four districts through micro planning. In fifty-three panchayats micro plan was developed with the participation of the communities in four districts and the entire process was captured and explained in this article.

Good governance is being discussed in every forum and it is being tested in local governance. The fifth article entitled "Good Governance at Grassroots" deals with the practices of good governance in the rural local bodies. Indicators have been evolved and through them the panchayat performance has been assessed. Sixth article is the report of training programme conducted in Gandhigram Rural Institute over a period of one decade. It has three parts covering the training of Gram Panchayat leaders, women Gram Panchayat leaders, women leader of the Block Panchayat and women leader of tribals. The seventh article entitled "Governance: From the Perspective of Elected Women Representatives" explains the perspectives developed by the women representatives on governance and to what extent their activities are governed by their perspectives. How they are different from others in governance is explained in this article.

Eighth article entitled "Problems faced by the Elected Women Representatives" gives a detailed account of the problems faced by the elected women representatives from their homes, relatives, community, political parties, traditional panchayat, politicians and bureaucracy. It is generated from the meetings organized by the women leaders and the training programmes organized in Gandhigram Rural Institute. Ninth article deals with the new phenomenon, namely a new governing culture at the grassroots with the active leaderships provided by the elected women leaders. How the elected leaders are different and how their activities are significant have been explained. Emerging new role models have been captured and explained. Tenth article entitled "Critical Mass to Critical Action" is the result of the analysis of the action project done in Tamil Nadu with the support of the Ford Foundation. Even though critical mass is formed among women as one-third of seats have been reserved for women in local bodies, women could not move forward to perform the critical function due to lack of support structure. As a result, the elected women representatives have formed their own association, organized meetings periodically and took their problems to the appropriate authorities for redressal. Many of their problems have been solved. How the whole exercise was done and what are the outcomes of all those exercises have been captured in this article.

In the eleventh article, the narration of the elected women leaders who have been elected twice and enjoyed power for two terms about their experience in office. Major observation of the elected women leaders are captured without any distortion or explanation. Twelfth article entitled "Media and Grassroots Governance" gives a detailed account of a media tie-up for helping the panchayats to expose their problems and highlight the major achievements of the panchayat leaders. With the support of the Hunger Project, Gandhigram Rural Institute under the aegis of Rajiv Gandhi Chair for Panchayati Raj initiated an action plan and partnership between Rajiv Gandhi Chair and Media to support grassroots democracy not only providing needed information to the panchayat leaders and people but also to cover the problematic area in governance at grassroots. Further the struggles and success of the panchayat have also been captured. The detailed process have been captured in this article.

When tsunami struck the Indian coastal area, people asked where panchayat had gone in terms of relief and rehabilitation work. Panchayat leaders from Tamil Nadu argued that panchayat leaders have been sidelined and the officials have been involved in relief and rehabilitation. When the whole group of panchayat leaders criticized the government for neglecting the panchayat, some of the panchayat have demonstrated their ability to do relief and rehabilitation work. Article thirteen gives a detailed account of the relief and rehabilitation activities carried out by the some of the gram panchayats in Nagapattinam and Cuddalore districts. Article fourteen brings to light the organized efforts taken by the gram panchayat in developing micro plan for reconstruction of tsunami affected areas in seventeen panchayats. There were conflicts among communities in all the stages from relief to rehabilitation. With the help of the Hunger Project, new initiative was undertaken by the gram panchayat to develop a micro plan in each and every gram panchayat. The process of micro plan preparation was captured.

Article fifteen explains the process of people's participation in governance at grassroots. It brings to light the existing conditions of people's participation in governance. Article sixteen gives a vivid account of the steps taken by various agencies in pushing the decentralization process further, especially efforts taken by the federal government. It further underlines the steps to be taken in decentralization of powers.

1

THE FRAMEWORK FOR DEVOLUTION OF POWERS

Introduction

The process by which the 73rd and the 74th Amendments to the Constitution of India were enacted, the subsequent enactment of conformity legislation in the states, the conduct of elections to grassroots institutions, the constituting of committees to suggest ways and means to devolve powers to the three-tier Panchayats, the constituting of State Finance Commissions to make recommendations to augment resources, the subsequent steps taken to implement the recommendations of the committees and commissions, the perception of the newly elected leaders of the new dispensation, the understanding of the new system by the officials in the administrative system, the outlook of the people towards the new institutions, the capacity of the leaders of the grassroots institutions and the activities carried out at the grassroots under the new dispensation have brought to light the conflicting tendencies in the whole range of activities of the institutions, procedures and processes, which, incidentally, indicate the confusion in the minds of the players and the stakeholders in the institutions about the new institutions. For any meaningful exercise perspective is more important than any other aspect. Obviously variations are bound to emerge. But conflicting tendencies need not and should not figure in the process as they will affect the whole system. While looking at the scenario of the process of devolution and decentralization taking place in India one notices the stagnation and the conflict which are the result of poor understanding of the package of devolution. Even academics, while writing articles and books on Panchayati Raj System, have not set the perspective as the backdrop for their analysis. To look at the issues of grassroots institutions, one has to have the right perspective. The prime objective of this write up is to develop a perspective for devolution of powers in the Indian context against the backdrop of the initiatives which have been taken in the political dispensation.

Backdrop

No doubt the new dispensation has come through a political resolution and constitutional provision. The political resolution and constitutional provision is not a sudden development in Indian polity. It has its own historical background. At the same time, the new dispensation is not an isolated event. It is contextual also When a perspective is developed against the backdrop of history one cannot wish away the context while looking at the historicity. Democratization, Decentralization, Devolution and Developmentalization are contemporary issues and movements all over the world. Though the process of creating democratic institutions in India has a history on its own, the very interface between national and global activity and global and local activity cannot be ignored. Both the Indian tradition of building up grassroots democratic institutions and the contemporary globalization and localization of economic and political activities form the core for building a perspective for devolution of powers in India.

In India, there are ample historical evidences to argue that democratic practices had been developed even in ancient India. But, in modern India, it started from Mahatma Gandhi. British administrators, excepting Rippon, had looked upon institution building at grassroots not as a part of democratizing the society but as an instrument to ease the frustration of the people by delivering some services. Rippon's resolution reiterated an important fact that the people of India should be given their first lessons in popular and political education through local boards. The same British had dismantled the existing system, despite knowing the fact that natural resources were being controlled and managed by the communities. The community structure was strong and hence they were able to manage the natural resources. By making the land to be owned by individuals, the British weakened the community structure and practices. It was only during the freedom struggle that the democratic process at the grassroots was initiated. Gandhiji's framework of Gram Swaraj was the basic foundation for subsequent discourses on empowering people. Jawaharlal Nehru initiated the process of looking for institutional framework at the grassroots within the established democratic politico-administrative system despite several oppositions. Next to Mahatma Gandhi, Jayaprakash Narayan made a fervent plea through his framework for developing a grassroots democratic system. In fact, he developed his thesis on the basic propositions of Mahatma Gandhi. Finally, Rajiv Gandhi started this exercise not as a dream but to find a solution to the unsolved problems of the people over three decades. His framework of devolution was not instantaneous. It is a framework evolved through a process of consulting the millions of stakeholders who are in the process of administering development and social justice. Rajiv Gandhi did not advocate an instrument to negate the state system as Mahatma Gandhi and Jayaprakash Narayan did. In the process of decentralizing governance and administering development and social justice Rajiv Gandhi wanted to rejuvenate and reinvent the government machinery both at the Centre and in the States.

Rajiv Gandhi's Framework

Devolution of powers for revitalizing Panchayat institutions is the outcome of a series of serious discussions and deliberations held among the Chief Ministers, Secretaries to Government, Ministers of Rural Development, officials and representatives of the people in local bodies. This process was started in the year 1985 itself. As a young Prime Minister Rajiv Gandhi wanted to look at administration from a modern perspective of new public management. He identified the crux of the issue, namely, the poor delivery of services and the reason for the poor delivery of services to the people. He lamented that our administration is unresponsive because it is not representative in character. He organised a series of workshops and conferences and analysed the reasons through the host of stakeholders. The framework he developed is the distilled essence of the views of thousands of elected local body representatives, hundreds of District Magistrates, scores of senior government servants and dozens of Ministers and Chief Ministers. His perception of development is of two types. One is macro and the other is micro. Governments have paid adequate attention to macro development but that much of attention has not been given to micro development.[1] When very big dams were constructed, we totally forgot to construct a small checkdam at the community level. When very big industries were established we failed to pay attention to small and tiny industries, including cottage industries. When universities and research institutions were developed, elementary schools and primary schools were not given that much of importance. When higher level medical facilities were developed, primary health care was not given that much of importance.

Rajiv Gandhi pointed out the neglect of the micro activities. Why this stagnation? Why this neglect? He tried his best to find answers through Gandhiji and hence he quoted Gandhiji "True democracy cannot be worked by twenty men sitting at the centre; it has to be worked from below by the people of every village".[2] Further he quoted Gandhiji: "Swaraj is to be obtained by educating the masses to a sense of their capacity to regulate and control authority".[3] To underline the importance of people's participation, he quoted Nehru: "It is not good enough to work for the people, the only way is to work with the people, and give them a sense of working for themselves; development work can be executed only if the people take the responsibility in their own hands".[4]

Rajiv Gandhi first listed the ills in the present system. He started arguing that the democratic structure at the top and the middle are strong because these two structures positioned only through the conduct of elections promptly whereas the third tier is weak because elections are erratic.[5] When the third level governance is weak, it will certainly affect the other two tiers. Without a strong structure at the grassroots, democracy cannot flourish at the Central and State level. It was promised during the freedom struggle that democracy and development would be ensured down to the lowest level. But those promises were not fulfilled after independence. People at the top were busy strengthening their own positions in politics as well as in administration. Democracy and development were part of our freedom struggle. When they have not been achieved, one can presume that the freedom struggle is not over and it will continue. The form and mode may vary.

Development programmes are designed in the capitals by intellectuals regardless of the needs at the grassroots and, as a result, the intended targets and results are not achieved. The centralized development planning initiatives improved the conditions of people who sitting at the top but did not remove the difficulties of the people at the grassroots. In the absence of elected representatives at the grassroots, power brokers have emerged in our country.[6] For any benefit people have to approach the power brokers. The administrative system is being managed by the best brains in the country and yet our administration is weak, unresponsive, inefficient, unsympathetic, often callous, sometimes even cruel to those whom they are meant to serve.

It is the considered opinion of talented civil servants that despite all the goodwill in the world, all their sincerity and all their dedication, a bureaucratic administration cannot be responsive until it is rooted in a democratic polity. A responsive administration needs must be a representative administration, an administration which is responsible to the people. The bureaucracy is responsible only to its masters at the next higher levels.

No one denies the importance of the bureaucracy. It is essential as they are experts in their art. But people should not depend solely on the bureaucracy. Excessive dependence on the bureau-cracy by the people will slow down progress. Normally people see the administration, not as servants of their representatives, but as a form of bureaucratic dictatorship.

Yet another problem Rajiv Gandhi identified was that our administration is plagued by enormous wastage. The cost of administration is eating up a disportionately high share of the total outlay for schemes and programmes.[7] Further there are leakages as power brokers are in the pipeline.

There is yet another malaise: people have increased their expectations and demands from the government. This is also the creation of our polity.[8] We have reduced our people to recipients of development benefits instead of being participants in the development process. There is a vast gap between what the people demand and what is possible to achieve. This is a dangerous trend in our polity.

Yet another issue in polity is the neglect of women in the progress of governance. Women are under-represented. At the grassroots they are totally neglected and marginalized.[9] It is women who undertake much more than half the economic activities of rural India. It is the women of rural India who are the main repository of India's great cultural tradition of moral values, which are fundamental to the survival of our civilization. As a result, many of the women issues do not surface in the decision-making bodies. Dalits and tribals are another marginalized segment and they have to be brought under the new dispensation. By pushing the people to the periphery the civic culture of the people has been dismantled.[10]

Framework for Action

Rajiv Gandhi emphasized two important concepts, namely, democracy and development which are cordinal principles. The two aspects are very important contextually. The rising aspirations of the people in respect of democracy and development are very high at present. How development is going to be achieved through a democratic process at the grassroots is now the main concern. First a system has to be created at the bottom through a Constitutional Amendment. Regular conduct of election to these institutions will stabilize the system as in the case of the National Parliament and the State Legislatures. Devolution of powers, functionaries and finance will ensure delivery of services to the people on a sustainable basis. Provision has to be made to induct women and Dalits into the portals of governance. To ensure the regular conduct of elections and regular flow of finance for independent activities, a State Election Commission and a State Finance Commission have to be created. The power given to the State Finance Commission is not the same as the power of the Central Finance Commission. A list of 29 subjects have been incorporated in 11th Schedule for decision-making. The Eleventh Schedule does not confer any legislative power on local bodies. To ensure people's direct participation in governance the Gram Sabha has been created. To involve the people in the development process, and to alter the trend of supply driven activities to demand driven activities, a District Planning Committee is created at the district level to develop a plan from the people. The planning process involves the people in the exercise and integrates the social justice component in the plan.

Diagram of the Framework

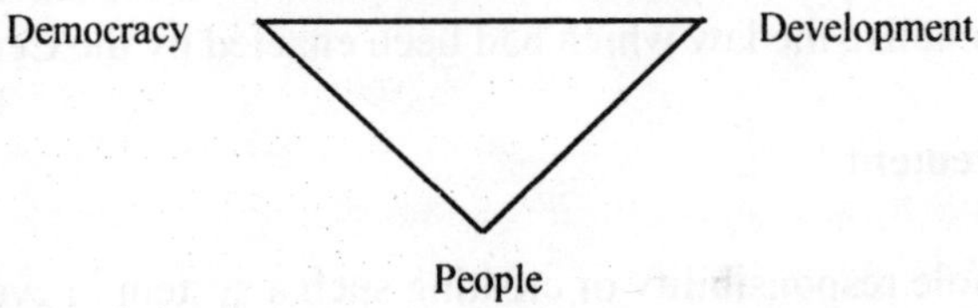

The System

- a. Three-tier structure
- b. State Election Commission
- c. State Finance Commission
- d. District Planning Committee
- e. Gram Sabha
- f. 11th Schedule — 29 subjects
- g. 33.3 per cent reservation of seats for women
- h. Reservation of seats for the marginalized proportionate to their population

The above system can be created through an amendment to the Constitution. This will be a charter for ending bureaucratic oppression, technocratic tyranny, crass inefficiency, bribery, red tapism, nepotism, corruption and the million other instances of malfeasance that afflict the poor of the villages, towns and cities.[11]

The essence of the framework is: "we trust the people, we have faith in the people, it is the people who must determine their own destinies and the destiny of the nation. To the people of India, let us ensure maximum democracy and maximum devolution. Let there be an end to the power-brokers. Let us give power to the people".[12] In this framework one can notice a few limitations: the 29 subjects mentioned in 11th Schedule do not give power to legislate, but only to take decisions. The State Finance Commission's recommendations are not mandatory in nature. The whole responsibility of giving power to the Panchayat system is given to the State Government. The Centre enacts the law and State has to operationalise the law which had been enacted by the Centre.

Requirement

The whole responsibility of creating such a system in every State is given to the State Government.[13] It is not an easy task. Formulating a legislation and passing the same is not difficult. But implementing the same is not so easy. This is not like implementing a decision or a policy. It is nothing but transfer of power. The transfer of power is not from the Centre to the State but from the State to the people. The normal presumption is that the State Government, which is enjoying only limited powers, has been asked to give power to the grassroots institutions.[14] To perform the task envisaged the total mindset of the leaders who are operating the State Government has to be changed.

It needs political will. A new governance structure has to be created. It is not in the hands of the Minister in charge of Rural Development. It is the normal mindset of every one that the Panchayati Raj is equated with rural development schemes and their implementation. It is not so. It is a process by which people have to be brought to the centre stage in the development activities as participants and not as beneficiaries, putting the people above the bureaucracy. So empowering the people is the essence. It brings into the main fold women and Dalits, hitherto marginalized in governance.[15] New tasks, new roles, new responsibilities, new collectivities in the orbit of governance at the grassroots require a new mindset. Political will is needed to pass a new bill to conform to the basic spirit of the 73rd Amendment to the Constitution of India. A new mindset has to be created among the bureaucracy for the smooth transfer of power and the removal of power brokers from the orbit of governance at the grassroots. At the same time, the capacity of the leaders at the grassroots has to be built up to the needed level. The mass have to be sensitized on the new dispensation and its implications. This process of sensitization has to take place as it happened during the period of the independence struggle.

NOTES AND REFERENCES

1. Rajiv Gandhi's Inaugural Address to the 13th All India Panchayat Parishad New Delhi on 22nd September, 1986.
2. Rajiv Gandhi's Inaugural Address at the Workshop of District Collectors and Magistrates on Responsive Administration held at Hyderabad on 13th February, 1988.
3. Rajiv Gandhi's Inaugural Address at the workshop of District Collectors and Magistrates on Responsive Administration held at Imphal on 2nd April, 1988.
4. Rajiv Gandhi's Inaugural Address at the Workshop of District Collectors and Magistrates on Responsive Administration held at Jaipur on 30th April, 1988.
5. Rajiv Gandhi's Inaugural Address at the Workshop of District Collectors and Magistrates on Responsive Administration held at Coimbatore on 18th June, 1988.
6. Rajiv Gandhi's Inaugural Address in the Panchayati Raj Sammelan of Northern States New, Delhi on 27th January, 1989.
7. Rajiv Gandhi's speech at the Conference of the Chief Ministers on Panchayati Raj, New Delhi on 5th May, 1989.
8. Rajiv Gandhi's Statement while introducing the Constitution (64th Amendment) Bill on Panchayati Raj in Lok Sabha 15th May, 1989.
9. Rajiv Gandhi's Address at a Seminar of Municipal Officers in New Delhi on 5th June, 1989.

10. Rajiv Gandhi's Address at a Conference of Chief Minister's, New Delhi 7th July, 1989.
11. Rajiv Gandhi's Statement in the Lok Sabha while Introducing the Constitution (65th Amendment) Bill, 7 August, 1989.
12. Rajiv Gandhi's Text of reply to the debate on the Panchayati Raj and Nagarpalika Bills Rajya Sabha on 13th October, 1989.
13. Government of India, *Powers and Functions of Panchayati Raj Institutions: A Framework* (Occasional Papers 5), New Delhi: Ministry of Rural Development, 1994.
14. Government of India, *Renewing Local Self Government in Rural India,* New Delhi: Ministry of Rural Development, 1994.
15. D. Bandyopadhyay and Amitava Mukerjee (eds.), *New Issues in Panchayati Raj,* New Delhi: Concept Publishing Company, 2004.

2

NEW PANCHAYATI RAJ SYSTEM IN TAMIL NADU

Introduction

Tamil Nadu had an experience of a century in local governance in the pre-Independence period which, in fact, forms the basis of the new local governance in the post-Independence era. Though it was intended to create Panchayats as institutions of self-governance, in practice, they were made institutions to implement the schemes and programmes of the Centre and State Governments. Till the enactment of the 73rd Amendment, the structure of the Panchayat system in Tamil Nadu was of three tiers and two tiers in two different periods. In the three-tier Panchayat system, District Boards, Taluk Boards and Village Panchayats constituted the structural arrangement in the pre-Independence period. Even after the enactment of the 73rd Amendment to the Constitution of India, discussion was on about the two-tier system. But to confirm the 73rd Amendment in 1994, the Tamil Nadu Government enacted a conformity legislation in which the three-tier Panchayat system was created. Originally, in the pre-Independence period, from 1884 to 1934, it was a three-tier structure and, when the Taluk Boards were abolished by the government, the two-tier system came into vogue. In post-Independence India, as per the 1950s, decision there were two tiers, namely, District Board and Village Panchayat, through two different Acts. With regard to powers, service functions were entrusted to local bodies during the pre-Independence period and development functions were entrusted to local bodies along with service functions in the post-Independence period. The Tamil Nadu Panchayat Act of 1994 has evaded assigning a precise role to Panchayats.

When the political climate prepared for the general elections in 1996, Panchayati Raj drew the attention of the political parties and it was incorporated in the manifesto of the political parties. The Dravida Munnetra Kazhagam (DMK) gave prominence to it in its manifesto. The DMK gave promises also during the elections that the DMK would conduct the elections to Panchayats and accused the All India Anna Dravida Munnetra Kazhagam (AIADMK) of not conducting the Panchayat elections. Thus it was the expectation at every level that 1996 would be a turning point for the Panchayats. In the general elections the AIADMK was defeated and the DMK won the elections and, to fulfil the poll promise, it conducted the Panchayat elections at one stroke.

Even before the conduct of the Panchayat elections, the Government of Tamil Nadu constituted the First State Finance Commission. After the elections a high level committee was constituted in the State Planning Commission under the leadership of L.C. Jain. In the meanwhile steps were taken to give assignments to all the three tiers. As a result the rural development schemes were distributed among the three tiers. In the meanwhile the First State Finance Commission submitted its report. Before finalizing the decision on functions and responsibilities among the three tiers, the State Finance Commission had made recommendations. Subsequently, L.C. Jain submitted his Committee's report. Based on the recommendations, orders were issued with regard to entrustment of responsibilities to the three tier Panchayats. Arguments and criticism were levelled against the government for poor devolution of powers. As a result, under the Chairmanship of the Local Administration Minister, a high power committee was constituted with representatives of the political parties. The above committee also submitted its report. Following the submission, orders were issued. From the above steps the following are the powers and responsibilities of the three-tier Panchayats in Tamil Nadu:

Panchayat's Structure

The New Panchayati Raj System came into being in Tamil Nadu after enacting a new law for local body institutions in the year 1994.

The salient features of the new Act are as follows:

(a) A three-tier system;
(b) Gram Sabha;
(c) Establishment of Election Commission;
(d) Constitution of Finance Commission;
(e) Reservation of seats for SC/ST proportionate to their population;
(f) One-third reservation of seats for women; and
(g) Constitution of District Planning Committee.

Gram Sabha

The Gram Sabha is the nucleus of the New Panchayati Raj System. All the registered voters are members of the Gram Sabha of that Village Panchayat. As per the Act it has to meet thrice a year and at least once in six months. The President of Gram Panchayat is the presiding officer of the meetings of the Gram Sabha. The Gram Sabha has to give approval to the budget proposal and annual plan of the Village Panchayat. Further it has to give approval to the annual audited statement of the expenditure of the Village Panchayat. One-third forms the quorum to transact the business of the Gram Sabha as per the Act. In Tamil Nadu the Gram Sabha is a neglected subject and unit in the local body arrangement as both elected leaders and officials have not shown any interest in it due to many reasons. As per the Government orders, even beneficiaries for many government schemes are to be selected only in the Gram Sabha. But in reality it does not happen. Beneficiaries are selected not in the Gram Sabha but in the Panchayat Council, which is violative of the provisions of the Local Body Act of Tamil Nadu. It is a government approved unconstitutional activity. The Government of Tamil Nadu emphasizes transparent activities in all government programmes and schemes but there is no way to execute it as the Gram Sabha is made defunct. It is a nightmare to many who have been enjoying power and resources all along. In order to strengthen the Gram Sabha, recently, the government passed an order that all Gram Panchayats have to convene the Gram Sabha meeting four times in a year on 15th August, 2nd October, 26th January and 1st May and transact the activities as per the provisions available in the Act. Further the quorum for the Gram Sabha has been reduced from one-third to one-tenth. Officials from all the Government offices related to development will also participate in the Gram Sabha meeting as observers of the meeting and will report the proceedings to the Inspector of Panchayats. The responsibility of the observer is to provide the details of the government schemes and programmes to the people in the Gram Sabha.

Village Panchayat

A Village Panchayat or Gram Panchayat is constituted for a minimum of five hundred population. The Village Panchayat has got members ranging from a minimum of five to maximum of a fifteen. In the Village Panchayat the Ward Members and the President, are to be elected directly by the voters. The Vice-President of the Village Panchayat is elected indirectly from among the elected Ward Members of the Village Panchayat. The Village Panchayat has to look after the following subjects:

(a) Construction, repair and maintenance of Village Panchayat roads;
(b) Lighting of public roads and public places;
(c) Providing drainage facilities;
(d) Cleaning of streets;
(e) Providing public latrines;
(f) Providing burial and burning grounds;
(g) Providing water for washing and bathing purposes; and
(h) Such other duties notified by the Government then and there.

To enable the Village Panchayat to perform its functions the following decisions have been taken and notified through Government orders:

(a) All Village Panchayats will get financial resources from the Government directly without any intermediary. Panchayati Union or Block Panchayat will not interfere in the process;
(b) Gram Panchayat Presidents have been designated as Executive Heads and they have been entrusted with powers and responsibilities;
(c) Village Panchayat roads can be taken up for works with the resolution of the Panchayats;
(d) Facilities like street light, water supply can be maintained and attended to if there is any disrepair;
(e) Part-time clerks can be appointed by the Panchayat President;
(f) House construction plan approval has to be given by the Village Panchayats;
(g) Beneficiaries for the Central Government Schemes and programmes have to be selected by the Gram Panchayat in the Gram Sabha; and
(h) New Library and information centre in the villages has to be established by the Village Panchayat.

Panchayati Union

For each development block a Panchayat Union is formed. Each Panchayati Union has a Chairperson and a Vice-Chairperson elected indirectly by the members of the Panchayat Council. Union Council Members are elected directly by the people. For every 5,000 population, one Union Council Member will be elected by the people. Members of Parliament and Legislative Assembly elected from that area are *ex-officio* members of the Panchayat Union Council.

The Panchayati Union has the following duties and responsibilities:

(a) Construction, repair and maintenance of public roads;
(b) Establishment and maintenance of dispensaries;
(c) Construction and maintenance of elementary schools;
(d) Preventive and remedial measures connected with any epidemic;
(e) Conduct of fairs and festivals;
(f) Veterinary relief;
(g) Opening and maintenance of Panchayat Union markets;
(h) Extension of village sites and regulation of buildings;
(i) Maintenance of statistics related to births and deaths;
(j) Improvement of agriculture and agriculture stock;
(k) Promotion and encouragement of cottage industries; and
(l) Other duties and responsibilities entrusted to Panchayati Union by the Government through Government notification.

To enable the Panchayat Union to perform its duties the Government of Tamil Nadu has issued a notification to take up the following activities:

(a) Construction and maintaining Panchayat Union roads, irrigation tanks, and lakes, initiating family welfare activities, executing noon meal schemes and implementing Schemes for Adi Dravidas;
(b) Works have to be identified from Employment Assurance schemes and they are to be executed;
(c) Draught relief works have to be identified and executed;
(d) MP and MLA area development schemes akin to union have to be executed;
(e) Panchayat Union buildings have to be maintained by the union itself; and
(f) Panchayat Union can supervise the activities in the domain of public health, primary education, drinking water supply, roads, small culverts, khadi and village industries works, technical training education, libraries, rural electricity and non-conventional energy.

The Panchayat Union administrative arrangement has been modified by which works have been classified into two divisions and entrusted to Block Development Officer and Assistant Block Development Officer. The two sections work independently with their supporting staff. Infrastructural facilities have also been divided and attached to the two divisions.

District Panchayat

The District Panchayat is constituted with directly elected members for every 50,000 population and indirectly elected Chairperson and Vice-Chairperson from among the Council Members. Members of Parliament and State Legislative Assembly of that area are the *ex-officio* members of the District Panchayat Council. The District Panchayat will have to perform the following functions:

(a) Advise the government in all matters concerning Panchayati Raj Institutions particularly on services and development programmes;
(b) Watching the progress of the measures undertaken by the government, Village Panchayats and Panchayat Union Councils in the districts as under the administrative control of the districts;
(c) Classification of markets, fairs and public roads in Panchayati Raj Institutions; and
(d) Collection of data, publication of statistics, demanding any information from Village Panchayats and Panchayati Union Councils.

To enable the District Panchayat to perform the earmarked functions, an administrative change has been effected by which the Divisional Development Office which is nearer to the district headquarters will supervise the District Panchayat activities. Yet another office which is away from the headquarters will look after auditing of the District Panchayat activities and the third-one will be attached to the District Panchayat.

District Planning Committee

The Government of Tamil Nadu shall constitute in every district a District Planning Committee to consolidate the plans prepared by the District Panchayat, Panchayat Union Councils, Village Panchayats, Municipal Councils, and Municipal Corporations in the district and to prepare a draft development plan for the district as a whole. The Committee shall consist of the Collector of the district, members of the House of People who represent whole or part of the district, members of the Council of States, Members of Legislative Assembly whose constituencies lie within the district, the Mayor of the City Municipal Corporation and all Chairpersons of the Municipalities of the district, Chairpersons of the District Panchayats, one-fifth of the total number of Chairpersons of the Town Panchayats and Panchayat Union notified by the government every year by rotation, and such number of persons not less than four-fifth of the total number of the committee as specified by the government elected from among the members of the District Panchayat, Town Panchayats, Municipal Councils and Corporations in the district in proportion to the ratio between the population of the rural areas and the urban areas. The District Collector is the Chairperson, the District Panchayat President is the Vice-Chairperson and Chief Executive Officer of the District Panchayat is the Secretary of the District Planning Committee. The Committee shall allocate funds to various schemes in the Panchayats and Panchayat Unions and shall monitor the implementation of the schemes. Now the Government has changed the chairmanship of the District Planning Committee from the Collector to the President of the District Panchayat. It is an irony that the District Planning Committees of the districts have convened their meetings and reviewed the activities of the sectoral departments but never took any step to prepare the District Plan. Further it is to be noted that even in the review meeting, district level officials do not participate. They send their officials to these meetings. It is a routine meeting without much of importance. But efforts are on in preparing Gram Panchayat level plans in four districts at the initiative of civil society organizations. Based on these activities a new scheme 'Namathu Gramam' was evolved by which each and every Gram Panchayat has to plan for social development.

Reservation

One-third of positions at all levels of the bodies are reserved for women. SC and ST get reservation of positions at all levels of the bodies in proportion to their population. In Tamil Nadu the rotation of positions, especially for women and Dalits, is for once in ten years. It is unique in the whole of the country. This change was due to the pressure given by the women Panchayat leaders through their federation.

Election and Finance Commissions

An Election Commission headed by the State Election Commissioner appointed by the Governor to conduct the local body elections is mandatory. The Election Commissioner enjoys the powers and privileges and status of a judge of the High Court. The tenure of office of the Election Commissioner is two years. However, the Commissioner can be given extension for four more years. In Tamil Nadu elections are conducted on party lines for District Panchayats and Panchayat Unions. Elections to Village Panchayats are not on party lines. In Tamil Nadu elections to Local Bodies, both urban and rural, will be conducted at one stroke. When the election was conducted in few places auctions were conducted, bidding was made, nominations were made by the traditional Panchayat leaders for Gram Panchayat Presidents' posts.

There will be a Finance Commission constituted every five years to review the financial position of the Panchayats and to make recommendations to the Governor to fix the principles to govern the distribution between the State and Panchayats of the net proceeds of the taxes, duties, tolls and fees leviable by the Government and to identify the logistics for making grants-in-aid to the Panchayats from the consolidated fund of the state and the measures needed to improve the financial position of the Panchayats. The Finance Commission shall consist of a chairman and four other members. In Tamil Nadu the 1st Finance Commission has recommended only 8 per cent of the total revenue to the Panchayats with an increase of 1 per cent every year. The Government have given already 8 per cent of the total revenue to local bodies. The State Government has not increased the amount of share to the Panchayats as per its commitment of 1 per cent more every year. It became stagnant at 8 per cent. The Government of Tamil Nadu have constituted the Second Finance Commission. The Second Finance Commission has also recommended the same 8 per cent of the total revenue to the Panchayats without any increase.

Critical Evaluation of Decentralization

The present Act does not provide much scope for giving life to the spirit of the 73rd Constitutional Amendment Act in Tamil Nadu. Subjects in the 11th Schedule do not find a place in the body of the Act, especially in the chapter on "Functions of Panchayat Bodies." Development officials who work in the Panchayat bodies are declared government officials and they do not come under the perview of local bodies. As a result, the local bodies cannot supervise the activities of the officials of local bodies. While comparing the old Act of Panchayati Raj of 1958 with the new one, one finds adequate powers to local bodies in the old act to supervise, regulate and control the officials working in the local bodies. In the new Act the District Collector is vested with the power of controlling the functioning of Village Panchayats. The District Collector's power to suspend and dissolve the Gram Panchayats is against the spirit of decentralization of powers. The DRDA (District Rural Development Agency) is a registered society, which is under the control of the Project Officer and the District Collector.

The Gram Sabha has not been activated to develop democratic culture in decision-making, to bring about transparency in the activities of the government and to involve the people in the development process of the community. Enactment of legislation and conduct of elections alone will not bring about any change in the functioning of the local bodies. Proper enhancement of the capacity of the leaders, enabling suitable government orders and provision of adequate resources can alone bring about needed change in the functioning of the local bodies.

Steps have been taken to train the Panchayat leaders for which training modules have been prepared. In the meanwhile training programmes have been conducted by a few institutions. Panchayat leaders have formed their associations to exert pressure on the government for more devolution of powers. Gram Panchayat Presidents have formed an association. Likewise the elected women representatives of Gram Panchayats have formed their own association. Dalit men and women elected to Gram Panchayats have formed their association. District Panchayat Presidents have formed their forum. Likewise the Block Panchayat Presidents have formed their association. Even among the Block Panchayat Presidents Dalit Women Presidents have formed their association. All these above associations prepare a charter of demands and sent it to the government periodically. Of the associations the Gram Panchayat Women Presidents Association is vibrant and active. It is always visible and highly articulate. As a result of the elected women representatives' continuous demand, the Government of Tamil Nadu has made an amendment in the existing arrangements for reservation in Tamil Nadu to reserve the constituencies in all the three tiers for two continuous terms to the women and Dalits by which whether it be a Ward of the Gram Panchayat or Gram Panchayat or a Ward of the Block Panchayat or Ward of the District Panchayat once reserved for women and Dalits will be reserved for two terms. The concept of rotation of reservation of position in Tamil Nadu is for ten years not for every five year term. The Government issued a directive to all the District Collectors that whenever the elected women representatives organization demanded a meeting with officials to sort out their problems, the District Collector has to organize such interface and sort out the problems faced by the women leaders. It is for women leaders alone.

In terms of resources, the Panchayat has to face a financial crisis due to the changes made in the formula for matching grant. Panchayats got matching grant from the State Government on a regular basis. If the Panchayat collects 100 per cent house tax it will get three times the amount from the State Government. Now it has been reduced to 125 per cent and that too only if the Panchayat has revised the house tax. Sizeable reduction of resources from the State Government has reduced the activities of the Panchayats. Further revenue from minor minerals and sand quarrying from the Panchayat area has been totally stopped as the activity of sand quarrying has been taken over by the State Government. Dues from Social Forestry is not being given as the money has yet to come from the Social Forestry Department.

The next important issue is that the tariff of the Electricity Board for the electricity consumption of Panchayats. Panchayats have to pay commercial rates for the consumption of electricity. It has been raised from Rs.1.20 to Rs. 3.40 per unit for public consumption by the Panchayats. This has increased the expenditure of the Panchayats. The entire electricity charge has been excluded from the State Finance Commission grant which is due to the Panchayats. The Block Panchayat Councillor is operating schemes which are meant for the village independently without consulting the Gram Panchayats. District Panchayat Councillors are also operating their schemes without consulting the Gram Panchayats. MLAs are operating their constituency development fund without consulting the Gram Panchayats. In the same way MPs are also spending their money without consulting the Gram Panchayats. Apart from the above the sectoral departments have their own funds. They carry out their activities without consulting the Gram Panchayats. Money is being spent in a huge quantities but not on the demands of the people. They spend the money as they prioritize the works. In all the four Gram Sabha meetings people project their felt needs but to meet the felt needs of the people there is no untied fund available at the disposal of the Gram Panchayat. Even the small quantum they get from the State Finance Commission is deducted at source for electricity charge remittance. Virtually funds are operated by different agencies on their own priorities and not on the priorities of the people finalized in the Gram Sabha. As a result the Gram Sabha has been weakened. It is being made a ritual. The District Planning Committee has been constituted and they meet periodically and review the works of the departments. There is no concerted effort on the part of the District Planning Committee to prepare a plan. Neither the District Planning Committee nor the officials show any interest in planning exercise at the grassroots level. The State Planning Commission has developed a module for training in multi level planning and conducted a training programme also. They have prepared guidelines for the preparation of perspective development plan for the whole of a district. Nothing moves in the absence of political will. Finally, the State Planning Commission has given instructions to all District Planning Cells to prepare Village Development Reports (VDR) in select Panchayats. It is a mere compilation of data. In select districts, the Village Development Plan was prepared in select Panchayats with the assistance of the development organizations for which the respective Collectors helped and in turn the District Collectors passed orders to all the sectoral departments to work on the prioritized activities of the plan prepared by the people. This new voluntary initiative of the Gram Panchayats drew the attention of the State Government and the State Government passed a Government Order to initiate such a planning exercise at the Gram Panchayat level which is called "Namathu Gramam"—Our Village. This initiative is to encourage the Village Panchayats to work on social development issues.

In the context of the non-functioning of the District Planning Committee, the recent notification of the Government Order, G.O.(Ms.) No.140 dated 10.09.2004, is a path breaking event as it envisages a holistic development plan for each and every Gram Panchayat with the participation of the people. The new proposal envisions the participation of the people in the sustainable development of villages and the improvement of the quality of life through good governance and convergence of schemes and programmes. It focuses on resource mapping and community mobilization for village development, micro planning and prioritization of needs among village communities, convergence of funds and functionaries of all schemes at the village level, and community led improvement in the overall quality of life.

It is a path breaking exercise in decentralized governance in Tamil Nadu, which is known for its centralized culture in carrying out development activities. It is a demand driven exercise and not a supply driven one. It envisages the participation of the people. It aims at improvement of the quality of life. It strengthens the physical resources for the improvement of the quality of life. It works for the convergence of the schemes and programmes of the government towards the needs of the community as identified by the people. It ensures the participation of sectoral departments in the implementation of the plan prepared by the Gram Panchayats with the participation of the people. It creates a synergy between the schemes and programmes of the governments (both the Centre and the State) and the needs prioritized by the people. It specifically focuses on such sectors as water, sanitation, environment, ecology, education, health, social security and on social issues (elimination of sex selective abortions, prevention of child abuse, age at marriage of women to be not less than 21, prevention of crimes against woman and immoral trafficking, prevention of untouchability and promotion of communal harmony).

The whole exercise is expected to be in a movement mode by carrying out specific campaigns by involving all the stakeholders in the field of rural development. Awareness creation, building and enhancing the skills and capacity of all stakeholders are continuous activities. Each and every Gram Panchayat will have a legal plan document ready for implementation in the next six months. Untied funds will be given to fill the gaps. To encourage the Panchayats to carry out the plan activities incentives will be given after assessing their performance. Each Panchayat will be given three lakh rupees as incentive money, based on its performance. Indicators have been evolved to evaluate the performance of the Panchayats. Most of the indicators are social development indicators which can be achieved without investment of much money. But it requires constant mobilization of the community. If the Panchayats are able to perform such functions, Tamil Nadu will become number one state in social development. Yet another change introduced in the Panchayati Raj System in Tamil Nadu is the inclusion of 611 Town Panchayats in the Rural Local Bodies as special Village Panchayats from the rubric of Urban Local Bodies. By making this change, in

Tamil Nadu there are two kinds of Gram Panchayats, namely Gram Panchayats and Special Village Panchayats.

Relevance

Panchayati institutions have brought people's representatives closer to the people. For the past several years below the State Government there was no representative democratic institution close to the people. Below the State Government level it was the rule of the bureaucracy. It is a well-known fact that the expansion of the bureaucracy will alienate the people. Middlemen establish links between the people and the bureaucracy and thereby brokerage becomes the accepted formula for all development activities. Now elected representatives are placed in all the areas and people can approach them easily. People will raise questions in the Gram Sabha. If water is not sufficiently available, people can raise the question face to face in the Gram Sabha. If the medical staff from the Primary Health Centre are not visiting villages periodically people will question the Panchayati leader. Likewise if the primary school teacher is not regular in reaching the school, it can be raised in the Panchayat. When they raise questions, the leaders cannot shirk the responsibility by saying that they have no power or resources. They have to seek power and finance for which they have to work hard and purposefully.

In the whole process, people have developed the attitude that these are the works to be attended to by the Panchayats for which the elected Panchayat leaders have to work. Panchayat leaders have developed the attitude that in the absence of required power and finance to fulfil the needs and demands of the people, people have to be mobilized to exert pressure on the government to get things done for the people. In the whole process, people are being mobilized by the Panchayats. Mobilization is being done in many ways of which the Gram Sabha is one and an important one. No doubt in India people are mobilized for cultural activities, religious activities and political activities periodically by various groups and the political parties. But they are not mobilized for development work. But now Panchayats are mobilizing the people for development activities. It is true that the Panchayat leaders are drawn from the place wherefrom MLAs and MPs are drawn. But MLAs and MPs can keep themselves aloof from the community. Panchayat leaders have to live with the people and in the community and hence they have to be responsible and responsive to the communities. Provision has been made in the structure so that the marginalised and women can find a place legitimately in the institution for governance. Women and Dalits, who never had any experience in governance, have come to power. A large number of them want to be transparent because the community has a hold over them. In many places a conducive atmosphere for transparent governance by women and Dalits which can serve as a model for others. Women have started attending the Gram Sabha meeting. A large number of SHG members attend the Gram Sabha meetings and they raise a lot of developmental issues in the meeting as they are oriented in social development activities by the NGOs. As a result, even the process of governance at the grassroots will be changed.

Electing a good leader is in the hands of the electorate. Shaping a leader and making him good lies in the hands of everyone. The leaders at the grassroots have to be conscientised on development and their skill and capacity have to be enhanced for proper management of institutions to achieve development and social justice. Once the leaders are properly trained, they will deliver the goods to the level of the expectations of the masses.

Potential Demonstrated

Leaders come to the Panchayat with different aspirations and levels of commitment. To make the leaders work for the society for its transformation and upliftment, they have to be conscientized on the roles to be performed and sensitized on the real issues of development. To manage the institutions they require management skills. To manage and mobilize the community for development work they need communication skills. To manage development the leaders need constant flow of information on all aspects through all tracks pertinent to development. As communities are uneven in terms of their socio-economic conditions, the leaders have to face several hurdles and, to overcome all those hurdles, they need a supportive structure. When the above requirements are fulfilled, the leaders will achieve what they wanted to achieve and then they will be recognized by the community. Once they win the recognition of the community, the leaders are recognized as path finders. They become visible in the media. They constitute the core group of potential performers. They are visited by Government officials, Panchayat leaders of other districts and leaders of political parties. They spread success stories and they become role models. When MPs and MLAs do not address social development issues who will address them is the main question. It is the Panchayat leaders who are addressing social development issues. Everyone is looking for such kind of Panchayat leaders. Such Panchayats are now visible in the society though their number is not large. Now the success stories are spreading through media. The media plays a predominant role in this regard. From our experience in Tamil Nadu, one would strongly argue that Panchayats are capable of tackling all the social development issues provided the needed support is ensured. Representatives of the people assume responsibilities and perform their role and function. Ten Gram Panchayat Presidents have demonstrated this by their constant attention to the services provided, enrolment of eligible children in school, reduction of dropouts in schools, ensuring antenatal care and postnatal care, family welfare, adoption of family planning methods, protecting the environment, establishing good sanitary conditions, providing safe drinking water, banning sale of illicit liquor, clearing channels which bring water to drinking water ponds and tanks for irrigation purposes. The above activities were carried out by the Gram Panchayat Presidents with the support of the communities. These activities were the result of the Population Foundation of India project executed in Dindigul District. It was made possible by the continuous training given to the Gram Panchayat Presidents, Vice-Presidents, community leaders and self help groups. The ten Gram Panchayat Presidents visited the Gram Panchayats in Kerala under the interface programme conducted by the Rajiv Gandhi Chair for Panchayati Raj Studies and acquainted themselves with the process of achieving social development. The Kerala visit provided enough input to them to work on social development issues. There are cases where the Panchayat Presidents have taken up the issues pertinent to social development on their own because of the commitment and the continued support of various development agencies.

Ms. Ponni Kailasam first took up the primary health centre issue. She made the doctor come regularly and made the paramedical and nursing staff visit the Panchayat. She made the staff of the PHC accountable to the people in the Gram Sabha. She first had a discussion with the doctor and listed the problems and the same was discussed with the District Collector. With the intervention of the District Collector she sorted out the problems in the Primary Health Centre. The Primary Health Centre doctor recognized her as a leader only after she sorted out the problems faced by the PHC through the intervention of Collector. Further she made the staff affix her signature in the Visitor's Book of Panchayat as evidence to show that she visited the Panchayat area. The PHC was surrounded by an area meant for open air defecation. She took efforts to clean the entire area and removed all the bushes with the help of the youth group and placed the area under the supervision of the same group. Now the PHC is functioning properly. To perform this task she had to struggle. Yet she did it and this brought recognition among the people to the effect that she is capable of doing things. Next the same leader identified the massive encroachment of common lands and she got orders from the District Collector and removed all the encroachments in the inflow channels of ooranies and tanks. After the removal of the encroachment, all the ooranies and tanks filled up during the rainy season because all the low channels had been cleared and as a result they brought rain water to the tanks. But she had to face a lot of problems during encroachment removal. She took earnest steps to put an end to the production and sale of illicit liquor in her Panchayat premises. All these activities were carried out with struggles. While experiencing the problems and struggles in the Panchayat activities, she thought that this should not happen to other women leaders. Hence, for collective action, she initiated steps to form a federation of elected women representatives at the Gram Panchayat level as in the other tiers the women necessarily act on behalf of their party. This elected women representatives' federation constantly mobilizes the women leaders to work together to sort out their issues. When they meet periodically they discuss their administrative problems and put them in a petition and submit the same to the Secretary and the Director of Rural Development. After submitting the same they meet the press also. The proceedings of the press meet used to appear in newspapers and hence the officials responded to their request. This outcome make the federation stronger. Further they started discussing the issues of women in their forum. Thus she was responsible for the critical action initiated at the Panchayat level.

Mr. Panneer Selvam of Keerapalayam Gram Panchayat of Cuddalore District provided toilets to all the households including those of daily wage earners. The entire village is clean and neat. He got several awards. His village is a total sanitation village. He mobilized the people for this public action and the people were sensitized. He was concerned about the utility of such facilities. So he developed a toilet culture in his village. He was supported by the DANIDA. It is an eye opener for many leaders, academics and bureaucrats.

Ms. Rani Sathappan, President of K. Rayavaram Gram Panchayat of Pudukkottai District, successfully abolished polythene usage in her village. The Government of Tamil Nadu abolished the use of plastics but revoked the same as there was public pressure. But she did it with the support of the community. The village is clean and neat. With the approval of the community she slapped a ban on the sale and use of polythene in the Panchayat area.

Ms. Sahaya Mary of Kakkanur Gram Panchayat President established a village based management system for drinking water supply. In fact she collected money from the people to manage the system. Her concept is that water should be given to all and should be brought very near to the people so that women's burden can be reduced. She collected water charges from the public and it is being managed by the people themselves. Her activities were also supported by the DANIDA. She constituted committees to look after the quality of the water supplied to the people. A separate bank account was opened for the management of water supply.

Ms. Jesu Mary of Michalepattinam Gram Panchayat established 100 per cent rainwater harvesting structure in her Panchayat area long before the Government of Tamil Nadu made it mandatory in every house. She was an eye opener for many and especially for the government.

Mr. Irudayam, President of Karisalpatti Gram Panchayat, fought with the community for establishing toilets in the streets for public use and in schools for students' use. There was no scheme at that time. With the help of the nuns who used to undergo internship programme in the convent, he created awareness among the people about the implications of sanitation. The Panchayat President asked the ANM to stay in the subcentre. She did not do so as she has got the support of the local minister. So he passed a resolution in the Gram Sabha and sent the same to the minister. Knowing fully well the implications of the resolution the local minister asked the ANM to obey the order of the Panchayats.

Mr. Sreerangam, President of Komberipatti Gram Panchayat eradicated the bad practice of arranging marriage for girls at the age of 14 or 15 in the Kurumbar community. It was an age old practice but it was stopped because of the intervention of the President. He even threatened them that he would inform the police. As a result he was defeated in the next election. He was happy that he stopped the age old practice of a community.

Ms. Jamruth Beevi, President of Devipattinam Gram Panchayat in Ramanathapuram District, took a firm decision to kill the pigs in her Panchayat area despite the opposition of hundreds of families who are responsible for rearing pigs. Based on the advice of the doctors and health inspectors, 146 pigs were killed and the Panchayat was made a clean Panchayat. She initiated yet another step to make compost manure out of the waste collected in the village with the help of an NGO. She was responsible for spreading the clean village concept.

Women Gram Panchayat leaders of Tamil Nadu have formed a federation with the objective of highlighting their problems in managing the Panchayats and to take up the issues of women. This federation is gaining momentum as they adopt a proactive approach. Many of the women leaders in the federation are drawn from self help groups and hence they are already oriented in social development issues. Whenever conventions are organised, they invite women activists to discuss the issues of women and to evolve strategies to combat the problems faced by the women through the Panchayati Raj. They pass resolutions and declarations for their future action. The women leaders use to invite consumer forum activists to explain to the members of the federation the methodology to be adopted to supervise the service providers. Further they demand activity charts showing how the service providers could be managed by the local body institutions and what powers the panchayats are enjoying in this regard and, if the service providers do not comply with the request of the leaders what action can be initiated. All these details are discussed in their meeting.

Mr. Ramanathan, President of Naalukkottai Gram Panchayat in Sivagangai District, ensured proper delivery of provisions to the poor through the ration shop by handing over the responsibility of the management of the ration shops to SHGs. It is a well known fact that the ration shop is yet another institution to help the poor by supplying the basic need of food material. It is also true that corruption keeps the poor away from it. He fought with the district administration and got it for a SHG. Now quality products in correct quantity are being supplied to the poor. SHG members are also earning from this service. It has become a model for others.

Ms. Chinnammal, President of Orathupatti Gram Panchayat, made it clear in her plan document that providing a nail cutter and mats and constructing a baby toilet in the balwadi were the priorities. Since the balwadi is located in a Dalit hamlet, she had a vision that all Dalit children should lead a decent human life, which, she feels, they are not leading now. Further she feels that the school is not clean and neat now. Such conditions have to be changed. Ms. Veera Kalaiarasi, President of Veppankulam Panchayat of Sivagangai District, explained that attending to the needs of the disabled, the destitute, widows and orphans is the priority work as she experienced torture at the hands of her husband and because of poverty. She feels that normally attention is not paid to the above sections. Hence she wants to pay more attention to these segments.

The above stated cases demonstrate the potential of the Panchayati institutions. The achievements projected here are the achievements of the leaders. How are these leaders able to achieve such results? They are sensitized, conscientized and capacitated leaders. They establish contact with community, NGOs and government officials. They establish contact with the media also. Government officials are taking these success stories to various places for dissemination. The message they want to spread across the state is that with the limited resources, powers and functionaries, they are able to achieve this much. Why can't others do the same by following these role models. The officials know pretty well that there is no political will and in the absence of political will they want to do something for Panchayats by which the leaders who want to break new ground can get the support of the higher level officials. Many of the higher level officials feel that Panchayats are competent to achieve social development provided needed support is given to the Panchayats. The cases quoted here are a few which have registered remarkable achievements. Likewise Panchayat leaders are breaking new ground in many areas and they are to be documented. Now the Government of Tamil Nadu has decided to form a training team and to conduct training classes for the Panchayat leaders. While sharing their experiences they can motivate others to do such things in the Panchayats. At present these leaders are identified and they are provided needed support individually, not through a system. Panchayat leaders want an activity manual. It is very difficult to create political will on the part of the leaders at the state level. But making the leaders perform by assuming responsibilities in achieving social development is possible. When the Government of Tamil Nadu announced a 15-point programme to make Tamil Nadu the number one State in the country, the Women Panchayat Presidents Federation convened a meeting and discussed all the major issues contained in the 15-point programme and they fixed the responsibility of the Panchayats in implementing the 15-point programme in the rural areas. They submitted a memorandum to the Minister, the Secretary and the Director of Rural Development, Government of Tamil Nadu. By sensitizing the masses through the Gram Sabha about the rights of the people *vis-à-vis* over the service providers, the people were prepared. By doing so people can be mobilized through the panchayats for social development activities. How can the above mentioned activities be done?

Process

The leaders who have broken now ground had commitment. They were in search of supportive structures. They were supported by many institutions. They enhanced their capacity and fixed targets for accomplishments. They developed their vision regarding the development of the community. They perceived their roles and responsibilities properly as they had undergone training continuously. By putting up exemplary performance they have developed contact with higher level officials. To manage the problems of the middle level officials, they have built an alliances with the media and formed a network with NGOs and other leaders. Because of their achievement the leaders have established strong contact with communities.

Communities are drawn towards the Panchayats by the transparent administration of the Panchayat Presidents. They cross the boundaries of caste and political parties for Panchayat work. When their achievements are brought to light they develop their self-esteem. Thus devolution for social development can achieved personal evolution. All social indicators can be achieved through evolution. Every Village Panchayat is a manageable administrative unit. All social indicators can be achieved at the micro level by enhancing the capacity of the Gram Panchayat leaders. By extending support to such leaders, their achievements will be increased to the next level. Their achievements are brought to light by the media as the media is constantly sensitized by The Hunger Project though its media workshop on building the perspective to cover the stories of Panchayats and women's empowerment. Panchayats ensure entitlements. People can claim their rights through Panchayats. By shaping a leader at the micro level, social development can be achieved.

Conclusion

It is true that there are very many weaknesses in the Act itself and a variety of existing Acts do not permit the state to devolve powers. The capacity of the leaders is not so high as to handle all the subjects earmarked for Panchayati Raj and yet leaders are alert and optimistic at present that the Panchayati Raj System is the only solution to solve most of the problems in the rural areas. Steps are on to rectify the defects. Local body leaders are putting out a one-point demand to the State Government to devolve adequate powers and resources to the local bodies. Expected pressure has come from the people for devolution of powers and the leaders of local bodies have come to a stage to take powers from the State Government on their own in the event of denial of powers to the local bodies.

Thus the Panchayat Raj System in Tamil Nadu is being kept in operation not because of the devolved powers and resources but because of the leadership at the Village Panchayat level. No doubt Panchayats are fulfilling the obligatory functions. A lot of innovations have happened in Panchayats due to the exceptional leadership qualities of the Panchayat leaders. Wherever Panchayat leaders are strong, vibrant, capacitated, and committed they perform very well. Whenever the District Collector and Project Officer, DRDA, is pro-Panchayat, the Panchayats perform very well despite several problems and constraints. District Collectors and Project Officers see this dispensation as very positive as they can achieve the targets in carrying out rural development schemes through the Panchayats. Thus it becomes a partnership between the district administration and the Panchayats. In Tamil Nadu Panchayats are evolving on their own. Devolution becomes evolution in Tamil Nadu.

Panchayats are instruments of the people created for governance with the participation of the people to achieve development. Though Panchayat leaders are drawn from the place wherefrom MLAs and MPs are drawn they cannot adopt the attitude and behaviour of the MPs and MLAs as they have to work with the community closely. By increasing their capacity and sensitizing them on developmental issues, Panchayats can be prepared to achieve development and social justice. Capacity building, continuous support extended by the support structure, forming network with the media and NGOs and providing needed information could make them achievers and path finders. If State Governments really want to achieve social development, it can be achieved through the Panchayats. People should be mobilized to participate in the development process. In the long run people will assert and claim their rights and entitlements through the Panchayats.

Panchayats in Tamil Nadu

1.	Total Village Panchayats	12,618
2.	Total Panchayat Unions	385
3.	Total District Panchayats	29

2001 Rural Population in Tamil Nadu

1.	Total Population	3,49,21,681
2.	Male Population	1,75,31,494
3.	Female Population	1,73,90,187

Village Panchayats Based on Population in Tamil Nadu

1.	Less than 3,000 population	8,945
2.	Above 3,000 population	3,673

Elected Panchayat Representatives in Tamil Nadu

1.	Village Panchayat Members	97,195
2.	Village Panchayat Women Members	32,485
3.	Village Panchayat Presidents	12,613
4.	Village Panchayat Women Presidents	4,329
5.	Panchayat Union Members	6,568
6.	Presidents of Panchayat Union	385
7.	District Panchayat Members	656
8.	District Panchayat Presidents	29

SUGGESTED READINGS

1. Athreya , V.B. and Rajeswari, K.S., *Women's Participation in Panchayati Raj: A Case Study from Tamil Nadu,* Chennai: M.S. Swaminathan Research Foundation, 1999.
2. Dharampal, *The Madras Panchayat System, Vol-II A General Assessment,* New Delhi: Impex India, 1972.
3. Government of India, *Powers and Functions of Panchayati Raj Institutions : A Framework,* New Delhi: Ministry of Rural Development, 1994.
4. Government of India, *Renewing Local Self Government in Rural India,* New Delhi: Ministry of Rural Development, 1994.
5. Government of Tamil Nadu, *Democratic Decentralization: Powers Entrusted to Panchayati Raj Institutions,* Chennai: Rural Development Department, 1999.
6. Government of Tamil Nadu, *High Power Committee Report on Entrustment of Powers to three-tier Local Bodies in Tamil Nadu,* Chennai: State Planning Commission, 1998.
7. Jennie Litvack, Junaid Ahmed, *Rethinking Decentralization in Developing and Richard Bird Countries,* Washington D.C.: The World Bank, 1998.
8. Palanithurai, G., "Building Alliances and Capabilities among the elected women representatives of Grassroots Institutions", *Womens Link,* Vol.10, No.1 (Jan.-Mar. 2004), pp.18-25.
9. Palanithurai, G., "Towards Participatory Governance at Grassroots: Synergisation of Rural Communities and Institutions", *South Asian Journal of Socio Political Studies,* Vol.4, No.1 (Dec. 2003).
10. Palanithurai, G., *Capacity Building for Local Body Leaders,* New Delhi: Concept Publishing Company, 2001.
11. Palanithurai, G., *Development Role Reversed: From Government to People,* Gandhigram: Rajiv Gandhi Chair for Panchayati Raj Studies, 2003.
12. Palanithurai, G., Dwaraki, B.R. and Narayanasamy, S., (Eds.), *Major Issues in New Panchayati Raj System* (Eds.) New Delhi: Kanishka Publications, 1997.
13. Palanithurai, G., *Empowering People for Prosperity: A Study in New Panchayati Raj System,* New Delhi: Kanishka Publications, 1994.
14. Palanithurai, G., *Evaluation of Process and Performance of Gram Panchayat Women and Dalit Presidents in Tamil Nadu,* Gandhigram: Rajiv Gandhi Chair, 2003.
15. Palanithurai, G., *Grassroots Democracy in Indian Society,* New Delhi: Concept Publications, 1997.
16. Palanithurai, G., *New Panchayati Raj System at Work: An Evaluation*, New Delhi: Concept Publishing Company, 2000.
17. Palanithurai, G., *New Panchayati Raj System at Work: An Evaluation,* New Delhi: Concept Publications, 1999.
18. Palanithurai, G., *New Panchayati Raj System: Status and Prospects,* New Delhi: Kaniska Publications, 1996, pp.57-64.

19. Palanithurai, G., *Panchayats, Communities and Social Development,* Gandhigram: Rajiv Gandhi Chair for Panchayati Raj Studies, 2003.
20. Palanithurai, G.,(Ed.), *Empowering People: Issues and Solutions,* New Delhi: Kanishka Publications, 1996.
21. Palanithurai, G. (Ed.), *New Panchayati Raj System Status and Prospects,* New Delhi: Kanishka Publications, 1996.
22. Population Foundation of India, *Empowerment of Panchayati Raj Institutions on Issues Related to Population, Health and Social Development, A Final Report,* New Delhi: Population Foundation of India, 2001.
23. Rajiv Gandhi Chair, *Functional Efficiency of Gram Sabha: A Report Submitted to II State Finance Commission,* Gandhigram: Rajiv Gandhi Chair for Panchayati Raj Studies, 2000.
24. Rajiv Gandhi Chair, *Problems faced by the Gram Panchayati Leaders,* Gandhigram: Rajiv Gandhi Chair for Panchayati Raj Studies, 2000.
25. Rajiv Gandhi Foundation, *Dialogue on Panchayat: Summary Proceedings of four Regional Tripartile Interface Interactive Workshops,* New Delhi: Rajiv Gandhi Foundation, 1999.
26. Rajiv Gandhi Foundation, *Panchayati Raj in India: Status Report,* New Delhi: Rajiv Gandhi Foundation, 2000.
27. Rajiv Gandhi Foundation, *Proceedings of the National Seminar on Panchayats,* New Delhi: Rajiv Gandhi Foundation, 1997.
28. Rajiv Gandhi Foundation, *Proceedings of the National Seminar on Panchayats,* New Delhi: Rajiv Gandhi Foundation, 1993.
29. Rajiv Gandhi Foundation, *Revitalization of Panchayati Raj in India,* New Delhi: Rajiv Gandhi Foundation, 1999.
30. Rajiv Gandhi Foundation, *Voices from Below: Summary Proceedings of Sub-Regional Workshops on Panchayats: Issues and Recommendations,* New Delhi: Rajiv Gandhi Foundation, 2001.
31. Rukmani, R., *Panchayati Raj Institutions in Tamil Nadu: A Historical Review,* Chennai: Madras Institute of Development Studies, 1996.
32. Rural Development Department, *Democratic Decentralization: Panchayati Raj System in Tamil Nadu,* Chennai: Rural Development Department, 1999.
33. Sarasvathi, *The Madras Panchayat System Vol-I A Historical Survey,* Delhi: Impex India, 1973.
34. Siddartha, Sivaramakrishnan, *Panchayati Raj Institutions in India - A Society Study for the World Bank,* Washington DC: World Bank, 1999.
35. Siddartha, Sivaramakrishnan, *Discussion: Challenges and Opportunities for Panchayati Raj,* New Delhi: World Bank, 1999.
36. State Finance Commission, *Summary of Recommendations of the State Finance Commission for Local Bodies,* Chennai: State Finance Commission, 1966.
37. State Planning Commission, *Report of the working group on Decentralized Planning and Panchayati Raj,* Chennai: State Planning Commission, 1997.
38. State Planning Commission, *Report on the Entrustment of Powers to Panchayats,* Chennai: State Planning Commission, 1997.

39. The Hunger Project, *Report on the Workshop on Panchayati Raj: Trials and Triumphs, Gandhigram:* Rajiv Gandhi Chair for Panchayati Raj Studies, 2003.
40. The Hunger Project, *Women and Panchayati Raj The Pathway to Social Transformation and a New Future for India,* Bombay: The Hunger Project, 1999.

3

FINANCIAL DEVOLUTION TO PANCHAYATS

Introduction

In the context of globalization of economy, power is being decentralized mandatorily through the Constitution. There are open protests against globalization of economy, but the globalization process is on and activities are being carried out speedily on the other hand decentralization of power draws support from various segments of the society and yet invisible hurdles and barriers hinder the process of devolution and it takes place at a slow pace. The State Government and its bureaucracy are the real barriers in the absence of political will on the part of the State Government. Ever since the Panchayat Raj System came into force, questions have been raised as to what extent Panchayats are autonomous in character. The Panchayat leaders have been lamenting on the paucity of funds available at their level to fulfil the responsibilities assigned to the Panchayats.

The cry has intensified and the Panchayat leaders have been pushed to the stage of resigning their positions as they are unable to meet the basic needs of the people with the funds available in the Panchayats. Over a period of time the responsibilities of Panchayats have been increased and financial resources to them have been reduced drastically and thereby Panchayat institutions have been crippled. The State Government has not enabled the Panchayats by providing the agreed resources. The financial constraints are so acute that the Panchayats to face a volley of problems. Major achievements are made in the social development sector by the Gram Panchayat Presidents and based on their performance and achievements they submit series of petitions to the government to improve the financial status of the Panchayats but nothing moves. Against this background, it was decided to evaluate the financial position of the Panchayats thoroughly and find ways and means to strengthen the Panchayats.

Emergence of New Panchayati Raj Set up in Tamil Nadu

New Panchayati Raj System was brought into force from 1994 to ensure continuity and stability and to improve the functioning of the grassroots institutions as a system of governance in the country to achieve economic development and social justice. For this purpose, chapter IX was newly introduced in the Constitution of India and thereby direction was given to the State Governments to devolve powers and authority so as to make Panchayat institutions self-governing institutions. Following this direction, State Governments enacted legislation on Panchayats by incorporating the salient features of the 73rd Amendment to the Constitution of India. In Tamil Nadu, the Tamil Nadu Panchayats Act, 1958 was repealed and reenacted as the Tamil Nadu Panchayats Act, 1994. The Tamil Nadu Panchayats Act, 1994 retained almost all the sections contained in Tamil Nadu Panchayats Act, 1958 and introduced some new sections to create a three-tier Panchayat structure. District Planning Committee, Gram Sabha, Finance Commission and Election Commission and reservation of seats in the three-tier structure for SC/ST people and women were provided for. Excepting the new provisions added as mentioned above, the 1994 Act was a replica of the 1958 Act.

Devolution of Powers

Article 243G of the Indian Constitution provides that "the legislature of a State, may by law endow with the Panchayats such powers as may be necessary to make them function as units of self-government". The Constitutional mandate requires devolving of powers by enacting necessary law whereas Section 257 of Tamil Nadu Panchayats Act, 1994 states, "save as otherwise provided in this Act, **government may** by notification and subject to such conditions and restrictions as may be prescribed therein, entrust to the Panchayats or any other committees constituted under the Act such powers and responsibilities etc." This is contrary to what is envisaged in the Constitution. But, the powers and responsibilities were not given to the Panchayats even by notification*. No doubt, some powers were given to the Panchayats by executive orders and these orders were not even communicated to the three levels of Panchayats and to the respective departments of the government properly. Certain powers relating to the 29 subjects mentioned in Schedule IV of the Tamil Nadu Panchayats Act, 1994 (Schedule XI of the Constitution of India) were given to the Panchayats by issuing executive orders. The concerned sectoral departments did not act on these orders in the spirit in which they were issued. By issuing executive orders an impression is given to the officials that they need not take them into account seriously. The officials know the difference between notification and executive orders. A notification has to be published for the consumption of the public and it comes out in the gazette. But executive orders need not be published and they are only meant for officials. Thus the Government

***Note:**

Notification: A notification will have more legal force and validity than an executive order issued by government. Section 257 of the Tamil Nadu Panchayats Act requires the powers to be given *by notification.* The courts have held that a notification issued under the Act will have the same force as the Act. Under Section 262 of the Tamil Nadu Panchayats Act, all notifications issued under this Act have to be published in the Tamil Nadu Government Gazette and should be placed on the table of the Legislative Assembly. Hence the orders issued under this Act other than by way of notification will have no validity. The Supreme Court in ITC Bhadrachalam Paper Board and another *Vs.* Mandal Revenue Officer, AP and others [(1996) 6 SCC 634] has held that the statutory requirement of publication of rules/orders in the official gazette is mandatory. The object of the publication in the official gazette is not merely to give information to the public also but to give final official confirmation to the rules/orders. The orders issued by the government giving powers to the Panchayats are not published in the Tamil Nadu Government Gazette. Hence the powers given to the Panchayats in Tamil Nadu by executive orders have no legal force.

of Tamil Nadu made the devolution a non-serious affair. Many of the orders giving powers to the rural local bodies merely state that the Panchayats can assist in identification of beneficiaries, watch and advise the government in implementation of schemes. Real powers were not given to the Panchayats. Power means authority to decide things. No such decision-making powers are given to Panchayat institutions.

Article 243G of the Constitution clearly states that the legislature of the State may, by law, endow the Panchayats with such powers etc. Taking advantage of the word "may" in the said article, the State Government considered that giving authority to the Panchayats is purely the discretion of the State Government and it is not a Constitutional mandate. In this context it is pertinent to note that the observation of the National Commission to review the working of the Constitution set out in Chapter IX of its report as below, as has been quoted in "Renga Reddy District Sarpanch Association *Vs.* Government of Andhra Pradesh, 2004(1) ALT 659 (L.B.) (para 54)".

"The National Commission to review the working of the Constitution, as part of its study, took up an analysis of decentralization and devolution of powers to Panchayats. The Commission's report records that the Union and the State Governments continue to exercise powers in planning and the Panchayats do not enjoy autonomy —financial or administrative —as institutions of local self-government. The Commission examined whether there has been devolution of powers and responsibility to Panchayats, *inter alia* in functional and financial spheres. The report records that Panchayats, having blossomed into institutions of self-government, have been reduced to an implementing arm of the State Government. On the financial domain the report observes, that to be an institution of self-government, a Panchayat should, as far as possible, be a viable and manageable unit. It should be capable of generating internal resources by using its own fiscal powers that include taxing power commensurate with the functions assigned to it. The Commission felt that major fiscal restructuring and financial resources are necessary to enable the Panchayats to function as viable local self-governing institutions. With regard to personnel of the Panchayati Raj Institutions, the report records that an institution of self-government must have the power to recruit and control the officers and other employees required for managing its functions. The Constitution is totally silent about this viability aspect of institutional autonomy. The failure to address the human resource issues has definitely affected the growth of Panchayats as self-governing institutions. The report also points out that since the task of assigning functions to the Panchayats was given to the State Legislature, State Governments retain the powers of the Panchayats with State Government. The conclusion of the Commission in this area is that the gap between the Constitutional hope and the reality in the area of empowerment of Panchayati Raj Institutions was on account of the inconclusiveness of the text. It recommended amendments to the provisions of Part IX and Schedule VII of the Constitution, among other provisions."

The political executive of the State did not have the will to make the Panchayats institutions of self-government. The bureaucracy also did not help in endowing the Panchayats with necessary powers intended to be given by government order. Both have joined together to see that the local bodies should not become a vibrant political force to challenge the State Government for its omission and commission. From the perception of the political and administrative executives Panchayats are only agents of the State Government.

Even though the Tamil Nadu Panchayats Act, 1994 incorporated certain provisions of the Constitutional Amendment Act, powers, functions, functionaries and finances are not given to Panchayats in the spirit in which the Constitutional Amendment Act was enacted. In fact some of the powers given to the Panchayats that are forward looking have now been taken away. For instance, prior to 1994, Village Panchayats and Panchayat Union Councils were empowered by rules to accord administrative sanction for estimates which have been prepared and approved by competent technical authorities without any financial limit as per the rules issued under the Tamil Nadu Panchayat Act, 1958. Now under the rules relating to execution of works issued in G.O. Ms. No. 286 RD dated 31.12.1998, Village Panchayats can accord administrative sanction only to estimates upto Rs.1 lakh. Any estimate beyond the above limit has to be sent to the District Collector for administrative sanction. If the estimate is beyond Rs. 3 lakhs it has to be sent to the Director of Rural Development for approval. Similarly, the Panchayat Union Councils can accord administrative sanction for estimates upto Rs. 5 lakhs only. Beyond that limit, it has to go to the District Collector and the Director of Rural Development for sanction. In the name of giving power to the people through the new dispensation, the State Government has taken away even the existing powers of the Panchayats granted by the Tamil Nadu Panchayat Act. It is nothing but one step forward and two steps backward. Thus, the powers already provided to Panchayats were taken away and the procedure now ordained only results in unnecessary delay and other undesirable consequences. Even simple works like black topping roads upto 1 km will cost more than Rs. 5 lakhs. So practically the functions of the Panchayat are crippled.

The various rules issued by the State Government are curtailing the powers and authority of the Panchayat. The State Government, in G.O Ms. 57, RD dated 22.02.2001, allowed the Village Panchayats to run the fair price shops under the Public Distribution System. The Public Distribution System is one of the items to be entrusted to the Panchayats under Schedule IV of Tamil Nadu Panchayat Act (Schedule XI of Constitution of India). Initially in the above rules it was stated that Village Panchayats which are willing to run the fair price shops under the Public Distribution System located in the Panchayat village shall be identified by the District Collector and the Collector shall grant permission to run the said shop. The word in this rule "shall" was changed to "may" by an amendment made on 14.08.2001 and thus gave discretion to the Collector. The spirit in which the rules were issued was negated by this amendment.

Many rules issued under this Act are not positive towards Panchayats. To cite an instance, the State Government, in G.O. Ms. No.108, RD dated 28.03.2001, issued the "Tamil Nadu Panchayats (determination of claim to trees growing on public roads and other property vesting in or belonging to Village Panchayats) Rules 2001", wherein certain provisions of the rules are obnoxious and do not stand to reason. In rule 7 of the above said rules it has been stated that the Village Panchayats shall have the powers to cut down or sell by auction the live trees on road margins or in water supply sources which are considered dangerous to traffic or dangerous to life or health. But certain conditions have been imposed whereby even in that situation the Panchayats can cut the trees only with the sanction of the Revenue Divisional Officer who shall accord sanction only after getting the report of the Tahsildar. Even if the Revenue Divisional Officer who is superior to the Tahsildar finds that the trees are dangerous to the public he should not give permission without getting the report of the Tahsildar. It is an unnecessary obstruction in the functioning of the Panchayats.

The Inspector of Panchayats District Collector has been given powers under Section 205 of the Tamil Nadu Panchayat Act to remove the elected President of a Village Panchayat. In the modern democratic setup, the powers of the executive to remove an elected representatives is considered undesirable. This power has been often misused. There are many instances to prove this point. In a particular instance one District Collector has threatened a Panchayat President that he will initiate action under Section 205 of Tamil Nadu Panchayat Act to remove him for the simple reason that he met him with certain public grievances.

Decentralization involves devolution of functions, powers and finance to the local bodies. No real power was given and this has been brought out by the study undertaken by the National Institute of Rural Development (NIRD) as per the direction of the Ministry of Rural Development. It has been pointed out that "the Ministry of Rural Development in its memorandum to the Central Finance Commission states that the requirement of funds by the Panchayats for performing the development functions under various centrally sponsored schemes and state sponsored schemes and regulatory and maintenance needs of the Panchayats should receive special dispensation from the Commission". The Eleventh Finance Commission entrusted with the NIRD the task of studying the position of devolution of functions to the rural local bodies, the powers to raise their resources to perform the core services, namely, primary education, primary health, rural roads, drinking water supply, sanitation and street lights. The NIRD study reveals that the 73rd Amendment has not significantally altered the functions of the

Panchayats at the various tiers. The Centre as well as States have sponsored schemes for rural development without associating the Panchayats in planning and implementation. This has further marginalized them (*Emerging Institution for Decentralized Rural Development*, Vol. I, NIRD, 2001, p. 180).

The Government of India releases more than Rs. 2000 crores every year to the rural local bodies to provide infrastructure and it is being spent and yet the people's felt needs are not met as there is no micro level planning at the grassroots which results in waste of funds and improper utilization. The Constitutional Amendment Act and the Tamil Nadu Panchayats Act, Section 243, enjoin that the Panchayats should prepare annual plans to achieve economic development and social justice. This is an important function assigned to them so that the felt needs of the people will be met through such planning. So far planning has not been done at the bottom level. Instead it has been imposed from above. The needs of the people have not been reflected in the planning exercise done above the Panchayats and therefore, it was realized at every level as early as 1970 that planning should be done at the grassroots. The District Planning Cell has been created and the District Planning Committee has been constituted and money is being spent for it and yet there is no constant effort to initiate micro planning as per the mandate of the Constitution.

I. STATE FINANCE COMMISSION (SFC) RECOMMENDATIONS

In accordance with Article 243(I) of the Constitution of India, the First SFC in Tamil Nadu was constituted in 1994 to make recommendations on devolution of funds to the Panchayats for five years from 1996-97 to 2001-02. It is to be noted here that the State Finance Commission started its exercise and came to the final stage before it was decided as to what powers and responsibilities have to be given to each and every tier of the three-tier Panchayat system. The First SFC submitted its report before the Committee which was constituted for making recommendations on entrusting responsibilities to the three-tier Panchayats submitted its report.

The First SFC made 462 recommendations, of which 49 were common to rural and urban local bodies, 107 were related to rural local bodies and 195 were related to taxation and other issues. Of these, only 93 recommendations were accepted in principle and 97 recommendations were not accepted by the government. Even for the 93 accepted recommendations, the government had not issued orders. The details are furnished in Table 3.1.

The First State Finance Commission recommended devolution of State owned tax resources (other than assigned revenues) from 8 to 12 per cent by increasing 1 per cent annually from 1996-97. But the State Government decided to freeze it at 8 per cent of its resources for the five years period in spite of the fact that initially in the "Action Taken Report" placed before the Legislature, a commitment was made by the State Government that payment will be made at the rate of 8 per cent, 9 per cent, 10 per cent, 11 per cent and 12 per cent during the period of five years starting from 1996-97. While considering the responsibilities assigned to the Panchayats, the resources devolved to Panchayats are meagre and insufficient. This poor recommendation was due to the fact that the First State Finance Commission considered the responsibilities given to the Panchayats with the 1958 Panchayat Act as a base and on that basis calculated the requirements and made recommendations.

Modifications

In some of the recommendations, the government made modifications which the First SFC had not suggested such as: (i) abolition of house tax matching grant, (ii) abolition of local cess surcharge matching grant, (iii) adoption of population as the only criterion for *inter se* distribution instead of population along with service indicators and per capita income. The modifications made by the government were detrimental to the interests of the Panchayats. The government, in its Action Taken Report placed before the Legislature in April 1997, had accepted the recommendation for direct remittance of the share of minerals and black granite to Village Panchayat account, but, subsequently, the Rural Development Department of the Government have rejected this

Table 3.1 : The Status of First State Finance Commission Recommendations for PRIs/ULBs

Sl. No.	*Topics*		*Accepted*	*Accepted in principle only*	*Not accepted*	*Orders not passed*	*Under examination*	*Total*
1.	Taxation and other related service		93	–	97	3	2	195
2.	Civic services	Urban	–	106	–	–	–	106
		Rural	–	–	–	26	–	26
3.	Organizations	Urban	–	5	–	–	–	5
		Rural	1	–	–	8	–	9
4.	Functions	Urban	–	1	–	–	–	1
		Rural	1	–	–	–	–	1
5.	Devolution of functions	Urban	–	1	–	–	–	1
		Rural	1	–	–	–	–	1
6.	Staffing pattern	Urban	–	5	–	–	–	5
		Rural	2	–	2	1	–	5
7.	Human resources development	Urban	–	11	1	-	–	11
		Rural	–	9	–	2	–	11

(Contd.)

(Contd.)

Sl. No.	Topics		Accepted	Accepted in principle only	Not accepted	Orders not passed	Under examination	Total
8.	Community participation	Urban	—	6	—	—	—	6
		Rural	—	—	—	6	—	6
9.	Adequacy of powers	Urban	—	8	—	—	—	8
		Rural	5	—	—	3	—	8
10.	Control system	Urban	—	7	—	—	—	7
		Rural	1	—	—	6	—	7
11.	Mechanism for performance	Urban	—	4	—	—	—	4
		Rural	2	—	—	2	—	4
12.	Database	Urban	—	6	—	—	—	6
		Rural	4	—	—	2	—	6
13.	Devolution of funds	Urban	—	—	—	—	—	—
		Rural	22	—	—	—	—	22
14.	Capital fund	Urban	—	—	—	—	—	—
		Rural	—	—	1	—	—	1
	Total		**132**	**169**	**100**	**59**	**2**	**462**

recommendation. As a result the money goes to the treasury and it does not come to the Panchayats. To get money from the treasury a cumbersome procedure has to be followed for which officials have to take steps from the district administration and they are to be pursued at the secretariat level. At present nobody bothers about it. As a result Panchayats are not getting their due share.

Unaccepted Recommendations

Some of the major recommendations made by First State Finance Commission which have not been accepted by the government are:

(i) Calculation of local cess and local cess surcharge based on average land revenue.
(ii) Compensation for local bodies towards local cess/local cess surcharge during the period of waiver/remission of land revenue.
(iii) Water tax.

This has also affected the financial resources of the Panchayats.

Utilization of SFC Devolution

The First SFC recommended specifically that the devolution is meant to cover maintenance of assets at the time of the award period as also the assets to be created during the award period and salary and wages of the personnel of the local bodies. This has been visualized with a view to maintaining the assets created and also to avoid delay in payment of salary to the employees of local bodies. In practice, the government have set apart a sizeable sum for capital works with a view to improving basic amenities in both rural and urban areas. Further, the government have deducted the debt payable by local bodies to other institutions from the State Finance Commission grant. On the other hand, the recommendations relating to remittance of PF dues (contribution) to the respective accounts has not been implemented. Moreover the entire devolution money has been credited to general fund accounts of the local bodies. When specific orders have been issued for the maintenance of separate cash book for utilization of devolution fund in urban local bodies no

specific orders have been issued in respect of rural local bodies. Experience shows that there is need for separate accounts to monitor the utilization of State Finance Commission devolution.
(*Source:* Second State Finance Commission Report)

II. STATE FINANCE COMMISSION RECOMMENDATIONS

The Second State Finance Commission was constituted on 01.12.1999 to make recommendations on devolution of funds for five years from 2002-2003 to 2007-2008. The State Finance Commission made 260 recommendations of which 60 are accepted in principle as mentioned in the Action Taken Report placed before the Legislature. The Second State Finance Commission recommended devolution of 8 per cent from State owned tax resources for the first two years and 9 per cent for the next two years and 10 per cent for last one year. But the government issued orders freezing the devolution of funds to 8 per cent for each year. When Finance Commissions are constituted a tradition has been established in Tamil Nadu that IAS officials are to be appointed Chairpersons. No doubt they have the capacity and capability to perform the job but it is a major question whether they have the needed mindset to look properly at the new paradigm. There are other experts in local body finance or public finance and they can also be appointed. With the minimum responsibilities to Panchayats the I Finance Commission recommended 8 to 12 per cent for a period of five years. But in the II Finance Commission, after fixing enormous responsibilities, the recommendation, instead of starting from 12 per cent, started from the same 8 per cent. It gives the impression that local bodies are not considered institutions of self-governance.

The government in its Action Taken Report placed before the Legislature during May 2002 indicated the extent to which the recommendations were accepted as indicated below:

Accepted in Principle	***Not Accepted***	***Accepted with Modification***
60	15	17

In respect of rural local bodies even though more than three years have lapsed after the submission of the report, the government have not passed any orders on the recommendations of the Second State Finance Commission.

One of the major recommendation which will give some relief to rural local bodies is payment of compensation for waiver of local cess and local cess surcharge whenever land revenue is waived due to drought or flood. For Block Panchayats, local cess surcharge is the most important source of income. This recommendation for payment of compensation whenever local cess surcharge is waived was also made by the First SFC. Though the government initially stated in the Action Taken Report that the payment of the compensation will be considered, the government have not taken any decision so far. During 2003-2004 the government have waived land revenue, local cess, local cess surcharge throughout Tamil Nadu. But no compensation to local bodies was thought of resulting in huge financial loss to rural local bodies roughly to the tune of Rs.33.30 crores.

Revenue dues to Panchayats not Settled

(i) Local Cess and Local Cess Surcharge

The Second State Finance Commission recommended in para 13.2.4 that local cess/local cess surcharge to the Panchayat/Panchayat Unions due during the period from 1997-98 to 2001-02 should be reworked and adjusted positively within two years, that is, 2002-03 and 2003-04 since local cess/local cess surcharge, which are legitimate dues of Panchayats and Panchayat Unions, are not at all being adjusted properly. This has not been done so far by the government. This results in loss of revenue to the Panchayats.

(ii) Mines and Minerals

The Second State Finance Commission in para 12 pointed out that the dues from mines and minerals have not been adjusted and it recommended that the remaining dues may be cleared by issuing suitable orders. But the government has not acted on this. Thus due share from the mines and minerals have not come to Panchayats.

(iii) Social Forestry

The Second State Finance Commission in para 8.7 stated that the share of the Village Panchayats from social forestry income from 1995-96 onwards is yet to be settled. The auctioning under social forestry is done by the Forest Department without any role assigned to the Village Panchayats. The Panchayats feel that their auction amount will be more if they are associated. Hence, the Second State Finance Commission recommended that the Village Panchayats' share may be directly credited to their own account after the conduct of auction to avoid delay. It further recommended the constitution of a committee consisting of Secretary to Government, Environment and Forest Department, Chief Conservator of Forests and DRD to monitor timely adjustment. The inaction of the government in taking steps to implement the recommendation to release the backlog dues to the Panchayats in respect of local cess/local cess surcharge, mines, social forestry has not helped the Panchayats to meet the core and basic requirements. A commitment by the government to rectify the above situation is urgently called for.

Release of State Finance Commission Devolution Fund

The Second State Finance Commission, in para 12 of Chapter XIII, pointed out that the release of SFC Devolution Fund for the first two years 1997-98 and 1998-99 was more or less regular while in subsequent two years there were erratic releases which affected any possible financial planning by the local bodies. It further pointed out that devolution has become discretionary with several local bodies finding it difficult even to pay salary to their employees.

The above instances amply make clear that the amount due to the Panchayats has not been released by the department in time even after a high level body, namely, the State Finance Commission, made positive recommendations to the effect that the dues should be paid immediately. As the entitlement due to Panchayats has not been released and hence they are unable to discharge the statutory duties entrusted to them. In order to make the Panchayats functional, the State Government should be made to release the dues in time. The Government is committed to releasing the State Finance Commission grant every month by modification to the Second State Finance Commission recommendations. But experience shows that the release of the State Finance Commission grant was not made every month. This has seriously affected the functioning of the Panchayats. The State Government should be made to honour its commitment and it should be watched by the Estimates Committee of the Legislature.

Unauthorized Diversion of Statutory SFC Grant due to Local Bodies by Government

The SFC grant is not being regularly released to the Panchayats. In many cases, the grant due to the Panchayats has been unauthorisedly diverted to other purposes and also paid to other departments. In some cases the grant has been adjusted at the state level towards electricity consumption charges (CC) due to the EB without verification with and intimation to the concerned Panchayats. As this is done at the State level, the release of grant is not reflected in the accounts of the Panchayats. Nay, the Panchayats are not even aware of their entitlement and the release. This further results in the improper maintenance of accounts by the Panchayats. "*The grant released through the right hand has been snatched away by the left hand without the knowledge of the body*".

The annual entitlement of SFC grant for rural local bodies for the year 2001-02 is Rs. 416.00 crores, of which the government, in G.O.Ms.18, RD dated 26.03.2002, restricted the SFC grant to the tune of Rs.175.00 crores for rural Panchayats in that year. Obviously, the Panchayats have been deprived of a substantial sum of Rs. 241.00 crores approximately during the year 2001-02. Even while releasing the above grant of Rs.175.00 crores, the government have adjusted the following amounts from Village Panchayats and Panchayat Unions during the year 2001-02:

Sl. No.	*Particular*	*Amount (Rs. in crores)*
1.	CC Charges (Electricity Charges)	1.78
2.	Payment of pensionary contribution towards Panchayat Union employees	31.85
3.	Contribution for loan amount sanctioned by government to Panchayat Unions for special Self-Sufficiency Programme	7.16
	Total	**40.78**

It is also observed that the entire equalisation and incentive grant from out of State Finance Commission funds for the year 2002-03 due to the three-tier of Panchayats has been diverted for undertaking drought relief works.

Responsibilities of Three-tier Panchayats

1. Village Panchayats

Onerous responsibilities are given to the Village Panchayats and they are listed as obligatory and discretionary functions in Section's 110 and 111 of Tamil Nadu Panchayat Act, 1994. The obligatory functions of Village Panchayats are:

(i) Construction, repair and maintenance of village roads.
(ii) Construction, repair and maintenance of water works for supply of water for drinking, washing and bathing purposes.
(iii) Light of public roads and public places in built up areas.
(iv) Cleaning of streets and removal of rubbish.
(v) Construction of disposal of drainage water and its maintenance.
(vi) Provision of public latrine and arrangements to clean public latrine whether public or private.
(vii) Opening and maintenance of burial and burning grounds.
(viii) Opening and maintenance of Public Distribution System.

Apart from this, the following discretionary functions are given to Village Panchayats:

(i) Planting and preservation of trees in the public roads.
(ii) Lighting in public roads and public places in non-built up areas.
(iii) Opening and maintenance of public market.
(iv) Control of fairs and festivals.
(v) Opening and maintenance of slaughter houses.
(vi) Opening and maintenance of reading rooms.
(vii) Establishment and maintenance of TV sets etc.

2. *Block Panchayats*

The obligatory and discretionary functions of Block Panchayats are listed in Sections 112 and 113 to 119 of Tamil Nadu Panchayats Act, 1994. The important obligatory functions are:

(i) Construction, repair and maintenance of Panchayat Union roads.
(ii) Establishment and maintenance of rural dispensaries and payment of subsidies to rural medical practitioner.
(iii) Establishment and maintenance of maternity centres.
(iv) Maintenance and expansion of elementary school buildings.
(v) Remedial measures considered with epidemic diseases.
(vi) Control of fairs and festivals classified as Panchayat Union festivals.
(vii) Veterinary relief.
(viii) Opening and maintenance of Panchayat Union markets.
(ix) Establishment and maintenance of chaultries.
(x) Improvement of agriculture.
(xi) Promotion and encouragement to cottage industries.

The discretionary functions given to Block Panchayats are:

(i) Entrustment and execution of NES and CD works.
(ii) Execution of any of the schemes or programme for economic development.

(iii) Provision and maintenance of common, burial and burning ground.
(iv) Lighting of public roads and public places in common areas of Panchayats.
(v) Maintenance of common dispensaries and child welfare centres.
(vi) Any other duty imposed by government.

3. District Panchayat

The functions of the District Panchayat as enumerated in Sections 163 and 164 of the Tamil Nadu Panchayat Act are advisory in nature. They have to advise the government on all matters relating to rural development.

Inadequate Finance and Manpower for Fulfilment of Responsibilities

Village Panchayats are given heavy and innumerable responsibilities which relate to the basic needs of the community. They have to necessarily carry out the functions. For this purpose, they are not equipped with either finance or the required technical or supporting staff. The main income of Village Panchayats is consumed by electricity charges for street lights and water supply and, even in respect of them, they are in huge arrears resulting in unauthorized adjustment at the State level from statutory grants made to them.

In respect of staff, they are provided with one part-time assistant and limited sanitary and water supply staff. More number of hamlets in Village Panchayats, expansion of population and execution of various water supply schemes with government assistance and other infrastructure development executed in the Village Panchayats require maintenance periodically and annually for which the existing staff and the funds now available are quite inadequate. Unless sufficient financial assistance and technical guidance with staff are provided, the various amenities provided at huge government cost will run into disuse and decay.

Block Panchayats were getting substantial assigned revenues during the pre-SFC period, viz., local cess surcharge matching grant, local roads grant, local education grant, minor irrigation grant, land revenue assignment etc., which are no longer in vogue and hence Block Panchayats now find it very difficult to run the administration with only the State Finance Commission grant. Though they are provided with adequate staff to carry out the above functions the increasing salary of staff and expenditure on pensionary commitments etc. have made them financially weak. The Block Panchayats should be provided with adequate financial assistance to attend to the various development schemes entrusted out of centrally sponsored schemes and state sponsored schemes besides the works carried out from their own finance in some Panchayat Unions.

As regards District Panchayats, the District Panchayats are having only an advisory role in the rural local body administration as per Section 163 of the Tamil Nadu Panchayat Act and no asset creation and maintenance are entrusted to them. Therefore, no separate allocation from out of SFC grant is called for after setting apart finance towards requirement of salary for District Panchayats till additional functions are entrusted.

Reduction of Sources of Income

(i) Village Panchayats

The main sources of income of the Village Panchayats are house tax, professional tax and advertisement tax and other non-tax items like building fees, Dangerous and Offensive (D & O) trades etc., and assigned revenues, viz., surcharge on stamp duty, entertainment tax, cable TV, local cess, mines and minerals etc.

The vehicle tax originally levied by the Panchayat as per Section 173 of the Tamil Nadu Panchayat Act, 1994 and the house tax matching grant provided as per Section 183 of the Tamil Nadu Panchayat Act were dispensed with. The surcharge on stamp duty which is the main and a substantial source of income to Village Panchayats has been drastically reduced *from 5 to 2 per cent and*

1 per cent in respect of mortgage of immovable property resulting in more than *60 per cent loss of income* to the Panchayats from this source alone. On the introduction of cable TV the income from Entertainment Tax (ET) has been reduced to a considerable extent. Originally the tax on exhibition of cable TV was levied by Village Panchayats but Village Panchayats could not assess the volume of tax properly due to inadequate staff. As a result it was taken over by the government. But the government have not paid any compensation to the local bodies after taking over the levy of tax on cable TV.

Regarding mines and minerals, the government have to apportion the lease amount to Village Panchayats and Panchayat Unions on a 50:50 basis. Now, the government have taken over the mines and the quarrying of sand directly but they have not issued orders for disbursing the dues to the local bodies so far. If the income from mines and minerals are not apportioned to the local bodies they will loose heavily.

In respect of the Block Panchayat, the Act still provides for the payment of land revenue assignment grant as per Section 170 of the Tamil Nadu Panchayat Act. But this has not been paid from 1997-98 onwards. Another important source of income is local cess surcharge matching grant under Section 180 of the Tamil Nadu Panchayat Act and now it has been deleted. Likewise local roads grant paid to Block Panchayats as per Section 182 has also been deleted. Now this is supposed to be merged with State Finance Commission devolution funds except land revenue assignment which is still in the Act but is not paid.

Income and Expenditure of Rural Local Bodies

Though the 73rd Amendment Act provides for more duties and responsibilities to Village Panchayats and Block Panchayats, mobilization of resources through taxes becomes increasingly difficult due to various factors. The expectations and aspirations of the people for receiving efficient service from the local bodies are more whereas the resources mobilized through taxes and non-taxes cannot meet the demands of the people especially in providing better basic amenities like water supply, maintenance of roads, street lights etc. There is a big gap between the pre-State Finance Commission and the post-State Finance Commission period in receipts. The expenditure has gone up.

An analysis of revenue and expenditure of Village Panchayats and Block Panchayats of the pre-SFC devolution period and the post-SFC devolution period are given below:

Village Panchayats
Source of Income for 1996-97 (Pre-SFC Devolution Period)

Sl. No.	*Particular*	*Average Amount per Panchayat (Rs. in lakhs)*	*Percentage*
1.	Tax and non-tax	0.27	21.8
2.	Assigned revenue	0.75	60.5
3.	Other grants	0.14	11.2
4.	Miscellaneous receipt	0.08	6.5
	Total	**1.24**	

Source of Expenditure details for 1996-97 (Pre-SFC Devolution Period)

Sl. No.	*Particular*	*Average Amount per Panchayat (Rs. in lakhs)*	*Percentage*
1.	General Administration	0.14	13.6
2.	Maintenance charge	0.69	64.14
3.	Maintenance expenditure	0.12	11.5
4.	Capital expenditure	0.11	10.15
	Total	**1.06**	

Break up details for Post-SFC Devolution Period (1999-2000)
Source of Income

Sl. No.	*Particular*	*Average Amount per Panchayat (Rs. in lakhs)*	*Percentage*
1.	Own source including tax and non-tax	0.53	17.51
2.	Assigned revenue	0.82	27.17
3.	Grants	1.48	48.88
4.	Miscellaneous receipt	0.19	6.43
	Total	**3.02**	

Break up details for Post-SFC Devolution Period (1999-2000)
Expenditure Details

Sl. No.	*Particular*	*Average Amount per Panchayat (Rs. in lakhs)*	*Percentage*
1.	General administration	0.55	15.14
2.	Maintenance charge	2.08	57.29
3.	Capital expenditure	0.90	24.71
4.	Miscellaneous expenditure	0.10	2.86
	Total	**3.64**	
	GAP	**–0.62**	

Prior to the SFC devolution, the major source of income derived by Village Panchayats was assigned revenue of surcharge on stamp duty, entertainment tax, etc., which constituted 61 per cent of the total income. Though there was not much resource gap between receipt and expenditure, Village Panchayats could not take up capital works (providing better infrastructure) since the major portion of expenditure was consumed on electricity charges and maintenance charges relating to streetlights and water supply which constituted 65 per cent of the total expenditure whereas the capital expenditure constituted only 12 per cent.

There is not much improvement at the receipt end even though the SFC devolution passed on income to Village Panchayats at the ratio of 47 per cent of total devolution due to rural local bodies.

Block Panchayat

Break up details for Pre-SFC Devolution Period (1996-97) Source of Income

Sl. No.	*Particular*	*Average Amount per Block Panchayat (Rs. in lakhs)*	*Percentage*
1.	Local cess surcharge and non-tax items	24.26	88
2.	Assigned revenue	3.20	12
3.	Miscellaneous receipt	—	—
	Total	**27.55**	

Break up details for Pre-SFC Devolution Period (1996-97)
Expenditure Details

Sl. No.	*Particular*	*Average Amount per Block Panchayat (Rs. in lakhs)*	*Percentage*
1.	General administration	16.84	52
2.	Maintenance expenditure	11.83	36.6
3.	Miscellaneous expenditure	—	—
4.	Capital expenditure	3.61	11.2
	Total	**32.35**	
	GAP	**–4.8**	

Break up details for Post-SFC Devolution Period (1999-2000)
Source of Income

Sl. No.	*Particular*	*Average Amount per Block Panchayat (Rs. in lakhs)*	*Percentage*
1.	Own source including tax and non-tax	6.52	11.99
2.	Assigned revenues	0.08	0.15
3.	Grants	47.76	87.86
4.	Miscellaneous receipt	—	—
	Total	**54.36**	

Break up details for Post-SFC Devolution Period (1999-2000)
Expenditure Details

Sl. No.	*Particular*	*Average Amount per Block Panchayat (Rs. in lakhs)*	*Percentage*
1.	General administration	45.05	67.56
2.	Maintenance charge	16.44	24.66
3.	Capital expenditure	5.19	7.78
4.	Miscellaneous expenditure	—	—
	Total	**66.68**	
	GAP	**–12.32**	

The above figures indicate that out of the total income derived by the Panchayat Union, local cess surcharge, local cess surcharge matching grant, local education grant, local roads grant and land revenue assignment etc., constituted 88 per cent. But in the post-SFC devolution period the financial assistance pattern has been changed and the income from local cess surcharge matching grant, local education grant, local roads grant and other statutory grants were dispensed with and assistance is given in the form of State Finance Commission devolution to Panchayat Unions. Even prior to the SFC devolution period, there was a gap of Rs. 4.80 lakhs between receipt and expenditure. This gap has widened to Rs.12.32 lakhs per Panchayat Union in the post-devolution scenario owing to the fact that the major portion of expenditure of 52 per cent in the pre-devolution period and 68 per cent in the post-devolution period is incurred for general administration. Under general administration, an expenditure 20 per cent of salary for Panchayat employees is incurred for pensionary contributions.

The above analysis will show that while the income to the Village Panchayats has sharply declined due to reduction in the surcharge on stamp duty which is a major source of income and also due to non-adjustment of receipts legally due to the Panchayats, there has been a steep rise in the expenditure due to streetlights and drinking water supply as well as increase in the establishment cost. The electricity board charged at the rate of Rs.1.20 paise per KWH till 15.03.2003 and it has been increased to Rs.3.60 from 16.03.2003, which is three times the earlier rate. Due to the three fold increase, many Panchayats are facing the problem of clearing electricity charges and are now in doldrums.

EB charges have increased three fold for supplying drinking water to the inhabitants as well as water supply for other essential purposes. Water supply and street lighting are obligatory duties cast on the Panchayats and they have to necessarily maintain them. In this connection electricity supply to the agriculturalists is now being charged only at the rate of 20 paise per unit. It is a well known fact that many of the agriculturalists availing of this concession are misusing this concession for pumping water and supplying the same to others and derive substantial income from this source. When such concession is being extended to the agriculturalists who are commercially exploiting it, it is a great injustice to charge heavily the Village Panchayats who are rendering social and public obligations. Now most of the Panchayats are in arrears and whatever little grant is given by government is being adjusted towards EB charges even without the knowledge of the Village Panchayats.

It is only proper that the electricity supply to Panchayats for water supply and streetlights is charged on par with the charges for agriculturalists.

Ways and Means to Augment the Resources of Panchayats

The Panchayats face several problems in raising local tax revenue such as narrow tax base, lack of administrative machinery, staff trained in tax collection, lack of guidelines to levy new taxes. Local tax collections can be improved by improving the administrative capacity of the local bodies before levying higher tax. The existing staff at the Village Panchayat level is highly inadequate for this purpose. The staff working in other departments connected with the duty of the Panchayats may be suitably redeployed and placed at the disposal of the Panchayats.

The rate of fee levied by the Panchayats for installation of machinery and D & O trades is very low since it was fixed as early as 1960. This needs revision and a higher fee may be fixed by suitable notification by government and thereby income can be raised.

Another major source of income is levy and collection of house tax. The present law provides for levy of tax on plinth area basis and it has not been resorted to by many Panchayats. The Panchayats should be made to levy the tax on plinth area basis and they should be suitably guided and motivated to do so through incentives.

At present the implementation of the recommendations made by Second SFC is left to the discretion of the State Government. This attitude should be changed and the recommendations made by such constitutional bodies have to be accepted in all seriousness and implemented unless it is beyond the resources of the State

Government. We find that even accepted recommendations have not been implemented on some pretext or other. This position should be changed by making suitable amendments to the Constitution.

Summary

1. Proper devolution of function, power and funds should be made available to the Panchayats so that they can effectively discharge their duties and functions as true local self-governing institutions as contemplated in the Constitution.
2. Recommendations made by the SFC and accepted by the government in principle should be faithfully implemented and arrears due to Panchayats should be paid without delay.
3. While releasing the SFC grant deductions should not be made at the State level. The funds should be credited to the accounts of local bodies and they should be made to pay the dues so that they can watch the receipt of grants and maintain the accounts properly.
4. To improve tax collection by Village Panchayats proper staff should be given by suitable redeployment of staff working in government departments and their salary should be continued to be met by the government. The Village Panchayats which come forward to increase the rate and assessment of tax and mobilize more new sources of income may be encouraged by suitable support through incentives.
5. For maintaining the cleanliness of streets and sanitation of the Panchayats suitable personnel and recurring grant may be sanctioned to the local bodies.
6. To improve the functioning of the Panchayat, the functions, staff and finance now provided to departments dealing with the 29 subjects (as per Schedule XI of Constitution) may be transferred to the Panchayats by issuing statutory orders.
7. Maintenance cost on drinking water supply and street lights have sharply increased (to almost 50 to 60 per cent of the income). Hence special grants may be sanctioned to Panchayats to make good the deficit.

8. The Central Finance Commission provides 29 per cent from centrally owned tax resources to State Governments as CFC grant. It is recommended that 1/3 of the amount from out of the CFC grant released be earmarked for local bodies and directly credited to the local bodies' accounts by the Central Finance Commission itself.

4

PLANNING FOR DEVELOPMENT AT GRASSROOTS

Introduction

"Planning" in India is believed by everyone to be an exercise that can be done only by top level bureaucrats and technocrats with the direction of the policy-makers for the development of the whole country. The concept of planning as an exercise and process which can be done at the lowest level in the hierarchy of governing structure with the involvement of the people has also been posited to the policy-makers ever since India adopted planning as a legitimate government exercise but it did not gain any support[1]. Committees were constituted to probe more into the details of the process and as a result reports were submitted[2]. In the beginning of 1970s the dominant thought of keeping planning at the top became flexible to some extent as such planning had not yielded the expected results to mitigate the problems of the poor and initiatives at the provincial level that too at the sectoral level were allowed. It went still further in the 1980s with the initiative for planning being undertaken at the district level. The 1990s marked a historic departure from the conventional arrangements to achieve development so as to match globalization of economy and decentralization of powers and planning at grassroots was made mandatory to achieve development and social justice with the participation of the people[3]. Though globalization gained currency and its operation is in full swing decentralization did not get that much of attention as the stakeholders of decentralization are weak.

To make decentralization work an array of support structures have to be created. Against this background, even for planning at grassroots one has to support the grassroots institutions. Though there were sporadic experiences in decentralized planning in the past, implementable strategies and devices could not be gained from all those experiments and experiences[4]. The new initiatives, following the 73rd and the 74th Amendments to the Constitution of India, have to take into cognizance the fact that the top down planning has not addressed the felt needs of the people, has removed people away from governance and participation in development. Development as an activity to be done exclusively by officials resulted in large scale corruption in rural development activities. This too has to be recognized while considering the new option. People were made beneficiaries, the self-respect of the people was jeopardized and people were not regarded as development participants[5]. It is so not only in India but also in many of the developing countries. Bridging the gap between the people and the government is a difficult task in third world countries. In this context, planning at the grassroots, initiated through the 73rd and the 74th Amendments to the Constitution of India, has to remove all the above stated obstacles and barriers in the process of development.

The Problem

Though provision has been made in the Constitution for planning initiatives at the grassroots, to what extent steps are being taken at the state level and the Panchayat level to plan for development at the grassroots is a question to be probed. Further at what level initiatives gain momentum and how this can be sustained is yet another question to be clarified.

Objectives and Methodology

This study has the following objectives:

(a) To study the efforts of the State Government in strengthening the planning process at the grassroots;

(b) To what extent planning is initiated from below by the Panchayats with the participation of people;

(c) How the planning process is initiated from the grassroots by the Panchayats and with whose support; and

(d) What are the implications of the intervention of the government and other agencies in the planning process at the grassroots.

The above stated objectives could be studied through documentary analysis and process analysis. The government's position on micro level planning could be evaluated from the steps taken by the government. A process analysis can be made on the initiatives of planning at the grassroots by the Panchayat institutions with the support of development organizations.

Context

To analyze decentralized planning, there are two approaches so far developed. One is historical in nature and the other one is contextual or critical analysis. Through the historical approach, ever since the concept of planning gained currency in India, discussions and deliberations had been conducted as to what alternative strategies have to be evolved to overcome the difficulties of centralized planning[6]. But all the discussions and deliberations were held against the backdrop of centralized planning. The issues and problems were looked at from the perspective of the centre and not from the perspective of the periphery. Macro economic activities through centralized planning did not mitigate the micro level problems particularly those relating to the basic needs[7]. Hence the policy-makers were compelled to think of planning units at different levels, namely, the district and the block. Yet there was no conscious and deliberate decision to establish planning units below the State level. Even to establish a planning unit at the State level, it took nearly about two decades after independence. Such a kind of rigid centralization had been practiced in Indian politics and administration[8].

But the decentralized planning enunciated at present is totally different and it makes a real breakthrough as it has been incorporated in the Constitution itself. It is not an isolated event that took place in Indian planning. It is a corollary of a worldwide event which pushes the economy to cross the boundaries of the nations and into every segment of the society. Both in economy and polity an overhauling took place by which the paradigm of governance, administration and development has been totally altered[9]. A new paradigm has been developed by which new opportunities, which are uncommon, can be harnessed by enhancing the capacity of the stakeholders[10]. Through this paradigm power is given to the people to determine their destiny[11]. People have been projected as the major stakeholders and they have to decide their course of action in the process of development. In the present context the concept "government" has been redefined. It is not a provider but a facilitator. The government takes a back seat and the community or the user group takes the front to take development initiatives. Thus the concept of government is no more relevant and it is only "governance" which is relevant at present[12].

How for the development of the community, activities have to be initiated through a new system of governance created at different levels below the State with the introduction of the Amendments to the Constitution of India. Governance structures have been created at the village level, the block level and the district level, including towns, municipalities and corporations. To activate the people to participate in the development process, powers have been devolved to different levels and the planning mechanism had been incorporated into the Constitution itself. By doing so the trend of development activities has been altered from "supply driven" to "demand driven" mode[13].

The major provisions and basic principles have to be conformed to through an Act at the provincial level. Hence all the states have conformed to the bases of the Constitutional Amendments in State Acts. Tamil Nadu also has passed conformity Act. Enacting a legislation is not a big task in a democracy since it is a representative democracy based on the principle of majority in Parliament and Legislative Assemblies. To pass a legislation the members of the decision-making body have to be managed through the established procedure. The difficult task lies in operationalizing the provisions of the Act which has to take place in the society among the people.

In India there are a large number of key provisions in the Constitution which are still not operated effectively because much of social conflict, social discrimination and illiteracy. Hence the focus should be on the operational part of the legislation. In the Tamil Nadu Panchayat Act due recognition was not given to the District Planning Committee and its responsibilities. The District Planning Committee and its functioning have to be seen and analyzed against the larger backdrop of devolution of powers in Tamil Nadu, because devolution of powers and planning at micro level will alter the existing mode of governance. To perform the above task the State Government and its leadership should have sufficient will, because this initiative to devolve powers, functions, finance and functionaries will cripple the existing exploitative and corrupt nexus between the ruling elite and the inert bureaucracy. It will mobilize the people for deepening democracy. People's perception has also to be changed as they regard themselves as beneficiaries instead of development participants having lost their self-confidence and self- respect. Further people have to be conscientized and capacitated. The whole exercise has to be done with the backing of the Central Government.

Perception

To undertake the gigantic and uphill task, normally any leader will pursue a normal course of action. In the Indian context, this new exercise of democratic decentralization starts only from the State Government not from the Central Government. Normally the term is used in development literature to refer to the transfer of authority to plan, make decisions and manage public functions from the national level to any organization or agency at the sub-national level and down below. Decentralization in India refers to a situation in which lower-ranking units below the State level acquire all powers and responsibilities from the State Government and also sole control over the determination of their goals and targets.

Tamil Nadu's ethnic political culture demanded adequate powers to the State Government since independence. Now these political parties, which are coming to power alternatively, view decentralization as a threat to the power of the State Government. These political parties, namely, both the Dravida Munnetra Kazhagam and the All India Anna Dravida Munnetra Kazhagam, forcefully opposed the creation of the three-tier Panchayat Raj System as it would emerge as a countering political force. Hence, they have developed a strategy to keep the Panchayat system a weak instrument while appearing to conform to the major provisions of the 73rd Amendment to the Constitution of India[14].

The Panchayat was created through the conformity legislation enacted during the period of the All India Anna Dravida Munnetra Kazhagam. The Act has many retrograde provisions[15]. The Act has not given any real power to Panchayats. The new Panchayati Raj was operationalized only during the period of the Dravida Munnetra Kazhagam. All the powers given to the Panchayat Institutions are supervisory in nature and not of the decision making kind. The powers given to Panchayats, however meagre, have not been given through Act but through Government Orders. The ruling parties at the State level somehow or other have managed to keep the local bodies in their party fold as the ruling parties have emerged victorious in the local body elections also. As a result most of the local body leaders never raise their voice against the State Government for more power, finance and functionaries to local bodies. Only the lowest units in the system, namely, the Gram Panchayats, which are freed from political contest raise their voice against the State Government and demand powers to local bodies. The District Planning Committee was created and it was under placed the Chairmanship of the District Collector. After a prolonged fight he was replaced by the District Panchayat Chairperson. Elections to District Planning Committee were conducted and now it is in position but no activity is undertaken.

Virtually planning at multi-level exists only in concept and theory but not in practice. But the State Planning Commission had prepared a report, guidelines and a training module for multi-level planning[16]. Both leaders and officials had been trained[17]. The elected representatives elected to the District Planning Committee have taken cognizance of the mandatory functions of the District Planning Committee. But there is no concerted effort to build up this process of planning from below and, as a result, the rural development activities are carried out still in the supply driven mode and people are not involved in the development activities. More than that the felt needs of the people projected through the Gram Sabha are not met, but a variety of activities are being carried out through sectoral departments[18].

In order to break the deadlock an exercise was initiated with the intervention of The Hunger Project by which ten Gram Panchayats in Sivagangai District and thirteen Gram Panchayats in Pudukkottai District have been set up as model Panchayats in terms of planning at micro level with the participation of the people who are willing to involve themselves in the preparation of plan for the development of the communities in the Panchayat area. Why these Panchayats in these two districts? The leaders of these Panchayat showed interest in this exercise and volunteered while they were undergoing training. Further these Presidents are supported by the respective District Collectors who have assured that they will extend all possible support and coordination to this exercise.

Initiatives of the Government

By going through the document entitled "Report of the Working Group on Decentralized Planning and Panchayati Raj" prepared by the Planning Commission, 1997 one can infer the poor interest evinced by the Government of Tamil Nadu in all the past experiments. In the 73rd Amendment, while there was a discussion in the Parliament, the two major political parties, namely, the DMK and the AIADMK being in power in Tamil Nadu State alternatively, made a categorical statement that they had not imagined a structure for Panchayati Raj above the Block Panchayats. They wrote letters to the Government of India that the District Panchayat has to be abolished. Both these parties opposed to the district level structure what would have been the fate of the District Panchayat in Tamil Nadu? Further when the District Planning Committee was formed the District Collector was made the Chairperson of the District Planning Committee. After a prolonged fight the District Panchayat President was made the Chairperson of the District Planning Committee. To fulfil the Constitutional obligation, the District Planning

Cell with a skeleton staff was created. It has to look after the day to day administration of the District Panchayats. Neither the State Government nor the District Planning Committee took any step with regard to the preparation of the District Development Plan. The State Planning Commission, though it took the initiative it did not have the backing of the State Government. As a result planning at the district level has not seen the light of day.

But organizations and activists engaged in public affairs, seeing the apathy of the State Government in taking the initiative for micro level planning, because interested in taking the initiative. Except in West Bengal and Kerala, micro level planning is the initiative of the development organizations. In this context in Tamil Nadu State The Hunger Project initiated the process of planning at Gram Panchayat level as Gram Sabha has got power to approve the plan document which becomes a legal and legitimate plan document. The Hunger Project has certain objectives, namely, ending hunger through micro plan mitigating malnutrition, empowering women and children through the micro plan, and working for social development through micro plan, all under women leadership. But The Hunger Project realized the fact that in the context of weak devolution of powers to the local bodies, micro level planning will be a meaningful exercise only when it is done with the partnership of the district administration as the sectoral departments are under the district administration. Since sectoral departments are not under the control of the Panchayati Raj System, for implementing the plans of the Panchayats, the cooperation of the sectoral departments is imperative. Against this background, working with the district administration becomes inevitable. Further, though the State Government is not interested in devolving powers, it is interested in achieving social development. This interest can be exploited to initiate micro level planning. The Hunger Project in Tamil Nadu is taking a major lead in initiating micro level planning at the Gram Panchayat level. Ten Gram Panchayats in Sivagangai District headed by women have planned and started working on the plan. Following Sivagangai District, in Pudukkottai District, 13 Gram Panchayats have been selected and planning is over. Another 30 Gram Panchayats have been selected for this exercise in Tuticorin District and Dindigul

District. Wherever the district administration is taking initiative, The Hunger Project joins them as partner and initiates micro level

Planning Exercise at Phase I

Table 4.1 : Model Panchayats for Community Based Micro Level Planning in Sivagangai District

Sl. No.	*Union*	*Panchayat*	*Name of the Panchayat President*
1.	Kallal	1. Veppangulam	Veera Kalaiarasi (SC)
		2. Nerpugapatti	A. Pushpam (BC)
		3. Kalipuli	S. Gandhimathi (SC)*
2.	Thirupathoor	4. Velangudi	A. Alphonsamary (BC)*
3.	Sigampunari	5. Vaduvanpatti	R. Rakku (SC)
		6. Sevalpatti	S. Poongothai (BC)*
		7. Kozhikudipatti	Nagajothi (BC)
4.	S. Pudur	8. Urathupatti	C. Chinnammal (SC)
		9. Manaloor	S. Gomathi (BC)
		10. Keelavayal	S. Sumathi (MBC)*

* The above Panchayats were included in this pilot exercise only at a later stage as per the suggestion of the District Collector.

planning. Panchayats are selected for this planning on two conditions, namely, the Gram Panchayat leader should have honesty, commitment and capacity and the Gram Panchayat should enjoy the support of the communities without any social and political conflicts. Table 4.1 presents some details of the Panchayats selected for the pilot exercise in Sivagangai District.

A total of 10 Gram Panchayats headed by women were selected in four Unions of Sivagangai District, Tamil Nadu. Out of the 10 Panchayat leaders, 4 belonged to the SC.

Methodology of the Plan Preparation in the First Phase

Before commencing the actual work, an intensive training was organised for three days to build the capacity of the leaders including the men and women who were all committed to this exercise. The training programme was organised from 27 to 31 May, 2002 in Gandhigram Rural Institute as a fully residential programme. Experts were drawn from different institutions including the government to conduct the training programme[19]. All the six Gram Panchayat Presidents initially selected wanted to have a common workshop to sensitize the Panchayat Ward Members, community leaders, SHG leaders, members of the youth groups and opinion makers on the importance and the implications of grassroots planning. The lead NGO, Rural Welfare Trust, agreed to help the Panchayats to organise the workshop and do the needful for planning also. The Hunger Council of Tamil Nadu agreed to share some of the responsibilities. As a result on 17 August, 2002, a workshop was organised at Tirupathur for all the six Panchayats and around 210 members from all the Panchayats participated in the programme[20]. The whole exercise focused on planning at the Gram Panchayat level and the discussion was on the steps to be followed in the planning. It was agreed that the planning exercise would be completed before October 2002 and that the Panchayats and the NGOs would take up the responsibility. Further it was decided to identify what could be done by the leaders and the people of the respective Panchayats. What could not be done by the Panchayats would be done by The Hunger Project.

The next step was to collect basic data about the people and their conditions. This could be done by the Panchayats. Before starting the exercise the statutory seven committees had to be constituted so that the number of members in the orbit of governance would be increased. For the data collection a well developed schedule prepared by the State Planning Commission was used. After collecting the data from each village a PRA exercise was carried out with the help of the staff of the Kottayam based NGO, Centre for Rural Management (CRM) to assess the needs of the people and to prioritise the needs. This exercise was done extensively and the staff of the CRM prepared a plan. Simultaneously the representatives of the people in the Panchayats also prepared a plan based on the PRA exercise. Finally, both the plans were synthesized and brought out in the form of a document. In the whole process the concept of development was critiqued, the role of the government was criticized and people expressed their willingness to participate in the whole process as the Panchayat leaders provided ample scope for people to participate in the planning exercise. When the document was ready for presentation in any forum for critical evaluation, The Hunger Council of Tamil Nadu organised a development seminar with a set of objectives, namely, of making this document legitimate, to sensitize the government on planning at the grassroots and to motivate other Panchayat Presidents to start this kind of exercise in their Panchayats also. On 26 and 27 October, 2002, the development seminar was organised in Gandhigram Rural Institute, inviting the State Minister for local bodies, secretaries, directors, planning officials, experts, representatives from the media, MLAs, community leaders, Panchayat leaders and women and youth groups from the six Gram Panchayats and women Gram Panchayat Presidents from all over Tamil Nadu numbering around six hundred.

The perspective plan document of the six Gram Panchayats contained a brief history of the Panchayats, details about the former Panchayat Presidents who held office during the pre-73rd Amendment era, basic data about agriculture, source of irrigation, veterinary facilities, land utilization, land ownership, landless families with social background, facilities available in schools, admission in schools, dropouts in schools, status of women and children, energy utilization, non-conventional energy sources, environmental conditions, skills available in the village, housing facilities etc. After projecting all these the document projected the needs and prioritized them. Further it stated how these prioritized needs are to be met[21].

Responsibilities were fixed on individuals and groups to take steps to meet the needs indicated in the plan document. Achievable indicators were fixed to monitor the activities of the Panchayats. It was stated unequivocally that the Panchayat would concentrate on 100 per cent school admission, ensure the normal weight of new born babies, institutional delivery, pre-natal and post-natal care, malnutrition, family welfare etc. Thus this plan document became a vision document. Responsibility was not fixed on the government alone. Activities were classified and accordingly responsibilities were fixed by which partners were identified for administering development and social justice.

Reactions and Responses to Plan Document

Officials from the State Planning Commission and the Project Office of the District Rural Development Agency of Sivaganga District first examined the document and offered their comments. They found certain deficiencies in the process of data collection. Apart from the basic data all other data were collected through PRA exercises and prioritization was also done through the same exercise. This was not approved of by the officials. The activities envisaged in the plan document could not be carried out under the available schemes of the government. The Panchayats had not identified the individual beneficiaries for the government schemes. While entering the activities in the plan document, the Panchayats had to indicate the source of funding to carry out all the activities. Further they questioned the legitimacy of the plan document in the absence of a planning exercise at the Block level and the District level. On certain issues such as agriculture, veterinary care, non-conventional energy and environment, the people in the villages had not consulted the government departments while projecting activities in the plan document. These subjects were highly technical in nature, but the Panchayats had taken the opinion of the people in deciding upon the activities. On the whole it was an expression of cynicism. It is to be noted here that, in the inaugural function, the Minister for Panchayati Raj and Rural Development, Government of Tamil Nadu, showered encomium on the women leaders for their exercise and he said that despite the implementation of a variety of schemes and programmes of the Central and State Governments, people's felt needs could not be met and that this kind of micro level plan would reverse the trend and the felt needs would be met and thereby wasteful expenditure could be avoided. He further said that this kind of exercise would trigger a movement for people's planning. He even appealed that in each district this kind of exercise should be initiated.

Despite the remark of the Minister, the officials recorded their negative remarks about the whole exercise. Following the reaction and response of the officials, some of the experts from the audience came forward to express their opinion. Prominent among them were B.S. Raghavan, retired Chief Secretary of West Bengal and adviser to the FAO, A.K.Venkatasubramanian, retired civil servant specializing in Public Distribution System, Dr. Rajagopalan of the M.S. Swaminathan Foundation, Mr.Vallinayagam, retired Additional Director of Rural Development, and Mr. N.S. Chidambaram, retired Additional Director of Rural Development. First all the experts appreciated the effort expended in taking up this cause and facing all the problems in collecting data and putting them in a plan proposal and getting the approval of the people in the Gram Sabha and the Panchayat Council. It is a plan of the people prepared by the people and not a plan prepared by officials. It is their vision. They have chalked out their activities on the basis of their felt needs. It is true that they have not chalked out activities to implement the schemes of the government and hence there will be a gap between the available schemes and the activities envisaged in the plan document of the Panchayats. The plan document is not a petition prepared by them to get sanction from the government. It is their plan and they seek to be partners in governance to administer development. They have indicated the possibilities to generate employment opportunity with the resources and skills available in their respective Panchayats. Further it is to be noted that social development issues have been projected in the plan document and it is indicated that they will take up the responsibility to achieve sustainable results in development in the social sector. While appreciating the efforts of the Gram Panchayat leaders, they addressed a few questions to the government officials and a few suggestions to the Gram Panchayat leaders.

In fifty years of democratic governance in India, no such document was prepared for village development by the government. Even after the introduction of the 73rd Amendment and the Constitution of the District Planning Committee, no systematic effort was made at the micro level, despite planning officials working at the district level. Having failed miserably in discharging duties and responsibilities at the government level, it was unfair on the part of the officials to criticize the efforts made by the women leaders for their small technical lapses. Further it was characteristic on the part of the officials to denigrate the people's efforts as unscientific. Since the officials have been oriented to act in the supply driven mode of development activities, they look at everything from the supply side and not from the demand side. While evaluating the proposal, officials had looked for proposals for the government schemes and programmes and that was why they were not in a position to suggest ways and means to meet the demands which could not be fulfilled by the government schemes and programmes. The experts said that the officials could have offered their suggestions rather than criticizing the plan. Even the model plan prepared by the officials in some of the villages in Tamil Nadu did not include social development issues. The model plans prepared by the officials have not seen the light of day.

It is a unique exercise in fifty years of governance because every segment of the rural community has been involved in this exercise to make a declaration that their destinies are going to be decided by their efforts only. Now owners have been found for the rural development activities. They have realistically projected their needs as felt by the community without looking into the supply side of it. Hence it is the responsibility of the officials to help in identifying the institutions to be involved in the process of fulfilling the needs of the people. The existing schemes of the government could be utilized for many of the demands and for some of the demands a slight modification is necessary in implementing the existing government schemes for which the District Collector as Chairman of the DRDA and Inspector of Panchayats can make use of his discretionary powers. Demands which could not be met through government schemes could be taken to various financial institutions for financial support with a viable action proposal prepared by professionals for which the Panchayats have to seek the support of NGOs. It is fortunate that the Rural Welfare Trust is working with all these six Panchayats. The same organization can be involved in preparing such proposals and approaching CAPART, DST, NABARD and other agencies. For the social development issues targeted, achievable and quantifiable indicators have to be fixed. For instance school enrolment of students, birth weight of newly born babies, institutional delivery, reduction of school dropouts, providing safe drinking water supply to all families, ensuring sanitation facilities to all families, eradication of plastics and so on have been identified as activities and responsibilities have also been fixed in the case all the above said activities. The seven statutory committees in the villages have to be activated to involve themselves in all these activities. What the Gram Panchayats now require is partners to carry this task further.

After making these observations the experts again requested the officials directly dealing with planning at the grassroots to give their feedback again. The officials from the State Planning Commission and the District Rural Development Agency informed the audience and more specifically the Panchayat Presidents of the possibility of making use of many of the Central and State Government schemes and programmes to meet many of the issues projected in the plan document. For other issues and demands the nodal agency, the NGO, Rural Welfare Trust, was to prepare and send proposals to NABARD, CAPART and other agencies. Achievable indicators have to be explicitly entrusted to the committees of the Panchayats and their activities have to be monitored every year. This was the assurance given to the Panchayats by the officials.

Finally, the Panchayat Presidents concluded their presentation by assuring the officials that they would take up the responsibility to achieve many of the achievable indicators on social development. Further they informed that they would meet all the sectoral departments to seek their help to fulfil all the demands of the people mentioned in the PRA meetings while preparing the plan for the Gram Panchayats. The women leaders, while expressing their gratitude to the officials, explained their struggle to make use of the power devolved to them.

The whole exercise and the presentation of the plan in the development seminar provoked the women leaders assembled in the seminar to think on the social issues highlighted by the women Presidents of the six Gram Panchayats. The women Presidents who assembled in the seminar from all over Tamil Nadu under the banner of the Tamil Nadu Federation of Women Leaders prepared a charter of activities and declared it a charter of activities for the next year. The charter is presented hereunder.

Declaration

We, the elected women representatives who are gathered here at Gandhigram Rural Institute on this 27th day of October, 2002, declare that we will address the following issues in the next one year:

(i) All the eligible children (girls and boys) will be enrolled in schools.
(ii) We will strive to remove malnourishment amongst children in the age group of 0 – 5 years. As elected representatives we shall ensure that no underweight babies are born in our villages. The mothers will be given proper nourishment before and after delivery.
(iii) Better anti-natal and post-natal care will be provided for all the women in our Panchayats.
(iv) Any injustice against women in our Panchayats will be dealt with firmly. As a collective we will fight against domestic violence and also any other form of violence against any women in our Panchayat.
(v) We will ensure that child labour is abolished in our Panchayats.
(vi) We will ensure equitable access to and distribution of Panchayat resources among all the people in the Panchayats and guarantee at least the provision of the basic minimum requirements for the poorest. The PDS system will be improved with our intervention.
(vii) Problems faced by the women Panchayat leaders and women in general will be addressed collectively by making alliance with supportive institutions and organizations.
(viii) The newly implemented sanitary complexes meant for women will be effectively managed by women's groups with the support of the Panchayats.

(ix) Our Panchayats will not suffer from lack of drinking water. Everyone will be entitled to safe drinking water.

(x) We will ensure that Gram Sabhas take place regularly and more and more people take part in these meetings. We will ensure that a minimum of 50 per cent of the total women in the Panchayat attend the meetings and that their issues are properly heard.

(xi) We commit ourselves to the implementation of the 15-point programme prepared by the Tamil Nadu Government and request the State Government to devolve necessary powers to the Panchayats and local bodies for the same.

Following the presentation of reports and the declaration of the charter of activities for women Panchayat Presidents, the Pudukkottai District Project Officer, DRDA, representing the Pudukkottai District Administration, pleaded that this kind of exercise be undertaken in the whole of Pudukkottai District for which he sought the help of NGOs and Gandhigram Rural Institute. Women leaders from Pudukkottai District who attended the development seminar expressed their willingness to undertake this kind of exercise in their Panchayats. Thus the micro plan exercise done in six Gram Panchayats and the presentation of all the six plans in the development seminar in the presence of the Minister for Panchayati Raj and Rural Development, Government of Tamil Nadu, officials of the State Government, experts in Micro Level Planning and six hundred Gram Panchayat women Presidents created an awareness among the minister, the officials and the local body leaders on the importance of micro level planning and, as a result, the State Planning Commission started the exercise of giving training to the local body leaders on planning exercises to be done at the grassroots.

Analysis of I Phase Efforts

Primarily, though it is a constitutional mandate that the planning exercise has to be initiated at the grassroots, beyond the State Governments and the Central Government producing documents on decentralized planning, nothing has been done on the ground in the 9th and the 10th Plans. These six Panchayats, under the leadership of women, have sensitized the minister and the higher officials to the implications of micro level planning.

Secondly, while carrying out this exercise, it could be seen at what level devolution of powers has taken place in the state as the Panchayats faced problems in getting the support of the sectoral departments. Empirically this proved the extent to which powers have been devolved to the Panchayats.

Thirdly, in the process of interacting with the officials and hearing views of the officials on the plan proposals of the Panchayats, the official attitude to this new dispensation and the exercise has been exposed and they have been sensitized to the legal and social implications of micro level planning.

Fourthly, the other women Presidents have gained confidence that this kind of exercise could be done in their Panchayats also as they heard the methodology adopted in the six Gram Panchayats for planning at the micro level.

Fifthly, social development issues came to the limelight because of the micro plans of the six Gram Panchayats. These six Gram Panchayat leaders gained this insight while they were in self help groups and thereby they quickly grasped the social development issues and fixed achievable indicators for the Panchayats. This kind of exercise motivated the other Panchayat leaders to take up this issue. As a result the women Panchayat leaders published a charter of activities to be undertaken by the Panchayats in the social development sector.

Sixthly, in the recent past people have been mobilized by various agencies for participation in the implementation of various schemes and programmes brought from above. But the position "we govern you receive" has not altered. By undertaking the planning exercise by the people, people's demands and priorities have been prominently projected in the plan document and thereby the old position "we govern you participate" has been replaced by "you govern and you participate".

Seventhly, the six Panchayat Presidents have started negotiations with officials, representatives of the people like MLAs and

MPs and NGOs for fulfilling the requirements of the plan. They have developed skills of negotiation.

Eighthly, the hidden potential of the leadership has been exhibited through this process. Class, caste and political organizations have their own roles in the activities of the rural society. While mobilizing all the groups cutting across these differences, the women leaders have exhibited a high decree of democratic leadership. Even the traditional Panchayat leaders have extended their fullest cooperation to the efforts of these Panchayat Presidents.

Ninthly, the conventional mode of looking at issues and demands from the supply mode has been done away with and instead issues are being looked at from the perspective of the people and thereby a sense of ownership has been cultivated among the people for the development of the community.

Tenthly, so far the Panchayats negotiated for schemes and programmes of the government. Now the trend has been reversed and they ask for the government's participation in their schemes and programmes. Petitioners have changed their role to that of negotiators because of this new exercise.

Eleventhly, the Panchayats have started mobilizing partners for their development activities. They have gathered many organizations to their support in implementing their schemes.

Twelfthly, the leaders have built a vision document through this exercise. They have gained rich input on vision building from the training undergone elsewhere by the Presidents. While doing so they are critiquing the very concept of development. They move around the skills and the resources available at their disposal.

Though they are women and, that too, three of them are of the Backward Class and another three are Dalits, their leadership is recognized, appreciated and supported by even traditional Panchayat leaders. The women leaders, by their performance, have won the recognition of the community. Since initiatives are taken jointly by the leaders, the administration becomes transparent and it reduces corruption to the maximum extent. The planning exercise has made the people volunteers in the development initiative.

Summing up of I Phase

Planning at the grassroots for administering development and social justice has long range implications in the paradigm of development. It alters the entire process of development. The roles of the government and the community have been reversed. All the loopholes in the development process in the existing paradigm have been exposed and people have developed a new perspective to look at issues and now plans of activities are chalked out on the basis of their demands and needs as prioritized by the people and not on the basis of the available schemes and programmes of the government. The concept of "we govern you receive" has gone and the new concept "you govern and you participate" has been ushered in. Social development issues have drawn the attention of the people because of this exercise and achievable indicators have been fixed for social development issues and people have taken up the responsibility of achieving the target. People have developed a sense of ownership as this plan document carries the demands of the people as schemes and programmes. Now the government finds itself in a tight spot as to whether this is to be allowed or not. There is no other option except to allow and continue the new practice. Over and above, at the earliest, the entire state has to take the initiative to plan for development from the Gram Panchayat to the District Planning Committee. The new paradigm will gain momentum and it will ultimately end in a movement for decentralized governance for development and social justice.

Exercise in II Phase

Based on the exercise undertaken in Sivagangai District micro level planning was started in Pudukkottai District. Pudukkottai District offered three advantages for undertaking this exercise. They were: the District Collector is pro-Panchayat and he believes in the potentialities of the Panchayats and the community; the link between Panchayats and the communities is strong; and, the capacity of the leaders is very high as periodical orientations apart from training were given to the Panchayat leaders. As the District Collector invited

The Hunger Project, it was decided to work with the Panchayats. The district administration provided office space for The Hunger Project in the District Panchayat office. Thirteen Gram Panchayats were selected from all the 13 Blocks. The main criteria adopted in the selection process is that the Panchayat leader should have commitment and honesty, the link between the leader and the community should be so strong, and there should not be any communal and political conflict between and among the collectivities. By adopting the criteria the following Gram Panchayats were selected in a meeting held in the Collecteroate with the participation of The Hunger Project staff, the District Collector, the Project Officer, DRDA, of Pudukkottai District. Table 4.2 presents the list of the selected Panchayats.

Table 4.2 : Model Panchayats for Community Based Micro Level Planning in Pudukkottai District

Sl. No.	*Name of the Panchayat*	*Panchayat Union*	*Name of the Panchayat President*
1.	Merpanaikadu	Aranthangi	Ms. Bhavani Ilango
2.	Poovalur	Avudayarkoil	Mr. Sarvana Perumal
3.	Melathur	Thiruvarankulam	Mr. Saravanan
4.	Edaiyathimangalam	Manamelkudi	Mr. Arumugam
5.	Elaikadaividuthi	Karambakudi	Ms. J. Manjula
6.	Melaputhuvayal	Kunandarkoil	Ms. Dhanalakshmi
7.	Parambur	Annavasal	Mr. Abdulwaheed
8.	Nerinjikudi	Ponnamaravathy	Mr. P. Ramnu
9.	Punalkulam	Gandarvakottai	Mr. Shanmugam
10.	Mookampatti	Pudukkottai	Ms. V. Mangalam
11.	Meenaveli	Viralimalai	Mr. Alagiri
12.	Virachilai	Tirumayam	Ms. Devi
13.	K. Rayavaram	Arimalam	Ms. Rani Sathappan

Out of the 13 Gram Panchayat Presidents 6 are men and 7 are women.

Planning Methodology in II Phase

After getting consent from the Panchayat leaders, the President was asked to constitute the statutory Panchayat committees along with the Panchayat Planning Committee. In all the committees it should be mandatory that women and Dalit representatives should find a place. Panchayat President, Vice-Presidents, Panchayat clerk, committee members, traditional Panchayat leaders, SHG leaders, youth leaders, retired officials of the Panchayat areas were drawn for training. A three-day training in planning at the village level was offered. It was a residential training programme and it was conducted in Gandhigram Rural Institute. In the training exercise emphasis was laid on participation of people, especially women and Dalits, and social development issues. Following the training in each Gram Panchayat a sensitization exercise was conducted to prepare the people for evolving a perspective plan for socio-economic development of the Gram Panchayat area. To change the mindset of the people, this exercise continued till the draft plan was approved in the Gram Sabha. Sensitization was also done on social development issues. When the training was over, responsibilities were fixed as to who and how the needed data have to be collected from both primary and secondary sources. After collecting the data, a neat profile of the village was developed which was termed a development report. After consolidation of the report a Participatory Rural Appraisal for every Panchayat was to be conducted to prioritize the works that were to be undertaken in the Panchayat.

After prioritizing the activities, The Hunger Project staff, with the help of the Panchayat leader and the clerk identified the vulnerable families and gave numbers to the families. A list of the disabled was made for constant monitoring. Schools, anganwadi, primary health centre service would be assessed by the staff of The Hunger Project. Thus social development activities became the primary concern of the Panchayat. A manual, listing the activities related to social development to be carried out in the Panchayat area by the Panchayats in partnership with other agencies was supplied to all the Panchayat leaders (activity chart). Malnourished children, pregnant women affected by anemia and poor women affected by diseases would be identified and all the lists would be attached to the plan document. Finally, responsibilities were fixed as to how these prioritized activities were going to be carried out and with whose partnerships. All the needs identified and prioritized through the PRA were to be matched with the schemes and programmes of the Central and State Governments that being operated through sectoral departments. For unmatched issues Panchayats were to seek the help of MLAs and MPs and to get substantial funds from their Local Area Development Fund. The whole plan document was placed before the Gram Sabha for evaluation, suggestion and approval. After getting the approval, with modifications, if any, the plan document was to be printed.

The printed plan document would be circulated to all the sectoral departments. The District Collector as Inspector of Panchayats would give necessary instructions to the sectoral department heads to carry out activities in the Panchayats based on their needs. The Panchayats with the help of the Planning Committee and the representative of The Hunger Project should do the follow-up activities.

Lessons Learnt

It is not a State driven planning activity. It is initiated from below. Though it was initiated by the leader of the Panchayat in the process of mobilization, people have been made to participate in the process of preparation of the development plan. Panchayat leaders and the members of various committees have developed negotiating skills in the process of the preparation of the plan. They negotiate with the sectoral departments, MLAs and MPs. Further they negotiate with Union Councillors and District Ward Members to make use of the funds available in the Block and District Panchayats. Since there was no initiative from the State Government and the Central Government for planning from below with the participation of people, these Gram Panchayat leaders took the initiative and followed the guidelines provided by the State Planning Commission for planning at the micro level, especially at Gram Panchayat level. Because of these initiatives, even the State Planning Committee has started doing this exercise in 250 Gram Panchayats throughout Tamil Nadu. It is also not planning but preparing a development report.

While engaged in this exercise it could be visualized at what level devolution of powers has taken place in the State as the Panchayats faced problems in getting the support of the sectoral departments. Empirically this proved the extent to which powers have been devolved to the Panchayats. Further while interacting with officials in the process of plan preparation the attitude of the officials towards planning could be seen. Thanks to this exercise the officials are exposed and sensitized towards planning and social development. The grassroots leaders have exhibited an extraordinary commitment towards communities social development. The micro level plan experience made the Panchayat leaders enhance their capacity and use the full potentiality of leadership. Panchayat Presidents and the people have prepared a plan. Now they have reversed the process of development activities from supply driven to demand driven mode. Realistically speaking the plan is a vision document and the activities listed in the plan document are only their wish list when there is no conducive atmosphere for micro level planning.

Summing up of II Phase

The new dispensation of micro level planning with the participation of the people to administer economic development and social justice envisioned in the Constitution through the 73rd and the 74th Amendments has far reaching implications in the development paradigm in the context of redefining the concept of Government against the backdrop of democratic decentralization of powers and globalization of economy. This new initiative has reversed the process from supply driven to demand driven activities. The old practice of the government providing and the people receiving has been reversed. Now people plan and participate and the government just supports. The whole development exercise moves in a different mode which is totally different from that of the government. People's wishes and vision have been projected as a major set of activities and people have taken up responsibilities.

There is yet another striking feature in the micro level planning process. In all such previous exercises only infrastructural facilities were projected as the major set of activities. But now people have focused more on social development activities because of the continuous sensitization and conscientization programme. This kind of people's initiatives in a few Panchayats has put the Government in a tight spot. As a result the State Planning Commission has taken efforts to prepare a development report in about 250 Gram Panchayat as a pilot project. Thus this new paradigm will gain momentum and it will ultimately end in a movement for decentralized governance for development and social justice.

Integrated Analysis

It has been tested in the process of planning at grassroots that planning is possible even without much power and the cooperation of the government departments. By initiating the process the gap between the Panchayat leaders and the community is bridged. People are mobilized constantly and conscientized on social development activities. Ownership is being developed among the people for many of the development activities. In the process of interaction with Panchayat leaders and officials, Gram Sabha members have established a grip over the Panchayat administration. While the Panchayat Presidents are organizing meetings with various committee members the Panchayat administration becomes transparent and non-corrupt. Planning initiative at the grassroots involves the women's and thereby women's issues have been dealt with. Slowly Panchayat leaders, Ward Members and committee members are sensitized towards gender issues. Committee formation is a process by which women members and representatives from the Dalit community are inducted and their participation in the meetings has created sensitiveness among all towards the issues of Dalits. Panchayat leaders have started bargaining with other representatives of the people, namely MLA, MP, Ward Members of Block Panchayats and District Panchayats. The leaders have developed bargaining capacity to deal with officials. Panchayat leaders have developed a vision for the development of the community. Panchayat leaders and the people have realized the fact that for most of the social development activities money requirement is minimum and that to accomplish the same what is needed is commitment on the part of the Panchayat leaders and the community. The District Collector and his team of officials have shown much interest in Panchayat activities as they have faith in the Panchayat's potential. Along with Panchayats, the officials also claim credit in achieving the target of all development activities. Without the cooperation of the Panchayats and the community, officials cannot achieve the target successfully and hence they now bank on the Panchayats. Further the quality of the works carried out by the Panchayats with the participation of the people is good compared to the work of the contractors. Each and every Panchayat is having a plan document which is regarded as it pride.

By developing a plan document at the village level, indirectly a compulsion has been placed on the sectoral departments to work in the villages with their allocation of resources restricted to the activities indicated in the plan document of the respective Gram Panchayats.

Conclusion

In the given context, however, poor devolution of powers, functions and finance in Tamil Nadu, planning at grassroots will compel the government to devolve the same. Administration becomes transparent and involvement of women and Dalits is remarkable in the activities of the communities. Both people and their leaders are sensitive towards the social development issues. Every Village Panchayat has a legitimate vision document which prevents the sectoral developments spending unilaterally. It bridges the gap between the people and the government. The entire State can replicate it.

NOTES AND REFERENCES

1. K. N. Raj, "*Some Thoughts on Decentralization of Development Planning and Implications*" keynote paper presented at Seminar on Decentralized Planning and Implementation, Nov. 29-1, Dec. 1984, ISEC, Bangalore.
2. K.V. Sundaram, *Decentralized Multi Level Planning*, New Delhi: Concept Publishing Company, 1997.
3. K.C. Sivaramakrishnan, *Power to the People? : The Politics and Progress of Decentralization*, New Delhi: Konark Publishers Pvt. Ltd., 2000.

4. T.M. Thomas Issac, and Richard W. Franke, *Local Democracy and Development,* New Delhi : Left Word, 2000.
5. N. Narayanasamy, M.P. Boraian and M.A. Jeyaraju (eds), *Corruption at the Grassroots : The Shades and Shadows,* New Delhi: Concept Publishing Company, 2000.
6. James Manor, *The Political Economy of Democratic Decentralization,* Washington DC : The World Bank, 1999.
7. G. Palanithurai, *Panchayat Raj System in Tamil Nadu : With Original Act,* New Delhi : Concept Publishing Company, 2003.
8. Jayati Ghosh, *"Development Strategy in India : A Political Economy Perspective" in Nationalism,* Democracy and Development : State and Politics in India (Eds), Sugata Bose and Ayesha Jalal, New Delhi : Oxford University Press, 1998, pp. 165/83.
9. M. Ajit Banerjee, and K.A. Chidambaram, (eds.) *Renewing Governance : Issues and Options,* New Delhi : Tata McGraw Hill Publishing Company, 1996.
10. International Commission on Peace and Food, *Developing Human Resourcefulness : Strategies to eradicate poverty in the 1990s* Draft Working Paper, California: ICPE, 1989.
11. The World Bank, *World Development Report, 2004 : Making Services work for Poor People,* Washington DC : The World Bank, 2003.
12. Rajesh Tandon and Ranjita Mohanty, *Civil Society and Governance,* New Delhi: Sanskrit, 2002.
13. G. Palanithurai, *Report of the Training Programme on Training of Trainers in Multi Level Planning Conducted for DRDA Officials,* Gandhigram : Rajiv Gandhi Chair for Panchayati Raj Studies, 2000.
14. G. Palanithurai, *New Panchayati Raj System at Work: An Evaluation,* New Delhi: Concept Publishing Company, 1999.
15. G. Palanithurai, *From Participation to Self-Governance : An Agenda for Restructuring Tamil Nadu Panchayat Act 1994,* Gandhigram : Department of Political Science and Development Administration, 1998.
16. State Planning Commission, *Report of the Working Group on Decentralized Planning and Panchayati Raj,* Chennai : Government of Tamil Nadu, 1997.
17. G. Palanithurai, *Report of the Training Programme on Training of Trainers in Multi Level Planning Conducted for DRDA Officials,* Gandhigram: Rajiv Gandhi Chair for Panchayati Raj Studies, 2000.
18. G. Palanithurai, *Report of the Workshop on "Panchayati Raj : Trials and Triumphs",* Gandhigram : The Hunger Project, 2003.
19. G. Palanithurai, *Report of the Training on Multilevel Planning,* Gandhigram: Tamil Nadu Council for Sustainable Livelihood, 2002.
20. G. Palanithurai, *Report of the Workshop on Multilevel Planning,* Gandhigram: Tamil Nadu Council for Sustainable Livelihood, 2002.
21. Veerakalaiarasi, *Perspective Plan for Development of Veppankulam,* Thirupathur : Grama Iyakkam, 2002; K. Rakku, *Perspective Plan for*

Development of Vadavanpatti, Thirupathur : Grama Iyakkam, 2002; Y. Pushpam, *Perspective Plan for Development of P. Nerpuhapatti,* Thirupathur : Grama Iyakkam, 2002; *Y. Nagajothi,* Perspective Plan for Development of Kozhikudipatti, *Thirupathur : Grama Iyakkam,* 2002; C. Chinnammal, *Perspective Plan for Development of Urathupatti,* Thirupathur : Grama Iyakkam, 2002; S. Gomathy, *Perspective Plan for Development of Manalur,* Thirupathur : Grama Iyakkam, 2002.

GRAM PANCHAYAT AND SOCIAL DEVELOPMENT

Activity Chart

INDICATORS

Sl. No.	*Activities*	*Responsibility*	*Outcome*	*Verification*
1	*2*	*3*	*4*	*5*
1.	100 per cent enrolment of eligible children	President, Vice-President, Ward Members, PTA, SHG Members, Youth Clubs, NGO, Retired Officials, Education Committee	Level of literacy increased.	School records
2.	Reduction of Dropouts	President, Vice-President, Ward Members, PTA, SHG Members, Youth Clubs, NGO, Retired Officials	Increase in Educational Standard	School records
3.	Ensuring protected Drinking Water Supply to School	President, Vice-President, Ward Members, School Teachers	Improvement of students Health, reduction of ill health of students	Physical verification
4.	Providing toilets to school	President, Vice-President, Ward Members, School Teachers	Increase in health of children	Physical verification
5.	Utilizing the toilets by the school students	President, other members of the Panchayat Council Teachers, PTA, Parents.	Toilet Culture Developed	Physical verification
6.	Cutting the nails of the students every Monday in Balwadi and School	Youth club, SHG, Panchayat Ward Members, School teachers	Health education, reduction of diseases, improvement of health	Physical verification
7.	Planting of saplings in the school premises	President, teachers, agriculture departments	Environment awareness eco-development	Physical verification

1	*2*	*3*	*4*	*5*
8.	Creating a school garden	President, teachers PTA, Youth Clubs, Agriculture Department	Increase in nutrition as the vegetables are given to noon mean centres	Physical verification
9.	Keeping the Balwadi clean and neat	Balwadi teacher, President, Vice-President, Ward Members	Health education, increase in status of health, culture of cleanliness is cultivated	Physical verification
10.	Providing a toilet in the Balwadi	President, Vice-President, Ward Members	Education, increase in health status	Physical verification
11.	Bringing a toilet culture among the kids	Balwadi teacher	Health education, increase in health status	Physical verification
12.	Adding vegetables to the noon meal by getting donations and getting the vegetables from the school garden	President, Vice-President, Balwadi teacher, School teachers	Nutritive food for students	Physical verification
13.	Taking steps to prevent the practice of child labour	President, Vice-President, Ward Members, School teachers, PTA, .NGO, SHG, Youth Club	School enrolment, literacy, HRD	Physical verification
14.	Cleaning over head tanks	OHT operators, under the instruction of panchayat regularly	Health status, productivity	Verifying the records
15.	Creating awareness among the people about the consequence of alcohol and stop brewing and selling the same in the panchayat premises	President, Vice-President, Ward Member, Health Committee, SHG, Youth Club, NGO	Economic status of poor, status of women and children, health of individuals and reduction of social problems	Physical verification
16.	Creating Awareness among the people about family welfare	PHC Staff, President, Vice-President, Ward Members, Health Committee, SHG, Youth	Livelihood security ensured	Verifying the records small family

1	*2*	*3*	*4*	*5*
17.	Identify the vulnerable fami- lies and ensure food security to them and constantly monitor them with the help of government schemes	President, Vice-President, Ward Members, SHGs	Income generation, reduction of poverty, status of women	Physical verification
18.	Building the skill of the women through training	Presidents, Vice-President, Ward Members, Training Institution, Social Welfare Department at the District Women Development Corporation	Income generation, reduction of poverty, status of women	Physical verification
19.	Establish link between the skilled persons and banking sector for the establishment of business venture by the women	President, Vice-President, Ward Members, Planning Committee Members, NGO, Banks, SHG	Development of rural economy, and increase of status of women	Panchayat profile
20.	Building the skills of the youth through training	President, Vice-President, Ward Members, Training institutions, NYK	Human Resource Develop- ment, Economic Development	NYK Report
21.	Establish link between the skilled persons and Banking sector for the establishment of business venture by the youth	President, Vice-President, Ward Member, Planning Committee Members, NGOs, Banks, NYKs	Development of Rural Economy	Panchayat Profile
22.	Ensuring proper function-ing of PDS	President, Vice-President, Ward Members and SHG, officials of Civil Supply	Food Security	Verifying the BPL List
23.	Prevent open defecation in the villages by creating awareness and construct-ing toilets in each and every house	President, Vice-President, Ward Members, SHG, Youth Club, NGO, Project Staff, TRSP, Retired Employees	Improvement in Health, Sanitation Environment	Physical verification

1	2	3	4	5
24.	Creating awareness about RCH by printing a card and giving it to every family	President, Vice-President, Ward Members, Health Committee, NGO, Staff of PHC	Improvement in women and children, health, economic status	PHC records
25.	Ensure the delivery of services from sub-centre and PHC to the people through the schemes available for pre-natal and post-natal care	PHC Staff, President, Vice-President, Ward Members, SHG, NGO, Health Committee	Increase in health status and economic status	Verifying the PHC records
26.	Creating awareness about growing medicinal plants and make it a business by involving SHG and youth clubs	President, Vice-President, Ward Members, SHG, Planning Committee, Youth Club, NGO, NABARD Bank Staff	Income generation for women-improvement of rural economy	Physical verification
27.	Creating awareness among the importance of water management	President, Vice-President, Ward Members, Community leaders, Planning Committee Members, NGO	Rational Utilization of Water	Physical verification
28.	Creating a common burial ground in to graveyard in the villages	President, Vice President, Ward Members, SHG, Youth Club	Social justice	Physical verification
29.	Taking steps to manage the solid waste and earn money from it for panchayats	President, Vice-President, Ward Members, Planning Committee, NGO, SHG	Environment development, income generation, better agricultural practices	Panchayat Records

1	*2*	*3*	*4*	*5*
30.	Organise workshop for pregnant women to dissemi- nate the needed information akin to ANC and PNC	PHC Staff, SHG, President and Vice-President	Increase of health awareness, health status, economic status, reduction of infant mortality and new born babies are in exact weight	Verifying with PHC Records
31.	Conducting medical camps for poor and school children	President, Vice-President, Ward Members, NGOs, SHG, nearby Rotary and Lions Club	Improved health status	Verifying with PHC Records
32.	Make the SHG and Youth Clubs to take up Panchayat works instead of employing contractor	President, Vice-President, Ward Members, SHG Youth Club, NGO	Employment opportunity, quality of work, reduction of expenditure, local needs	Panchayat records
33.	Regularly conducting Gram Sabha meetings	President, Vice-President, Ward Members	Peoples participation, Good Governance	Panchayat Records
34.	Ensuring 60 per cent attendance in Gram Sabha meeting.	President, Vice-President, Ward Members, all eligible members, SHG members, NGOs working in the Panchayats	Transparency, accountability of Panchayats	Panchayat Records
35.	Ensuring Women / Dalit parti-cipation 50 per cent of attendance	President, Vice-President, Ward Members, SHG, NGO	Social justice, status of weaker section	Panchayat Records
36.	Information disseminations • Income/Expenditure display • Report on schemes implemented display • List of schemes proposed to be implemented • List of beneficiaries	President and Panchayat Clerk	Transparency, accountability credibility of Panchayat, Better participation	Seeing the Display Board of Panchayat

1	*2*	*3*	*4*	*5*
37.	Participatory decision making • Opportunities for discussion to all communities • Equal status to all in seating • Developing consensus	President, Ward Members, Community Leaders/ retired government officials, School teachers, Planning Committee Members, Dalit Leaders, NGOs and other association members	Achieving communal harmony, evolution of social capital	Verifying the records of Panchayats
38.	Develop a system of communication to give information about Gram Sabha meeting	President, Clerk, Ward Member, SHG, Youth Clubs, NGOs	Transparency, accountability	Physical verification
39.	Provision of water supply to Dalit hamlets	President and the concerned Ward Members, Committee for water supply	Receiving the services continuously	Physical verification
40.	Removal of untoucha-bility by • Preventing the two tumbler system • Participating in temple festival	President, Ward Members, SHG, Youth Clubs, Community Leaders	Social justice, Communal harmony	Physical verification
41.	Training to Dalit Youths in skill development and availing THADCO schemes	President, Youth Clubs, NGOs, Education Institutions	Economic development, social justice	Physical verification
42.	Identification of all CPR verifying the status of encroachment details	Panchayat President, Vice-President, Ward Members, Government Officials, Police, Department	Environment development social justice, income generation	Verifying Panchayat Records

1	2	3	4	5
43.	Removal of encroachments	Panchayat President, Vice-President, (Revenue and Police Department	Productive use of resources, equity, income generation for Panchayats	Verifying Panchayat Records
44.	Utilizing the Common Properties and developing the same	Panchayat President, Ward Members, NGO, SHG, Youth groups	Environment development, income generation	Verifying Panchayat Records
45.	100 per cent house tax collection	President, Clerk, Vice-President, Ward Members, SHG, Youth	Financial status of Panchayat more government funds	Verifying Panchayat Records
46.	Panchayat functioning as a system	President, Clerk, Vice-President, Ward Members	Accountable	Verifying Panchayat Records
47.	Records maintenance/ transparency	President and Clerk	Good Governance	Verifying Panchayat Records
48.	Preparing a perspective plan through village planning forum	President, Ward Members, Planning Committee, School Leaders, NGO, Youth, SHG	Planned development better use of resources	Verifying Panchayat Records
49.	Formation of Statutory Committees	President	Efficiency of panchayats accountability	Verifying Panchayat Records
51.	Old age, Physically and mentally disabled, destitute, orphan and other vulnerable sections	President, Ward Members, SHG, NGO, Government and Planning Committee	Social security, social harmony	Verifying Panchayat Records

The above projected activities could be carried out easily if the Panchayat meets some key assumption. They are:

Key Assumptions

- Harmony prevails in Panchayat.
- Panchayat is perceived as development space.
- Community supports the Panchayats.
- Panchayat leader has got commitment.
- Panchayat leader has vision.
- Panchayat leader has got skill and capacity.
- Panchayat is not leader centric.
- Panchayat is people and system centric.

5

GOOD GOVERNANCE AT GRASSROOTS

After four decades' experience of democratic governance in India, academics and intellectuals have started exercising on the theme of good governance by accepting the fact that it is not in vogue and further that governance has become bad also[1]. But one can get solace by projecting the same experience of bad governance, poor governance and absence of governance in many countries in the world. One can become complacent only when remedies are found out. Exercises are on in the whole of the world to contain corruption, reform the government machinery at the managerial level and fix indicators to establish good governance. Approaches and strategies vary from country to country and society, to society depending on the need of the country and the society[2]. A variety of definitions have been offered and roughly eighty definitions are being discussed and deliberated over a period of one and half decade and it is a pity that the direction came for such discussion from the donor agencies who have lent heavily for development works in the developing countries as they have not been used properly.

Even before the start of this kind of discussion in the academic institutions many of the democratic regimes have been changed due to poor governance and bad governance. It is pertinent that more than 50 per cent of the population of the world are coming under the parliamentary form of governance. More and more number of collectivities have expressed their aspiration to move towards democracy and started struggles to achieve the same. The countries which are having representative democracy are now inclined to move towards participatory democracy[3]. Right from the recognition of the concept of government either for the community or for the nation state, value premises have been developed as to how a good government has to perform and how not to function. Thinkers and theorists have pondered, upon the concept continuously[4]. Yet there was no such intense discussion on this concept as now as the necessity has arisen only now. To operationalise good governance, "new public management" is being considered as a vital input. The last two decades of the present century have witnessed a great deal of structural adjustments and a new type of state intervention to seek cooperation and help from community organizations for the empowerment of the citizens. Most of the countries have attempted to limit the role of the state, including downsizing the bureaucracy, devolution of authority, cost reduction, contracting out some of the operative functions of the government, developing and designing result oriented appraisal systems, and commercialization as well as market orientation of the governmental activities. This has been supported by effective accountability through an open reporting system. The administration is apparently moving from rule to result orientation, from systems to enterprise, from obedience to reward, from inaction to action, from centralization to decentralization and from the duties of administrators to the rights of citizens. Starting from the World Bank all the donor agencies have discussed the establishment of good governance at every level with a view to keeping their money back in the track[5].

For some time good governance was for resource management. Good governance has always been a subject in the political discourse in the world right from Socrates down to Mahatma Gandhi. Ancient literature provides ample evidence for the establishment of good governance[6]. What is more important is that good governance cannot be established in a bad society and it can be achieved only in a good society. A good society will create good governance[7]. Studies are abundant on good governance at federal and regional levels from the donor perspective and indicators are evolved specifically to evaluate governance in terms of its goodness. There were reports submitted by various commissions to reform government, administration and bureaucracy but nothing moved as expected in the absence of political will[8]. But now it is a donor driven exercise and they are compelled to do the exercise as it is mandatory to ensure uninterrupted fund flow for development activities. The whole exercise of achieving good governance in the Indian context is a mechanical process and not an organic one. Studies are rare at grassroots level as if it is meant for federal and state level governments[9]. Good governance has to start from the grassroots as it works closely with the community and the society. Of all governing institutions, grassroots institutions are the only institutions that can establish linkages with the community and society on a day to day basis. Hence it is necessary to visualize it from the perspective of the people. The whole of governance, democracy and development are always being debated and discussed from the perspective of the rulers, donors, academics and bureaucrats but not from the perspective of the people who are the participants of democracy and development. In the whole process nobody dare ask the people how a good government should be. People have their own perception of governance and good governance. Is it different from the governance indicators evolved by the donor agencies and administrators and social thinkers. To discuss the above issues a study has been initiated. An attempt is made to study governance at the grassroots from good governance perspectives and that too from the perspective of the people and their representatives at the grassroots.

A Framework for Analysis

Governance and good governance have been seen from different perspectives. The donor perspective dominates now[10]. There is another perspective called ideology. There are a variety of approaches and strategies and they have been developed over a period of time. Adequate literature is also generated from both empirical analysis and normative analysis. Indicators have been fixed to evaluate the performance of governments. Yet these are all pertinent to Central and State Governments. Of the variety of indicators fixed by different agencies, the indicators fixed by the UNDP have been recognized all over the world. They are:

(a) participation, (b) transparency, (c) responsiveness, (d) accountability, (e) legitimacy, (f) partnership, (g) rule of law, (h) consensus orientation, (i) equity, (j) effectiveness and efficiency, (k) strategic vision, (l) resource prudence, (m) ecological soundness, (n) empowering and enabling, and (o) spatial grounding in communities.

Recent developments in that subject have crept into the orbit of governance after the enactment of the 73rd Amendment to the Constitution of India, which provides enormous scope to look at governance at the grassroots. But studies are scanty in this area. Hence it is necessary to look at governance at the grassroots from the perspective of the people.

To analyse Panchayat performance at the grassroots from the people's perspective, parameters have to be evolved. To evolve parameters to evaluate good governance at the grassroots from the perspective of the people a serious exercise was done with a set of elected representatives and, based on the exercise, indicators have been fixed for good governance at the grassroots. The elected representatives have conceptualized the concept of good governance only from the perspective of the people[11]. The indicators derived from the above exercise are matched with the indicators evolved by UNDP. To suit the grassroots institutions the following indicators are fixed as referral indicators for this study. They are: (a) putting all the activities on a demand driven basis; (b) development activities are people centric and undertaken with the participation of people; (c) ensuring transparency in administration and decision-making process; (d) increasing efficiency and effectiveness in delivery of basic services; and (e) ensuring equity in the process of distribution of benefits to the needy.

It is to be analysed to what extent Panchayats are taking decisions and carrying out activities based on the demands of the people and how these activities are carried out in a transparent way, to what extent people are involved in Panchayat activities from decision-making to evaluation of Panchayat activities, to what extent the services delivered by Panchayats are effective in terms of quality and quantity, and, to what extent the problems of the vulnerable and marginalized are addressed through Panchayats.

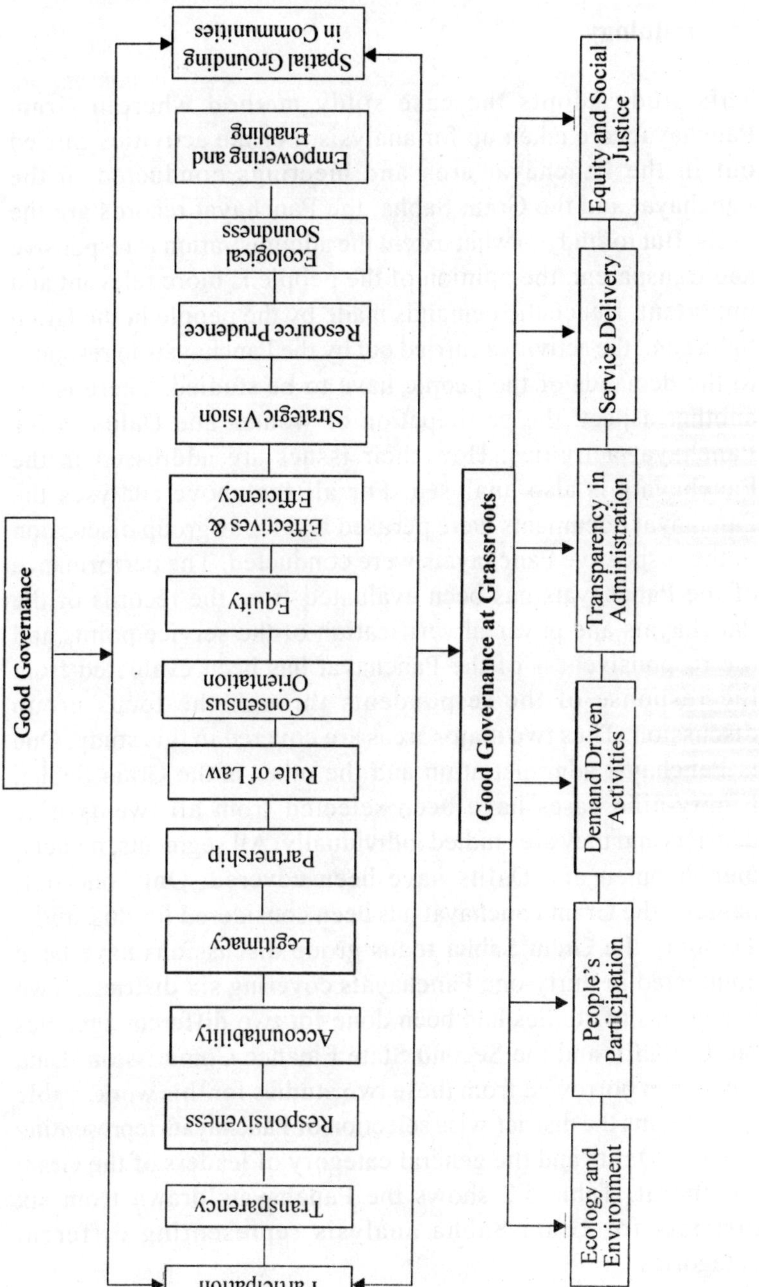
Good Governance
Participation
Transparency
Responsiveness
Accountability
Legitimacy
Partnership
Rule of Law
Consensus Orientation
Equity
Effectives & Efficiency
Strategic Vision
Resource Prudence
Ecological Soundness
Empowering and Enabling
Spatial Grounding in Communities
Good Governance at Grassroots
Ecology and Environment
People's Participation
Demand Driven Activities
Transparency in Administration
Service Delivery
Equity and Social Justice

Methodology

This study adopts the case study method wherein Gram Panchayats are taken up for analysis. For the activities carried out in the Panchayat area and meetings conducted in the Panchayat and the Gram Sabha, the Panchayat records are the basis. But to study to what extent the administration is responsive and transparent, the opinion of the people is more relevant and important. Hence the demands made by the people in the Gram Sabha and the activities carried out by the Panchayats in response to the demands of the people have to be studied. There is yet another aspect: the participation of women and Dalits in the Panchayat activities. How their issues are addressed in the Panchayats is also analysed. For all the above analyses the Panchayat documents were perused and focus group discussion in the respective Panchayats were conducted. The performance of the Panchayats has been evaluated from the records of the Panchayats and physical verification of the service points and the responsiveness of the Panchayat has been evaluated from the response of the respondents through the focus group discussion. Thus two major areas are covered in this study. One is Panchayat administration and the other is the Gram Sabha. Eighty-nine cases have been selected from all twenty-nine districts and they are studied individually. All segments, namely, men, women and Dalits have been covered. Only one-tier, namely, the Gram Panchayat has been considered for this study. To study the Gram Sabha focus group discussions have been conducted in thirty-one Panchayats covering six districts. Two categories of studies had been done for two different agencies the UNICEF and the Second State Finance Commission. Data have been borrowed from these two studies for this work. Table 5.1 explains the district-wise selection of Panchayats representing women, Dalits and the general category of leaders of the Gram Panchayat. Table 5.2 shows the Panchayats drawn from six districts for Gram Sabha analysis representing different categories.

Table 5.1 : Details of Case Studies for Panchayat Management

Sl. No.	*District*	*Women (General)*	*Women (SC)*	*Men (General)*	*Men (SC)*	*Total (G.P.)*
1.	Tanjore	2	1	1	1	5
2.	Ooty	1	-	1	1	3
3.	Nagapattinam	4	-	-	1	5
4.	Theni	1	3	-	2	6
5.	Cuddalore	1	2	1	-	4
6.	Dindigul	-	3	-	-	3
7.	Ramanathapuram	1	3	1	1	6
8.	Sivagangai	1	2	2	-	5
9.	Ariyalur	-	1	1	1	3
10.	Thiruvallur	-	1	1	-	2
11.	Virudhunagar	1	1	1	-	3
12.	Coimbatore	1	1	2	1	5
13.	Vellore	-	2	-	1	3
14.	Madurai	-	-	-	1	1
15.	Villupuram	-	-	1	1	2
16.	Thiruvarur	1	1	-	-	2
17.	Namakkal	-	3	1	-	4
18.	Thiruvannamalai	1	2	1	1	5
19.	Kancheepuram	1	-	2	-	3
20.	Kanyakumari	1	-	-	1	2
21.	Pudukkottai	2	1	1	-	4
22.	Tirunelveli	1	1	-	-	2
23.	Karur	1	-	-	1	2
24.	Perambalur	-	-	1	-	1
25.	Tuticorin	1	-	-	1	2
26.	Dharmapuri	-	-	1	1	2
27.	Salem	-	1	-	-	1
28.	Erode	-	-	-	1	1
29.	Trichy	-	2	-	-	2
	Total	**22**	**31**	**19**	**17**	**89**

Source : Computed.

Table 5.2 : Details of Case Studies Conducted for Gram Sabha

Sl. No.	*District*	*Name of the Panchayat*	*Total Panchayat*
1.	Madurai	Maganakulam Uchapatti A. Kovilpatti Valayankulam Katchakatti	5
2.	Dharmapuri	Chandrapatti A. Mallapuram Thimmapuram Madehalli Kottaipatti	5
3.	Kancheepuram	Mevalurkuppam Orikkai Pulleri Thiruvancheri Pullalur Mudichur	6
4.	Thiruvarur	Ammayappan Varambiyam Anaikuppam Bharatimoolangudi Kallikudi	5
5.	Kanyakumari	Erachakulam Eraipudur Karumpattur Shenbagaramanpudur Pallamthurai	5
6.	Coimbatore	Arasur Jameekottampatti Kongeyampalayam Servakaranpalayam Okkilipalayam	5
		Total	**31**

Source : Computed.

Table 5.3 : Gram Sabha Meeting

Sl. No.	*District*	*% Attendance*	*Women Participation*			*Dalit Participation*		
			G	*M*	*P*	*G*	*M*	*P*
1.	Tanjore	13	✓	-	-	-	✓	-
2.	Ooty	10	✓	-	-	-	-	✓
3.	Nagapattinam	12	✓	-	-	✓	-	-
4.	Theni	12	✓	-	-	✓	-	-
5.	Cuddalore	11	-	✓	-	-	✓	-
6.	Dindigul	13	✓	-	-	-	✓	-
7.	Ramanathapuram	12	✓	-	-	-	✓	-
8.	Sivagangai	12	✓	-	-	-	-	✓
9.	Ariyalur	11	-	✓	-	-	✓	-
10.	Thiruvallur	11	-	✓	-	-	✓	-
11.	Virudhunagar	12	✓	-	-	-	✓	-
12.	Coimbatore	12	-	✓	-	-	-	✓
13.	Vellore	11	-	✓	-	-	-	✓
14.	Madurai	12	✓	-	-	-	-	✓
15.	Villupuram	11	-	✓	-	-	-	✓
16.	Thiruvarur	13	-	✓	-	-	✓	-
17.	Namakkal	13	-	✓	-	-	✓	-
18.	Thiruvannamalai	11	-	✓	-	-	✓	-
19.	Kancheepuram	12	-	✓	-	-	✓	-
20.	Kanyakumari	12	✓	-	-	✓	-	-
21.	Pudukkottai	13	✓	-	-	✓	-	-
22.	Tirunelveli	11	✓	-	-	✓	-	-
23.	Karur	12	✓	-	-	-	✓	-
24.	Perambalur	11	-	✓	-	-	✓	-
25.	Tuticorin	10	✓	-	-	-	✓	-
26.	Dharmapuri	12	✓	-	-	-	✓	-
27.	Salem	13	✓	-	-	-	✓	-
28.	Erode	12	✓	-	-	-	✓	-
29.	Trichy	12	✓	-	-	-	✓	-
	Total		**18**	**11**	-	**5**	**18**	**6**

Source : Computed.

Gram Sabha

The Gram Sabha is a mechanism by which equality can be achieved, participation of people can be ensured, democratic culture can be inculcated in the Indian context. More particularly, the gap between the people and the government can be narrowed down only through the Gram Sabha. Further it is only with the Gram Sabha that Indian democracy changes its character from representative to participatory. The Gram Sabha has got such vibrancy and vitality. Its utility depends on proper understanding of the new devise and application of the same in the life of the people.

The participation of the people in the process of development at the grassroots is verified only through the Gram Sabha as it has to be convened four times in a year with a quorum of one-tenth of the total members of the Gram Sabha. Both the Gram Panchayat Presidents and the members of the Gram Sabha have accepted the fact that the attendance at the Gram Sabha is to show the officials that the quorum is achieved. There is no voluntary participation of the people in the Gram Sabha meeting as the demands projected and prioritized in the Gram Sabha meeting are not honoured by the sectoral departments of the Government of Tamil Nadu. Women's participation in the Gram Sabha is more than that of men as the SHG women have to get many certificates for their activities. Hence they feel that it is their obligation. Likewise, Dalit participate in the Gram Sabha meetings only because they want their names to be included in the BPL list to get the benefits from the schemes of the government. Only in a few places the members of the Gram Sabha participate in the Gram Sabha meeting with voluntary spirit as the Panchayat Presidents have performed very well. In order to support such Gram Panchayat Presidents, people participate in the Gram Sabha meetings. In all Gram Panchayats accounts are placed properly and the Gram Panchayat Presidents inform that they not only placed the accounts in the Gram Sabha but also made announcement in the Gram Sabha that the accounts of the Panchayat are always kept ready for verification by the public. But the people never bother to ask questions on the accounts. They continue to give petitions to the Presidents thinking that the Gram Sabha is a place to collect petitions. Since the Gram Panchayats selected for the study are good Panchayats in terms of their performance, people did not bother to ask questions. Further the Presidents informed the investigators uniformly in all the Panchayats that the people are not ready to take up any responsibility as they have been oriented in the past five decades to act as beneficiaries and petitioners. Now it is the responsibility of the Panchayats to change the mindset from beneficiary to citizen. Further Panchayats are weak in terms of power in the governance system. Yet people are participating in the Gram Sabha because Panchayat Presidents are responsive to the call of the people. One important profit society has gained in the process of conducting the Gram Sabha meetings irrespective of the powers it enjoys is that people have an opportunity to discuss their issues and problems. Further the women have started discussing their problems in the Gram Sabha. In many Panchayats gender and livelihood issues are being discussed in the Gram Sabha meetings. Social development issues are gaining momentum only because of the women who participate in the Gram Sabha meetings.

Demand Driven Activities

The new dispensation has to act on the basis of demand and not on the basis of supply[12]. Both the Panchayat Presidents and the Gram Sabha members have categorically stated that the Panchayat activities are still in the supply mode. In 18 districts the respondents recorded very poor relationship between the supply and the demand. People continue to demand services from the government. The Panchayat system is also created with an objective of altering the existing arrangements from supply driven to demand driven mode. The list of demands projected in the Gram Sabha by its members continues to increase and continues to remain unattended to by the sectoral departments. Panchayat Presidents have to move from pillar to post to meet the demands of the people. Since the Presidents have commitments and responsiveness they seek the help of all the sectoral departments to fulfil the demands of the people. A few departments cooperate with the Presidents to fulfil the demands by utilizing the allotted money of the sectoral departments. Many do not come to the rescue of the Panchayat leaders. They seek the help of the MLAs and the MPs since they have discretionary funds.

Table 5.4 : Demand and Supply

Sl. No.	*Districts*	*Demand and Supply Relations*			
		Poor 0 – 25	*Average 26 – 50*	*Moderate 51 – 75*	*Good 76 – 100*
1.	Tanjore	-	✓	-	-
2.	Ooty	✓	-	-	-
3.	Nagapattinam	✓	-	-	-
4.	Theni	✓	-	-	-
5.	Cuddalore	✓	-	-	-
6.	Dindigul	-	✓	-	-
7.	Ramanathapuram	-	✓	-	-
8.	Sivagangai	-	-	✓	-
9.	Ariyalur	✓	-	-	-
10.	Thiruvallur	✓	-	-	-
11.	Virudhunagar	✓	-	-	-
12.	Coimbatore	-	✓	-	-
13.	Vellore	✓	-	-	-
14.	Madurai	✓	-	-	-
15.	Villupuram	✓	-	-	-
16.	Thiruvarur	-	✓	-	-
17.	Namakkal	✓	-	-	-
18.	Thiruvannamalai	✓	-	-	-
19.	Kancheepuram	✓	-	-	-
20.	Kanyakumari	-	✓	-	-
21.	Pudukkottai	-	✓	-	-
22.	Tirunelveli	-	✓	-	-
23.	Karur	✓	-	-	-
24.	Perambalur	✓	-	-	-
25.	Tuticorin	-	✓	-	-
26.	Dharmapuri	✓	-	-	-
27.	Salem	✓	-	-	-
28.	Erode	✓	-	-	-
29.	Trichy	-	✓	-	-
	Total	**18**	**10**	**1**	**0**

Source : Computed.

Our development activities are still in the supply driven mode as it is inferred from the Panchayat leaders. It is interesting to note that money is being spent in the villages through various schemes by various departments. But there is no match between the demands of the people and the activities carried out in the rural areas by the sectoral departments. MLAs and MPs are also spending a lot of money without consulting the Gram Sabha and the Panchayat. On an average, as per a rough estimate, seven to ten crores of rupees are enough to fulfil the demands of the people in every district barring two big districts in Tamil Nadu. But roughly forty to seventy crores are being spent annually in every district for development activities. One prime message one can gain from this kind of practices in the development domain is that the government departments and the people's representatives, excepting the local body leaders, have scant respect for people's demands. The whole purpose of decentralization of power is to alter the existing paradigm from supply driven to demand driven activity. But it is not so easy. To achieve this the Central Government and the State Government have to work purposively. One remarkable achievement has been made in Panchayats in Tamil Nadu: people have been oriented to ask the sectoral departments to work on the issues prioritized by the people in the Gram Sabha meeting. Now the government has issued an order through G.O. (Ms) No.140, dated 10.09.2004 that all the sectoral departments have to work on the priorities mentioned in the plan documents prepared by the Gram Panchayats under the new scheme "Namathu Gramam".

Service Delivery

It is unequivocally clear from the literature that in most of the developing countries, public institutions have failed miserably in delivering basic services to the people, especially the poor. It is clear from the World Development Report 2000-2001 that many poor people around the world perceive the large public institutions, especially those of the State, to be distant, unaccountable and corrupt[13]. India is no exception. Arguments are developed among scholars that service delivery can be transferred from the government to the private sector. As a result service users have to pay for service delivery. Those who are using roads, hospitals, and water have to pay. By giving the responsibility of delivering services to the private sector, the government reduces its expenditure and abdicates its role. The rich can pay and use the services. What will happen to the poor? But in India, now, basic services are transferred to the Panchayats. It is inferred from the reports that, in 25 districts, the service delivery of the departments

Table 5.5 : Service Delivery

Sl. No.	*Districts*	*Sectoral Departments*			*Panchayats*		
		Good	*Mode-rate*	*Poor*	*Good*	*Mode-rate*	*Poor*
1.	Tanjore	-	✓	-	✓	-	-
2.	Ooty	-	-	✓	-	✓	-
3.	Nagapattinam	-	-	✓	✓	-	-
4.	Theni	-	✓	-	✓	-	-
5.	Cuddalore	-	-	✓	✓	-	-
6.	Dindigul	-	✓	-	✓	-	-
7.	Ramanathapuram	-	-	✓	✓	-	-
8.	Sivagangai	-	✓	-	✓	-	-
9.	Ariyalur	-	-	✓	✓	-	-
10.	Thiruvallur	-	-	✓	✓	-	-
11.	Virudhunagar	-	-	✓	✓	-	-
12.	Coimbatore	-	-	✓	✓	-	-
13.	Vellore	-	-	✓	✓	-	-
14.	Madurai	-	-	✓	✓	-	-
15.	Villupuram	-	-	✓	-	✓	-
16.	Thiruvarur	-	-	✓	✓	✓	-
17.	Namakkal	-	-	✓	✓	-	-
18.	Thiruvannamalai	-	-	✓	-	✓	-
19.	Kancheepuram	-	-	✓	✓	-	-
20.	Kanyakumari	-	-	✓	✓	-	-
21.	Pudukkottai	-	-	✓	✓	-	-
22.	Tirunelveli	-	-	✓	✓	-	-
23.	Karur	-	-	✓	✓	-	-
24.	Perambalur	-	-	✓	-	✓	-
25.	Tuticorin	-	-	✓	✓	-	-
26.	Dharmapuri	-	-	✓	-	✓	-
27.	Salem	-	-	✓	-	✓	-
28.	Erode	-	-	✓	✓	-	-
29.	Trichy	-	-	✓	✓	-	-
	Total	**0**	**4**	**25**	**23**	**6**	**0**

Source : Computed.

is reported to be poor. When they are transferred to the Panchayats, service delivery has drastically improved. The reason behind the improvement is not increasing the quantum of resource allocation. It is because of the intervention of the local body institutions. Panchayat leaders have identified the responsibilities of all the service providing institutions and they have made continuous supervision on them, and, as a result, the quality of service and the quantum of service have improved drastically.

Further, the relationship between the sectoral departments and the people has improved. Slowly people are also aware of the nuances to have supervision over the public departments. It brings a message to the scholars that service delivery need not be privatized and they can be handed over to the local bodies or they can be kept under the control of the government and the local body leaders may be asked to supervise the departments. It brings an alternative approach to the existing paradigm of governance and development. Yet another aspect is that people now gain the confidence that public institutions will also deliver goods. In the past two decades the public had lost confidence in the public institutions whether it is a primary school or a primary health centre. Now people have gained confidence in public institutions because of the service of the local bodies[14]. Further people have started analyzing and evaluating the performance of the service providing institutions. Now service delivery will be effective and thereby social development issues will gain currency among the people.

Equity and Social Justice

Achieving equity and social justice at the grassroots has been handed over to the local bodies but, in reality, the Panchayats are struggling to perform the same due to the given social fabric and the political polarization of the communities. Social divisions and political polarizations have compelled the Panchayats to remain under the influence of the dominant caste groups and dominant party leaders. Yet, in many of the Panchayats, leaders have started charging the mindset of the people. Further the marginalized have also developed aspirations and claim their rightful place through their representatives. The overall political climate is also favourable to them. As the whole of the development exercise is transparent with the advent of new Panchayati Raj System, the marginalized and underprivileged come with their charter of demands to the Panchayats and the Gram Sabha and participate in and deliberate over their issues. As many schemes are available for them and they are aware of them, their inclusion is imperative and they demand it. It does not mean it is smooth without barriers. In many places Panchayat Presidents cannot implement schemes which are meant for the marginalized as the dominant communities resist the whole process. Whenever Panchayat Presidents are well

Table 5.6 : Equity and Social Justice Activities

Sl. No.	*Districts*	*Works for Equity and Social Justice*		
		Considerable Attention	***Moderate Attention***	***Poor Attention***
1.	Tanjore	-	✓	-
2.	Ooty	✓	-	-
3.	Nagapattinam	✓	-	-
4.	Theni	✓	-	-
5.	Cuddalore	-	✓	-
6.	Dindigul	✓	-	-
7.	Ramanathapuram	-	✓	-
8.	Sivagangai	✓	-	-
9.	Ariyalur	✓	-	-
10.	Thiruvallur	✓	-	-
11.	Virudhunagar	-	✓	-
12.	Coimbatore	-	✓	-
13.	Vellore	-	✓	-
14.	Madurai	-	✓	-
15.	Villupuram	-	✓	-
16.	Thiruvarur	✓	-	-
17.	Namakkal	-	✓	-
18.	Thiruvannamalai	✓	-	-
19.	Kancheepuram	✓	-	-
20.	Kanyakumari	✓	-	-
21.	Pudukkottai	✓	-	-
22.	Tirunelveli	-	✓	-
23.	Karur	✓	-	-
24.	Perambalur	✓	-	-
25.	Tuticorin	✓	-	-
26.	Dharmapuri	✓	-	-
27.	Salem	-	✓	-
28.	Erode	✓	-	-
29.	Trichy	-	✓	-
	Total	**17**	**12**	**0**

Source : Computed.

informed and have a grip over the Gram Sabha they are able to overcome the barriers and implement the schemes for the marginalized. But in many places, that too in Panchayats headed by Dalit leaders, men and women find it difficult to work and deliver the schemes due to them. In 17 districts considerable attention has been paid to the issues of social justice. One important transformation one can notice visibly in all Panchayats in that Panchayat Presidents and a section of the people have realized that social justice is part of Panchayat administration. Secondly, the marginalized have also got awareness about their condition and started asking for their share in the development activities. Out of compulsion government departments have started supporting the Panchayats for social justice activities. Panchayats in seventeen districts have paid considerable attention to social justice and equity issues. It does not mean that all the Panchayats have achieved what they wanted to achieve. They have started working on it with several limitations and barriers. Panchayats in twelve districts have paid moderate attention to these issues. In the Indian context, taking up the cause of social justice issues itself is a success. It was reported by many elected women representatives and elected Dalit representatives that they were not permitted by the dominant caste group leaders to take up the issues of women and Dalits for discussion and decision making both in the Gram Sabha and in the Panchayat Council meetings[15].

Ecology and Environment

One interesting observation emerges from the analysis of the performance of the Panchayat Presidents. Most of the Panchayat Presidents, barring a few, are sensitive towards environment and ecology. They address the issues of livelihood security through the Panchayat works on environment and ecology. They borrow models from community based organizations to manage the natural resources. In the context of over-exploitation of natural resources, especially water, soil, sand and minerals, Panchayats are the institutions to rationalize the whole thing and protect and enrich natural resources. All water bodies are taken care of by the Panchayats. Climate management, water management, natural resource protection and enrichment activities are on the agenda of the Panchayats. The Panchayat mobilizes the people for all the above activities. It is proved beyond doubt that institutions which are working nearer to the communities on management of natural resources as communities are vibrant in managing the natural resources[16]. For many years the higher level governments struggled to perform these functions but now the Panchayats are doing it easily.

Table 5.7 : Ecology and Environment

Sl. No.	*Districts*	*Works for Equity and Social Justice*		
		Considerable Attention	*Moderate Attention*	*Poor Attention*
1.	Tanjore	✓	-	-
2.	Ooty	✓	-	-
3.	Nagapattinam	✓	-	-
4.	Theni	✓	-	-
5.	Cuddalore	-	✓	-
6.	Dindigul	✓	-	-
7.	Ramanathapuram	✓	-	-
8.	Sivagangai	✓	-	-
9.	Ariyalur	-	✓	-
10.	Thiruvallur	-	-	✓
11.	Virudhunagar	-	-	✓
12.	Coimbatore	-	✓	-
13.	Vellore	-	✓	-
14.	Madurai	✓	-	-
15.	Villupuram	-	✓	-
16.	Thiruvarur	✓	-	-
17.	Namakkal	✓	-	-
18.	Thiruvannamalai	-	✓	-
19.	Kancheepuram	-	✓	-
20.	Kanyakumari	✓	-	-
21.	Pudukkottai	✓	-	-
22.	Tirunelvelli	✓	-	-
23.	Karur	-	✓	-
24.	Perambalur	-	✓	-
25.	Tuticorin	-	✓	-
26.	Dharmapuri	✓	-	-
27.	Salem	-	✓	-
28.	Erode	-	✓	-
29.	Trichy	✓	-	-
	Total	**15**	**12**	**2**

Source : Computed.

Now the multinational companies have come to exploit the natural resources in India. Globalization has provided an opportunity for the multinational organizations to make profit out of exploitation of natural resources, be it water, or sand or minerals. But decentralization has provided an opportunity to the local populace and their leaders to protect them for their advantage. Whenever Panchayat leaders and people are sensitive towards the issues, they are in a position to manage the same. Panchayat Presidents and the people are very active in this regard. NGOs are playing a catalyst role in creating awareness about the importance of natural resource management. A number of cases have been registered in courts by the Panchayats on the matters of ecology and environment[17].

Analysis

Normal analysis of good governance in the Indian setting is always from the donor agencies. For conceptualization, the academics trace it from the perspective of history and ideology. Now feverish analysis on governance is on the supply driven exercise. This study is different from the conventional type and it anchors on the perception of the leaders of grassroots institutions on governance. They perceive the concept of good governance from the viewpoint of the people. But it is strange to note that in no way it is different from that of the donor perspective. Donor perspective analysis is centered round reforming the institutions. But the grassroots perspective is centred round the people. Ultimately it touches upon the major indicators evolved by the UN agencies.

From the perspective of the people, ecology and environment, demand based activities, transparent development activities, effective delivery of services, social justice and equity are important. It perfectly concurs with the indicators developed by the UNDP for good governance. While analyzing the functioning of Panchayats, it is inferred that Panchayats are heading towards achieving all the indicators. Despite an array of obstacles, the leaders from different segments have tried their best to achieve the major indicators. In all the aspects they have progressed well and they have found several structural and functional problems. With their critical input the Panchayat institutions have started delivering quality service. With their performance they have attracted the people towards the Gram Sabha. With their honesty, they have displayed the accounts in the Gram Sabha meeting. With their vision, Panchayats are made to work on ecology and environment, with their humane attitude, social justice issues are addressed in Panchayats. Bureaucracy is still dominant, society is still caste-ridden and politically polarized, the governance system is corrupt, people still hold the perception that they are beneficiaries and petitioners. With all these barriers the Panchayat leaders, with their leadership quality, have performed their role and function effectively and thereby they have fulfilled the indicators of good governance. It does not mean that the Panchayat is borrowed from heaven and Panchayat leaders are decended from angels. They are also part of the larger socio-political systems afficted by the same malaise[18]. Yet they are in the control of the communities and, as a result, corruption has started declining though not arrested. By giving more powers to the Gram Sabha and the Panchayat institutions good governance can be achieved at the grassroots level first and from the grassroots it can be effected to higher levels of governing institutions.

Conclusion

Many myths are broken in the world now by empowering the people and making them participate in the development process. Good governance is spoken of and debated at a higher level with the thinking that it has to come from above. The process is slow as it is donor driven and in the absence of political will. From the above good governance is always a talk if there is no political will. It has been reiterated by the speaker of the Lok Sabha in a recent memorial lecture. But, at the grassroots, it happens with the active participation of the people in governance and with committed leadership. With the advent of Panchayat institutions, good governance is being perceived from the people's perspective and practiced at the local level with the active support and participation of the people. To make it happen at the grassroots level with the participation of the people leadership matters much. Devolution takes place with an array of barriers and obstacles. With the limited powers devolved to Panchayats, Panchayat leaders are able to achieve tremendous results. Simultaneously two important transformations are going on in society silently. One struggle has started at the local level to demand power for the people to decide their destiny and alter the paradigm of governance. Devolution is being evolved and democracy is being deepened and good governance is emerging at the grassroots.

NOTES AND REFERENCES

1. Mohit Bhattacharya, "Conceptualizing Good Governance", *The Indian Journal of Public Administration,* Vol. XLIV: No.3, (July-September, 1998) pp. 289-91.

2. O.P.Minocha, "Good Governance: New Public Management Perspective", *The Indian Journal of Public Administration,* Vol. XLIV: No. 3, (July-September, 1998) pp. 274-275.
3. International Commission on Peace and Food, *Developing Human Resourcefulness: Strategies to Eradicate Poverty in the 1990s,* California: International Commission on Peace and Food, 1990.
4. Hobbes, Locke, Rousseau, Paine, Mill, Marx, Gandhi and Rawls also discussed the concept of good governance when they discussed about state in their writings.
5. World Bank, *Governance: The World Bank's Exercise,* Washington: World Bank, 1994.
6. O.P. Dwikedi, "Common Good and Good Governance", *The Indian Journal of Public Administration,* Vol. XLIV: No. 3, (July-September, 1998) pp. 253-264.
7. Manmohan Malhotra (ed.), *New Century: Whose Century,* New Delhi: UBS Publishers and Distributors, 2001, pp.142-187.
8. For more details P.R. Dubhashi, *Administrative Reform,* New Delhi: B.R. Publishing Company, 1986, pp.18-34.
9. B. Bandyopadhyay, "Administration, Decentralization and Good Governance", *Economic and Political Weekly,* Vol. XXXI: No.48, (November 30, 1996).
10. Niraja Gopal Jayal, "The Governance Agenda: Making Democratic Development Dispensable", *Economic and Political Weekly,* Vol. XXXII: No. 8, (February 22, 1997), p. 407.
11. G. Palanithurai and J. Vanishree, *Governance: from the Perspective of Elected Women Representatives* (Monograph), Gandhigram: Rajiv Gandhi Chair for Panchayati Raj Studies, 2004.
12. G. Palanithurai, *New Panchayat Raj in Tamil Nadu,* New Delhi: Concept Publishing Company, 2003, pp. 3-6.
13. The World Bank, *World Development Report 2000-2001 Attacking Poverty,* New York: Oxford University Press, 2001 and D. Narayanan, R. Chambers, M.K. Shah and P. Petesch, *Voices of the Poor: Crying over for Change,* Washington DC: World Bank, 2000.
14. Path Breaking Achievements are documented through a series, for more details, G. Palanithurai, *Path Finders Series – Leadership Matters in Grassroots Governance,* Gandhigram: Rajiv Gandhi Chair for Panchayati Raj Studies, 2004.
15. G. Palanithurai, "The Empowerment Process: Women Representatives in Grassroots Institutions in Tamil Nadu", *Indian Social Science Review,* Vol. 6 : No.1 (January-June 2004), pp. 78-106 and G. Palanithurai, *Dalit Leadership in Panchayats* (Monograph), Gandhigram: Rajiv Gandhi Chair for Panchayati Raj Studies, 2003.
16. V. Ragupathy, *Participatory Management of Natural Resources: Irrigation Tanks in Panchayats,* New Delhi: Concept Publishing Company, 2004.
17. The Hunger Project, *Report of the Workshop on New Panchayat Raj: Trails and Triumphs, 2003,* Gandhigram: Rajiv Gandhi Chair for Panchayati Raj Studies, 2003.
18. Suresh Mishra and Rajvir S. Dhaka, *Grassroots Democracy in Action,* New Delhi: Concept Publishing Company, 2004, p.162.

6

CAPACITY BUILDING

PART - I

Capacity building is an imperative for the elected representatives of the people at all levels from Grassroots to National Parliament. Capacity building for the elected representatives is not perceived in perspective and hence it is the most neglected area in governance. For the establishment of the three-tier governance at grassroots as an institution of self- government, conscientisation and capacity building are needed exercises to be done on a war footing. It not only builds the skills and managerial capacity of the elected representatives but also builds a movement for prosperity at the grassroots as the system has been created in such a way that the performance of the Panchayats can be evaluated and monitored constantly by the people. Cleansing operations for the establishment of good governance must start from the bottom. The present article highlights the capacity building exercises conducted in Tamil Nadu against the backdrop of the prevailing negative setting and its implications. The experience brings to light the emergence of the grassroots movement to utilize power and authority to decide on issues which affect the life of the people. It also indicates what is further needed to strengthen the grassroots democracy.

Introduction

'Capacity Building' is the most urgent and imperative step in every sector to cope with the pace of development at present. In market driven development activities enhancement of capacity plays an important role in placing individuals, organizations and associations in competition. Development sectors take conscious decisions to enhance the capacity of the professionals and personnel working in organizations and institutions. New technologies and institutional mechanics require conscious steps to enhance the capability of individuals who are handling technologies and new organizational mechanisms to use the full potential of the technologies and institutional structures to bring out the maximum competence.

The 73rd Amendment to the Constitution of India has created a structure at the grassroots for governance. It has come with a set of promises and assurances to the people[1]. Compelling global, national and regional contexts make everyone look at the new system contextually. The new system has its own roles and responsibilities and, to perform the assigned roles and responsi- bilities, the leaders who are managing the new system should build up their skill and capacity[2]. The new system has been created to break new ground in governance and to tackle the problems and issues which are unmet and unsolved through the policy options of the governments at the State and the Central level. It should be clearly noted that the new institutions have to perform a variety of activities at the grassroots for which the grassroots leaders should have a clear-cut perception of the roles and responsibilities that are to be discharged and the skills needed to manage these institutions which are under the purview of the elected Panchayat leaders[3].

It is unfortunate that, in India, capacity building is not a serious issue for the representatives of the people who determine the fate of millions of people[4]. The elected representatives of the people do not feel that it is an imperative as it is considered in other sectors. In all sectors capacity building is a much valued exercise for the enhancement of their activities in their respective domains. But in politics it is not so and, as a result, one can notice a retrograde trend in politics.

However, in the Panchayati Raj scenario, it has been felt that, to manage the Panchayats, training is essential even though there is no training policy and no conscious steps have been taken by the government to build the capacity of the elected representatives of the people in the grassroots institutions. It has been argued time and again that training is an imperative and needs to be undertaken on a war footing. Yet only a few states have taken conscious steps and in many places it is only the voluntary organizations who have imparted training to local body leaders despite several constraints, like the absence of well developed training centres, training material and well equipped trainers[5].

In Tamil Nadu it is the demand of the Panchayat leaders that training should be given to Panchayat leaders and Panchayat functionaries to manage the institutions efficiently[6]. To cater to the needs of the local body leaders, there are enough training centres in Tamil Nadu. The Government of Tamil Nadu has established Rural Extension Training Centres in different regions and, at the State level, the State Institute of Rural Development. It is unfortunate that the Government sends unwanted employees to these training centres. As a result the training centres have lost their importance and value. They are mostly defunct. Further there is no training manual to train the Panchayat leaders and functionaries[7]. Realising the problems involved in training, the Rajiv Gandhi Chair for Panchayati Raj Studies took a conscious decision that it has to train Gram Panchayat Presidents for which a training manual has to be prepared.

Training in the First Phase

When the decision was taken to train Gram Panchayat leaders, what powers were going to be devolved, how much of fiscal devolution was going to be effected and what functionaries were going to be part of the Panchayats had not been spelt out. The Government of Tamil Nadu had allowed the Panchayats to perform the old civic functions along with agency functions to carry out the schemes and programmes of the Central and State Governments. Based on these activities a training module was prepared and training programmes were conducted. It was just a conscientization programme to change the mindset of the leaders by indicating the spirit of the 73rd Constitutional Amendment Act and the basic details about the Panchayati Raj Act of Tamil Nadu and its implications in the socio-economic and political transformation of the rural society. Gradually the sensitization programme was extended to other tiers with the financial support of various agencies.

Table 6.1 : Training Programmes Organised in Gandhigram Rural Institute

S. No.	*Title*	*Sponsored Agency*	*Total No.of Leaders Trained*
1.	Empowering Panchayati Raj Institutions on Issues of Population, Health and Social Development	Population Foundation of India	6834
2.	Capacity Building for Gram Panchayat Presidents	CAPART	1369
3.	Training of Presidents and Vice-Presidents in Panchayat Administration with Special Reference to Water and Sanitation	DANIDA	814
4.	Training of Women Presidents of Gram Panchayats	Social Welfare Board	825
5.	Training of Trainers in Multi Level Planning	State Planning Commission	71
6.	Capacity Building for Weaker Sections in New Panchayati Raj System	CAPART	271
7.	Capacity Building Exercise for Gram Panchayat Women Leaders	The Hunger Project	390

Source : Computed.

Capacity Building Programmes

Total number of elected local body leaders trained	:	10,584
Total number of Panchayats covered	:	4,426
Districts covered	:	11

In the whole process of training what was achieved was that the Panchayat leaders were sensitized on the issues of democratic decentralization of powers and the bases of the 73rd Amendment to the Constitution of India and the issues of social development.

In the meanwhile the First State Finance Commission submitted its recommendations and they were placed before the Legislative Assembly[8]. Subsequently the L.C. Jain Committee[9] constituted for making recommendations on entrusting responsibilities to the three tier Panchayati institutions submitted its report. Based on the report, decisions were taken and the action taken report[10] was placed before the Legislative Assembly. Political parties, Panchayat leaders, academics and NGOs criticized the Government for not devolving needed powers to the local bodies and, as a result, yet another committee was constituted, with the Local Administration Minister[11] as the Chairperson and representatives of the major political parties as members, to look into the devolution process and to make recommendations. This committee also submitted its recommendations to the Government and action has been taken on the recommendations[12]. As a result many changes have been effected in the Act and several Government Orders have been passed. Thus the first period from 1996 to 2001 marked a transition period wherein steps were taken to transfer power to the local bodies in Tamil Nadu. For the Panchayat leaders, it was a period of guessing and the officials were also in the same predicament. Virtually all the three Panchayat tiers shared the Government schemes and implemented the same and, as a result, the Panchayats became agents of the State Government. Leaders elected to Panchayats became contractors.

Initiatives of Rajiv Gandhi Chair

During this period the Rajiv Gandhi Chair for Panchayati Raj Studies took a series of steps to prepare a training manual to train the Panchayat leaders with the support of the Ford Foundation. The manual was tested and published for the benefit of the NGOs who are interested in organizing training programmes for Panchayat leaders[13]. Following the preparation of the training manual, steps were taken to collect the needed information, namely, the amendments introduced on the Act, orders passed by the Government as well as rules and schemes and programmes of the Government of India and the Government of Tamil Nadu relating to rural development. They were collected and compiled as a basic referable document and published for wider circulation and for distribution in the training programmes for Panchayat leaders[14]. Even today the Government offices do not have the updated Panchayat Act. So far the Government has passed eighty-four orders for Gram Panchayat administration alone. But not even a single Government Order has been sent to the Gram Panchayats. Yet Panchayat Presidents have been taken to task by the District Collectors as they have not followed the Government Orders. Panchayat Presidents ask how the Panchayat can follow the Government Orders in the absence of the GOs. So, with the help of retired staff, all Government Orders were collected from various departments along with the updated Act and rules. It took about a year to do this.

With the training module and the information package ready, the Rajiv Gandhi Chair identified a band of retired officials at the level of Additional Director for Rural Development based on their commitment, honesty and sincerity, as resource persons to impart training along with the Rajiv Gandhi Chair team. The Rajiv Gandhi Chair team has been already oriented on social development issues besides Panchayat administration. Along with the retired officials and the Rajiv Gandhi Chair team a few resource persons were drawn from NGOs as they run organizations for specific problems in the rural society such as environment, health care of child and women, RCH, child labour, human rights and natural resources management. Thus a comprehensive team was developed.

Apart from these arrangements, a specific initiative was taken to prepare a separate module for women as they require special leadership training. The Hunger Project, New Delhi, helped the Rajiv Gandhi Chair to prepare the training module on leadership and the same was published[15].

Along with the training modules, training materials to be used in the classroom were prepared. Because the educational background of the trainees varies from illiteracy to post-graduation,

Table 6.2 : Training Programmes Organised in Gandhigram Rural Institute

S.No	*Name of the District*	*Total No. of Presidents*			*No.of Presidents attended the training*			*Percentage of Panchayat Presidents*		
		Men	*Women*	*Total*	*Men*	*Women*	*Total*	*Men*	*Women*	*Total*
1.	Pudukkottai	326	172	498	275	140	415	84	81	83
2.	Dindigul	200	105	305	191	100	291	96	95	95
3.	Tiruchirappalli	275	132	407	255	131	386	93	99	95
4.	Sivagangai	292	153	445	242	112	354	83	73	80
5.	Ramanathapuram	282	147	429	229	116	345	81	79	80
6.	Theni	82	48	130	66	43	109	80	90	84
7.	Karur	109	49	158	91	49	140	83	100	89
8.	Virudhunagar	303	144	447	245	103	348	81	72	78
	Total	**1869**	**950**	**2819**	**1594**	**794**	**2388**	**85**	**84**	**85**

Source : Computed.

training aids were prepared in the form of charts. An artist was inducted in the team of resource persons, as his services were needed in the vision building class. Trainees would be asked to portray the existing conditions of the villages and to project their vision of how to develop the village. The entire vision was to be brought out in a chart.

With these preparations, the Rajiv Gandhi Chair approached the CAPART (Government of India) and The Hunger Project (New Delhi) for financial support to conduct training programmes for Gram Panchayat leaders of eight districts. The two agencies extended their support to conduct the programme. With the financial support of the CAPART, men leaders were trained and with the financial support of the Hunger Project women leaders were trained.

Collaboration

Before starting the training programme, a conscious decision was taken that the training programme should be conducted in collaboration with the Government of Tamil Nadu for two reasons. Gandhigram Rural Institute should be recognized as a nodal centre for training and officials should recognize the training programme which should not be duplicated by any other agencies. Secondly, Panchayat Presidents have to be brought to the training centre by the officials. It was very difficult to bring the Panchayat Presidents to training programmes in previous exercises. Further it was decided to have at least three officials dealing with Panchayats at the Block level from every Block in the training programme. To ensure attendance in the training programme Gandhigram Rural Institute needed the support of the Government. The training had to be made official. In this regard the Government issued an order[16]. As a result it is fully a Government recognized programme.

It was a fully residential programme. The Panchayat Presidents had to stay for five days in the campus of Gandhigram Rural Institute. Of the five days, three days would be devoted to Panchayat administration and two days to social development issues. Subjects such as the bases of decentralization of powers in the context of the globalization of the economy, Panchayat administration,

Panchayat finance, common property resources management, people's participation, micro level planning, economic development, accounting and auditing procedures, Gram Sabha and its implications, social justice, and, the implications of reservation of seats for women and Dalits were covered in three days. Social development issues such as sanitation, water supply, gender bias, child care, pre and post-natal care, school environment, child labour, RCH and other issues were covered in the remaining two days of the five day programme. In each one and half an hour lecture, half an hour was set aside for a question and answer session. Men and women had separate training classes. Special sessions were arranged in the night both for men and women and all their doubts were cleared. Local and specific problems of the Gram Panchayats were discussed with the resource persons individually in the Gandhigram Rural Institute Guest House. It was an advantage that the entire team of resource persons stayed in the Gandhigram Rural Institute Guest House.

A special session was devoted to eliciting the Panchayat Presidents' problems in Panchayat administration. On the last day of the training programme the trainees were taken to the field and finally, they were asked to give their feedback.

Feedback from the Training

Before starting the training programme a questionnaire was circulated among the participants. This was done with the aim of assessing their level of understanding of Panchayat administration. It was noticed that excepting the Panchayat leaders elected for a second term, all the trainees knew only that the Panchayat provides an opportunity to serve people better and deliver services and were aware of a few schemes of the State and Central Governments. It was observed that the Panchayat Presidents were virtually under the control of the Panchayat clerks and lower level officials working in the Block Development Offices. After imparting training their feedback was recorded. The Panchayat leaders had now learnt the details of their powers, duties and responsibilities, sources of income to the Panchayats, Panchayat management, common property resource management, removal of encroachments and accounting and auditing procedures. They further insisted that they need periodical refresher courses at least for a day every year and that, apart from the refresher courses, they need help, information and counselling regularly for which the Rajiv Gandhi Chair has to work as a nodal centre for Panchayats[17]. From the experience of the Panchayati leaders, suggestions were made for appropriate follow-up. The following are their suggestions:

Acts which contradict the provisions of the Tamil Nadu Panchayati Raj Act of 1994 have to be identified and suitable amendments have to be made. All officials have to be trained and sensitized on the New Panchayati Raj System. Many officials at lower levels do not understand the Act and the rules and, as a result, Panchayats and themselves in trouble. For proper Panchayat administration, an administrative manual has to be prepared and published. All Government Orders pertinent to Panchayat administration have to be compiled and kept in all the Panchayat offices as it has been done in Pudukkottai District. A review has to be undertaken of the actions taken by the District Collectors on Panchayat leaders by using provision 205 of the Tamil Nadu Panchayat Act of 1994. This suggestion was made because 80 per cent of the dismissals and suspensions have been stayed by courts. It means that the officials have erred somewhere.

No proper handing over and taking over takes place in Gram Panchayat administration after the election to the Panchayats. Records created by the previous Panchayat administration are not handed over to the newly elected Presidents. A sizeable area of common properties encroached upon by influential individuals are to be recovered. It can be done by the Revenue Department as a special drive. Though a Government Order has been passed, no Village Administrative Officer has handed over village maps to the Gram Panchayat Presidents and the properties of the Gram Panchayats have not been shown to the Gram Panchayat Presidents. The higher officials of the Revenue Department, preferably the Secretary for Revenue, has to instruct the Village Administrative Officers through an order that all poramboke lands of the Panchayats have to be identified and shown to the Gram Panchayat Presidents and that village maps have to be given to the Panchayats. House tax collection has to be made rigorous and revision has to be enforced. In most of the places the Panchayats want a direction from the State Government to enhance the house tax as the Panchayat is seen as leader centric. Minor minerals revenue should go to Gram Panchayats. But now it is in court. Nobody takes action in this regard. As a result minor minerals are being lifted for the advantage of the mafia. The State Government has to take the initiative to expedite the case in the court.

Drinking water supply is going to become a difficult task in the years to come in the rural areas. There is no proper water management system, no regularization of illegal tap connections. All these problems have to be solved. Water policy and water regulation rules have to be evolved. Panchayats have to take the initiative for micro level plan which would turn the activities from a supply driven mode to a demand driven one. Huge sums have been spent in the villages by different agencies but the demands of the people projected in the Gram Sabha meeting remain unmet. Departments and representatives of the people have spent the money at their disposal in the rural areas as per their wish and perception. To avoid this kind of wastage, micro planning has to be initiated and thereby planned activities have to be carried out by pooling the resources of all the Departments and representatives of the people. Panchayat leaders have to be sensitized on social development issues. Awareness has to be created among the leaders about the status of rural areas in terms of social development. Panchayats have to keep the Electricity Board (EB) cards in the Panchayat office. Panchayat leaders have to monitor the electricity consumption and meter reading. In many Panchayats, the cards are not available in the Panchayat office and the Panchayat Presidents are not aware of the expenditure on electricity, because the cards are in the EB office. Wherever the Panchayat leaders are sensitized and conscious about the expenditure, they take action to reduce electricity consumption by fitting tubelights for streetlights, removing sodium vapour lights and regulating the water supply.

It should be made mandatory that all development works, whether sponsored by sectoral departments or the Central or the

State Government, should be carried out in the Panchayat area with the approval of the Gram Sabha. Panchayat Presidents are being criticized for not convening Gram Sabha meetings seriously as the Gram Sabha attendance is poor. When the proceedings, resolutions and demands of the Gram Sabha are not seriously considered by the officials, MLAs and MPs, how can one expect people to participate in the Gram Sabha meetings? People know that the Collector is powerful, the Project Officer, DRDA, is powerful, the MLA has Rs.77 lakhs and the MP two crore rupees at his/her disposal every year and hence people meet all these representatives and the Collector. Issue of birth, death and community certificates should be entrusted to the Panchayat administration. Certificates issued by the Panchayat should be provided for public verification. Funds earmarked for Panchayat activities should be directly given to Panchayats. The District Planning Committee has to take the initiative for evolving a perspective development plan for the district. The District Planning Committee has been constituted but there is no work assignment for the committee. A District Panchayat Secretary has been appointed planning officer but no planning work has been entrusted to him. Manuals have been prepared for planning, training has been conducted for officials in multi-level planning and yet there is no systematic planning at the grassroots.

Officials should not allow the husbands of the women Panchayat Presidents either to participate in the official meetings or to sign any of the papers which are to be signed by the elected women representatives. In many of the districts, lower level officials encourage the male family members of the women leaders either to attend meetings to carry out activities. If officials are very strict in this regard either genuine women will emerge as leaders or the men of the women leaders' families will change their attitude. Most of the women leaders insist that a very strict order has to be issued to the officials not to encourage the husbands of the women leaders to participate in the official meetings.

For each Panchayat an untied fund up to a maximum of Rs. 5,00,000 could be given with an instruction that the amount should be spent only for economic activities, particularly employment generation and social development, as it has been done in Kerala.

For women and Dalits a special development component plan could be developed. Panchayati Raj Institutions require a State level Director to look after the functioning of Panchayati Institutions as per the recommendations of the Swaminathan Committee. At present there is no State level authority to monitor the functioning of the Panchayati institutions. All officials, top to bottom, are interested in monitoring the implementation of schemes though they are not legally authorized to intervene in Panchayati affairs. As a result the Panchayat administration is not properly monitored and helped. To make the Panchayati institutions from District Panchayat to Gram Sabha institutions of self-government, their functioning has to be monitored and corrective steps have to be taken then and there, for which a State level officer has to be given charge of these institutions. Revenue from forestry has to come to Panchayats. But no effort has been made in this regard. Panchayat leaders have repeatedly pleaded in vain for the dues to Panchayats. Appropriate initiatives have to be taken by the district administration in this regard.

Village Panchayats which are very near to industrial estates can get a lot of revenue by way of house tax, building tax, layout approval fee and plan approval fee. But now it does not happen so in many of the cases because the Panchayat Presidents are not aware of the rules. In certain cases the rules are misused for the advantage of some leaders. In many of the cases house tax assessment is very poor or sometimes it is wrong. Proper assessment has to be made. In many places, huge amounts of revenue are being lost due to improper assessment. This has to be rectified. Cheque transactions could be avoided and the entire amount could be sent to the bank account of the Panchayats for all activities by which corruption could be eliminated since all Panchayats maintain bank accounts. This suggestion is made because of the demands made by officials whenever they issue cheques to Panchayats. Unless the Panchayat President pays a sum, cheques will not be released. Still a major portion of the common properties are vested with traditional Panchayats. They get huge amounts of revenue from common properties but they pay very little to the Gram Panchayats. In many places auctions of commons are taken by the traditional Panchayats at a nominal rate and the same commons are re-auctioned for a huge sum. The traditional Panchayats keep the lion's share after remitting the meagre dues to the Panchayats. In many places the traditional Panchayats work in tandem with formal Panchayats. In some places they are at loggerheads. This is to be studied seriously and appropriate action has to be taken.

All sectoral departments have to inform the Panchayat Presidents about the schemes and programmes they are going to carry out in the Panchayat area. The Panchayats are given powers, not to decide about the works to be carried out but to help the sectoral departments to implement and carry out the activities. But, at present, the sectoral departments do not even consult or inform the Panchayats about the programmes being carried out in the Panchayat areas. If the annual plan preparation is done in every Panchayat, the sectoral departments' activities could be integrated with the plans of the Panchayats. Whenever a licence is issued for quarrying, a copy of the licence should be sent to the Panchayats.

Panchayat leaders at Gram Panchayat level feel that the District Collectors have to convene a meeting of Gram Panchayat leaders once in a while and help the Panchayat administration by eliminating hurdles created by lower level officials. It would help not only the Panchayat administration but also the district administration for speedy implementation of schemes and programmes. Wherever the District Collector establishes direct contact with Gram Panchayat leaders, the Panchayat administration is streamlined and strengthened and innovative practices are developed while implementing the schemes and programmes. The best innovative practices have be documented properly and scientifically and they have to be disseminated through the media[18].

At present Panchayat institutions are not functioning as a system but discretely and individually in a leader centric or officer centric manner. Both officials and leaders perceive Panchayat affairs as their affairs. Both leaders and officials are not well versed in the rules of the game. To make the Panchayat an institution of real self-government a series of steps have to be taken[19].

Integrated Analysis

Of the two-phase training, the second phase was scientific as it was conducted with the guidelines of the manual and by a good training team. The participants, namely, the Panchayat Presidents, attended the programme with a volley of questions. The precise roles and responsibilities to be performed by the Panchayat leaders and the resources and grants which are due to Panchayats were clear. Information to be supplied to the leaders were compiled and distributed to them. In the training programme they were briefed about their destination and where they are now and how they have to reach their destination. In the first phase the Panchayat leaders were groping in the dark but now they were enlightened leaders with a sense of commitment. Finding the environment not positive towards devolution of powers to Panchayats, the Panchayat leaders had formed their own associations region-wise and integrated them in to a federation. Women leaders had formed their own federation and Dalit Panchayat leaders had formed their own outfit[20]. These associations and federations demanded powers. Further, to clarify day to day administrative problems, Gandhigram Rural Institute with the collaboration of a popular vernacular (Tamil) daily, namely, *Dinamalar* had started a weekly supplement (every Monday) under the caption 'Panchayat Malar' which carries Panchayat news and information. For the 'Panchayat Malar' the Rajiv Gandhi Chair does all the work for the entire page, recording the struggles and the successes of Panchayats, providing useful information for effective Panchayat administration, and, giving answers to the questions of the public and Panchayat leaders on the affairs of Panchayats[21]. Gandhigram Rural Institute, with the support of The Hunger Project, New Delhi, conducted a workshop for journalists and sensitized them on the issues of Panchayati Raj and development. Now the media is focusing attention on the successes and struggles of the Panchayats[22]. Gradually the grassroots movement is emerging as a popular movement, gaining momentum from the people, wherein training plays a major role.

Conclusion

Capacity building and information dissemination are the two prerequisites for the effective functioning of local bodies at present. But it is unfortunate that serious thought has not been given to training since there is no policy on training. Conducting training programmes is not easy as it requires several facilities and a well trained team of trainers. Further it requires a volley of information pertinent to Panchayati administration. By imparting training, the skills and the capacity of the Panchayati leaders have been enhanced. The existing conditions and the way in which Panchayats are being administered have been identified only through the training programmes. Steps which are to be taken to put the Panchayats on the proper track have been identified. From the experience of Gandhigram Rural Institute it is perceived that by building the capacity of the leaders of grassroots institutions, a movement can be generated with the active participation of the people for the establishment of the Panchayati system as an institution of self-government. One need not wait for the initiative of the government either for the preparation of a manual and a module for training and for conducting capacity building exercises. If a few NGOs join together the right kind of leadership can be developed at the grassroots and through them the people could be mobilized for the establishment of grassroots institutions. Through the capacity building exercise, the leaders can be sensitised as to where they are now in terms of devolution of powers and where they have to go in consonance with the spirit of the Constitutional Amendment for devolution of powers and a strong people's movement can be mobilized with the initiative of the grassroots leaders. As a result Panchayats can move to the right track to reach the destination.

PART - II

Background

India has a rich tradition of management of natural resources by the local communities of independent village republics. The common resources like forests, fisheries, grazing lands and water bodies were managed by diverse decentralized community based system. Particularly tribal communities lived inside the forests protected and used forest resources for centuries without damaging them. Tribals had a simple lifestyle with minimum needs and they used resources absolutely necessary for their subsistence. Due to socio economic changes and changes in the public policies the tribals control over common resources and their organic linkage with nature have been damaged. This allowed large scale degradation of natural resources mainly by the exploitation of outsiders. Degradation of natural resources critically affects the life of tribals. It makes them vulnerable to hunger and poverty.

73rd Constitutional Amendment Act has opened opportunities for the empowerment of marginalized groups. Social justice and economic development are two important objectives of the New Panchayati Raj System. Reservation for women, SC and ST in various positions in Panchayats ensures participation of these marginalized groups in governance. Elections provides opportunities to ST women in Panchayats. But ST women are doubly affected. Gender and caste are their disadvantages.

Against this background, State Institute of Rural Development, Government of Tamil Nadu and Gandhigram Rural Institute — Deemed University came forward to organise a two days workshop for ST Women Panchayat Presidents on Common Property Resource Management on 28th and 29th March, 2005 at Gandhigram.

Objectives of the Workshop

1. To provide an opportunity to Women ST Panchayat Presidents to freely articulate their experiences, ideas and opinion on the functioning of the tribal Panchayats.
2. To generate information on the status of Common Property Resources in tribal areas.
3. To facilitate a brain storming on the social development issues by the ST Women Panchayat Presidents.
4. To facilitate an interface between ST Women Panchayat Presidents, Government Officials.

Participants

In the two days workshop 14 Women ST Panchayat Presidents, 8 Community Leaders, 8 Government Officials, 2 Resource Persons and 12 Academicians participated.

Methodology of the Workshop

The workshop gave importance to generate open and free participation of tribal leaders. The programmes were informal and flexible. In general sessions were open and speeches of resource persons were very much limited. Group discussions were organised. Free interaction was arranged between government officials, experts, academicians and ST Women Panchayat Presidents. Women ST Presidents had more time to express their opinions, ask questions and give their suggestions. Discussions were arranged in evening and after dinner with experts.

Setting

The proceedings of the workshop are summarized here.

Dr. V. Ragupathy, Coordinator of the workshop, Reader and Associate Coordinator of Rajiv Gandhi Chair for Panchayati Raj Studies, Gandhigram Rural Institute in his introductory remarks highlighted the significance of the workshop and explained the objectives of the workshop. The natural resources particularly forests play a key role in the livelihood of poor and particularly women. Forests in the state is gradually degraded and there is a need for involving local people in development of forest resources. In this, Panchayats in forest area could play a critical role. The women scheduled tribe Panchayat Presidents must be trained and motivated to take up participatively programmes to achieve this objective. The community based organisations in tribal areas are playing central role in the life of the tribals. Panchayats should remember this fact while undertaking any programme in tribal areas. At the same time presidents should not permit the vested interests to exploit natural resources in the name of community based organisation. Panchayats, particularly women Panchayats have made remarkable contribution for the social development of rural areas. So tribal leaders also must understand their responsibilities in the areas of health, sanitation, primary education and child welfare. The status of women is a grey area and special focus must be give to improve the condition of women. Schools and hospitals are two important institutions. Unfortunately forest areas have schools but teachers are not there. There are primary health centres. But there are no doctors.

Dr. G. Palanithurai, Coordinator, Rajiv Gandhi Chair for Panchayati Raj Studies, in his special address highlighted the role of building the capacity of the women ST Panchayat leaders. The scope for participation and collective action is very high in tribal areas. This potential has to be fully used by the Panchayat leaders. Particularly in the management of common property resources tribal Panchayat could play critical role and create models for others. Panchayats as constitutionally created institutions provide require opportunities to take up activities related to water, grazing lands, forests and other resources. This resources must be effectively used to provide livelihood opportunities for the local community. Forest based crafts and industries must be promoted. Here self-help groups could play vital role. Panchayat Presidents must use the services of good non-government organizations in developing livelihood opportunities. Particularly forests based economic activities like production of honey, handicrafts, herbal products have great scope. The DRDA's and Women Development Corporation are always ready to provide training and marketing facilities. Panchayat leaders should have a vision to use such possibilities effectively.

Identifying Problems and Challenges – Key Issues Affecting Panchayats in Tribal Areas

After the inauguration the women Panchayat Presidents shared their views. The tribal leaders expressed extraordinary interest in articulating issues related to Panchayat administration. In spite of many problems they had, they were very optimistic and forward working in general they could identify some key issues affecting the working of Panchayati Raj in tribal areas.

Connectivity is the Greatest Challenge

Connectivity is the key issue identified them. Tribal villages do not have roads, electricity and telephone. Due to this, problems are multiplied. As there are no proper roads, buses are not regular so teachers are not coming to schools regularly. Children are also not able to reach school safely. Particularly women children are not permitted to attend schools. Enrolment and dropouts have increased. Students are not able to get higher education. Health status is also affected because of the problems related to connectivity. Doctors posted in tribal areas do not join or take long leave. Doctors and para-medical staff posted are not regularly coming to PHCs. The para-medical staff are also not regular. Because of this health status is critically affected. The ANC and PNC are not given properly to tribal women.

Need for Basic Infrastructure

Apart from road, electricity is another problem. Protected drinking water supply is not available to the expected level. The repair of motors and pumps are not attended in time because of absence of trained technicians. In the hills water lines are often broken. Hamlets in remote places do not always get protected water supply. Due to the changes in the environment water has become scarce. Electric connections are given to many villages but still many hamlets do not have. Telephones are not available and cell phones are also not used because of the absence of coverage.

Interface with Forest Department

There is no proper coordination between Village Panchayats and Forest Departments. Forest department officials do not understand the role of Panchayats in the management of natural resources.

Many of the schemes of forest departments are implemented without the knowledge of the Panchayats. Panchayats are not able to take many of the construction activities because of the objections from the forest departments. Particularly roads are not provided because the absence of coordination with forest department. Forest department officials must be oriented on the role of Panchayats and Gram Sabha in management of tribal and forest areas.

Need for Social Development Plan

Panchayats in tribal areas very much need an integrated social development plan. Literacy, school enrolment, anti and post-natal care, child health are some of the priority areas of these Panchayats. Due to certain cultural practices related to marriage tribals are affected by large number of health problems. Child marriage and marriage within close family circles affect the health of tribals. Only very few female children gets higher education. Tribal Panchayats need special arrive on social development plan.

Support for Effective Functioning of Tribal Panchayats

Tribals, particularly women tribal Presidents require special support from government officials in managing Panchayat affairs. Panchayat officials particularly officials at grassroots must be sensitized on the problems of ST women leaders. Particularly there must be special efforts to help them in financial planning and administration.

Training ST Women Panchayat Presidents

ST leaders expressed that the training programmes to them must be arranged immediately after elections. They found training programmes given by institutions like SIRD and Gandhigram Rural Institute very useful. They need refresher programmes also once in a year. Training should cover members of the Panchayats and Panchayat Clerks. They do not aware many of the schemes available for ST Panchayats special inputs on such schemes are very much required.

Panel Discussion on Challenges and Opportunities

A panel discussion was arranged to help the Panchayat Presidents to understand critical issues affecting the integrated development of Panchayats. In this Mr. Vallinayagam, Additional Director of Rural Development (Retd.) and Mr. Subramaniam, Additional Director of Rural Development (Retd.) and Dr. V. Ragupathy, Reader in Gandhigram Rural Institute served as experts. Presidents wanted to know more details on various schemes and development programmes useful for tribals. They also asked questions related to the management of national resources in forest area. Mr.Vallinayagam explained how various schemes could be integrated to bring all round development. Mr. Subramaniam highlighted the need for improving the financial administration various sources of resources discussed. Dr.V. Ragupathy requested Presidents to take up social development issues. He also highlighted the need for developing hamlet level development plan. Poverty and Hunger must be reduced with the help of education and employment generation. Available opportunities must be effectively used. Gram Sabha must be used to generate peoples participation in the development activities of Panchayats. The discussions were helpful for Presidents to clarify their doubts and it gave them new ideas on development.

Brain Storming

The second day programme started with the brain storming session.

Sri Ramamoorthy, Director, SIRD, Chennai initiated a brain storming session with the Panchayat leaders, in which the Faculty Members of SIRD participated actively. SIRD, Director in his initial remarks highlighted the achievements of women leaders in states like Rajasthan in developing natural resources for the benefit of the community. He explained the methods through with water bodies in tribal areas were regenerated to provide water for agricultural purpose. A large number of women leaders also shared their experiences in this session.

Semmedu Panchayat President narrated her experiences in fighting the problem of alcoholism in her village. Outsiders are brewing and selling arrack in the tribal areas. She passed a resolution against such practices in the Gram Sabha meeting. Members of the Gram Sabha collectively decided to fight against the problem of alcoholism because it created problems to women and children and many families were ruined. They made complaints with the police station and gave pressure on the police to take strong steps to stop the problem. The problem has been completely eliminated from the Semmedu Panchayat.

Two Presidents explained how the collective effort of their community resulted in the improvement of the Public Distribution System in their village. The President of the Sellore Panchayat explained the functioning of Primary Health Centre. Because of the problem of transport doctors and para-medical staff do not attend their work in time. Due to this tribal women are not able to get proper ANC and PNC. Presidents explained that the cost of construction of group houses is very high in tribal areas. Budget for group houses must be increased in forest areas. Tribal leaders narrated their problems with the forest department. Tribal youths are often arrested by forest officials without sufficient reasons. The youths have to enter in the forest area for various reasons. So they must be provide with permits to do so. In Muthumalai Village Panchayat there are many resorts and cottages. They do not pay any property tax. The owners of the resorts are powerful. They do not professional tax even though they have employed many staff in their establishments. The Panchayat President explained her efforts to collect taxes from the resort owners and the problems related to it. Many of the Panchayat Presidents explained the problems they have with forest committees formed by the forest department. There is no coordination between those two bodies. Forest committee members do not cooperate with the Panchayat activities.

Feedback

In two days group discussions were organised to generate solutions from the leaders for the problems they face. The women leaders discussed among themselves and gave many useful feedbacks some of them are highlighted here.

- District Collector must arrange special monthly meetings with tribal Panchayat Presidents in which officials from all development departments must participate.
- A Coordinator/official must be appointed at district level to take up the issues of tribal Panchayats with the forest officials.
- All the programmes of the forest department in a Village Panchayat must be intimated to the Village Panchayat Presidents. The schemes must be discussed in the Gram Sabha meetings.
- The villagers must get permission to collect firewood and minor forest products in the forests for their personal use and Panchayats may be given power to issue permits for this.
- Grazing of the cattles of tribals must be permitted in the forest area and Panchayats may be given powers to issue grazing permits.
- These activities may be monitored by the Village Panchayats.
- In Panchayats must be encouraged to plant trees in the Panchayat area, protect them and use them.
- Forest department should organise training programmes to Panchayat Presidents and members about various programmes of the forest department.
- Revenue officials must undertake special programmes to remove encroachment in tribal Panchayats.
- User groups must be formed in Panchayats to manage grazing lands and other common property resources in Panchayats.
- Watershed committees must be formed to harvest water and store it for the use.
- Hamlet level planning for the conservation and development of common property resources must be formed.
- The cultural and traditional practices and local knowledge systems must be preserved and protected.

- Forest department, Panchayats and local CBOs must always work together and local coordination committees must be formed.
- Link roads must be provided to all Panchayats and government should arrange mini bus facilities.
- School teachers and medical staff must be made accountable to Village Panchayats.
- Local education unemployed tribal youths must be given opportunities to work in schools, hospitals and other government offices and programmes.
- PDS must be strengthened and in each hamlet self-help groups must be given the responsibility of managing self-help groups.
- All Panchayat offices must be provided telephone facility. Based on need and requirement computer with internet connection must be given.
- Rural Libraries and Rural Knowledge Centres must be established in every tribal Panchayats.
- Self-help groups must be promoted in tribal areas with special assistance.
- The skill development training must be provided to self-help groups members and youth groups.
- Marketing outlets for the tribal products must be arranged in Chennai and District headquarters.

Outcome and Conclusion

Two days workshop gave ample opportunity to the tribal women leaders to articulate their experiences and opinions on issues related to the management of Panchayats. In general women Panchayat Presidents expressed optimism and positive attitude. They became more confident and motivated. Their demands were limited and reasonable. From the workshop it is found that periodical interaction between government officials and ST women Panchayats is very much required. It is also found that there is a need for facilitating a network among the ST tribal leaders. They formed an informal group of ST women Panchayat Presidents. It will facilitate the spirit of self-help and mutual learning. The ST Panchayat Presidents have proved that their capacity and leadership quality. They are ready to accept new ideas without any hesitation. They demand at least two such workshop in a year. The SIRD Director agreed to this request and he promised to make arrangements for more such workshops in the future.

PART - III

Background

The 73rd Amendment to the Indian Constitution has created a self-governing Panchayati Raj Institution to administer economic development and social justice. Reserving one-third of seats for women is a unique opportunity for women and a pathway to work for poor and disadvantaged sections. This legislation mandated the transfer of decision-making powers to three million people, of whom one-third are women-powers to decide their destiny on their own. Women play a major role in ensuring the well-being of the poor, women and Dalits. Therefore, empowering people and particularly women means making them realize their worth and assume responsibilities. Hence, the leadership of elected women representatives and the active participation of women in governance are crucial for effective governance at the grassroots. But due to lack of skill and capacity, they cannot manage the institutions. This is the case of women in general. The position of Scheduled Caste and Scheduled Tribe women is more pathetic. They are the most disadvantaged because they are women and more particularly they belong to the SC/ST. Administering a Village Panchayat which is the lowest level institution itself is a difficult task for them. Then, one can imagine their ability in administering the higher level institutions like Panchayat Union. In order to inculcate leadership qualities in them and to ignite and foster their efficiency a capacity building exercise was organized for SC/ST Women Panchayat Union Chairpersons from 27th to 31st January, 2004 at Gandhigram with the support of the State Institute of Rural Development, Maraimalainagar, Chennai.

Objectives of the Programme

The following are the main objectives of the programme:

- Enable SC/ST Women Panchayat Union Chairpersons to realize their worth.
- Develop a sense of self-esteem and dignity.
- Engineer a shift from a mindset of 'I cannot' to 'I can'.
- Instil a sense of political citizenship, social citizenship and make them realize their fundamental rights and responsibilities which is crucial to making them effective leaders.
- Make them build a vision for the development of communities and more particularly the Dalits.
- Inculcate in them skills needed to be effective Chairpersons to manage the institution by familiarizing them with the rules, procedures, regulations, various schemes and programmes of the government, management of finance and accounts in the Panchayat Union Office.
- Make them realize the importance of community participation in development activities.
- Create a sense of solidarity with others (with other women, e.g. Gram Panchayat women leaders and self-help groups) committed to this cause.
- Make them aware of gender, inclusion and exclusion.

Methods of Training

The participatory training method, which includes small group discussion, reporting to the larger group, one to one discussion and role play and lectures, was adopted. A question and answer session was arranged everyday to clear doubts. A field trip was arranged to visit Vedasandur Panchayat Union Office to interact with Panchayat Union Chairperson.

Resource Persons

1. Dr. G. Palanithurai, specialist in Governance at Grassroots.
2. Dr. V. Ragupathy, specialist in Common Property Resources and Management.
3. Mr. N. S. Chidambaram, specialist in Panchayat Administration.
4. Mr. K. Vallinayagam, specialist in Panchayat Administration.
5. Mr. Subramanian, specialist in Panchayat Administration.
6. Dr. A. Suriakanthi, specialist in Gender Sensitization and Women Empowerment.
7. Ms. Ramani Mathew, specialist in Women Legal Rights.
8. Dr. N. Lalitha, specialist in SHG : Concept and Practices.
9. Ms. Logeswari, specialist in Women's Empowerment.
10. Ms. Vasantha, specialist in Women's Empowerment.
11. Mr. A. Thangathurai, specialist in Schemes and Programmes of Government.
12. Ms. G. Uma, specialist in Women Empowerment.

Course Material Provided

- A book listing the powers and functions of the Panchayat Union, the role and the responsibilities of the Panchayat Union Chairperson, GOs pertaining to Panchayat Union administration, the role and the responsibilities of Union Councillors, schemes and programmes of the State and the Central Governments to be operated by the Panchayat Union, was provided to the participants.
- A book narrating Dalit history, prepared by the SIRD, was also provided.
- A well designed bag.
- A writing pad.
- A pen.

Nature of Training

The training was fully residential. All the participants stayed in the hostel in the Krishi Vigyan Kendra, Gandhigram Rural Institute.

The resource persons stayed in the Guest House. Both in the morning and in the evening the Chairpersons went to the Guest House to meet the resource persons to discuss personal problems pertaining to their Panchayat Union. This was extremely useful to the participants.

Regularity

All SC/ST Women Panchayat Union Chairpersons in Tamil Nadu attended this training in all seriousness.

Content of the Programme

In this training programme the following areas were covered:

- Basic objectives of decentralization of powers.
- Framework of new Panchayati Raj System.
- Features of 73rd Constitutional Amendment Act.
- Tamil Nadu Panchayat Act of 1994 and its basic features.
- Emergence of caste system in India.
- History of the Panchayat Union and its structure.
- Details of Scheduled Tribes in Tamil Nadu.
- Provisions for SC/ST in the Indian Constitution.
- 1989 Protection of Civil Rights (Central Act).
- Importance of women in Panchayat Administration.
- Government schemes for SCs and STs.
- Non-governmental organizations working for SCs/STs.
- Financial schemes for SC/ST students for education.
- Economic development schemes.
- Women development schemes.
- Drinking water schemes.
- Elections to Panchayat Union.
- Tamil Nadu Panchayat Act of 1994 – power and functions of Panchayat Union Councils.
- Power and functions of Union Chairpersons–Tamil Nadu Panchayat Act, 1994.
- Power and functions of Panchayat Union Councillors.

- Travelling allowance to the Panchayat Union Councillors.
- Passing the resolution in the Council and raising questions.
- Structure of the Panchayat Union staff.
- Power and functions of Panchayat Union officials.
- Links with other tiers.
- Links with sectoral departments.
- Special powers of the District Collector.
- No confidence motion.
- Dissolution of Panchayat Union Council.
- Interface between elected representatives and officials.
- Self-sustained programme.
- MLA Area Development programme.
- MP Area Development programme.
- Total Sanitation programme.

Administering Office

- Office rooms and equipments.
- Correspondence and routine activities.
- Council meetings.
- Inspecting line department works.
- Review meetings with officials and conducting camps.
- Vehicle usage.
- Arranging village level meetings.

Powers of Commissioner

- Control over Commissioner by the Chairperson.
- Tour programmes of the Commissioner and the Extension Officer.
- Arranging Panchayat functions.
- Rooms for MLAs.
- Council meeting.
- Passing of resolution and taking necessary steps to implement it.
- Formation of committees and their functions.
- Formation of joint committees.

Income and Expenditure

- Surcharge.
- Entertainment tax.
- Fees.
- Government subsidy.
- Expenditure.

Pre-Training Evaluation

Among the 27 SC/ST elected women Panchayat Union Chairpersons, only one has been elected for a second term. When they were asked about their entry into the Panchayat Union more than 40 per cent of the Chairpersons said that it was due to the party which allotted tickets to them and so they contested, adding that they are proxy to someone in the party. This is the reality. This is the situation of many of the cases but they did not want to tell all this openly. A few disclosed this with the intention that someone has to break the silence. They felt that it is a shame on the part of the party, the males of their family and themselves. This kind of programme gives the confidence and hope for better performance and they will be able to manage the Panchayat administration independently. They are able to interact and discuss with MPs, MLAs and District Collectors boldly. One Chairperson stated that the Minister for Sports and Youth Affairs, Government of Tamil Nadu, encouraged her to contest in the election. Another Chairperson stated that her party's Union Secretary motivated her to contest in the election. Only a few stated that they themselves wanted to contest in the election to do social development activities better than others.

When they were asked about what factors contributed to their success in the election, divergent views emerged, and some of them are listed below: It was a party matter and party functionaries worked for the success. No one could take the credit. Some of them claimed that it was due to their participation in public life that they won.

Next their idea about the new Panchayati Raj System was inquired into. Many of them were able to spell out the basic features of the new Panchayati Raj System. They were:

- Reservation of seats for SC/ST.
- Implementing State and Central Government rural development schemes by involving the people.
- Protecting women's rights and enhancing the leadership qualities of women.

When they were asked to list the features of the 73rd Constitutional Amendment Act, only 30 per cent of the respondents reacted positively. Others said that they did not know. Some said that they were attending the training programme to learn the features of the 73rd Constitutional Amendment Act. Those who listed the features of 73rd Constitutional Amendment Act mentioned the following:

- Gram Sabha for people's participation.
- One-third reservation for women.
- Reservation of seats for SCs/STs based on their population and reservation for SC/ST women.
- Fixing the Panchayat Union Council term as five years.
- Creating a three-tier structure.
- 29 subjects.
- Giving importance to economic development and social justice.
- Elections have to be conducted within six months of the dissolution of the Council.

The next question was about the roles and functions of the Panchayat Union Councillors, according to the Tamil Nadu Panchayat Act, 1994. All the participants answered this question and most of them gave the same answers. They were:

- Implementing development activities effectively.
- Providing basic amenities to the villages.
- Identifying beneficiaries for government schemes and ensuring that the schemes reach the beneficiaries without fail.
- Fulfilling the people's needs step by step.
- Providing drinking water.

- Imparting cleanliness habit to the people.
- Taking care of women and children.
- Participating in the Gram Sabha meeting.

They were also inquired about the functioning of the Gram Sabha in their Panchayat Council area. All responded to this question and a few gave elaborate answers. Their responses were the following:

- This is people's Parliament.
- If more and more people participate in the Gram Sabha, then developmental works will be implemented effectively.
- Discussion should be based on people's thoughts.
- It is a place to explain about the Government schemes and it should reach the poor through the Gram Sabha.
- Selecting the BPL list.
- It is a place to redress the grievances of the people.
- It is a chance for the people to directly explain their grievances to the leaders and government officials who participate.
- The public can know about the income and expenditure of the Panchayats.
- Gram Sabha members can plan for development.

All SC/ST women Chairpersons stated that they regularly attended the Gram Sabha meetings. They expressed that this is the place to boost their popularity among the masses. While replying to a question about their experience in previous training pro- grammes, some Chairpersons from Kancheepuram District said that they attended training programmes conducted by District Rural Development Agency and the State Institute of Rural Development, Maraimalainagar, and a few of them had attended a training programme conducted by an NGO named Deepam. One Chairperson visited New Delhi in the year 2001 and another Chairperson attended a training programme organized by RETC, Bhavanisagar.

Next, they were asked about the various schemes offered by the State and Central Governments. Most of them (more than 90%) were aware of the available schemes implemented through them. They mentioned a few schemes such as:

- Distribution of free cycle to SC/ST school going children.
- Social welfare schemes.
- Cradle baby scheme.
- Free noon meal to the poor at temples.
- 11th Finance Commission.
- SGRY.
- Namakku Naame Thittam.
- Small savings.

Finally, in the pre-evaluation training the participants were asked about their expectations and requirements from the training programme. They expressed the following as their needs:

- To know about the procedures in administration.
- To know the rights of the Panchayat Union Chairpersons.
- How to approach various departments to implement schemes effectively.
- To know about the conduct of Council meetings and about the powers of the Union.
- To know about the powers of the Union Chairpersons of other states.

From the pre-training evaluation it can be understood that their expectations from the training programme were high and they wanted to enhance their capacity for administration. Their interest in public life is very much appreciable and this should be channellized through capacity building exercise. While talking to them informally, they stated that once they increase their capacity they want to perform better and aspire for higher posts both in their party and in the Panchayat. They need regular capacity building exercise programmes and follow up workshops. Regular capacity building exercise programmes would enable them to realize their roles and responsibilities. They wanted to work for the marginalized and the poor. Even though they faced a lot of obstacles from the male Councillors and party people, they wanted to fulfil the aspirations of the people. For this they needed proper guidance and support from officials, training institutes and the party to which they belong but the conditions now are not positive.

Post-Training Evaluation

After training the Chairpersons with the help of resource persons and specialists, the impact of the training programme was assessed with the help of a questionnaire which was administered at the end of the training.

The first question was about the objectives of the Panchayat Raj system. The participants' responses were:

- New Panchayat Raj system was established to administer development and social justice.
- It provides opportunity for providing benefits to socially disadvantaged people.
- It was established for providing food security to the poor.
- It was established to empower women in society.
- To provide the basic amenities.

The second question was about the special features of the new Panchayat Raj system. The responses were:

- Participatory governance.
- Demand driven.
- To deepen democracy.
- To empower people.
- To empower women.
- To empower Dalits.

The third question was about their roles and responsibilities. After the training, the participants were more conscious of their roles and responsibilities than before. They came to know the roles and responsibilities to be discharged by the Chairpersons, especially women SC/ST Chairpersons. They admitted that now they could work cordially with Union officials and MLAs. They also admitted that they understood the meaning of 'leadership'. They also realized the importance of harmony. The other functions and responsibilities that they indicated were:

- Convening and conducting the Union Council meeting.
- Discharging all roles and responsibilities stated in the Tamil Nadu Panchayat Act, 1994.
- Providing basic amenities like roads, drinking water, electricity, sanitation, etc.
- Make people participate in developmental activities.
- Improve the economic activities in the Panchayat Union area.
- Preparing plan from below.
- Using human resources to develop the same.
- Assigning responsibilities to the people preparing the need based plan.
- Improving the status of women and abolishing differences among communities and between genders.

Fourthly, their suggestions and strategies for making people participate in the activities of the local bodies were elicited. Their suggestions were very much helpful for further enhancement of the system and in policy advocacy also. They suggested the following:

- Making people prepare a plan for their requirements in the area of basic amenities and involving them during the implementation.
- Integrating all the Gram Panchayat activities and preparing a comprehensive plan for the Panchayat Union and implementing the same.

The fifth question was about fund mobilization. Except a few every participant listed the sources of income to the Panchayat Union Council. They knew much about:

- Entertainment tax.
- Surcharges.
- Licence fee for factories.
- Licence fee for market.
- Temporary licence fee.
- Getting money through leasing fishing pond, trees, orchards, etc.
- Construction of shopping complex.

In the training programme, they were taught how to mobilize funds through common property resources management.

The seventh question was about how to prepare the development plan and the steps to be followed in the preparation of the development plan. The participants listed the following:

- It should have the goal of development and social justice.
- It should have the goal of health.
- It should contain a plan to protect the environment.
- Proper coordination should be ensured.
- People's participation should be given top priority.
- Priorities must be determined in decision-making and planning.
- There should be a separate plan for each line department. It helps the Panchayat Union to involve line departments in implementing the plan.
- Underdeveloped Panchayats should be given top priority.

The participants were oriented well in the planning process their suggestions were useful to the trainers.

The next question was on how to maintain records. Only 30 per cent of the participants answered this question. Their answers were:

- Checking vouchers regularly and properly.
- Diesel bills should be maintained properly.
- While preparing balance sheet, opening balance has to be taken into account.
- State Government funded capital income should be maintained as it is.

- There should not be much difference between budget estimate and revised estimate.

The ninth question was about how to establish social justice in society. Again only 30 per cent of the participants answered this question. The suggestions were:

- Providing basic amenities to the poor, Dalits and women properly and involving them in maintaining them.
- Proper implementation of Government schemes for the poor, Dalits and women.

The tenth question was about how to develop leadership qualities. The participants did not respond to this question.

The next question was about how to uplift the Scheduled Castes and Scheduled Tribes. All the participants gave suggestions:

- Providing basic services to them, namely, drinking water, streetlights, housing facility.
- Construction of CC road to SC/ST colonies.
- To fight for their basic rights.
- Implementing State and Central Government schemes properly and making sure that benefits reach them properly.
- Creating employment opportunity specially for them.
- Construction of sanitary complex.
- Establishing library, creche etc.
- Giving subsidy for the establishment of cottage industries.
- Giving entrepreneurship training to women.
- Tie up with NGOs.
- Identifying training institutions.

Next came the most important topic 'women empowerment'. All the women Chairpersons were concerned about the upliftment of their own segment. They came out with important suggestions to empower women. They were:

- Formation of SHGs at village level and giving training to them to start cottage industries for economic independence.

- Formation of women federation and making them participate in politics.
- Giving leadership training to women who are willing to become leaders.
- Creating self-confidence among women.

The next question was about their priorities in Panchayat administration. All the participants listed the following items as their priorities:

- Development of women and Scheduled Castes and Scheduled Tribes.
- Cultivating good habits among school children, especially those from the Dalit families.
- Formation of SHGs among Dalit women.
- Providing basic amenities to the Dalit hamlets.
- Running Panchayat Union administration efficiently.

Finally, their opinion about the training programme was also asked for. Only 3 participants said that they needed a 10-day training programme. The others were fully satisfied with a 5-day training programme. However they offered the following suggestions:

- They need refresher course once in 6 months.
- Training content should be intimated to them much earlier.
- They need purely participatory method; they are not interested in the lecture method.
- They need more explanations with regard to government orders and laws.

The participants express the following opinions about the training programme:

- They came to know the laws related to Scheduled Castes and Scheduled Tribes.
- They came to know about the roles and responsibilities of the Commissioners, Chairpersons and members and about the administration of the Panchayat Union.

- They came to know about District administration and the Gram Panchayat administration.
- They came to know the strategies to be followed for the development of women.

They also opined that the training was given without break and this was very useful to them. They stated that the training was like providing nutritious food to them. They now knew the rules and regulations of Panchayat Union administration. It has given them confidence to run the Union efficiently. They now know how to control officials and how to work with officials cordially. They have gained confidence to point out officials' mistakes. The training programme was more satisfactory than what they had expected.

Socio-Economic Background of the Participants

Following is the profile of the leaders:

Table 6.1 : Age distribution of respondents

Sl. No.	*Age Distribution*	*No. of Chairpersons*	*%*
1.	21-30	8	29.63
2.	31-40	8	29.63
3.	41-50	6	22.22
4.	51-60	3	11.11
5.	61 & above	2	7.41

Source : Computed.

Table 6.2 : Educational Qualification of respondents

Sl. No.	*Educational Qualification*	*No. of Chairpersons*	*%*
1.	Illiterate	-	-
2.	Neo-literate	1	3.70
3.	Primary	7	25.93
4.	Secondary	9	33.33
5.	Higher Secondary	6	22.22
6.	Degree/diploma	4	14.81

Source : Computed.

Table 6.3 : Distribution of respondents by Religion

Sl. No.	*Religion*	*No. of Chairpersons*	*%*
1.	Hindu	26	96.29
2.	Muslim	-	-
3.	Christian	1	3.45

Source : Computed.

Table 6.4 : Occupational category of respondents

Sl. No.	*Occupation*	*No. of Chairpersons*	*%*
1.	Agriculture	27	100
2.	Non-Agriculture	-	-

Source : Computed.

Table 6.5 : Distribution of respondents by annual income

Sl. No.	*Income*	*No. of Chairpersons*	*%*
1.	Less than Rs.10,000	11	40.74
2.	Rs.10,001 to Rs.25,000	12	44.44
3.	Rs.25,001 to Rs.50,000	1	3.70
4.	Rs.50,001 & above	1	3.70
5.	Don't say	2	7.40

Source : Computed.

Table 6.6 : Landholding of respondents

Sl. No.	*Land Particulars*	*No. of Chairpersons*	*%*
1.	No	10	37.04
2.	0-5 acres	16	59.26
3.	6-10 acres	1	3.70
4.	Above 10 acres	-	-
5.	Landless	-	-

Source : Computed.

Table 6.7 : Distribution of respondents by type of family

Sl. No.	*Type of family*	*No. of Chairpersons*	*%*
1.	Joint family	14	51.85
2.	Nuclear family	13	48.15

Source : Computed.

Table 6.8 : Type of houses owned by respondents

Sl. No.	Type of house	No. of Chairpersons	%
1.	Huts	4	14.81
2.	Tiles	15	55.55
3.	Pucca	-	-
4.	Group house (IAY)	4	14.81
5.	Rent	3	11.11

Source : Computed.

Table 6.9 : Distribution of respondents by household facilities

Sl. No.	Facilities	Yes	%	No	%
1.	21-30	27	100	-	-
2.	Toilet	16	59.26	11	40.74
3.	Drinking water connection	17	62.96	10	37.04

Source : Computed.

Table 6.10 : Party affiliation of respondents

Sl. No.	Name of the party	No. of Chairpersons	%
1.	AIADMK	18	66.66
2.	DMK	5	18.51
3.	CPI (M)	2	7.41
4.	Puthiya Tamizhagam	1	3.70
5.	Congress	1	3.70

Source : Computed.

Table 6.11 : Respondents' connection with social organization by respondents

Sl. No.	Contact with social organization	No. of Chairpersons	%
1.	Yes	5	18.51
2.	No	22	81.48

Source : Computed.

Table 6.12 : Reading habit of respondents

Sl. No.	Reading Newspaper	No. of Chairpersons	%
1.	Yes	27	100
2.	No	-	-

Source : Computed.

Field Visits

The participants were taken to Vedasandur Block of Dindigul District. Ms. Kavitha Parthiban is the Chairperson of the Vedasandur Block. She is an agriculture graduate. She shared her experience with the participants. She is working cordially with officials and she is working independently. The participants raised many questions and got clarifications. The questions raised were:

- How to maintain cordial relationship with the Commissioner? How to get cooperation from the Commissioner in accordance with law? Is there any possibility of asking the District Collector to intervene or to get an order from the District Collector?
- How to allocate resources for development work?
- Do we have rights to allocate IAY houses to BPL families?
- How to renew BT road?
- How to allocate DPAP funds?
- Is Panchayat Union letter correspondence through the Chairperson or through the Commissioner?
- Protocol is not maintained in most of the government programmes–how to rectify it?

The participants also raised questions on general fund and budget. They are:

- Do Chairpersons have the right to check the BDO and other field staff daily?
- Who should decide on the tender–the BDO or the Chairperson?
- Do Chairpersons have the right to conduct staff meeting once a month?
- How to get the jeep for the Chairperson's tour programme?
- How to prepare a 5-year plan? Who will take charge of preparing the 5-year plan–BDO or Chairperson?
- Does the Chairperson have the right to maintain the CL register of the Panchayat Union staff?

- Does the Chairperson have to submit work estimate to the Council meeting or to the BDO?

Vedasandur Block officials and Union Engineers also participated. They took the participants to a nearby village where construction of toilets was going on. Practically the participants learnt the day-to-day affairs of Panchayat Union administration. They stated that this training programme gave strength to them to act confidently as Chairpersons. They would be able to run the Panchayat Union administration efficiently.

Problems faced by the Women Representatives

1. The Block Development Officer, colluding with the MLA, functions independently, disregarding the Union Council. The officials yield to the pressure/influence of the MLAs in selecting the Panchayats, finalizing the activities and other developmental activities carried out in the Block. Hence more clarity is needed on the roles and the responsibilities of the Union Council in carrying out various developmental activities initiated by the government within the jurisdiction of the Block.
2. The ruling party men establish good contact with Block officials and easily influence them for their own interest. Guidance is needed on how to tackle the BDO who deviates from the resolution of the Council.
3. There is a provision for 75 litres of diesel every month for the Union Chairperson for official and field visits in connection with the Union activities. But in reality, the vehicle is not available for such visits and sometimes it is said that the allotted diesel was utilized by the District authorities. The details are not shared with the Chairpersons in this regard.
4. Council members are generally active members of political parties. They group themselves on party basis and try to stall the proceedings in the Council meeting. They use 'no

confidence motion' as a weapon against the Union Chairpersons.

5. In general, the various activities going on in the Union are not shared with the Union Chairperson. The BDO and the Engineer join hands with the Vice-Chairman and do not properly disclose things to the Union Chairperson. SC/ST women Chairpersons are mostly in the hands of the Vice-Chairmen and they are under the control of party functionaries.
6. Vice-Chairmen organize their own group of members and overrule the Chairpersons.
7. The Tamil Nadu Panchayat Act, 1994 is not known to Union Chairpersons or is not available at the Union office for reference. Without knowing the Act and its provisions the administration of the Panchayat Union is a problem.
8. The women Chairpersons have to encounter challenges from three sides: from the officials, from the Ward Members and from the Vice-Chairmen.
9. There is a nexus between the District level members and the MLA of the ruling party. They decide on many activities without any consultation with the Union Chairperson on the pretext that the District Collector advised them to do so.
10. Without any genuine reasons, a no confidence motion is introduced due to political rivalry.
11. There is no support base for the SC and ST women Chairpersons. This is the first time they have met together and shared their problems and they thanked the government for this initiative of training them separately.
12. Ruling party men side with the Vice-Chairperson if the Chairperson belongs to the opposition and so the Council deliberations are disturbed.
13. Officials of the Department of Rural Development are behaving as if they are the masters and they treat the leaders as subordinates. They do not have orientation in Panchayati Raj. Proper orientation to them is also needed. It would be better if both the Union Chairperson and the Block Development Officer are put together in the training.

14. Casteism is deeply rooted even among government officials. They do not give equal treatment to SC Chairpersons.
15. The details of the Union budget are not known to the Chairpersons. Officials do not give much importance to enabling them to learn administration.
16. The Eleventh Schedule the 29 subjects, the role and responsibility of the Union–all these details are not properly shared with the Chairpersons. In fact they are not aware of any government order in this regard.
17. In the context of social inequality, male chauvinism, caste hierarchy and political rivalry, it is a very tough task to ensure social justice to the marginalized sector.
18. The absence of an organic link with the Gram Panchayat should be rectified legally. The Chairpersons realize the importance of the relationship between the Gram Panchayat and the Union Panchayat.
19. Procedures related to conducting the Council meeting are not properly known to the Chairpersons. Instead of explaining these to them the Block Development Officers just reject the Chairpersons' pleas.
20. The Council members demand so many things. They ask to provide photocopies of the minutes book. But the Chairpersons do not know what the rules relating to the rights of the Union Councillors are.
21. All issues are considered on party lines.
22. The officials fail to give due regard to the Union Chairpersons. They are not aware of the protocol pertaining to organizing government meetings. But the Block officials do not include the name of Union Chairperson. The officials decide individually and run the show.
23. Refresher training and other capacity building exercises have to be organized at the District itself for the sake of the convenience of the women representatives.
24. In general the State Government does not have any vision to improve the socio-economic conditions of the SC community.
25. The SHG activities are not known to Union Chairperson.

Officials and NGOs work together without giving any space to Union Chairperson.

26. The BDO conducts review meets with the Block staff without inviting the Union Chairperson. It would be better if the review meet is held in the presence of the Union Chairperson. As the Chairperson of a Union, by attending the review meet, the Chairperson can learn details of various works being carried out and, if necessary, suitable intervention can be made for their successful implementation.

What They Have Learnt

1. Self-confidence and determination in performing the roles and responsibilities.
2. The strength of teamwork.
3. They are to act on their own.
4. Significance of social justice and vision to work for the betterment of SCs and STs.
5. The art of human resource development.
6. Building alliances with SHG members to empower womenfolk.
7. Drafting of schematic plan to materialize the vision.
8. Gender issues.
9. Building rapport with government functionaries and the art of lobbying with the authorities, if necessary.
10. Total involvement with a sense of commitment.
11. Sustaining the interest and spirit and steadfast leadership.
12. Developmental perception rather than scheme implementation.
13. Adherence to rules and regulations.

Observations

- It seems that they are not only in the hands of their husbands but also in the hands of the party's representatives as they were nominated by the party.

- Their aspirations and learning capacity are very poor and so it is very difficult to change their mindset.
- Many of the leaders have left their roles and responsibilities to the Vice-Presidents.
- It seems that they do not regularly attend the office. They are told by both the Vice-President and the BDO not to go over to the office and that the files will be sent to them.
- They have to learn a lot from the Gram Panchayat women leaders.
- Their economic condition is poor and that is why they have to rely on others who helped them financially to become the President of the Block Panchayat.
- Without the knowledge of the Chairpersons the entire administration is being carried out. They merely affix their signatures.

NOTES AND REFERENCES

1. Rajiv Gandhi Foundation, *Charter of Panchayats,* New Delhi: Rajiv Gandhi Foundation, 1998.
2. Government of Tamil Nadu, *Democratic Decentralization: Powers Entrusted to Panchayati Raj Institutions,* Chennai: Rural Development Department, 1999.
3. D. Bandyopadhyay, Amitava Mukerjee and Mitali Sen Gavani, *Empowering Panchayats, Handbook for Master Trainers using Participatory Approach,* New Delhi: Concept Publishing Company, 2003.
4. G. Palanithurai, *Role Perceptions of Legislations: A Case Study of Tamil Nadu,* New Delhi: Konarak Publishers, 1991.
5. M. Aslam, *Directory of Panchayati Raj Training Institutions in India,* New Delhi: Rajiv Gandhi Foundation, 2001.
6. Panchayat Leaders have made such demands in their federation meetings and while submitting petitions to the Government.
7. In the month of June 2003, the Government of Tamil Nadu released the training module along with a G.O. 14440/2003 dt. 28.4.2003. It is stated in the G.O. that wherever Gandhigram Rural Institute conducts training for Local Body Leaders the Government should not conduct similar training.
8. State Finance Commission, *First State Finance Commission Report,* Chennai: State First Finance Commission, 1995.
9. State Planning Commission, *Report on Entrustment of Responsibilities to Three-Tier Panchayats,* Chennai: State Planning Commission, 1997.

10. Government of Tamil Nadu, *Action Taken Report on the Entrustment of Responsibilities to Three-Tier Panchayats,* Chennai: Department of Rural Development, 1998.
11. Government of Tamil Nadu, *Report on Roles, Responsibilities and Powers Devolved to Panchayats,* Chennai: Government of Tamil Nadu, 1998.
12. Government of Tamil Nadu, *Action Taken Report on the Entrustment of Responsibilities to Three-Tier Panchayats,* Chennai: Government of Tamil Nadu, 1999.
13. Rajiv Gandhi Chair, *Training Module for Panchayat Training Progress,* Gandhigram: Rajiv Gandhi Chair for Panchayati Raj Studies, 2002.
14. G. Palanithurai, *Tamil Nadu Panchayati Government Act, Rules and Schemes (in Tamil),* Chennai: South Vision, 2002.
15. The Hunger Project, *Training Module for Leadership Training for Women in Panchayat,* Gandhigram: Rajiv Gandhi Chair for Panchayati Raj Studies, 2002.
16. Letter from the Director of Rural Development, Government of Tamil Nadu Rc. No. 85678/2002/Training dt.17.9.2003.
17. Since the participants demanded a service and support centre to provide information to the Panchayat leaders, the Rajiv Gandhi Chair decided to launch an on line service and the Panchayat leaders have been asked to contact the phone number 0451-2451775 for any help.
18. All the points drawn from the Panchayat Presidents were submitted to the Secretary to Government, Department of Rural Development and Director of Rural Development, Government of Tamil Nadu on 30th June, 2003.
19. In the meanwhile an interface meeting between the higher officials and women representatives of Gram Panchayats was arranged and facilitated by the Rajiv Gandhi Chair on 11th July, 2003 at Chennai.
20. Gram Panchayat Presidents have formed a Federation which is called the Federation of Gram Panchayat Leaders of Tamil Nadu. Women Gram Panchayat Leaders have formed their own federation called the Tamil Nadu Federation of Women Panchayati leaders. Dalit leaders in Panchayats have for their federation. These three federations periodically meet and discuss their problems. They are drawing the support of NGOs. These federations are independent and not politically affiliated. District Panchayat leaders have their own associations but they are not effective.
21. This newspaper has a readership of 5 lakhs. The entire exercise is being done with the support The Hunger Project.
22. The media has not developed an appropriate perspective to look at Panchayats and as a result it has only projected the official versions of the Government on local bcdies. After the media workshop was conducted, the media has started covering the struggles, successes and innovations of the Panchayats and the media has started helping the Panchayats.

7

GOVERNANCE : FROM THE PERSPECTIVE OF ELECTED WOMEN REPRESENTATIVES

Introduction

The concept of 'governance' has gained currency now as it signifies and brings a new connotation contextually, which is different from the concept of 'government'. In the same way, the presence and the participation of women in governance is also new contextually and it gains significance as they are new to the job and they function as the representatives of the people against the backdrop of patriarchy. There is yet another category of collectivity, namely, the Dalit women, who have come to power and function against the backdrop of patriarchy and also the hierarchy of the caste system in India. Thus newly recruited women to grassroots institutions have come to the institutions with different barriers and obstacles. Their style of governance depends much on their perception of governance. There are, of course, a series of questions that have been raised on the capacity and capability of the elected women representatives to discharge their role and function as they come to positions with inherent difficulties at personal and social levels. Studies have been conducted to evaluate the performance of the elected women representatives. These studies reveal that the style of governance of women is different from that of men. Certainly, it brings to light new information and new insights. Women's voices in governance were not so far heard due to their under-representation and non-participation in institutional structures for decision-making. Despite obstacles, women are in the decision-making process at present because of the 73rd and the 74th Amendments to the Constitution of India. They have already begun to make their mark by scoring achievements in governance at the grassroots. The political space provided for women can be considered an opportunity for expressing their opinion and raising their voice on the issues of people's development in the governing institutions as they perceive and understand them.

The World Bank defines governance as "the manner in which power is exercised in the management of a country's economic and social resources for development". 'Governance' a comprehensive term and, as a phenomenon, it can be looked from different perspectives. Generally, it is perceived as the process of governing the institutions which ought to bring about an orderly change in the environment, leading to social and economic development of the society. The UNDP defines governance as "the exercise of political, economic and administrative authority to manage the country's affairs. It comprises the mechanisms, processes and institutions through which citizens and groups articulate their interests, exercise their legal rights, meet their obligations and mediate their differences". Governance is a multi-faceted complex situation of institutions, systems, structures, processes, procedures, practices, relationships and leadership behaviour in the exercise of social, political, economic and managerial/administrative authority in the running of public or private affairs. Good governance is the exercise of this authority with the participation, interest and livelihood of the governed as the driving force. The exercise of political authority to a large extent influences decisions and the political participation of men and women occupies a prominent position in governance. At present women in governance draw attention and a series of studies have been carried out on gender and governance to give a holistic perspective to the development process through governance. The space provided for these women in the process of governance has added value to their voices which was suppressed earlier in the patriarchical society. A study on gender in governance must look at all these areas and their interactions. The success of democracy doesn't result in the development of the country. Further, no society can be called developed if one half of it remains voiceless, invisible and undervalued. At the Fourth World Conference on Women held in 1999, 189 governments committed themselves to "take measures to ensure women's equal access to and full participation in power structures and decision-making" and to "increase women's capacity to participate in decision-making and leadership". To fulfil these strategic objectives, they pledged to take action to "establish the goal of gender balance in governmental bodies and committees". Even though the action was taken much earlier in India in the existing situation, women representation at grassroots is under supervision and evaluation.

To understand about women's governance it becomes imperative that their perception of governance be studied. Against this backdrop an attempt is made to study the perception of the elected women representatives on governance.

Problem to be Studied

In this study, an attempt is made to analyze the perception of the EWRs on governance. Primarily the focus will be on the gap between their perception and the actual process of governance. Specific emphasis will be laid on governance at the grassroots. Women are in all the tiers of the Panchayati Raj System. Of these chairpersons, that too at the lowest unit of the Gram Panchayat, have been fixed for this analysis as they are heading the institutions and managing the institutions. Others are only members of the constituent body and hence they are left out. Of the three-tier structure, Gram Panchayats have been selected as these institutions are legally free from political party based electoral contests. So the Gram Panchayat Presidents are having more autonomy in terms of their functions. Hence the Gram Panchayat Women Presidents are fixed as respondents for this study.

Methodology

Elected women Panchayat Presidents of Cuddalore District and Tirunelvelli District, Tamil Nadu, visited Gandhigram Rural Institute and underwent a Capacity Building Programme for five days. A schedule was prepared and a focused group discussion was conducted, where in 217 EWRs of Cuddalore District and Tirunelvelli District were divided into 14 groups, and their perceptions and views on governance were recorded. The topics for their discussion were categorized into four divisions, viz. governance-conceptual, governance-practical, governance-participation and governance-gender. The EWRs were motivated to express their views on the above four subjects.

Governance—Conceptual

It is crystal clear that the elected women representatives conceived government as an institution which has to provide facilities needed by the people to lead a decent human life with peace and dignity. The government should be humane and look after the well-being of the people. People should not have any fear of the government. People should have faith and confidence in the government. To create such a feeling among the people government institutions have to work positively towards the people. People should not develop aversion towards the government. They should have a feeling that government institutions are always responsive to the demands of the people. The government should respect the people by making officials responsive to the people.

Women conceptualize governance as the process of implementing government schemes sponsored by both Central and State Governments which are aimed at poverty reduction and infrastructure building. Recently these women have witnessed a great change in women's life and the government has started focusing on empowerment of women also. The organization and the functioning of SHGs have effected a tremendous change and now opportunities are provided to women to enhance their economic capacity. These SHGs serve as a motivating factor to many women headed Panchayats in implementing their ideas and lend a helping hand in many activities of the Panchayat from participating in Gram Sabha to supporting the women Panchayat Presidents during periods of crisis. These Presidents also consider the Panchayat a viable unit for successful implementation of government schemes, but fee that most of the schemes are supply driven and not demand driven. Even five decades after the attainment of Independence, the government has failed to provide safe drinking water, transportation, medical facility to the poorest of the poor, ensure 100 per cent enrolment in schools of eligible children, health and hygiene, sanitation and so on. These Panchayat Presidents are trying to do their best in order to achieve the above-mentioned facilities, which have been entrusted to them as their responsibility in the Eleventh Schedule of the Constitution through the list of 29 subjects. Since most of the Panchayat Presidents are not in a capable position to plan for their Panchayat they merely act as agents of implementing government schemes and many equate the Panchayats with contract work. Women Presidents want these attitudes changed. The government should introspect on its outlook towards the Panchayats in devolving funds and powers to them. Further they expect that the present wage employment programmes are not sufficient and more industrial zones should be created in rural areas which will pave way for the upliftment of the poor people in the rural areas. In relation to agriculture, these women consider government intervention necessary but they can not explain it in concrete terms. These women also assert that the funds allocated for Panchayat activities should reach the Panchayat in the stipulated time so that delay may be avoided. They also plead that the Panchayats should not be forced to perform certain activities which are not necessary at all. For example, they cite the construction of retaining walls in some places which is not necessary at all, and say that this money can be utilized purposefully by performing other necessary activities. Overall these women are satisfied with their mode of functioning and all the women tried to explain their achievements and their mode of operation in implementing government schemes. Women and nature are close to each other and they need orientation in this direction also. They advise the government to take earnest steps to protect the environment from degradation and assure of their help to the government as and when required.

Generally, women's conception of governance encompasses all areas like poverty alleviation, infrastructure building, women empowerment, health and sanitation and nature conservation. Their ideas are profound, their capacities are enormous, their curiosity is sky high but they need constant motivation and information to encourage them to achieve in the political arena dominated by males. They want to capacitate themselves and hear their voices, which have been suppressed in history for a long time.

These women have witnessed a series of changes in the past five years from providing basic facilities to women empowerment. They are aware of environmental issues. Apart from these things they talked about the changes brought about by the Panchayati Raj Institutions like convening of the Gram Sabha, action taken through resolutions and allocation of funds. They expect some changes to be brought about by the government by giving representation to women in the State Legislature and Parliament. All facilities provided in the urban areas should also reach the rural areas with particular reference to information technology. Even though they agreed that they got transportation facility which was not provided earlier, they stressed that the roads laid should be of high quality and the frequency of buses visiting their villages should be maximized. They also expect the selection of beneficiaries for various schemes to be increased, since most of the people in the villages are below the poverty line. They also assert that most of the resolutions passed in the Gram Sabha are not put into practice due to paucity of funds. So, allocation should be made proportionate to the requirements. They also expect that functional autonomy should be provided to the Panchayat and that the State and the Central Governments should recognize the Panchayat as an institution of self-government and sufficient resources should be devolved to the Panchayat.

When they were asked whether all the help from the government was useful, they replied positively, but expressed their grievances against politicians and bureaucrats. The schemes proposed by the government are of good scope but they are not practised in the spirit due to corruption and nepotism. When they were asked to suggest a solution to the problem most of the responses stated that functional clarity regarding Central, State and Local Government should be ensured and interfering in others functions should be curbed. The implementation of government schemes should be demand based not supply based. In turn people should also be more responsive to the administration and they should watch all the actions of the government. After the enactment of the 73rd Amendment to the Constitution of India, it was expected that, with the new system at the grassroots created by the Central and State Governments, people's immediate needs would be met. When women leaders come to local bodies, women will consider the space as meant for development and hence they would attend to development works. It is believed that since in Indian society women are valued much, when they come to power, they will be respected by all. It was expected that the new dispensation included power to provide work to the energy of the people and skills. Panchayats can ensure social justice by using the power vested with the Panchayats. They enumerate the qualities of good governance as people friendly, pro-poor, pro-labour, pro-nature, pro-community, pro-women, pro-Dalit and functioning purely by understanding people's needs. They said that the leaders of the people should have humaneness, good judgment, tolerance, vision, self-confidence, faith and hope in people, self-respect, information and capability to forge alliance with different partners. Apart from these things they also said that the leader should have honesty so that he/she can be free from corruption and lead the community. Effective leadership lies in perceiving the barriers, problems and obstacles in handling power and turning them into opportunities and challenges and responding to the challenges.

Governance—Practical

While sharing their views on the governance in vogue, they are not satisfied with the present situation since they are not getting proper information from the government. The government orders passed by the State Government relating to Panchayati Raj Institutions are not reaching them. Even the officials at the block level are not giving them proper and needed information. Their solution to this problem is telephone facility in each Panchayat office so that they can be informed and they can get information promptly. About corruption they say that it has become part of the administrative system and officials and the public have to change their attitude to getting their things done. Many government officials demand money to perform their duties. Government officials do not like being questioned, people claiming their entitlement, and coming to their offices without having a deal. Many officials discourage the women representatives to come to their office. They asked the EWRs to send their male family members. They never listen to the EWRs. They make the EWRs listen to them. They expect the EWRs to behave as subordinates and obey the orders of the officials. Awareness can be created among the public but it is very difficult on the part of the officials to change their mindset and so training should be given to them on how to be honest. On the part of people also an attitudinal change is needed and people should be vigilant and participate in the civil society activities to remove corruption from society. Because poor people are the worst sufferers they should know their rights and claim them. Vigilance committees may be formed at the grassroots level to look into the matter of corruption and their report should be taken into account in taking decisions, said one of the Presidents. Finally, all concluded that people should take a resolve to curb corruption. Severe punishment should be given to those who practice corruption. While sharing their views on people's relationship with government officials and how this can be enhanced, they said that bureaucrats behave in an autocratic way and they are not people friendly. The people did not follow their language and they always tried to force their knowledge on innocent people. Even though there are some kindhearted and people friendly officials, their number is small. Officials should understand the needs of the people and should act as servants of the people. They should understand the condition of the people by visiting their place and people should send confidential reports on officials to the government and the government should act upon them. Their remuneration and promotion should be purely based on this evaluation.

Their experience of practical governance is mixed in nature and they expressed both positive and negative views regarding the modern practice of governance. The advancement in information technology is amazing according to them but they are not well informed by the government promptly in spite of this advancement. Hence, they requested that telephone connection to all the Panchayats be made mandatory and information can be made available to them by the block officials promptly. Even though information technology has grown beyond our imagination information is not available to the poor and they serve only rich and educated people. The government should take necessary steps to enable the poor to use information technology. One of the Presidents said that the government is taking necessary steps for the development of the country in all aspects from poverty alleviation to advancement in information technology but these things are not informed to the public through a proper mechanism. Instead the government is propagating its political agenda through information technology. Only pole gimmicks are played by the political parties through this medium and the government has failed to achieve the end it is meant for. Institutions which are delivering services to the people are in the hands of the sectoral departments and they continue to post dismal performance. Even though they are listed in the 11th Schedule they are still under the control of the sectoral departments. Primary education, noon-meal, anganwadi, primary health and public distribution shops are with the officials. They never listen to the people's representatives. People expect these institutions to be geared up for better service delivery by the intervention of EWRs. But it does not happen.

The practice of corruption and mal-administration are the two factors which hinder the development of our country. The Presidents stated that these things can be eradicated at different levels with the strong determination of the people as well as the representatives of the people. Corruption, according to them, varies from office to office. Nobody pays heed to the words of the poor. A gap has been created between the people and the Government by the officials. It is wantonly created to make use of the gap for the advantage of the officials through power brokers. The new Panchayati Raj System has been introduced only to bridge the gap between the people and the Government and to remove the power brokers from the middle. But officials want only power brokers. Officials get jittery when EWRs come to them for help as they won't give bribe like the brokers. If EWRs are allowed to come to the office continuously and interact with officials the administrative setup has to be made transparent. Further the relationship between the people and the officials has been strained. The strained relationship between people and Government can be improved only when the Government adopts a people friendly approach. They said that officials from the development sector are corrupt and they adopt corrupt practices as if it is their prescribed duty and personnel from the police department terrorize the people as though they are the messiah sent to protect law and order. Police atrocities against Dalits are severe and the experience shared by one of the Dalits Presidents was heartbreaking. She was beaten up by the police to make her withdraw a criminal case which she filled against a caste Hindu. In spite of her complaint against these police personnel of violating human rights she was not paid attention to till now. Due to the cruel treatment of the police her intestines were damaged and now a part has been replaced by surgery using fiber. The government cannot come to the rescue of Dalits and women in this age of globalization. These Presidents are very critical about the behaviour of Government officials and they don't know the redressal mechanism to get rid of this menace. Anyhow they asserted that they are respected by some of the officials who are mostly kind hearted and duty conscious. The reservation of seats for Dalits was made with the aim of establishing social justice in society and nearly 33 per cent of the participants in the discussion were women from the Dalit community. Most of these women were elected unopposed and the reason behind this was that the caste Hindus of the Panchayat selected the women of their choice who were bound to work according to their command. Since the seats were reserved for Dalit women no election was conducted in these Panchayats. In spite of the serious efforts taken by the Government to bring about social justice in society, in practice the domination of caste Hindus over Dalits still persists. On many occasions they discovered the poor capacity of the officials. Officials have been trained to satisfy their higher officials and to make money for their personal use. Unless their capacity is enhanced, one can not expect any change in their functioning. In the whole process of interface between the women leaders and Government officials one can find an undercurrent, namely, the power of the organized group. When an EWR approaches an officer individually she cannot get anything, but if she goes with a group, she can achieve things.

Governance—Participation

Governance and participation as the topic for discussion aroused their interest and they expressed their views enthusiastically and appreciated the introduction of the Panchayati Raj System and making the reservation for women mandatory, since it has provided them an opportunity for participation in the political space as decision-makers. SHGs in this aspect are helping a lot to Gram Panchayats and they mobilize people to participate in the Gram Sabha. They also provide strength to the women Panchayat Presidents in implementing many schemes and most of the programmes regarding sanitation were thriving successfully because of their full participation. Normally people tend to participate in the Gram Sabha expecting many benefits from it. But the SHG members are aware of the need for participation and group involvement in many activities since they have been sensitized to the need for collective action. Community based organizations and women should be encouraged to participate and awareness should be created among the public about the necessity for and implications of participation in public life, said these Presidents. Further people should be assured of benefits for their participation and this will help to increase the level of participation.

Only with the introduction of Panchayati Raj System and through the reservation of seats for the weaker sections participation in governance to a larger extent is ensured, according to these Presidents. The Presidents cited various examples of how they did certain activities with the participation of the people like construction of mud roads, tank desiltation, and temple renovation. SHGs, most of the time come to the rescue of the women Panchayat Presidents in performing their activities perfectly. But they feel guilty that the selection of beneficiaries in the Gram Sabha for various schemes has become more eyewash, because they were influenced by the elected members at the block level or by the local politicians. These things should be changed and the sole responsibility should be vested with the Gram Sabha. Only this will make more people participate in the process of governance. People should be ensured the benefit of their participation. Participation takes place only in the fora where the participants have a feeling that they are going to decide things on their own. Here, from the perception of the government officials, people have to participate and officials have to decide. Still officials hold the view that people are to receive and government is to give. People participate vibrantly in different activities where they feel they are the decision-makers. Even though the Constitution provides such a fine opportunity to the people, it is not facilitated by the officials properly. Instead they create many barriers as they perceive that it is a threat to their power over the people. It is proved that wherever a little opportunity is provided to women, they prove their efficiency.

The maintenance of women's sanitary complex and the participation of the people in the Total Rural Sanitation programme have added a new dimension and more women have now come forward. The EWRs appreciated schemes of this type and expressed their hope that, in the course of time, people will participate in all activities if opportunity is provided to them. One thing that deserves mention here is the role of the traditional Panchayat and village heads and their helping hand to the Panchayat in making the people participate in the village activities. These Presidents on most occasions seek their assistance if they want to organize the people for any common cause. The traditional Panchayats are positive and transitional in nature. Hence they cooperate with the formal Panchayats. There is yet another category of traditional Panchayats which are working against the interests of the elected women representatives who have to fight against the domination of the traditional Panchayat leaders over the formal Panchayats.

Governance—Gender

Women in the process of governance have attained a new strength through the reservation of seats and they express their hope that they could try their maximum for the betterment of womenfolk even though they represent the whole community. But a few things bother them very much like the influence of males of their family on their functioning which they are trying to overcome with great mental trauma. The focused group discussion with these EWRs showed that most of the women are under the control of their husbands and they are mere proxies. Even though they are willing to work on their own, their husbands don't have faith in them and some of them ever refuse to send them to attend the training programmes since they doubt their capacity to comprehend and consider the capacity building programme for these women a mere waste and they fear that they may not in a position to function independently. Due to the pressure from the officials these males have sent their female counterparts to this training programme. These EWRs, after coming here, have realized the importance of their role as Presidents but have a question in their mind: when they go back, will they be allowed to function independently? Anyhow constant self-motivation and training makes them work and they hope to learn a lot in the process of governance in the near future. First they accept they are not so serious about the issues of women. They are serious about the issues of children. After listening to the presentations in the training programme, they have come to the conclusion that they have committed an error so far. Now they feel that they are sensitive to the right issues. The question before them is whether they can take up the issues immediately, because they are not able to stand on their own. Further the Government, which passed several laws in Parliament and State Legislatures has not implemented the same in letter and spirit, which means that governments are not having the needed will. But they have come to that conclusion that these issues can be tackled with the support of women's organizations, especially SHGs. They further feel that men should be sensitized to the issues of women. With their partnership, many of the problems can be tackled. They expressed their gratitude for asking their opinion about governance. Till now they considered themselves well-versed only in the kitchen and in rearing children. Now they raised a volley of questions regarding women in governance such as the role of women in good governance, qualities of women in public life, methods for enhancing participation of women in politics, protection for women in public life, expectations of women from the patriarchal society and the role of the media in women empowerment. Their voices are presented in a nutshell in the following:

- Women know equally as men the process of governance since women manage the family in spite of the severe economic and social constraints imposed on them.
- If their family trusts them they can function effectively and in the same way they can perform well if people and the bureaucracy have faith in them.
- If opportunities are provided for women in Legislature and Parliament a large number of women can enter into the public space and effect an alternative approach to governance.
- Besides reservation in political spaces, they also demanded reservation in employment and administrative sectors so that women can be empowered. Alliances can be formed in different segments for women empowerment.
- Women should be educated in public life and they should be well trained.
- For their better functioning they seek the help of their family members and so they are to be oriented.
- The media should stop projecting women as a sexual symbol and women should join hands in protesting against these projections. The media should take up the responsibility of expressing the problems faced by women and bring out their calibre by broadcasting their success stories. Specific slots can be allotted for women empowerment programmes in the media and space can be created in the print media.
- Media programmes should attempt to change the attitude of both men and women on gender issues.
- They cannot share time with their children and sometimes they get into quarrels with their family members because of an overburden of work since they have to play a dual role.
- Women in public life easily succumb to character assassination. They need counselling.
- Officials do not respect EWRs properly if they are from poor economic and social background.
- If the officials are women, the EWRs are relaxed to some extent, since they believe they can understand them better. But they find that the women officials also behave like men.

- They don't get needed information from government officials.
- They are not aware of the allocation of funds by the government. They are aware only of the funds allocated to their Panchayat and that too only if it is communicated.
- Even though there are enormous schemes for women's welfare, the government doesn't take proper steps to devolve these schemes to the needy. Most women are unaware of the programmes earmarked for them.
- Women are still not thinking about themselves. They are very much worried about the family and they feel happy when their family is happy. They reflect upon the happenings in the family and they don't think about themselves and their problems.
- But they are aware of the issues affecting women and they are not in a position to bring them out for resolution as women have been oriented to internalize them.
- Even though they think the judiciary can come to their rescue, they feel that the procedure is too complicated and time consuming.
- The presence of SHGs in the villages has created a remarkable change on the part of women and the society's outlook towards women has also been changed and the EWRs hope for a better future for womenfolk.
- Women's voice relating to governance at Centre, State and Local Government level is much louder but they are concerned with the framing and implementing of suitable schemes.
- Finally, they said that if women are trained properly and opportunities are provided in political and administrative structure, social development will not be a distant dream. It could be achieved by women leaders.
- Reservation of seats for women in the local government may be extended to 50 per cent and reservation should be ensured in State and Central Government. This may provide more opportunity for the women to come forward to perform development work.

- All Gram Panchayats can be reserved for women representatives.
- The capacity of the women in governance should be enhanced.
- Officials should be trained properly on how to behave with women. They infact need gender training.
- Women in politics should also be supported by their family members and they should give them proper protection.
- Women should be relieved of household chores.
- Men should change their attitude towards women and supporting organization should come to the rescue of women whenever they are in trouble. They should criticize the actions of officials who remain anonymous in their action.
- They said that the government mechanism is still complex in nature and they cannot comprehend some procedures.
- They are not aware of the budget procedure of the government and felt that they should be educated on this.
- The schemes meant for women and children are of good use but most of them are not noticed by the women. So the government should take the schemes to the needy. Being Presidents and women they came to know about these schemes and are trying to implement them for the welfare of the women.
- A woman's will and wish always centres round her family and this circle should be further enlarged to the community, the village and the nation.
- Even though they are aware of the gender disparity, they continue to live with it since they are accustomed to it and not sensitive.
- Through SHGs women have learnt the importance of group action and this has gained momentum in rural areas. It is a lesson to the EWRs.
- They don't believe that their discussion will change the society and they underestimate their knowledge since they are not educated and they don't have a high level of mobility in public places.
- Finally, they hope that women in governance will lead to great

achievements but they have a blurred vision due to lack of clarity in their perception of their role and their position.

Observations

From the above statements the following observations are deduced:

1. Women in political space largely depend on the family.
2. Even though they have many ideas on governance, they fear that they cannot be put into practice.
3. They consider government a delivery mechanism but they want to deliver things based on the needs of the people.
4. Their opinions about the bureaucrats are not positive.
5. They think that the media is not women friendly.
6. They want the government to devolve more functions and finance to the Panchayat.
7. They think that the collective action of women in the form of SHGs is creating a tremendous change on the part of women and this will lead to social development and economic development.
8. People's participation will bring benefits to the people and participation will serve as a tool to achieve change and development.
9. Women in public life should be relieved of household chores and their family members should be oriented accordingly.
10. Women in public life should be well educated and sensitized.
11. Finally, attitudinal and behavioural change on the part of both men and women will lead to women empowerment. The bureaucratic and patriarchal society should modify itself accordingly. Then a great measure of women empowerment can be achieved.

Conclusion

The voices of women are not fully represented in the political arena even after one million women have reached different levels within the local government system in India. They are lacking influence over public decision-making even though they form a 'critical mass' to ensure adequate political representation in local government. They can create a significant impact on governance but women in society do not enjoy opportunities as men and they succumb to the domination of the patriarchal and hierarchical social structure. Women want to influence the decisions that affect their lives and the lives of their families. A profound understanding of the barriers to women in politics will help to transform the present condition and this may suggest ways and means for increasing women's representation and help women to achieve what they want. The greatest opportunity for women is given through the 73rd and 74th Amendments to the Constitution of India. There is a visible gap between their perception of governance and the reality. They have come to power with a lot of dreams, expectations and aspirations. They perceive the space as development space. But, in practice, it is full of barriers and obstacles. The obstacles and barriers are created by different sections of the society which continue to enjoy power. But now it all moves towards the poor and marginalized. The concepts of democracy and development have met with severe resistance in Indian society. Women are working in the governance system which is full of systemic corrupt practices. To overcome this menace they have to struggle. Hence they have to work together. They should work with moral and spiritual strength. On many occasions, problems are created in the society itself as caste and patriarchy strongly work together to stop democratizing the society. The lacuna is obvious with the social setup of the Indian society with the added disadvantage of the bureaucratic setup. The institutional structures have failed to recognize women as a factor to reckon with for human development. The government has also started looking into the development of women and development through women only after women figured in the Human Development Report of the United Nations Development Programme from 1995 through Gender Development Indicators (GDI) and Gender Empowerment Measures (GEM). Gender Development Index that ranked each nation upward or downward based on its record of gender equality in the core areas of life expectancy, educational attainment, and income. The gender empowerment measure gives a different perspective on women's programmes by focusing on women's access to economic, professional and political opportunities. Thereafter, the measures taken by the government for the enhancement of women in politics and economy, try to dismantle the patriarchal society. In the meantime, women in their new role in politics are undergoing a different experience and in governance they have begun to mark their achievement in spite of severe obstacles but their number is meagre. They are in need of orientation towards politics in addition to making them to enhance their capability through capacity building, skills building training programmes to effect a significant change in women's political life.

Indian polity has developed an authoritarian system of governance dominated by authorities and officials and this merely reflects the society wherein men tend to dominate over women and other weaker sections of the society. Women were suddenly brought into this system as a part of development approach and both of them find it difficult to adjust with the new system. It is very difficult to gauge the performance of women amidst the conditions favouring patriarchy and the bureaucracy. The continued absence of women's voices in governance now draws the policy makers' attention and women tend to assert themselves and have started claiming their rights. Still due consideration its yet to be given. Much more still needs to be done. Women should be capacitated in such a way that they directly influence the broader political and economic measures. Understanding governance requires that the perception of women on governance should be altered. Constraints on women within the family and society have a direct impact on their capacity for public engagements. Suitable measures should be taken to eradicate these constraints and a conducive atmosphere should be created for women to perform in the public domain.

From the understanding of these women, it can be concluded that the present situation is complex and the system is not favouring women to their fullest extent even though serious efforts have been made. It ultimately leads to the question of how we ought to proceed from here and whether the voices of these women are valuable or not.

PROFILE OF THE EWRs

Two hundred and seventeen Gram Panchayat women Presidents participated in the focus group discussion in fourteen groups.

Table 7.1 : Age group of respondents

Sl. No.	*Age Group*	*Number of Participants*	*Percentage*
1.	20-35	79	36.40
2.	36-50	120	55.30
3.	Above 50	18	8.30
	Total	**217**	**100**

Source : Computed.

Table 7.2 : Education

Sl. No.	*Level of Education*	*Number of Participants*	*Percentage*
1.	Illiterate	18	8.30
2.	Primary	78	35.94
3.	Secondary	99	45.62
4.	Higher Secondary	9	4.15
5.	Degree/Diploma	13	5.99
	Total	**217**	**100**

Source : Computed.

Table 7.3 : Religion

Sl. No.	*Religion*	*Number of Participants*	*Percentage*
1.	Hindu	202	93.09
2.	Muslim	10	4.60
3.	Christian	5	2.30
	Total	**217**	**100**

Source : Computed.

Table 7.4 : Community

Sl. No.	*Community*	*Number of Participants*	*Percentage*
1.	FC	10	4.61
2.	BC	72	33.18
3.	MBC	57	26.27
4.	SC	78	35.94
	Total	**217**	**100**

Source : Computed.

Table 7.5 : Affiliation with Political Party

Sl. No.	*Respondents Affiliation*	*Number of Participants*	*Percentage*
1.	Yes	83	38.25
2.	No	134	61.75
	Total	**217**	**100.00**

Source : Computed.

Table 7.6 : Tenure as a President

Sl. No.	*Tenure*	*Number of Participants*	*Percentage*
1.	I term	177	81.56
2.	II term	40	18.44
	Total	**217**	**100.00**

Source : Computed.

Table 7.7 : Factors behind their interest to contest in the election

Sl. No.	*Factors*	*Number of Participants*	*Percentage*
1.	Own interest	1	0.46
2.	Family	137	63.13
3.	Caste	8	3.69
4.	Political Party	11	5.07
5.	Village community	60	27.65
	Total	**217**	**100.00**

Source : Computed.

Table 7.8 : Annual Income

Sl. No.	*Income*	*Number of Participants*	*Percentage*
1.	Less than Rs.10,000	79	36.40
2.	Rs.10,001 to Rs.50,000	129	59.45
3.	Above Rs.50,001	9	4.15
	Total	**217**	**100.00**

Source : Computed.

8

PROBLEMS FACED BY THE ELECTED WOMEN REPRESENTATIVES

Introduction

Ever since the enactment of the 73rd and 74th Amendments to the Constitution of India, "empowerment of women at the grassroots" has become a popular concept used by all segments of society with varied meanings and explanations. One-third of the seats at all levels of the grassroots institutions have been reserved for women of all categories. This has raised the expectation among all the sections of the community that this group of women will become a 'critical mass' which, in turn, will stamp an indelible mark on the management of these institutions at the grassroots. The expectation has grown to such an extent that the existing development paradigm will undergo a drastic change in the distributive system of benefits.

Women elected to these institutions have been performing their roles and functions for the past five years. The impact and the implications of the management of these institutions by the women leaders have been felt in many spheres. But the 'critical mass' of women formed by the reservation system has not performed the critical role on the scale expected. Yet, changes have been brought into the system, though not to the expected level. The problems which are being faced by women are expected to be addressed by these women leaders, since these leaders are assumed to be sensitive to the issues affecting women. Women's issues are expected to be pushed to the centre to draw the attention of all, especially the policy-makers.

From a cursory analysis, it is deduced that the representation provided to the women at the grassroots has not been fully utilised. Instead of tackling the problems of the womenfolk, the elected representatives have started facing a plethora of problems because of their gender. The problems of the women representatives are many and the challenges encountered by them are innumerable. As a result, more failures have been projected in the media than success stories. Such projections are largely based on assumptions rather than facts. As per the statistics provided by the government, failures are not more than five per cent.

An in-depth analysis will prove that it is a systematic effort on the part of the mainstream system to project the failures of women leaders rather than their problems in handling power and institutions. It is also observed that in the name of training and capacity building, the women leaders have been oriented to lose their identity and to co-opt in the maligned administrative system. The women leaders' vision and their self have been eroded. For the past five years silent withdrawal and silent coopting have been noticed while analysing the functioning of the women grassroots leaders.

A concientised move to equip the women leaders to stand on their own legs has been initiated at the Gandhigram Rural Institute, founded as an institution for empowering women by the disciples of Mahatma Gandhi at the dawn of independence. This new initiative has highlighted scores of problems faced by the women representatives on various fronts. The problems highlighted in this article are drawn from the exercise conducted in many parts of Tamil Nadu State. Based on these exercises, associations have been formed and they are federated with other associations in South India.

Caveat

The problems, issues and encounters faced by the women leaders and dealt with herein are location specific and they are confined only to Tamil Nadu. The observations, analyses and explanations are not to be generalised. All the problems are to be seen against the backdrop of the environmental setting of Tamil Nadu.

The Issue

This write up throws light on the problems faced by the women representatives of the grassroots institutions of Tamil Nadu. Further, it highlights the major encounters experienced by them while trying to achieve their avowed goals. It will also indicate the needed support to sustain their position of power in the space created for women.

Methodology

The problems of the women representatives were collected fro two channels. First, while conducting training programmes for th women representatives, a specific sharing session was arranged, in which all the problems faced by the women representatives were discussed and documented in detail. Second, when the women representatives formed an association and federated themselves with the support of Gandhigram Rural Institute, they organised regional meetings in several places in order to consolidate the demands of the women representatives in the local bodies. The above exercise was carried out in four zones and the exchanges and interactions of the women leaders have been documented.

Backdrop

While looking at the issues of the women leaders, one has to bear in mind the environment in which the institutions have been created through 33.3 per cent reservation of seats for women and how they have carried out the duties and responsibilities assigned to them. From the report of the Sub-Committee of the National Planning Committee of 1941 to the recent report of the Committee on Status of Women in India, every report has emphasised that the condition of women is unacceptable and that they have been denied their rights and opportunities. While commenting on women's predicament, Justice V.R. Krishna Iyer observed : "Rethinking on the separate terms from the perspective of women who, despite the constitutional guarantees, had not achieved real justice or liberty or equality or dignity produced the holistic concept of gender justice which united all the principles into one to challenge the persistent denial of these promised objectives to the overwhelming majority of the women of India within a quarter of a century after the birth of the Republic."

It is true that Indian history provides ample proof that the rights and freedoms enjoyed by women change in inverse proportion to the status of their families, especially the men in their families, within the social hierarchy. Further, it is horrifying to note from the observation of an IAS officer, based on the latest two censuses, that the only section of India's multiple people who neither destroy their baby daughters before or immediately after birth, nor allow them to die in infancy through discrimination in nutrition and health care are the Adivasis whom the rest of us have been taught to regard as the most backward and least developed/civilised members of our nation. There have been a series of reviews and observations about the condition of women based on which new schemes and programmes have been chalked out for the welfare of women. Yet one cannot see any significant impact on the society. In fact, women had been increasingly viewed by the planners as not being in need of an independent livelihood to the point where women's decreasing work participation rate and share of employment, increasing poverty and insecurity in certain sectors of the economy in which they used to dominate earlier were not even viewed as unfortunate problems of change. This kind of marginalisation of the majority of women in the economy and their consequent neglect and demonstration of gender, class and urban bias led to a complicated situation in the general political framework of the society.

It is also true that even the opportunities that have been provided to the women have not been properly used by them for their upliftment as they are trained to be insensitive towards their own issues. In a democratic country, power is always with the people and they should have the strategy to handle power. It is not the government that gives power to the people. The government derives power from the people.

To liberate the oppressed women, steps have to be initiated from the side of the oppressed and not from the oppressor's. The government in a patriarchical society will look at issues only in a patriarchical way. To overcome these problems, feminists have fixed two long term goals— freedom and empowerment. Freedom from oppression for women involves not only equity but also the right of women to freedom of choice and the power to control their own lives within and outside their home. Control over their lives and bodies is essential to ensure a sense of dignity and autonomy for women. 'Power' refers to the sense of internal strength and confidence to face life, the right to determine choices in life, the ability to influence the social process that affects their lives as well as the direction of social change.

Empowerment of women is prominent everywhere and has gained currency among academics and policy-makers now. Empowerment has been defined differently by different scholars contextually. But, at present, most scholars have come to give a broad meaning to the concept. It is a method of tackling powerlessness in encountering and combating personal and social problems. It is distinguished by its focus on developing critical awareness, increasing the feeling of collective and self-efficacy and developing skills for personal, interpersonal or social change. In other words, empowerment can be defined as control over material assets, intellectual resources and ideology. Thus empowerment is a process of awareness, capacity building, leading to greater participation, to greater decision-making power and control and to transformative action.

This process takes shape in two forms, internal and external. Women should realise their inner worth and they should be made to realise their worth. In order to perform the above tasks, the problems faced by the powerless should be first eliminated from the social environment. In the 1970s and 1980s, systematic steps were taken through the five year plan proposals. Consequent to the pressure brought on the government by the women's movement at the national and international levels commissions were constituted. Yet, the struggle is still going on to acquire a legitimate space in all spheres of life for women. Thus, the position of women has not changed drastically or dramatically as dreamt of. The problems of women representatives at the grassroots have to be looked at against this background.

Problems Faced by Elected Women

To empower women, the elected women representatives have to be first empowered through the available means. In this process, it is essential to understand the problems faced by the women representatives while performing their roles and functions and to solve these problems as far as possible.

Elected women representatives to the grassroots level institutions have been facing numerous problems, apart from within their families, in their social, political and administrative setting. This has led to ineffective administration of the bodies by the women leaders. They don't have a common platform to express their grievances and get them redressed. Experiences from capacity building exercises conducted in various parts of the state have propelled us to prepare an action programme for empowerment of women leaders at the grassroots level. This can be done by forming an association of women representatives and federating it with similar associations of women representatives in local government in different parts of the country and making them articulate their issues on their own.

In the Indian context empowering women is a herculian task as social and cultural moorings have established strong roots in the belief system of the people. As a result, there has always been an uncommon disparity in the upbringing of women and men. All social reconstructions took place only through political activities, that too through political systems. Democracy provided enough scope for such reconstructions through polity. Hence every social segment is moving towards power. Yet, women hesitate to take part in politics as if the space is for men alone. In order to break this barrier at the micro level, a new device has been worked out through the 73rd Constitutional Amendment Act. This act provided women with one-third reservation of seats at all levels in all positions of the Panchayat institutions. But this provision has not yielded the expected results as this space is not perceived properly by the women leaders, because the elected women representatives of these grassroots institutions are facing a variety of problems in their social, political, administrative settings. They have been made ineffective in administration since they have come to these institutions as freshers. Yet, laudable achievements have been scored by women leaders in panchayats.

In order to achieve success in panchayats, the women leaders have to face numerous problems. They are engaged in constant struggle. The leaders have been made insensitive to their own and women's issues. They have been oriented to lose their identity. They have been made instruments to operationalise certain processes for others. This process has made them sink in localism and voicelessness. As a result, their space is still severely limited. In order to overcome all these hurdles, an attempt has been made to associate the women leaders on their own to address all issues in the general cause of women in their day-to-day functioning.

Need for this Programme

The finding of the capacity building programme is that women leaders are in need of an alternative arrangement for the continuous flow of information and consultancy to stabilise their activities for development. The existing grassroots leaders' organisations do not provide space for grievance redressal of the women leaders. Moreover, the requirements of the women leaders are not adequately fulfilled by these organisations. Hence the demand for a full-fledged professional organisation to assist the women local body leaders. Against this background, a series of programmes covering the entire State of Tamil Nadu was organised in four zones. The details of the programmes are given hereunder.

Table 8.1 : Network Meetings of the Elected Women Representatives

Sl. No.	*Category of Participants*	*Programme*	*No. of Leaders attended*	*Venue*
1.	Panchayat Union Chairman, Village Panchayat Presidents, Ward Members and Self-Help Groups	South Zone Network Meet on Associating Women Representatives in Local Bodies	25	Madurai
2.	Village Panchayat Presidents, Ward Members and SHG leaders	North Zone Network Meet on Associating Women Representatives in Local Bodies	32	Chenglepet
3.	Village Panchayat Presidents, and Ward Members	East Zone Network Meet on Associating Women Representatives in Local Bodies	23	Thiruvarur
4.	Panchayat Union Chairman, Village Panchayat Presidents, Ward Members and Self-Help Groups	Central Zone Network Meet on Associating Women Representatives in Local Bodies	48	Karur
	Total		128	

Source : Computed.

A facilitating centre for grassroots women leaders is being considered at the Gandhigram Rural Institute. Before proceeding further, it is necessary to take a glance at the problems of the women leaders.

The problems are drawn from the elected women representatives who have attended training programmes organised by Rajiv Gandhi Chair for Panchayati Raj Studies funded by various agencies. The details of these programmes are given hereunder.

Table 8.2 : Details of the Training Programme Conducted for Elected Women Representatives

Sl. No.	*Training Programme*	*Funding Agency*	*No. of Participants*
1.	Empowering Panchayati Raj Institutions on the issues of Population, Health and Social Development	Population Foundation of India	6834
2.	Capacity Building for Gram Panchayat Presidents	CAPART, Hyderabad	681
3.	Training of Presidents and Vice-Presidents on Panchayat Administration with special reference to Water and Sanitation	DANIDA, Villupuram	815
4.	Training of Presidents and Vice-Presidents on Panchayat Administration with special reference to Water and Sanitation	DANIDA, Cuddalore	416
5.	Training of Women Presidents of Gram Panchayats	Social Welfare Board	825
6.	Training of Elected Women Representatives of Urban Local Bodies	Tamil Nadu Institute of Urban Studies	2150
7.	Training of Trainers in Multi-Level Planning	State Planning Commission	71
8.	Capacity Building for Weaker Sections in New Panchayati Raj System	CAPART, Hyderabad	317
9.	Capacity Building for Gram Panchayat Presidents	CAPART, Hyderabad	317
10.	Training Programme for Panchayat Leaders in Nilgris District on Ecological Empowerment of Panchayats	Rural Development Organization, The Nilgris	102
11.	Training for Village Panchayat Presidents and Vice-Presidents in Total Rural Sanitation	DRDA, Cuddalore	682

Source : Computed.

Total number of elected local body leaders trained	=	13,318
Total number of panchayats covered	=	2,354
Total number of urban local bodies covered	=	294
Districts covered	=	17

The problems of the women representatives of local bodies are classified under two categories, based on their perception as women and as women panchayat representatives respectively.

Increasing Workload

The moment the women filed their nomination, their workload increased doubly and so did constraints. No women representative from the rural areas reported that her workload in the home front decreased due to her work in the public space. In a joint family system, attention to the routine work cannot be reduced. At every stage, the elected women representative has to tackle the problems carefully in the family; otherwise, she will court trouble. The family burden, coupled with the workload in the panchayat, made the elected women representatives tired of the activities in the public space. Their efficiency could neither be exhibited nor improved as they had no time. On most occasions, the elected women representatives opted for a joint workshop with the males of their families. Instead of discussing the problems faced by them among themselves, a workshop could be organised to which the elected women representatives and their husbands or any family males assisting them could be invited. All the issues of the women representatives could be discussed and that could bring about change in their attitude.

Implications of Micro Politics

Politics has its own ramifications and dimensions—whether it is State politics or National politics. Till they entered grassroots institutions, women had confined themselves to voting. After the reservation of seats for them in the grassroots institutions, they have also been made players in the political game. So far, they had not been dragged into this game and hence they are novices in this art. In order to acquaint them with politics, they need the support of men. But, while drawing upon the support of men for their work, they run the risk of the men trying to coopt the women representatives in their work. Now they are gradually learning the art of politics.

Illiteracy

Illiteracy is a basic problem among the newly elected women representatives. They are not able to write and read, but they are allowed to file nomination. After they are elected to positions, they feel very much annoyed about their inability to read and write. They have the aspiration to read and write and are prepared to undergo training but their husbands prohibit this since they are operating the panchayat at present on behalf of their spouses. Wherever the elected women representatives establish contact with NGOs, they are properly oriented and trained to manage the institutions on their own by the intervention of the NGOs.

Usual Shyness

Having traditionally secluded themselves from society, especially the menfolk, women face difficulties in interacting with men in office and in public life, after being elected to Panchayati Institutions. Further, they have had no experience of sharing their views on issues and matters with men. But when they become the leaders they have to interact with the community—both men and women. Such kinds of inhibition prevent the women from interacting with men in public places without any reservation.

Domination of Males

It is clear from the experience of the elected women representatives that their capacity had not been recognised by the males of their families. After their election, they have been attending meetings and training programmes. They learn many things from the training. Initially the men in the family, under the guise of helping them, accompanied the elected women representatives to offices and public places. Over a period of time, the women have learnt the art of administration through interaction and training. But the male family members will not accept that their family women, who have been elected to panchayats, have equipped themselves to manage the institutions. It is an irony that though the elected women representatives feel that they could manage the affairs of the panchayat on their own without the help of any male from their families, this cannot be communicated to the males of their families. Further, the elected women representatives are facing problems in Panchayats when the males of their family interfere in the administration. In the absence of interference in administration by the males of the families of the elected women representatives, trouble from male representatives would be minimal and negligible.

Further, the men sincerely feel that the women are elected not on their own merit but because of their men's support. When such an attitude has been formed, it is very difficult to change it. Further, the women leaders have been oriented to believe that they have been elected to Panchayat institutions only because of the influence of their husbands or the other males of their families.

Movements are Restricted

The women representatives pointed to yet another problem—their restricted social mobility. Village people used to bring problems to the representatives at any time. Though the women representatives indicated their willingness to attend to such work any time, they were not permitted by their husbands/other family members to do so. They need the permission of their husbands or in-laws if they want to go to the police station or the hospital at night. On such critical occasions, people want the support of the leaders. If the leaders are not coming out to help the people, the public criticise the panchayat leader.

Forced not to Raise Issues of Women

Although women in the rural areas are facing a multitude of problems, men ensure that such problems are never raised openly in public fora. The women representatives feel suppressed by this. Alternatively, the women representatives feel that those problems could be raised by the affected women in the fora. However, the affected women feel that those problems should be raised by the women representatives. The family members of the elected women representatives, however, prevent the elected women representatives from articulating women's problems in public.

Environmental degradation and depletion of natural resources are affecting the life of women in rural areas, especially the poor women. Even though the elected women representatives are aware of the gravity of the problem, they are unable to raise the issue in public fora as some mafia gangs are involved in such despicable activities. Only NGOs are creating awareness about this problem among the Dalit women and the poor in the rural areas.

The menace of alcoholism breeds all sorts of troubles for the family, especially women. Women are facing innumerable problems in the family and in society because of alcohol. Every woman and every child is affected and yet nobody has the will to oppose this practice, since everybody knows that this illicit trade takes place with the active support of the government and politicians and with the connivance of the police. No one need create awareness about this menace among the people as they are all aware of it. But they are all afraid of the police who are behind it.

The health of womenfolk is not seriously viewed in rural areas by men. Even women themselves do not realise the importance of their health. In every respect, women are discriminated against in the family. No one dares to create awareness among the women. Even in carrying out activities in the panchayat, men are not sensitive to the issues confronting women. Worse, the women are not sensitive to their own issues, be it guiding the pregnant women to avail themselves of ANC or motivating girls to go to schools. In such circumstances, the elected women representatives taking up these issues are not appreciated and, instead, they are being criticised.

Negative Attitude of Officials

Elected women representatives find it very difficult to convince the officials in the government offices as they have a poor opinion about the women representatives. The officials feel that the elected women representatives are in position simply because of the reservation policy and that they do not have any opinion or vision of their own. The officials assume that the women representatives will accept whatever the officials advise. Contrary to expectation, women representatives who go to offices with aspirations and expectations from the officials feel frustrated.[1]

Ill-treatment

It is a sorry state of affairs in government offices that the elected women representatives with high social and economic background get respect while the poor elected women representatives, especially the Dalits, face only ill-treatment. To illustrate the tragedy of Dalit leadership, a case is narrated here. A poor Dalit woman who served as a construction worker assisting the mason got elected as Gram Panchayat President. She went to the Panchayat Union office to clear a file for her panchayat. The moment she met the concerned clerk, she was asked to bring a cup of tea from the nearby tea stall by the clerk. She readily agreed to do so and picked up a glass tumbler and got a cup of tea for the clerk without minding it. Later she was asked to meet him at his residence. She went to his residence and she was asked to do some work in his garden. She also did that work. Later, she got the cheque from him and went home happily. When she narrated the incident in a training programme she was asked why she did not resist. She said that previously it was her routine to bring tea to the mason at the construction site. Now she was asked to do so by an official and so she obliged. Ill-treatments continue unabated, despite the Dalit movement.[2]

Information Blockade

There are several blocks and barriers to the process of women empowerment. Information blockade is the most powerful weapon used by the officials to disempower the women. Generally, women do not have access to newspapers. Moreover, all government information is transmitted from one department to another only among officials. The officials circulate the information booklets and details only among the men and not among women. Even the elected men representatives are not willing to share their knowledge with the women representatives.[3]

When women representatives are invited for training programmes permission is not accorded by many of the families. When the elected women representatives insist, they are allowed to attend the training programme along with their husbands or other males of the family. Now, the government insists that the elected women representatives should not be accompanied by their husbands or others while attending training programmes.

Domination of Caste Panchayats

Traditional caste panchayat leaders are yet another barrier to the elected women representatives as they impose conditions and restrictions on the women leaders. If the elected women representative belongs to the caste of the traditional panchayat leader, he extends all support to her to be in power but not in attending to the works on her agenda. The traditional panchayat leader expects that elected women representative should adhere to the advice of the traditional panchayat. She is expected to carry out the works from the agenda of the traditional panchayat. If the elected women representative belongs to other castes, particularly Dalit, she cannot do any work at all. Invariably, she has to be under the control of the traditional panchayat leader. Otherwise, she has to spend sleepless nights.

Party men also expect the same. Normally, women in the panchayat do not have any political identity and hence they look at issues on the basis of the reality. On the contrary party men want the elected women representatives to look at the issues from the party angle, failing which the women representatives will face problems from the party high command. Why do party men take such a stand? Because, it is a normal practice that when a seat is reserved for women, a male of the party gets permission from the party to field his wife or sister in that place. Hence, the party men feel that it is the responsibility and duty of the elected women representative to adhere to the dictum of the party men at the local level.

Lack of Communication Skills

Communication skills are most important for the success of any leader in the modern era. The elected women representatives never had a public space experience and hence they lack communication skills. The elected women representatives have to manage the councils and the public. Since they feel that they lack skills, they can not achieve what they want to.

When the elected women leaders are presiding over the council of local bodies, some men use unparliamentary words with the intention of making the elected women leaders nervous. The men councillors or ward members even threaten the women leaders. This is common in many places.

Poverty Prevents

There are elected women representatives from the working class who have to rely on their daily wages. Though the elected women representatives have been entrusted with so much of responsibilities and duties there is no means of reimbursing their loss of wages. This deprives them of their livelihood and hence some are forced to use proxies in their office.

Oriented to Loose Self

Commonly, we could expect that women would be very sensitive to women's issues. However, it is not true in the case of the elected women representatives as they have been continuously oriented formally and informally not to be sensitive to the women's issues. In the same way, Dalit women representatives are unmindful of

Dalit issues. One argument put forwarded is that they are the representatives of not only women or Dalits but the whole village community. Therefore, they address neither all the women's issues nor the issues of Dalit women effectively.

Interference of MPs and MLAs

They face yet another botheration in their administration, i.e. the interference of MPs and MLAs. The elected women representatives feel that everyone has his or her own domain for action. Roles are different for all the representative institutions. MPs and MLAs feel that the panchayats are under their control and that the local body leaders have to accept whatever they say regarding rural development.[4]

Lack of Managerial Skills

In order to achieve success, one should possess managerial skills. Managerial and administrative skills are essential for any successful administrator. The elected women representatives are lacking in accounting and managerial skills. Since they have this deficiency they are misguided by the officials and the males of their families. Sometimes women are trapped on this count and thereby they are coopted in all the under hand dealings of the officials. They say that they need managerial and accounting skills to overcome the problems which they have been facing.

Women Leaders Coopted

When the elected women representatives meet the officials with the males of their family, the officials talk to the males and not to the representatives. Even the reserved seats are offered to their husbands and the other males of their family and not to them. Initially, they felt this very much and later they developed a practice of ignoring such things. Only after attending training programmes, they have realised the mistake. Most of the matters transacted between their husbands and officials were not known to them. The training programmes which they attended made them understand the issues in administration. At every level the ignorance of the women representatives is exploited.

However minor the politics at the local level, muscle and money power have their due role and hence, all activities are planned in the context of managing the muscle and the money. In order to overcome this problem, the women have to rely on either the family or caste leader or party heads. At a later stage, whoever comes to the rescue of the women representative comes to the panchayat for personal favours and obligations. When such obligations are denied, the women representatives are criticised and castigated.

Social Cleavage

The caste division in the villages has been another kind of hindrance to the elected women representatives. While forming Self-Help Groups (SHGs) all women are united and do not entertain any cleavage. But, after forming the same and functioning for a period of time, the women are compelled by their menfolk to look at issues from the perspective of caste. As a result, many groups have collapsed. In the same way, while distributing the benefits to the poor, women leaders are compelled to distribute the benefits on the basis of caste considerations. Caste has entrenched itself everywhere and become a barrier to the smooth functioning of panchayats. Elected women representatives are often put into trouble because they look at issues beyond the perspective of castes.

Lack of Motivation

To perform any job motivation is important. The elected women representatives are new to this job. All of them have not taken up this assignment willingly or voluntarily. Further, they have been facing problems without any support. There is no motivation for them. As a result, many elected women representatives are in a state of mental depression. How to solve this problem? Nobody knows the solution. The problem has reached such a stage that they are searching for a counselling centre for the mentally depressed elected women leaders.

They are asked to carry out a variety of programmes and schemes. Before one starts his or her work, one should know what role one has to perform. They filed their nominations without knowing what for! They are not aware of the 73rd Amendment to the Constitution of India and the State Conformity Act of 1994. Without their knowing the basis of decentralization of powers, they have been assigned the task of realising it in practice.

Caste Discrimination

Untouchability is in practice in the rural areas. For the Dalit leaders, it becomes a problem. Whenever a Dalit heads the Panchayat Council and Gram Sabha, we may witness pandemonium. Dalit leaders are not respected and, in many villages, the traditional leaders conduct the proceedings. In the meeting the elected women representatives merely serve as spectators. Further, the two tumbler system prevails in the rural areas where the Dalit leaders are the presidents. They are not able to speak on those issues as they have developed mortal fear. It is the duty of the panchayats to administer social justice but, in reality, they are not able to do so. Only a few political parties highlight the issues and plight of the Dalits and submit critical reports to the government periodically.

Dalit Women Leaders Marginalised

Dalit women representatives, unless oriented by some political party, are powerless and voiceless. Dalit leaders are not allowed to speak and that too about the problems of Dalits. Even if some Dalits oriented decisions are taken in the panchayat, they are not allowed to be executed. Genuine and basic facilities to Dalits are not allowed to be provided. In certain areas, the traditional panchayat leaders ask the Dalit women representatives to hand over the office to them. In many places, the Gram Sabha is being organised and conducted by the traditional panchayat leader and the elected women representative remains one among the participants. She has no voice and she has to sit along with other Dalit women in the audience section.

Husbands Coopted

When the husbands of the Dalit women representatives are working on the farms of the traditional or caste Hindu leaders, it is all the more easy to take over the panchayat office. Her husband insists that she has to obey the dictum of the caste leaders in order to avoid conflict and to lead a peaceful life. Officials, on their part, terrorise the Dalit women leaders to execute whatever programme, they want to be executed in the rural areas, irrespective of the needs of the panchayats. Dalit women representatives are easily coopted in the corrupt administrative system without any resistance. Whenever the misdeeds are found out, the poor Dalit women are penalised and not the officer.

Non-Cooperation of Police

It is a well known fact that police officials are always in the hands of the upper class or upper caste people. Despite the repeated steps taken by the Dalit women representatives, nothing favourable comes to the Dalits from the police. Police officials are not taking cognizance of the genuine grievances of the Dalit representatives. Dalit representatives complain to the police about the encroachment of the common properties by the caste Hindus and influential party men in the rural areas. As per the government order, the police have to take action and eviction has to be carried out. But, contrary to expectation, no action is taken against the encroachers despite repeated complaints. Common property resources are the lifeline of the poor. But now several hundred acres of common properties have been encroached upon by party men. When they are identified, action is being initiated by the panchayat president. But there is no action from the police. But police act in accordance with the government order in the panchayats headed by caste Hindu women leaders. The basic question here is why do we have such discrimination?

Design of Caste Hindus

Since the Dalit women are poor, they hand over the panchayat responsibility to someone, mostly caste Hindu traditional leaders– with a view to earning their livelihood. No one can refute this. But one has to look at the reality. Why is the poor Dalit woman preferred by the caste Hindu leaders, when a Dalit woman with sufficient economic background contests in the election? It is the design of the caste Hindus to elect a poor Dalit woman so that the woman could be easily coopted in their design, whereas the economically sound Dalit women could not be easily coopted in their design, as they have needed economic background to manage their livelihood.

Paucity of funds is a general problem for all the panchayats in Tamil Nadu. For the Dalit women, it is a serious problem because the women of the Dalit community expect that a woman representing their community would do many things in favour of the Dalits. But, contrary to expectations, the elected women Dalit representatives could not do anything for Dalits due to paucity of funds. The caste Hindus are not allowing the elected women Dalit Presidents to carry out programmes earmarked for Dalits as they also need such programmes, for which there is no sanction from the government. Even the allotted works for Dalits could not be carried out in the rural areas. Hence, the Dalit Presidents have got a poor name among the people of their own caste. They get neither the support of Dalits nor the support of non-Dalits.

Dalit Problems not Focused

Dalit representatives face another constraint in all public fora. They realise that there are a large number of problems unattended to so far but could be attended to now through the reservation system. But it is deliberately ensured that the elected women Dalit representatives do not take up Dalit issues either in Gram Sabha or in Panchayat Council meet or in any meeting. This kind of prevention keeps Dalit representatives aloof from the Dalit community and they continue to be in the hands of others. Even if they are ready to take up such issues, their family members are not ready to support them as they are in the fold of the caste Hindu families. Thus, their expectations are belied and the Dalit youth are in an agitative mood, paving the way for social and communal conflict in the villages.

Non-Cooperation of Caste Hindus

Another silent attempt is made by the caste Hindu leaders in their panchayats through non-cooperation, which makes the elected women Dalit leaders non-functional and unsuccessful. Thereby they declare that Dalits, especially women of that caste, are totally incompetent to manage the public institutions. In many places they have successfully done this. Wherever the elected women Dalit representatives agree to co-opt with the caste Hindus, they are allowed to carry out certain works which are not favourable to the marginalised.

The elected women representatives face yet another problem in panchayats. The caste Hindus have cleverly created a design of usurping the power of Dalits. Even during the time of election, in many Gram Panchayats, the caste Hindus resort to a ploy by which they get an assurance from the candidate that the Vice-President would be elected from the caste Hindus, especially a male. After the election, the President is asked to agree to the proposal that the Vice-President could be elected from the caste Hindus, particularly a male so that they can get cooperation from the caste Hindus. As a result the Dalits are victimised as the panchayat administration is virtually under the control of the Vice-President. The elected woman Dalit President has to accede to the proposals of the Vice-President. In many places, Vice-Presidents are making the Presidents commit mistakes and become victims of Clause 205 of the Tamil Nadu Panchayat Act. Further, in these panchayats infrastructure facilities are created in the settlements of the caste Hindus and not in the Dalit settlements. This has been raised many times in the Gram Sabha by the Dalit youth to which the Vice-President gives a vague reply whereby the President is made to face the problem in the Dalit community.

Neglect of Vital Issues in Training

Training and orientation is given to the elected women representatives by the government but these programmes do not touch upon the vital issues of the marginalised people. In the training programme, orientation is given to the leaders to take up the schemes and programmes of the government. There is no scope for discussion on gender issues, issues of the Dalits and participation of the people in the planning process. Proper orientation is not given to women leaders in the training programme conducted by the government and some of the non-governmental agencies.

No Support Base

Another pertinent question discussed by the women is the support base of the women leaders. Discussions have been held on all the aspects based on which the women leaders have taken the initiative to carry out certain schemes and programmes. They have faced a variety of problems in the field. To overcome these problems they are in need of some supportive organisations. But, in reality, there is no support base for women leaders. In the absence of such support mechanism, one cannot expect exemplary achievements from the women leaders at the grassroots level.

Encroachment Encounters

As per the New Panchayat Act, the President of Gram Panchayat can take action against encroachments. To evict an encroacher, Panchayat Presidents have to get the village map from the village administrative offices. In many of the villages, the administrative officers do not give the village map to the Presidents of the Gram Panchayats. With great difficulty the Gram Panchayat Presidents take the initiative to retrieve the common property from the encroachers. This act has propelled the encroachers to fight against the women leaders. This is yet another challenge to the elected women representatives.

Crowd Management

Another problem they face is the problem of crowd management. Gram Panchayat Presidents have to convene Gram Sabha meetings four times every year. Our rural masses have not been oriented in the orderly presentation of issues in public fora. In a crowd they normally tend to shout. Even the speaker of the Lok Sabha is not able to manage enlightened representatives and the Legislative Assemblies do not fare any better. But in a Gram Panchayat, even if it is four hundred in an open place, it is always a free for all. When women representatives are presiding, anti-social elements deliberately use unparliamentary words in order to drive away the womenfolk. Nobody regulates the meeting except the family members of the elected women representatives. When family members come to the rescue of the elected women representatives other members of the Gram Sabha oppose it. But the same Gram Sabha members do not help the elected women representatives while they are facing problems in the Gram Sabha due to anti-social elements. People under the influence of alcohol participate in and disturb the proceedings. But no one is ready to control them. What is the way out of this?

Local body leaders are invited for public functions and they are asked to address the public. The elected women representatives are not in a position to speak like others in the public meeting as they don't have the required communication skill. It is the felt need of every elected woman representative. This deficiency is responsible for poor management of crowds also.

Procedure of Accounting Procedure

Another hardship they undergo is the accounting procedure. In the computer era, Gram Panchayat Presidents have to maintain a total of 31 records. All the 31 records are to be regularly maintained. Even post-graduates with a Commerce background find it difficult to manage the thirty-one records. How can a poor uneducated Dalit woman representative maintain so many records? They are not properly oriented in account-keeping but they are taken to task when they commit mistakes in accounting. Most of the elected women representatives are the victims of this procedure. Either the procedures have to be simplified or the women's capacity has to be enhanced.

Representatives' Perception of Women's Issues

The above posited issues are the problems faced by the women leaders in the Panchayat Administration. They have perceived the problems faced by the women in the rural areas. The issues are classified and presented. They are:

Primarily, the aspirations and feelings of the women are not respected and are not taken into consideration for decision-making.[5] It is common at the family level and at the community level. There is not much difference between the rich and the poor.

Gender discrimination prevails in the family, community, office, parties, cultural organisations, and religious organisations. Women are discriminated against in providing facility, service and benefits. From the family level to the Central Government level one can find discrimination on the basis of gender. Girl children are poorly fed and malnourished. They are not given fair treatment on par with the male children. Women are harassed in the family and sexually exploited in the workplace.

Girls are generally not permitted to go in for higher studies or even beyond primary school. Women are discharging dual responsibilities with great difficulty, yet, their burden is not appreciated properly. When women move beyond the routine, their workload increases with nobody to share the workload. For the poor women, there are no proper amenities in the workplace. Health facilities are not provided to the women as extended to the men. Women are also not sensitive to their health problems. Female infanticide and foeticide are the problems that women face in many villages. Due to non-availability of water, fuel wood, medical facilities, proper public distribution system, women are the worst victims.

Women are denied property rights even though the Equal Property Rights Act has been passed in Tamil Nadu Legislative

Assembly. Women workers are paid poor wages compared to men. Women are made to be dependent. Assertive women are subjected to character assassination. Panchayats have no perspective plan on gender development.

What They Need

These are some of the vital issues they have perceived as problems of the elected women representatives. Solutions could be found to all these problems. The women representatives have identified some solutions. They are:

Proper orientation has to be given to the elected women representatives by way of periodical training. The women representatives are to be sensitised on the issues of the women. They have to be organised at a larger level and enabled to address their issues on their own by creating a suitable support base. Institution based legal support has to be provided to the women who take up the struggle to administer social justice. Periodic interface between successful women and women leaders who lead struggles has to be organised. Managerial skills, leadership qualities, accounting skills and communication skills have to be developed through periodic capacity building exercises.

Comprehensive awareness programmes have to be conducted in rural areas on the problems of the women. Information has to be provided to the women representatives on all vital matters pertaining to improvement in the quality of their life. Womens participation has to be ensured in Gram Sabha meetings. Women component plan has to be initiated at every level. Stringent laws are to be enacted to deal with individuals committing atrocities against women.

The women segmented on the lines of political party, caste, religion and class have to be united and they should be helped to stand as a single entity. As a prelude to this, the elected women representatives have to be organised at state level and further federated with other state level organisations so that they will gain added strength. They can espouse the cause of women and legitimately claim the political space in order to address the women's issues effectively.

Where They Are

Though the elected women representatives face innumerable problems while discharging their duties, they continue their struggle to succeed in their mission. But their perception of their self and their desire vary from individual to individual and from group to group. There are six kinds of leaders, namely, aggressive leaders, sober capacitated leaders, ambitious capacitated leaders, leaders with aspiration, leaders with a mood of withdrawal and leaders without an idea. A few cadre parties and a few committed NGOs have been continuously orienting a set of leaders and extending all their support to the women leaders having links with the party and NGOs. They always exhibit an aggressive character which enables them to discharge their duties more effectively than the other leaders. Twelve per cent of the representatives belong to this group.

There is yet another category of leaders, who have been oriented and trained but are not committed to any ideology or organisation. But they are committed to their work. They have participated in the programmes organised by the NGOs but they do not have continuous linkage with the NGOs. They are capacitated leaders concentrating much on their responsibilities and they have performed very well as they have enhanced their capacity. They have aspiration to continue in public service but no specific position. Whether they win the next election or not they will remain in the public sphere. This group constitutes 22 per cent.

There is another category which is slightly different from the previous one. The capacitated leaders have concentrated much on enhancing their capacity continuously and performing their duties. While performing their duties, they see the response of the people, based on which they have a desire to continue in office. But this category has an ambition to continue in the same position, for which they have developed an art of managing the people in the local bodies. All their deficiencies are compensated by their public relations. Their linkages with the people are strong as they are always with the people. Nearly 24 per cent of the leaders belong to this category.

The fourth category of leaders have a different aspiration. Though they have a number of deficiencies, by keeping themselves very active in discharging their duties, they want to demonstrate to their party leaders that they are the apt candidates for membership in the Legislative Assembly. They are always busy meeting the people and familiarizing themselves with the people. They consider the Panchayati Institution as a launching pad for their political career. Though their number is very small they are certainly the models for emulation. Eighteen per cent of the leaders have this type of aspiration.

Another category of leaders are unable to meet the challenges of their role and unable to bear the pressures of the society and the family. They have expressed their desire to withdraw from public life. These leaders were brought to the public life by force by their husbands. In most of the cases the relationship between the husband and wife has undergone a change in the whole process of administering development through Panchayati Raj Institutions. Many husbands realized the fact that their wives have acquired needed capacity and, hence, they have to withdraw from the support space. But there is another segment of men who have determined not to allow their wives to attend to their duties on their own. Most of the women leaders have stated that they have been facing problems in the local body institutions because of the interference of their husbands. This factor cannot be explained to their husbands by the women leaders of panchayats on their own. This group constitutes 20 per cent of the leaders.

There is yet another category which has no idea. They are in the hands of the males of the family, despite the pronouncements of the Government. The women leaders do not move out of their houses for public work. They do not meet the people. Virtually their husbands are operating the machinery. They are not bothered about it. It is a money spinning device which is ably tackled by their husbands by their muscle and money power. Officials are also cooperating with such leaders. They have no idea about the panchayats and they have no aspiration to contest in the next election. If their husbands ask them to contest they will contest;

otherwise, they will not bother about it. They are only 4 per cent; yet their cases have been repeatedly quoted in public places. It is true that withdrawal symptom is visible among the women leaders in local bodies. They face a volley of problems from the officials, caste groups, own family members and even their own political party leaders.

Yet the majority of the leaders have exhibited their determination to occupy the public space. Having entered and tasted power, the women leaders have come to the stage of enlisting themselves as members of various organisations to fight for their rights and legitimate spaces. In their struggle, they have identified the organisations and institutions which are supporting empowerment of women and, through them, they have determined to continue their struggle. Further, they have started forming their own organisations and federating their organisations with other organisations. Another interesting development is that a large number of women are being trained in the self-help group (SHG) to move over to this power domain. Women leaders have come to the public sphere and they will continue to keep their hold over the institutions and try to expand their space.

Observation and Conclusion

Women have come to positions in the local bodies as provision has been made in the Constitution. The attitude of society towards women has started changing. But, in the process of empowering women, the hurdles are continuing. Steps are being taken by the women on their own to overcome the hurdles. It is a long drawn process. A structure which has been created over centuries to work against the interests of women cannot be dismantled within a short span of four or five years. It can be changed only by creating a movement by the masses for which this provision of one-third reservation of seats to women will help. To fight against the designs of the structure, an organised movement of the masses is an imperative. In order to make the women achieve results in their positions an array of interventions are necessary.

They need orientation, sensitization, capacity building, information and counselling continuously through organisations. The ongoing experiments and experiences suggest that periodical training, orientation and sensitization make the women leaders perform the assigned role in a better way than the novices. When the women leaders are responding to the socio-political challenges in society, they are to be supported by the organisations and institutions which are working for empowerment of women. Wherever such interventions are available the achievements of the women leaders are substantial and impressive. The Government will respond to the needs of these women leaders only when they are supported by organisations well-known for their credentials and to be reckoned with as a force.

NOTES AND REFERENCES

1. G. Palanithurai, *Report on Empowerment of Panchayati Raj Institutions on issues related Population, Health and Social Development (sponsored by Population Foundation of India),* Rajiv Gandhi Chair for Panchayati Raj Studies, 1997.
2. G. Palanithurai, *Report of the Training Programme conducted for Gram Panchayati Presidents Dindigul and Sivagangai Districts (sponsored by CAPART),* Rajiv Gandhi Chair for Panchayati Raj Studies, 1998.
3. G. Palanithurai, *Report of the Training Programme conducted for Women Presidents of Gram Panchayats in Five Districts (sponsored by Social Welfare),* Rajiv Gandhi Chair for Panchayati Raj Studies, 1998.
4. G. Palanithurai, *Report of the Training Programme conducted for Presidents and Vice-Presidents on Water Supply and Sanitation in Villupuram and Cuddalore Districts (sponsored by DANIDA),* Rajiv Gandhi Chair for Panchayati Raj Studies, 1998.
5. V.B. Athreya and K.S. Rajeswari, *Women's Participation in Panchayati Raj : A Case Study from Tamil Nadu (sponsored by Women Commission),* M.S. Swaminathan Research Foundation, Chennai, 1998.

9

ELECTED WOMEN REPRESENTATIVES AND EMERGING ALTERNATIVE GOVERNANCE

Introduction

The last decade has seen a growing awareness of the importance of the roles to be performed by women in the public sphere and their impact on the process of development and establishment of good governance. Studies have adequately demonstrated the correlation between the women's participation in governance and decision-making and the delivery of services to the people for their livelihood security and economic development. More specifically, the World Bank's studies confirm that a strong correlation between low levels of female involvement in public life and high levels of government corruption[1]. Barriers prohibiting women from access to resources, jobs, education and participation in governance inhibit a nation's economic viability. Gender inequality will result in greater poverty, slower economic growth and lower quality of life.

By involving women, delivery of services in the sectors of education, health, credit and governance will become effective. Enhancing women's rights, access to resources and participation in decision-making will not only benefit the women's segments but also the whole community. It is recognized throughout the world that grassroots women's groups are redefining governance and development in their orbit of action. They significantly alter the process of administering development. By their local action significant progress and changes are made in the life of the communities which, in turn, draw the attention of the academics, administrators and the media. After seeing the implications of women's involvement in governance throughout the world, steps have been taken at the grassroots to build their capacity and skill, sharpen their leadership, and forge alliances with varied partners to project the emergence of the alternative governance. Grassroots women deal with everyday survival and livelihood issues from their own perspective and with the most ingenious solutions as they have a knowledge base which is local in character[2].

Against the above backdrop, the position of grassroots women leaders in India and their role in governance in administering development and social justice as envisioned in the Constitution of India has to be analysed.

After enacting the 73rd and the 74th Amendments to Constitution of India, the legitimately created space for women in the orbit of governance has raised a question about whether the women who have come to power at the grassroots can achieve what they have to achieve. It is obvious that the entire public space was occupied by men for five decades but no question was raised as to the ability of those leaders. It is understandable that the women who have come to power with different kinds of disabilities have to perform the task assigned to them. The task assigned to them is not easy. Since the State and Central Governments have failed in solving many of the nation's problems, they are being entrusted to the grassroots institutions. Unless the newly recruited leaders equip themselves with skill, capacity and capability to manage the people, the bureaucracy, the resources and the Panchayats, they cannot deliver the goods.

It is an axiomatic premise that the task to be performed in the grassroots institutions and the capacity of the women leaders do not match, as the women elected as leaders face different barriers, disabilities and obstacles. There is yet another proposition that the general expectation is that the women leaders have to perform certain duties which are not expected from men leaders making their task all the more difficult. The following observations of the women Panchayat leaders learn out the above statement:

"Many of the women leaders of Gram Panchayats were driven by the District Administration to the venue of the five day training programme in Gandhigram as they were driven to the public areas by a combination of forces. Now they have realized their worth and started feeling ashamed of keeping themselves aloof from attending office and allowing their male family members to run the office execute the activities and affixing their signatures on the dotted line as per their instructions", observed by Ms. Juliet Susila, a second time Gram Panchayat woman President while evaluating the training programme conducted in Gandhigram Rural Institute on 3rd March, 2004[3].

"We came here for the training, as we were asked to by our Block Development Officer, without knowing what to do here. We were accompanied by our male family members and party cadres as we were their captives. After the five day training we came to know our worth and the role and responsibilities that have to be performed by us. We face two inherent problems. One is that we belong to the category of women and the other is that we belong to SC and ST category. As we are in the middle tier of the Panchayat system we have to face the election on a political party basis. We do not belong to any political party. But we were made and branded party candidates as our family members belonged to political parties. We were considered horses and on us the party functionaries tied to ride. To get back their money they kept us in position and obtained our signatures. Many of us were asked not to come to the office as the Vice-Chairperson, being a man, would manage. This advice was endorsed by the Block Development Officer also. But now we feel that our space has been used by someone else. It is the shame of the system. We feel we have also been a party to the shame. This five day training programme has created a hope among us that we can also manage the institution with the input we have gained here. In order to strengthen our efforts jointly we have formed an association called 'Dalit Block Panchayat Women Leaders Association' and that Association will project our problems to the appropriate authorities for redressal", observed S. Ponnammal while making an evaluation of the five day training programme organised by Gandhigram Rural Institute on 30th January, 2004[4].

In one of the conventions of the State Level Federation of Elected Women Representatives, a series of resolutions were passed requesting the State Government to pass an order prohibiting the male family members of elected women representatives to attend the official meetings at the district headquarters and affixing the signature of the elected women representatives to get the cheques for the Panchayats. Further they made a plea that when the seat of Chairperson is reserved for women, along with the Chairperson, the Vice-Chairperson's position should also be reserved for women. Otherwise the Vice-Chairperson will usurp the power of the elected woman President.

The above lamentations no doubt reflect the reality and, at the same time, despite all the problems and troubles, the elected women representatives have drawn the attention of many toward them by their excellent performance, that too in the social development sector[5]. Hence, this article will focus on how the elected women representatives have performed their role and function and how they are different from men. This study makes an investigation into what are the responsibilities assigned them, how these responsibilities are discharged, how differently they perform in governance and how they overcome the problems in the domain of governance. All these questions will be addressed against the backdrop of the established theory on women governance.

Backdrop

Women, governance and development are the major subjects for debate and discussion among academics and policy-makers all over the world at present and they draw the attention of the public. Debate and discussion have further deepened after grassroots institutions were created legitimately through the 73rd Amendment to the Constitution of India for governance and development[6]. Ever since women were elected to local bodies after the Amendment was passed in the Indian Parliament, a major question has been raised in every forum as to what extent the elected women representatives (EWRs) can change the agenda of gover-nance and the process of development. It is a well-known fact that the state of the art of governance, the condition of women in Indian society and the current trend in the process of development are not what they ought to be in terms of major achievements in their respective domains. Yet the question has its relevance in the present context as an opportunity has been provided to the women in governance to achieve development by changing the development paradigm by changing the agenda of governance. The present study makes an attempt to analyse the role played by EWRs in governance to achieve development at the grassroots. Further it is essential to analyse how they are different from men in terms of their approach and strategy in managing the institutions, delivering services and achieving development. The analysis is more of the process than of the works carried out in the Panchayats.

Five decades of conscious struggle by women groups at the national level have brought the subject of women to the forefront for discussion, deliberation and to the level of policy-making[7]. As a result of all these activities a series of legislations have been enacted to free women from the existing clutches of bondage and slavery. Yet the conditions have not radically changed. Women are evolving themselves in the context of globalization and governance to face challenges and achieve sustainable development. In looking at the issues of women, perspectives vary from school to school. Micro and macro movements are on in the world in addressing the issues of women from different perspectives. As a result a space has been reserved for women in the orbit of governance legitimately in India by which one million women have come to power at the grassroots as a critical mass to perform a critical function. As an exclusive space has been created for women at the grassroots, they have to work with the community, which is totally engrossed in the local feudal hierarchical social system and patriarchy[8]. One can imagine how the community perceives the role of women in governance. It matters much in governance. Further, it is a factor to be visualized that, in a patriarchal system, the men who have lost their political space because of the space reserved for women tend to think that it is their legitimate space which can be occupied by any one of their family members and so these women have been mobilized to occupy their position.

How these women perceive their role and perform their responsibilities is a matter of deep concern for every one. In this context empowerment plays a crucial role[9]. While visualizing the women's perception and performance, one has to consider the prevailing views on women's space in governance. One school of thought emphasizes the fact that it is a political space and it has to be insisted that they treat the space as governance space and act accordingly. Even though they are elected as representatives of the people, they have an additional responsi-bility to bring to light the problems of women in general. But the other side of the argument is that they are not the representatives of women alone. They are the representatives of all. There is yet another view that the governments at the Centre and the provinces have not considered many of the development and gender issues as issues of governance. As a result many of the development issues have been totally relegated to the background at the grassroots. Against this background the women leaders have to consider this space as development space. Without moving the political frontiers much, they have to continue their activities in the development domain. It is in such a context of conflicting perceptions that they have to perform their role and responsibilities.

Governance has been a much debated topic in the past one decade, ever since the Government of India announced through the budget of 1991 that the concept of government has to be redefined to suit the context. The government had assumed several responsibilities and taken over several of the responsibilities of the community and thereby the government had become omnipotent and monstrous. People had abdicated their major responsibilities and regarded themselves as beneficiaries. The Government perceived itself and was perceived by others as the provider of benefits and services for which the structure was expanded to the maximum size. In the process of expansion of the government a wide gap was created between the people and the government. The Government became so big that the people could not bear the weight of the government. A new class of brokers emerged to negotiate with bureaucrats and thereby corruption became entrenched in every facet of government. Thus governance became bad. International aid agencies who provided development aid to India expressed concern and demanded good governance to deliver services and goods to the people effectively and efficiently. Consequently the introduction of reform packages, reduction of government institutions, reduction of cost of delivery of services, handing over of responsibilities to the communities to manage the livelihood security issues are on the cards. Building alliances and partners for governance is currently on. The participation of civil society organizations in the delivery of services has increased. Thus governance has become an important subject for debate among academics and policy-makers[10]. It is in this new context that the elected women representatives have to perform their duties and responsibilities.

Development is yet another concept subjected to scrutiny in the context of over exploitation of the natural resources and causing damage to the ecological foundations of nature. Internalizing the concept of development has changed the lifestyle of the people. Producing more, consuming more and market-oriented activities have caused severe damage to the livelihood security of the people. Enabling the rich to become richer and allowing the poor to be marginalized has created a wide divide between the rich and the poor. The growing pace of development causes intense social conflict and thereby peace and equity are jeopardized. To overcome the obstacles and barriers created by the development activities, a new concept has evolved—sustainable development, which provides security to the poor, protects nature, maintains balance in ecology, provides the needs of the individuals and communities. Thus the concept of development[11] has been localized and it enables the communities to maintain their cultural heritage. Against this backdrop this study makes an attempt to evaluate the performance of the elected women representatives in Tamil Nadu.

Theoretical Framework

Before evaluating the performance of the elected women representatives, it is necessary to examine the postulates evolved over a period of time on the basis of the experience in the wide world of women's way of governing[12]. In Political Science women representative and participation in decision- making bodies are looked at against the backdrop of the 'critical mass'; which refers to the quantity needed to start a chain reaction, an irreversible take off into a new situation or process[13]. Based on the studies conducted, Drude Dahlerup set out six changes expected when women achieved critical mass and they include change of political discourse, social climate of political life, policies, culture, behaviour, political attitudes, policy priorities, legislative styles and decision making roles[14]. Of the several assump-tions about women in governance in the world, for this study a few are considered vital and relevant to the Indian context. First, women will bring a different approach to governance. It is a strong notion among development organizations and women activist groups who have rich experience with women that women will bring in new ideas, nuances, energy, enthusiasm and approach to governance and that hitherto unutilized potentials will be used. It is expected that women's participation will transform the quality of the political life and agenda. There is yet another view that women leaders come to power with several inherent barriers and, weaknesses and as a result, they follow the men as role models and lose themselves.

Second, women perceive the concept of development comprehensively rather than narrowly. They have a broad vision of development. Their notion of development is sustainable development. Their concentration is more on natural resources management. To women bringing service providing institutions to their area is development. Women believe and perceive that service providing institutions, whether a school or a primary health centre or a public distribution system shop, should be near to them as it will reduce their hardship and misery. Further they consider removal of child labour, alcohol and violence and reducing competition part of governance and development. Further, to them governance is always good governance and it is equated with government.

Third, elected women representatives play an important role in pushing the women's issues forward for public discussion and decision-making. It is pertinent to mention here the view that women have been oriented to think like men as patriarchy is strongly entrenched in the family and the social system. They do have their own distinctive thought process. But there is no space for it in the public fora. On certain issues, elected women representatives show greater concern in the decision-making process. It is true that they are not in one group. They have their own different affiliations. In order to bring the women's issues to the public they need a support structure. They establish links with SHGs and through them the issues of women are being discussed. They are also divided on caste, class and religion. Yet they show their distinctiveness in the process of governance.

Fourth, elected women representatives ensure more participation of the people in the process of development and governance. Women leaders at the grassroots in the Indian context always evince simplicity, transparency and accountability. They further demonstrate that they maintain their closeness and contact with the clients and the people. Fifth, elected women representatives have different sets of skills and they enhance the leadership qualities of others. Women have developed skills to carry out works despite the limited resources and differences of opinion with their family members. Working in adverse circumstances is not new to them. Further they have patience to listen to others, which men do not have. On many occasions elected women representatives are honest and accurate in presenting issues to the decision-making authorities. Sixth, elected women representatives are the pathfinders in attacking social issues. They assume powers to perform certain roles and responsibilities. Several of the problems need to be attended to for which no power is needed. Women leaders who have a service orientation in their attitudes and behaviour assume responsibilities and carry out activities in society and they become role models and they are able to set new agendas and perhaps create new styles of leadership[15].

Seventh, elected women representatives tend to maintain secular values in dealing with matters of governance. They never tend to give room for discriminatory practices in society based on caste and religion. Having got orientation in managing schemes such as agriculture, water management, fuel and fodder, poverty alleviation programmes, education, health, family welfare, child development, public distribution and social welfare the women leaders' concentration is always on development and on the segment of people who are left out in the process of development. Eighth, the elected women representatives are less corrupt. As per the gender ideology women are always honest, pure, simple and non-corruptible. Corruption is always found in the public domain and not in the private domain. All public systems are corrupt and whoever comes to the system will be afflicted by the disease of the system. As a result they will also be coopted. Since women are at the tail end of the public system and remain with the community the women leaders tend to keep the image which they have acquired in the family system and the community. The above-mentioned postulates have to be tested for which this work relies on the studies conducted earlier for PRIA, the UNICEF and The Hunger Project. The reports of all these studies form the database for this work.

It is imperative to put forth the factors which are responsible for delivering services to the people effectively through efficient governance by the women leaders. Whether the women leaders occupy the National Parliamentary Institutions or Regional Legislative Institutions, their participative, deliberative and decision-making pattern varies from that of men. It is normal that whenever a large number of women representatives are elected to such representative decision-making bodies at any level, the expectation of the academics is the difference in their functioning. Women's role in those institutions has been probed all over the world whenever large number of women leaders are elected to decision-making bodies at National and Regional levels[16]. Academics have termed it a critical mass by fixing the number of representatives from women at more than 10 per cent of the total membership in the house. No doubt women leaders in the authoritative bodies do bring a new culture and new values and add a new dimension to Legislative Politics[17].

Even in the West European countries[18], such studies have been conducted and extended to African and Asian countries. Results vary sharply in terms of performance[19]. When women are elected, they are being considered representatives with varying emotions, distinct problems and capabilities. It is to be noted that they are elected as representatives not because they are women but because they are sponsored by a political party. Such representatives are well regulated by the party whips and their emotions, problems and difficulties can be sorted out within the party structure and they cannot go beyond the party. When they go to legislative institutions they are the mouthpieces of their party and not womenfolk. But the general expectation from the womenfolk and women organised groups when they move into policy-making bodies is for certain key changes[20]. Women's problems have to be articulated in the policy-making and decision-making bodies. Conscientized women on the issues of women and women drawn from women's organizations to political parties are aware of the barriers and hurdles in party politics and parliamentary politics as they are under the clutches of men. To go beyond the party regulations, they formulate devices and mechanisms by which they form alliances with different categories of groups working within the political system and the administrative system to push forward the issues of women to the centre stage for decision-making. The variations observed in the performance of women in different parliamentary institutions are attributed to an array of factors[21]. They are the educational background of the representatives, the capacity of the representatives, the support structure created to help the women representatives, the women representatives' alliance building strategy, the women representatives' capacity in orienting their party structure to take up women's issues and the external support of women groups to the women representatives.

The above factors are mostly responsible for the effective functioning of Parliamentary and Legislative institutions. In the Indian context, the critical mass is formed only in grassroots institutions. These institutions have to work with the community. In India, grassroots institutions, however constitutional and legal they are, are affected by several obscurantist practices as they are drawn from the communities. The grassroots institutions reflect more of the community practices than the political, legal and governmental practices. So, to study the behaviour and performance of the grassroots level women leaders, that too at the Gram Panchayat level, a distinct analytical framework is necessary.

In India, the general capacity of the leaders, their support structure, their linkages with organizations and associations and their orientation distinguishes them from men leaders in terms of their behaviour and performance.

Diagram of Analytical Framework

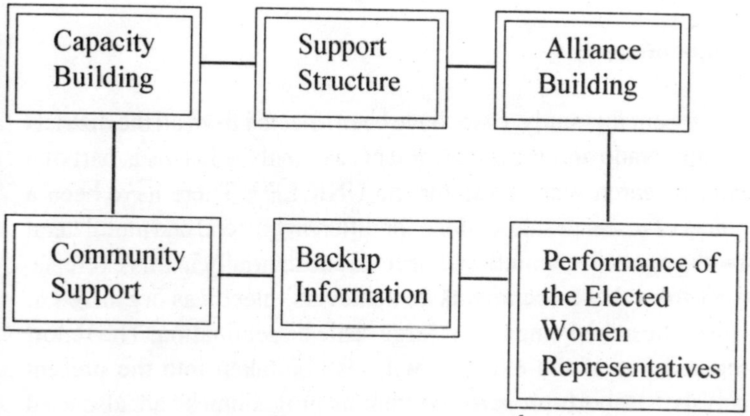

This is based on the experience in other countries and the limited experience from Indian local bodies, that too from the action research carried out in many places. For effective performance of the women leaders, their capacity, community support, support structure at higher level to break the barriers, information backup, and building alliance with various stakeholders are essential factors in the Indian context. Capacity building is not limited to building the managerial and communication skills alone. It includes changing the mindset of the leaders towards the issues of women, children and other marginalized segments. The support structure must extend a helping hand when they take up the issues of women, children and other weaker sections and the marginalized and face an array of problems. Information is the key to managing the institutions and decision-making. The bureaucracy survives and establishes its control over the leaders by keeping the information from the leaders. To break this deadlock, an information gateway has to be created and through the flow of information, their articulations are to be made authentic and appropriate. Alliance building is a process by which they establish contact with women groups, the media, development organizations, women's wings in political parties and other practice organizations, groups and institutions. They get periodical support from them for their effective functioning. In the light of the above analytical framework the performance of women leaders is analyzed and explained hereunder.

Methodology

To carry out this study, cases have been selected from all the districts of Tamil Nadu and the achievements are analyzed. This is part of a major research work done for the UNICEF[22]. There have been a number of research studies done for different bilateral and multilateral funding agencies, which will be used substantially in this exercise. Apart from these documents an achievers' meet was organized to project the achievements for large scale dissemination. The report prepared out of the exercise will also be taken into the present analysis[23]. Reports prepared on training programmes[24] are also used in this study. It is more of a narrative history of the development that took place in the rural areas with the intervention of the elected women representatives.

Limitations

This chapter reflects only the process of activities, initiatives and performance of the elected women representatives of Gram Panchayats of Tamil Nadu. This study excludes the elected women representatives of Block and District Panchayats. Even in the case of the Gram Panchayats headed by women, limited cases have been documented and analyzed. The reason for excluding the Block and District Panchayats is that they are elected on party tickets whereas Gram Panchayat Presidents contested in the election on their own as party based contest is not allowed under the Panchayat Act. Moreover political parties do not have any hold over them. Opportunities to exercise their will and vision are more for the Panchayat Presidents. At the same time possibilities for confrontation are also more as they have to work with and in the community. The analysis will project a trend that is emerging but it can not be generalized.

Socio-Economic Background

The elected women representatives have come to the grassroots institutions with varying socio-economic backgrounds. Their educational background varies from neo-literate to retired college teachers. There are leaders drawn from self-help groups and political parties. Leaders who are drawn from political parties and self-help groups are oriented in politics and social development issues respectively. Of the women elected representatives 65 per cent are from the middle class, lower middle class and the poor. They have entered into the power structure with all drawbacks and barriers due to the existing socio-economic structures in the society[25]. How they perform their roles and responsibilities in administering development and social justice is probed in this paper.

Leaders' Perception

The elected women representatives who have occupied positions in the Panchayati Raj System perceive that the Panchayati Raj Institutions are to provide services to the people to the level of the satisfaction of the communities. Their entry into the political domain was sudden and their activities were driven by many in the background as they could not do anything on their own. They never dreamt of such positions in their whole life. The elected women representatives were fully directed by the male family members while discharging the duties and responsibilities. But there is a small segment of elected women representatives who have come from SHGs and political parties as branded candidates, who have taken up the responsibilities on their own. There is yet another section gaining the spirit to act independently after participating in the training and orientation programmes and enhancing their skills and capabilities. Hence the elected women representatives have a perception that the Panchayat Institutions have to attend to the needs of the people. A small section of the representatives have focused their attention on development, more particularly on social development[26]. They are the opinion makers now in the Panchayat system.

Performance in Governance

Fifty-two case studies have been conducted in all the Districts of Tamil Nadu. These cases were selected on the basis of the information provided by the District Rural Development Agency of the respective districts. Further it was verified with the NGOs working near the Panchayats. Of the fifty-two cases, it is observed that 45 representatives said that in the first period women came to Panchayats as leaders because of the space created by the State by reserving one-third positions for women. In course of time, the EWRs developed nuances to manage the obstacles in the family, political parties, communities and offices and started delivering services. They enjoyed the response of the people. During the second term they decided to contest and the EWRs openly said that they were able to win the election based on their performance. While managing the Panchayats a variety of models have been evolved by the EWRs[27]. One finds variations between blocks and between districts.

Elected women representatives touched upon the basic needs of the community. Their focus was more on drinking water supply, primary health care, child care, public distribution system, common property resources management and environmental protection. They strove to achieve communal harmony to carry out development activities. They felt that social conflict would hamper development. The leaders who have got orientation in Panchayats with the intervention of the training institutions and Non-Governmental Organizations focused their attention on social development issues[28]. But on most occasions social development issues were not discussed in the Gram Sabha. But activities relating to social development issues could be seen in the performance of the Gram Panchayat Presidents. The EWRs said: "We are oriented and sensitized on social development issues but people are not conscientised and they continue to harp on only services like water supply, street light and roads"[29]. Thus EWRs have to respond to popular perceptions also as they need the support of the community. To regulate the public distribution system a woman representative (Leelavathy) gave her life. To retrieve the common properties from the encroachment of the mafia, another woman representative (Menaka) gave her life. To stop the illegal brewing and sale of liquor, a woman representative with her family (Ponni) had to spend several sleepless nights in the same village and face all kinds of ill-treatment. Despite opposition they did all these activities simply because of their vision, social commitment and the fire in them for the cause of the people[30]. But the elected women representatives have slowly evolved strategies to keep the masses with them. They transact all the Panchayat activities in a transparent manner and display the accounts on the Panchayat notice boards. This transparency draws the people towards the Panchayats[31] and the self-help groups towards the Gram Sabha to discuss the issues of women and children. The women leaders have allowed all sections of the community to express their opinion freely and they listen to them. There is a striking difference between the Elected Men Representatives (EMRs) and the EWRs in conducting the Gram Sabha meetings. When the EMRs, except the Dalits, conduct the Gram Sabha meetings, the leader takes more time and the members of the Gram Sabha take less time. They speak from authority. When the EWRs listen to the public patiently and accommodate their views in the decisions, a sense of collective action is created. People start believing that the leaders are under their control.

The EWRs have developed a practice of mobilizing the people through the SHGs. Men resisted the entry of SHG members into the Gram Sabha meeting as they raised issues which warrant discussion whereas EWRs brought the SHGs to the Gram Sabha and made them partners[32]. This is a new culture developed by the elected women representatives and they have developed nuances and methods by which they raise the issues. They have developed a practice of lobbying with political leaders at the state level for redressal of their problems through the legislature.

They further wanted to bring services nearer to the people and especially to women as they are the worst sufferers if services are drawn from far-away places. Normally elected representatives lament upon the poor devolution of powers whereas the elected women representatives assume responsibilities and demonstrate their capabilities in delivering services which receive appreciation from the provincial government. The EWRs attend to minute things like providing nail cutter to the balwadis (Anganwadi), construct-ing baby toilets, providing mats to the balwadis by making use of the available development schemes[33]. The EWRs assume responsibilities to deliver services. They say that service channels have to be identified and after that representatives have to watch whether the services are properly delivered by the officials.

Before the Government of Tamil Nadu passed an order for 100 per cent rainwater harvesting, Jesu Mary of Michael Pattinam Panchayat installed 100 per cent rain water harvesting structures and won appreciation. The Government of Tamil Nadu passed the order only after two years. She said that to do service leaders need no power from above, they need only the community support. Sahaya Mary of Kakkanur Gram Panchayat evolved a Village Based Management System to ensure clean water to all the houses without any difficulty by involving the community and getting their monetary contribution. In the whole of Tamil Nadu no Panchayat was collecting water charges but she collected the same with the active backing of the community. The Government considered it a model and made water an affair of the community and passed an order in this regard. Likewise Rani Sathappan of K. Rayavaram Gram Panchayat totally abolished the practice of using polythene from the Village Panchayat area. Ms. Kala of Noothulapuram Gram Panchayat created a citizens' centre where she provided all information related to development and governance and the citizens' centre was made a place to discuss public issues. Informed citizens go through all the documents provided in the centre and render assistance to the needy. To create well informed citizens she has created this centre. Further the centre discusses issues of the public in the interests of the community. Thus the women Presidents have brought about changes in governance. They have brought about all changes through mobilizing the community for the sustenance of the changes which they have brought about. They strongly believe that the community alone can bring about changes and the leaders are only facilitators.

For men development means laying of roads, black topping roads, constructing community halls, school buildings and more of hardware. As MLAs and MPs they also want to show the physical structures created by them whereas the elected women represen-tatives have started looking at development as all inclusive. They perceive more of software activities. They touch upon ecology, environment, employment, women's literacy, health, livelihood security and so on. When the Government of Tamil Nadu introduced a 15-point programme to make Tamil Nadu a premier state in terms of development, the EWRs convened a meeting of their federation and discussed the document at length and formulated an action plan and submitted it to the government[34]. No other organization has done this exercise. Further, they have indicated the role of the Panchayats in implementing the 15-point programme and for effective implementation they demanded adequate powers and finance for the Panchayats. The issues of Dalits, women, destitutes, orphans, widows and the differently abled are found in the agenda of the elected women representatives. In the EWRs annual convention they have a fixed agenda and they discuss all the social development issues which are not discussed either in the Gram Sabha or in the Panchayat Council. The popular perception was originally different from that of the women leaders. Gradually they have tried to change the popular perception of development. To honour the popular perception of development they have taken steps to put up hardware structures. Chinnamal of Orathupatti Gram Panchayat declared that, by providing nail cutter and toilet to the school, a new culture could be created among the kids. Providing assistance to the differently abled, destitutes and widows is the priority of Veerakalaiarasi of Veppankulam Gram Panchayat. Stopping the sand mining in their Panchayat area is the main target of Eswari of Appipalayam Gram Panchayat and Rani Muniyakannu of Vanduvancherry Gram Panchayat. To them it is livelihood security and protecting ecology and environment.

Further the elected women representatives, with the support of self-help groups, have brought the issues of women to the forefront. Initially the elected women representatives formed their own association and they discussed the women's issues in their forum.

They used to invite women activists and feminists to their Association for interaction. By constantly conscientizing the women leaders the elected women representatives have grown highly sensitive to women's issues. Women leaders have taken conscious steps to bring the issues of women to the public at the grassroots level. A long list of activities has been identified for the women Panchayat leaders, including combating domestic violence. The women Panchayat leaders have started associating themselves with the State Women's Commission to address their problems. Many of the Gram Panchayat women Presidents have started associating themselves with SHGs and, with their support, many of the women's issues have been discussed in the Gram Sabha. While prioritizing the activities in the Gram Panchayat women have identified a few works for which they had fought against men in the PRA exercise done in model Panchayats. This kind of activities are getting recognition at the grassroots because of the presence of women leaders and the self-help group members.

Having proved their credentials in managing the Panchayats, women Gram Panchayat leaders draw more members of the Gram Sabha to all public activities. They exhibit all the accounts on the Panchayat notice boards. In many of the Panchayats, women Gram Panchayat Presidents give work to Ward Members and self-help group members. They never indulge in corrupt practices. It is natural that when women take up such works, all in the community are interested to see their works. Further the women are always watched by the men. Moreover they are morally bound and hence they carry out all the activities transparently without giving any room for criticism.

Elected women representatives have acquired skills which are totally different from those of men. This enriches the leadership qualities of the elected women representatives. Women representatives act upon common sense and they suggest practical solutions to problems. Whenever they speak to the higher officials they speak with exact details as otherwise they feel that they will not be listened out. They have patience and, hence, they are able to manage the crowd and the officials. While analyzing the skills of the women leaders one finds a distinctive pattern wherein they want to excel men in their performance. They build alliance with the media and NGOs for their effective functioning. The media has covered extensively the struggles and achievements of the women leaders. NGOs are extending their support to the activities of the elected women representatives. A large number of NGOs are working in the areas where women are leaders of the Gram Panchayats.

The women leaders are interested in breaking new ground. They are known for their pathbreaking activities. Rainwater harvesting was initiated long back in Tamil Nadu by Jesu Mary, a Gram Panchayati President of Michael Pattinam of Ramanathapuram District. The Government of Tamil Nadu issued an order for rainwater harvesting in all the houses only after two years. Likewise, to eradicate plastics, the Government of Tamil Nadu issued an order but could not withstand the opposing pressure and so later it was withdrawn. But K. Rayavaram Gram Panchayati President Ms. Rani Sathappan has successfully eradicated the use of polythene in her Panchayat area. In the same way in Kakkanur Gram Panchayat Ms. Sakaya Mary collected water charges from all families for water management. Ms. Ponnikailasam, the President of Annai-kuppam Gram Panchayat of Thiruvarur District, formed a federation of elected women representatives to get the problems of the women leaders in Panchayats solved. She got a government order in this regard for a regular interface between government officials and the women leaders. After she formed the Association men formed their Associations. Now at all levels Associations have been formed. Before she did so nobody dreamt of such Associations and Federations.

Yet another striking factor among the women leaders is maintaining the secular character. A notable example is Jamruth Beevi of Devipattinam Gram Panchayat, who fulfilled a long felt need of the pilgrims who visit Rameswaram. An important shrine, a water pond, lies on the otherside of a water-logged stretch and the devotees had to cross the water to reach that pond. After a long struggle she constructed a bridge between the road and the shrine. It was appreciated by all the communities. In the same way she created a small tank for a Hindu temple which generated tremendous support from the Hindu families. She did several works in the Panchayat. But she did not consider all these works important. According to her perception, constructing a bridge to the holy shrine and providing a tank for the temple of the Hindus were her major achievements for which she got the support of all the communities. She has been the President of the Gram Panchayat consecutively for two terms with the support of all the communities. Those who instigated communal feud were defeated in the election. She said that she is of the opinion that communities are always secular and not communal. If the leaders are secular it is good for the society. Following the model of Jamruth Beevi, Noor Mohammed of Sakkaraikkottai Gram Panchayat helped the Hindu organizations to construct a temple in the Panchayat area. Appreciating the enthusiasm and help rendered by the Panchayat President, his name was inscribed on the front elevation of the temple. A Musalman's name is inscribed on a Hindu temple! The President drew the support of all the communities in his Panchayat area. He is a model to many Panchayat leaders belonging to the Muslim community.

Women Panchayat leaders are not corrupt as it is evident from the studies conducted among the Gram Panchayat women Presidents. They are open and their activities are transparent. They give accounts periodically to the people through the Panchayat meetings and display the accounts on the notice board of the Panchayats. It is seen in the study conducted for PRIA that the women Panchayat leaders are always honest, as observed by the officials.

Evaluation

From the above narration, the postulates formulated from the experience in the world have come to be formulated as hypotheses and they have to be tested in many provinces and a large number of empirical studies have to be conducted to test the hypotheses. The narration includes evidence to argue that the women leaders have joined together to promote the best practices developed by them in governance and development activities to other places and to make them successful. A variety of support structures have been created in different domains to extend support to the elected women representatives to continue their struggle to achieve efficiency in performing their duties and responsibilities. The elected women representatives face several inherent barriers. Their role on the uneven ground becomes difficult. Yet, in the context of the market driven economy and rights based development, they assume several social responsibilities and perform their duties and responsibilities very effectively to the satisfaction of the communities. They are always open to learning. They enjoy learning and listening. When the needed support structure is provided they perform their duties perfectly. Their concentration and achievements are always at an appreciable level. When their achievements were appreciated by Secretaries of the Government at a seminar held in Chennai, they developed the argument that if Panchayats are regarded as a service delivery mechanism, the entire system can be handed over to the women and everyone can then see the power of women leaders.

There is yet another argument that they picked up, namely, that in Tamil Nadu the Gram Panchayat election is not fought on party lines and hence individuals contest on their individual strength. In no way are they answerable to any political party. They are answerable only to the people. Hence women in Gram Panchayats perform well whereas in Block and District Panchayats they are in the hands of the political parties through their husbands or any other male of their family. When they deal with government officials, they follow a different approach. Normally the accepted norms for bribery are not acceptable to women. Hence officials are reluctant to speak to the women leaders and they prefer to speak to their husbands or any other male of their families.

To project the issues of the women they formed alliances with SHGs and the media. It is unequivocal that women in India have been oriented to think like men. But proper orientation and discussion have now made them think differently. They project the women's issues gradually in public fora. Now it is not a difficult subject for public debate. Their conceptualization of development is different and all inclusive and more particularly it is relationship between human beings and nature. It is for men, women and nature.

They demonstrate their ability, credibility and accountability. Their actions are transparent. Their performance draws the attention of the public. Leaders have to enable the public for participation. Men militate but women tend to listen and discuss. Therefore, the public have an interest in attending the Gram Sabha meetings as their views are considered. Women exhibit extraordinary skill in managing the Panchayats. In all adverse circumstances they tend to work and produce results. It is a common belief that women act only from common sense and not on the basis of facts and data. This belief has been disproved. Before they go to any office they prepare themselves well with all necessary facts. Women leaders react to the policy discussions of the government then and there. Thus they are pathfinders. Secular values are being upheld by the women leaders. They are above communal perceptions. They perceive that conflict cannot bring about prosperity and development. Hence they concentrate on communal harmony. They never entertain conflict among caste groups and religious groups. They work towards harmony. Thus the performance of Gram Panchayat women Presidents is influenced very much by the factors like capacity which they develop, skills they acquire, alliances they build, support from support structure, needed and adequate information and their work with the community.

Conclusion

The elected women representatives consider the space which they occupy as a space for development. However illiterate they are, however backward they are, they want to achieve something in life when an opportunity is given. They tend to seek a support base for their activities, especially for increasing their efficiency and capability. They improve their skills constantly and their skill is used for managing the Panchayats. Issues of women and development are brought to the public for debate. They are open to learning and patient to listen. They convert challenges into opportunities. They assume responsibilities and attempt innova- tions. By their actions, they create new contours of decentralization of powers. They build alliances to get support for their activities and to spread their innovations and achievements. They run the administration transparently and reduce corruption. They develop alternative governance to achieve development with the participation of the people. A new culture is being evolved and a new value profile is being evolved at the grassroots by the women leaders through their handling of powers. They are emerging models to be emulated. They have registered a striking difference in governing the grassroots institutions. Now the women federation leaders are voicing a demand that all Gram Panchayats should be reserved for women since, in Tamil Nadu, the Gram Panchayat is freed from political contest. All these observations are based on the study conducted in fifty-two Gram Panchayats headed by women in Tamil Nadu spread over 28 districts.

NOTES AND REFERENCES

1. World Bank, *Endendering Development Through Gender Equality in Right, Resources and Voices,* 2001.
2. Huairou Commission, *Advancing Governance through peer Learning and Networking — Lessons Learned from Grassroots Women,* 2002.
3. Palanithurai, G., *Evaluation of Performance of Gram Panchayat Presidents in Tamil Nadu,* Vol. I & II. Gandhigram: Rajiv Gandhi Chair for Panchayati Raj Studies, 2004.
4. Palanithurai, G., *Report of the leadership Training Programme Conducted for Gram Panchayat Women Presidents of Tuticorin District in Tamil Nadu,* Gandhigram: Rajiv Gandhi Chair for Panchayati Raj Studies, 2004.
5. Palanithurai, G., *Report of the Leadership Training Programme Conducted for Block Panchayat SC and ST Women Chairpersons of Tamil Nadu,* Gandhigram: Rajiv Gandhi Chair for Panchayati Raj Studies, 2004.
6. Buch Nirmala, "Decentralized Governance, Women's Participation and Poverty Eradication", *Women and Political Empowerment* (eds) B. Mohanty and S. Haider, New Delhi: Institute of Social Sciences; Devaki Jain, 1996, *Panchayati Raj: Women Changing Governance,* New Delhi: UNDP.
7. Ray Sumita, "Women's Struggle in India" *Advocacy Internet*, 5:4, (July-August, 2003).
8. Palanithurai, G., *Empowerment of Women: Experience of the Elected Women*

Representatives in Grassroots Institutions, Gandhigram: Rajiv Gandhi Chair for Panchayati Raj Studies, 2002.

9. Sharma Kumud, "Grassroots Organizations and Women's Empowerment: Some Issues in the Contemporary Debate", *Samya Shakti,* Delhi, CWDS.
10. The Indian Institute of Public Administration published a special volume of the Journal on "Towards Good Governance", for more details about the new context refer to *The Indian Journal of Public Administration,* Vol. XLIV: No. 3 (July-September, 1998).
11. The Indian Institute of Public Administration published a special volume of the Journal on "Governance for Development", for more details about the concept refer to *The Indian Journal of Public Administration,* Vol.L: No. 1 (January-March, 2004).
12. Sharma Sumedha, 2000, "Women's Ways of Governance", *Participation and Governance,* 7:19 (Nov., 2000).
13. Dahlerup, D., "From a Small to a Large Minority: Women in Scandinavism Politics", *Scandinavism Political Studies,* 11:4, 1998.
14. Kanter, R.M., "Some Effects of Proportions on Group Life: Skewed Sex Ratios and Responses to Token Women" American Journal of Sociology, 82 (1976) p. 966; Norris. P., "Women Politicians: Transforming West Minister"?, *Parliamentary Affairs,* 49:1, 1996.
15. Jackquette, J., Women in Power: From Tokenism to Critical Mass", *Foreign Policy,* (Fall 1997).
16. T. Studlar Danley and Mc Allister Ian, "Does a Critical Mass Exist? A Comparative Analysis of Women's Legislative Representation 1949-1997" paper presented at the American Political Science Association, Atlanta 2nd to 5th September, 1999.
17. Norris Pippa, and Lovenduski Joni, "Blair's Babes: Critical Mass Theory, Gender and Legislative Life" paper presented in the weekly seminar on women and public policy programme on 28th September 2001 in Kennedy School of Government, US.
18. Mac Dougal Linda, *Westminster Women,* London: Vintage, 1998.
19. Norris Pippa, "Women in Eurpean Legislative Elite", *West Eurpean Politics,* Vol. 8, No. 4 (1985).
20. Dahlerup, D., "From a Small to a Large Minority: Women in Scandinavism Politics", *Scandinavism Political Studies,* 11:4, 1998.
21. Grey Sandray, "Women and Parliamentary Politics: Does Size Matter? Critical Mass and Women MPs in the New Zealand House of Representatives", Paper presented in the 51st Political Studies Association Conference from 10th to 12th April 2001, Manchester, UK.
22. Palanithurai, G., *Report of the Leadership Training Programme Conducted for Gram Panchayat Women Presidents of Tuticorin District in Tamil Nadu,* Gandhigram: Rajiv Gandhi Chair for Panchayati Raj Studies, 2004.
23. Palanithurai, G., *Report of the Leadership raining Programme Conducted for Block Panchayat SC and ST Women Chairpersons of Tamil Nadu,* Gandhigram: Rajiv Gandhi Chair for Panchayati Raj Studies, 2004.

24. Palanithurai, G., *Report of the Capacity Building Exercises Conducted for Gram Panchayat Women Representatives,* Gandhigram: Rajiv Gandhi Chair for Panchayati Raj Studies, 2003.
25. Palanithurai, G., *Report of the Training Programme Conducted for Women Leaders of Gram Panchayats,* Gandhigram: Rajiv Gandhi Chair for Panchayati Raj Studies, 2004.
26. Palanithurai, G., "The Genre of Women Leaders in Local Bodies: Experience from Tamil Nadu", *The Indian Journal of Public Administration,* Vol. XLVII: No. 1 (January-March 2001).
27. Palanithurai, G., *Evaluation of Process and Performance of Women and Dalit Panchayat Presidents,* Gandhigram: Rajiv Gandhi Chair for Panchayati Raj Studies, 2003.
28. Rajiv Gandhi Chair, *Report of the Second Annual Meet of the Elected Women Representatives,* Gandhigram: Rajiv Gandhi Chair for Panchayati Raj Studies, 2002.
29. Rajiv Gandhi Chair, *Report of the Regional Workshop of Elected Women Representatives of Local Bodies,* Gandhigram: Rajiv Gandhi Chair for Panchayati Raj Studies, 2004.
30. Tamil Nadu Federation of Women Presidents of Panchayati Government, *Voices of Women Presidents of Panchayat Government in Tamil Nadu,* Chennai: TNFWPPG, 2002.
31. Rajiv Gandhi Chair, *Functional Efficiency of Gram Sabha in Tamil Nadu: A Report,* Gandhigram: Rajiv Gandhi Chair for Panchayati Raj Studies, 2001.
32. Rajiv Gandhi Chair, *A Report on Interface between Elected Representatives of Local Bodies and Self-Help Groups,* Gandhigram: Rajiv Gandhi Chair for Panchayati Raj Studies, 2001.
33. Palanithurai, G., *Evaluation of Process and Performance of Women and Dalit Panchayat Presidents,* Gandhigram: Rajiv Gandhi Chair for Panchayati Raj Studies, 2003.
34. Rajiv Gandhi Chair, *Report of the Second Annual Meet of the Elected Women Representatives,* Gandhigram: Rajiv Gandhi Chair for Panchayati Raj Studies, 2002.

10

CRITICAL MASS TO CRITICAL ACTION

PHASE - I

Introduction

The decentralization process has opened up opportunities for women and other marginalized groups to influence the allocation of Government and community resources in their favour and to protect and promote their human rights. However, there are several barriers to women hailing from marginalized sections in exercising their powers. It is really a challenge to work for the social, economic and political empowerment of women, particularly those from marginalized sections. Undoubtedly, it is necessary to work towards the goal of empowering women for which the oppressive power of the existing gender relations is to be exposed and challenged. Further the gender relations have to be reshaped. This exercise could be started at the level of the elected women representatives of rural local bodies as they constitute a critical mass since one-third of seats have been reserved for women. The critical mass will be able to perform the critical function only if they are oriented, conscientized and trained in the methodology of deconstruction and reconstruction of gender relations.

Background

The first task undertaken by the Gandhigram Rural Institute (GRI) was to conduct a series of capacity building programmes for leaders in local government. Initially, these programmes were offered to both men and women simultaneously. Then, the GRI received a request from the women that they should be granted separate training programmes from those of the men. Even when they were interested in the materials and processes, they were unable to participate because the centuries of inhibited behaviour of women in the presence of men who were not family members, in a public space, did not allow them the opportunity to speak or fully engage with issues at these workshops. Consequently, special training programmes were organized for the women. In these programmes, women were trained in leadership skills that would enable them to undertake work in their local bodies.

The sensitized and conscientized EWRs were keen on the Panchayat issues after attending the training programmes, namely, ensuring entitlements to the poor, evicting the encroachers from the encroachment of common properties and creating awareness among the women about their problems and the remedy for the same. But conditions were not conducive for the EWRs to tackle all those issues and they had to face a volley of problems in the Panchayat administration. At this juncture, they were looking for an agency to help, guide, support and counsel them. To perform the above tasks, GRI had been also looking for an agency and at this juncture GRI contacted Ms. Devaki Jain, a well known woman activist and development economist and the Managing Trustee of SSF, Bangalore. GRI had several rounds of discussions and finally, the Ford Foundation came forward to support its activities along with such activities in other states, namely, Kerala, Karnataka and Andhra Pradesh through the Singamma Sreenivasan Foundation.

While taking up this project we (GRI) deliberated on a dual strategy to be adopted to empower the EWR to overcome all their problems. Tamil Nadu was known for women development activities during the day of the Dravidian Movement under the leadership of E.V. Ramasamy Naicker and C.N. Annadurai and an array of legislations were enacted during the period of the Dravidian Parties in government. This had its own impact on the social transformation process of Tamil Nadu.

Women leaders in Local Bodies, from their experience with men leaders, felt the need to form an association of EWRs. They formed some associations but these associations did not had any structure. All the same they used them as a forum to meet the officials collectively to represent their problems. Upon seeing this development we felt that the elected women representatives only need facilitation. We started working on this line since the Rajiv Gandhi Chair for Panchayati Raj Studies has similar objectives.

The primary objective of the Chair is to activate grassroots democracy by conducting action research and extension programmes. It has to work with the Panchayat leaders for regeneration of the rustic folk and to create awareness among the people about the new system of governance through the new institutional arrangement called Panchayati Raj System. The Chair works at different levels. It acts as a policy research cell and give advice to the policy-makers. It also acts as a nodal centre to offer training to the elected local body leaders in governance, especially in administering development. Further it acts as a coordinating agency for NGOs for people oriented participative action for sustainable development and good governance. This approach emanates from the basic premise that people are capable, honest, and sincere and committed in deciding their destiny and hence all the issues are visualized from the perspective of the people.

Against this background it was planned to keep the following as objectives and activities of the project:

- to enable elected women representatives to be courageous with self-confidence and not to be affected by atrocities or yield to pressure in carrying out their role and responsi-bilities;
- to empower the elected women representatives to assert their rights;
- to facilitate the sharing of experiences among the elected women representatives not only within districts and states but also between states;
- to build a movement of women political leaders to address issues on their own;
- to make the government listen to the collective voice of the elected women representatives;
- to institutionalize a gender perspective in decision-making.

With these objectives, reputed action oriented feminists, gender specialists, lawyers, representatives from NGOs and academics were invited to deliberate upon the strategies and the approaches to be adopted for a transformation process through the women's organizations. The elected women representatives were invited to share their experiences with the feminists and gender specialists. On 26th August, 2000, they deliberated upon the prevailing environment in the rural society for the functioning of the local bodies under the leadership of the women drawn from different socio-economic conditions.

In this consultation exercise, the following actions and approaches were evolved. As a first step, the loosely organized associations have to be federated into a cohesive movement to address the issues of the women and the marginalized. To do this, regional meetings have to be organized and zonal or regional units have to be created for furthering the activities of the federation. While organizing such regional meetings, the problems faced by the women leaders have to be properly documented for policy advocacy and they have to be published through the media. Leaders from different regions are to be gathered for periodical meetings and they have to be sensitized on the basic issues of development like food security, livelihood security and more specifically on the issues of women. While sensitizing the women these issues are to be discussed contextually and futuristically. To gain confidence, they need hands on experience for which meaningful interface programmes could be organized on demand by taking these leaders from Tamil Nadu to Kerala and even from one region to another region within Tamil Nadu where success cases are reported.

An annual Elected Women Leaders Convention has to be organized where the documented problems of different regions have to be discussed in front of dignarities and the media for popular dissemination and corrective action. The discussed issues have to be taken to the policy-making level for lobbying for which Gandhigram Rural Institute should take up the responsibility. Through the regional outfits, needed information has to be provided periodically to the Panchayat leaders. The elected women representatives who are struggling in the Panchayat administration to deliver services should be given a helping hand by which it can be demonstrated to the other leaders that they are not alone and that there are thousands of leaders behind them and many civil society organizations. To develop this movement the elected women representatives have to be trained in Panchayat management. They should be provided with needed skills and capability. Further the leaders of the Association in different regions are to be oriented in providing leadership to other elected women representatives. To adduce visibility to the issues of women and the organization, a proper media tie up has to be established. The media has to be sensitized on women in governance and the issues of women. The media's role in the movement is felt to be imperative. There are certain issues which are to be fought only through legal means for which the leaders are to be oriented for such an eventuality. To push forward the movement, the strong support of the NGO network is required. It is to be underlined that the NGOs' activities should always be at the back of the Women Leaders Association and not *vice versa.* After finalizing the strategy, approach and action programme, another meeting was organized to create an NGO network to support the women's organization. It was held on 23rd October, 2000. The NGOs who have been working on the issues of women development were invited to participate in the meeting. The NGO representatives participated and deliberated upon the strategies and approaches evolved in the previous meeting. It was almost a workshop for women's solidarity activities and expressed their commitment to this work. They agreed upon the objectives and offered to extend their support in carrying out the activities as partners. It was decided to divide Tamil Nadu into five zones. The activities had to be carried out in all the five zones through the NGOs and the NGOs had to act as nodal agencies and resource centres for the activities of the elected women representatives.

Following this commitment of the NGOs, regional meetings were organized at Madurai on 21st December, 2000, at Thiruvarur on 2nd February, 2001, at Chengalpattu on 16th February, 2001, and at Karur on 21st March, 2001. In all the regional or zonal meetings, the problems faced by the elected women representatives in administering development were discussed and they were documented. The documents were published and circulated among the representatives of the media for wider dissemination. The problems had to be taken to different levels for redressal. So they were classified and they were taken to the Block Development Office and to the State Legislative Assembly for redressal. On 5th August, 2001 an annual convention of the women leaders was organized at Gandhigram and it discussed the basic issues of the women, strategies to overcome the problems and the problems faced by the Panchayats. As they discussed the issues thoroughly, all the issues were fully covered in the media which brought visibility to the women's federation.

Interface Meetings

After the zonal or regional meetings and the annual convention, it was decided to undertake the interface programme under which the federation leaders were to be taken to Kerala to visit some of the Panchayats and hold discussion with the leaders and functionaries on the issues of development. They concentrated more on the issues of social and economic development. Almost all the federation leaders got an opportunity to visit Kerala to have a glimpse of the social and economic development activities of the Gram Panchayats.

The elected women representatives tried to bring the Minister of Rural Development, Government of India, to their programme and succeeded in their attempt. On 20th February, 2002, Mr.Venkaiah Naidu participated in their programme wherein the elected representatives discussed their issues with him and appealed to him to intervene at the appropriate level to redress their grievance. Along with the Minister, State level officials also participated and they were all asked by the Rural Development Minister to give replies to the questions raised by the representatives.

They organized the Second Annual Meeting in Gandhigram on 3rd May, 2002. In the second annual meeting, they discussed the 15-point programme of the Government of Tamil Nadu. In the course of the discussion they pointed out that, out of the 15-points, about 13 come under the purview of the Panchayati institutions. They went on to clarify at what level they can work and to what extent officials have to work to achieve the target. They compiled guidelines by which the details of the earmarked responsibilities could be identified. For the annual meet they invited the Director of Rural Development, Government of Tamil Nadu, Mr. S. Ayyar, IAS. They made a powerful plea that in each and every district the District Collector has to convene a meeting of Gram Panchayat women leaders and redress their problems in the management of the Panchayats. He agreed to do so and promised to issue an order in this regard. They further decided to form an advisory council consisting of retired officials, representatives from NGOs, academics and representatives from the media to facilitate the functioning of the federation. Subsequently, based on the deliberations of the Second Annual Convention, a regional leaders' meet was organized on 9th May, 2002 to make an in-depth study of the 15-point programme and the problems faced by the women leaders and consolidate their demands to be presented to the Government of Tamil Nadu.

Implications

So far the sequence of events has been presented. But the implications of the activities have to be explained. One should not assume that the federation met once a year and deliberated only in Gandhigram. They organized several meetings in several places with the help of other NGOs also. They met political party leaders and officials for presenting their charter of demands. They used to meet the press periodically and express their opinions on vital issues which affect the life of the people, particularly women, children and Dalits. Based on the training programme, we have collected the problems faced by the Panchayati leaders generally, and women and Dalit leaders specifically, and those problems have been documented by our centre. These documents have been used by this Federation for policy advocacy. It was very difficult for them to get information regarding Government orders, rules and schemes. But now they are being received from Gandhigram Rural Institute and so they regard it as a resource centre. Contacting Ministers, higher officials, MPs and MLAs is no more a problem for them.

Women leaders who are in this federating arrangement are highly sensitized on the issues of social development and more specifically on the issues of women and children. When the State Government's proposal to introduce cheap liquor came as the most unkindest cut of all for the women heading village Panchayats, the women Presidents reacted sharply that they were let down by a woman Chief Minister. They unequivocally argued and made it clear that they would launch an agitation if the Government refused to drop the proposal. When the regional leaders of the Federation met at Gandhigram, they discussed this issue at length and spoke to *The Hindu* Special Reporter Mr. S. Annamalai that they have been fighting at the village level for the past five years to eradicate illicit liquor, but now the Government itself seeks to introduce liquor to make money. Subsequently the move was withdrawn in the rural areas. It was considered a victory for the women Panchayati Leaders' Federation.

Subsequently, in the month of December 2002, when they met at Gandhigram, they made a plea to the Government of Tamil Nadu to increase the revenue of the Panchayats. The women Panchayati Leaders' Federation suggested that the State Government can hand over the common properties to the Panchayats. They indicated that quarries, tanks and trees which were now under the control of the Government agencies and individuals would fetch adequate revenue to make the local bodies self-reliant. They projected an alternative model of resource mobilization for Panchayats.

As they attended periodical meetings of the Federation, the restrictions imposed on them were gradually removed. Without the assistance of the males of their family they travel to Chennai, Madurai and Trichy to attend the meetings of the Federation. Further their communicative ability has improved to a surprising level as the grassroots women leaders have developed their own style of communication which has been accepted as a formal mode of communication. Their bargaining capability has been enhanced to strike a deal with officials, MLAs, and MPs for the benefit of the people. The feeling of isolation that prevailed among the elected women representatives has gone as they meet frequently and share their joys and difficulties. When the elected women representatives face problems in administration, the Federation leaders take the issue to the District Collector and to the level of the Director for Rural Development. They get their problems redressed, failing which they go to court and get suitable legal remedy which has raised the morale of the women leaders. Frequent sharing has built up the idea that this kind of exercise is necessary for their success. Their media contact is frequent and its implications are also positive.

Though Tamil Nadu has a District Panchayat Presidents Association, a Block Panchayat Association, and a Gram Panchayat Association, only the Federation of Women Panchayat Leaders Associations is visible and reacts sharply on many of the vital issues. Even though the elected women representatives have a charter of demands, they are more keen on getting reservation of seats for women for ten years, retrieving common properties from encroachment, and, ensuring the entitlements of the poor through the public distribution system. Active leaders in the Federation are very much sensitized on these social development issues after visiting the Kerala Panchayats. During the first period the women leaders were harping on transfer of power, finance and functionaries. Now they speak about issues and problems. They have gained voice and bargaining power.

One major achievement that they have scored through their work is getting the reservation of seats for women in local bodies extended for one more term. It is unique in the whole of the country. Another important achievement is that the Federation has made the State Government to withdraw the plan for cheap liquor. They pleaded with the Government that every month higher level officials at the district level should convene a meeting of the women Panchayat leaders and solve their problems. The Director, Rural Development, Government of Tamil Nadu, issued an order immediately to District Collectors to convene such meetings and solve the problems of the women leaders.

Because of their repeated pleas and activities, the Federation of Women Leaders Associations is visible to the policy-makers and 33.3 per cent of seats have been reserved for women even in cooperatives societies also. Likewise an order has been issued that in all statutory committees one-third reservations should be provided for women. Some of the women Panchayat leaders were in deep trouble. It was only the Federation which saved them. Menaka, the President of Oorappakkam, was murdered in the Panchayat office due to her stern action against encroachment. No FIR was filed till the Federation leaders went to the Panchayat. It was only because of this Federation that the culprits were booked. Another interesting noteworthy feature is that more number of office-bearers in the Federation is now from the Dalit community and the Federation has focused its attention on Dalit issues.

Thus the women have started realizing the potential of the Associations and the Federation. Political parties have started identifying the potential leaders from Gram Panchayats and enlisting them as their party members and proclaiming their achievements as the achievements of the party. The media has been sensitized on the women issues and as a result the media has given wide coverage to the activities of the Women's Federation. Elected women representatives have learnt the art of managing bureaucracy. They have picked up communication skills. They have developed bargaining power. Moving with higher officials has become a routine affair and the fear to meet the District Collector and other higher officials has gone. A large number of new leaders are drawn from self-help groups towards the Panchayats. Sharing the struggles and achievements in the regional and annual conventions has motivated other women leaders to emulate them. The fear syndrome and the dependency syndrome have gone. The group activities have developed a positive attitude among the women leaders to strive for achievements.

PHASE - II

Background

As a result of the First phase activities the EWRs have formed their association and conducted their activities in many places, with the active support of Rajiv Gandhi Chair for Panchayati Raj Studies apart from the help received from some NGOs. Thus, the EWRs have come to realize the importance of the association and yet there are encounters from all sections to weaken the association. After forming the association, they got success in many of their demands. But still, they are in need of documents to highlight their issues for policy advocacy. Further, to sensitize the EWRs, periodical meetings among themselves are very essential. Moreover the EWRs are to be concientised on the women issues. Hence they put forth a few more demands like:

- Periodical meetings among themselves to keep the tempo of the organizational and association activities;
- To concientize the members of the association on the basic issues of women and the EWRs;
- Leadership training for the EWRs;
- Concrete documents on their issues for which a supportive research team is necessary; and
- To overcome the information blockade, an information channel is needed.

Thus the past one year the first level leaders have struggled to concretize the association and the existence and continuation of the association itself is a very big success. To move further the support provided to them should continue. Keeping in view the second phase activities were planned.

To proceed further Rajiv Gandhi Chair for Panchayati Raj Studies, with the assistance of Singamma Srinivasan Foundation planned to evolve an approach, to take the federation further based on the input of the colleagues working with women and their problems throughout Tamil Nadu for the three decades. Against this background it was planned to keep the following as objectives and activities of the project:

- to extend support to the EWRs association to continue their activities of the association;
- to conscientize the EWRs on the basic issues of the women and EWRs;
- to provide research support to document all problems they encounter while performing their duties and responsibilities;

- to extend support for their periodical meetings in different regions to sensitize the EWRs on gender issues and social development issues;
- to conduct periodical leadership training of EWRs;
- to supply needed information to the EWRs to perform their duties and discharge their responsibilities;
- to arrange interface programmes between the EWRs of Tamil Nadu and EWRs of Kerala and Karnataka;
- to arrange for interface programme between the EWRs and the Media.

So, a state level consultation meeting was organized on 21st October, 2003 in Gandhigram by inviting women activists, feminists, scholars, gender specialists, lawyers, academics and representatives from women's organizations to discuss the problems involved in strengthening the federation for empowering the women to take up the issues on gender and social development.

In this consultation meeting our activity chart as well as our approach was presented. They included:

- All the members and leaders need orientation on the issues affecting the women and the poor.
- For state level activities all associations can be invited and involved.
- Since political leniency prevents some of the women leaders, appropriate strategy has to be worked out and by which those who are willing to project the issues could be projected.
- EWRs can work with political parties which are taking up the issues which are projected by the EWRs.
- Regional meetings could be organized at the district level.
- Periodical capacity building exercises have to be carried out.
- Innovative practices developed by the EWRs in tackling issues and managing the affairs of Panchayats could be documented properly and initiatives have to be taken for proper dissemination.

- More number of interfaces could be organized for EWRs to address the issues by drawing the attention of the officials.
- Federation can allow the SHG members and leaders to become the members of EWRs federation. It will bring sustainability to the federation.
- EWRs federation can retain the membership even after the tenure of the leaders in position. They can play a supportive role to EWRs federation.

Regional Workshop

Based on the decision taken in the consultation meeting a Regional Workshop was organized at Thiruvarur on 27th December, 2003. It was attended by office-bearers of the District Units and Block Units of the EWRs. Representatives of Thanjavur, Thiruvarur and Nagapattinam Districts attended the meeting. In this workshop, Ms. Ponnikailasam, Association President mentioned the major achievements of the federation and highlighted the struggles of the women leaders. She appealed to the participants to discuss the steps to be taken to strengthen the Federation of Women Leaders to ameliorate the conditions of women and children. She listed the major efforts taken by the Federation and the solid achievements scored by them.

To Strengthen the EWR Federation

The following are the problems indicated by them were:

1. Visibility at a higher level (at State level).
2. No visibility at the grassroots as they are part of Union Federation with men.
3. Existence of many associations – Block level, District level.

> *EWRs should work united for achieving the task, which is not only to fulfil the demands of the EWRs but also to provide sustainable development to all the Panchayats of Tamil Nadu.*
>
> ***Ms. K. Ponni, President, EWRs Association***

4. EWR needed active support only on the ground as challenges are on the ground.
5. Women leaders are not aware of the problems of the women.
6. No sensitization of the women leaders on gender and social development.
7. No proper capacity building for women leaders.
8. Women leader's achievements are not highlighted.
9. Press is underutilized.

Solutions

- Deepen the federation.
- Encourage federation at lower levels.
- Partnership with press has to be created.
- Using the Government order issued earlier periodical meetings have to be organized at the district level.
- For official intervention at local level, the District level leader has to be contacted.
- To contact the officials at State level, the State level leaders have to be contacted.
- While meeting in the convention, the issues of women have to be discussed.

Ms. Jesumary, Vice-President, EWRs Association, *all EWRs should work together and fight against severe crises united. Cordial relationship will ensure the achievement of their goal and vision. Women should not confine to the home but come out to the outside world where they have to learn a lot. She insisted that courageous attitude, efforts and experience could cope with any kind of threat. She advised the EWRs that this type of attitude made the officials to render positive efforts in favour of them.*

A New Partner in Our Exercise

From the experience of the EWRs of Thiruvarur District it was learnt that the elected men representatives have extended a helping hand to the women leaders to perform their roles and responsibilities very effectively by forming a federation of Gram Panchayat leaders of a particular Block, namely, Kudavasal. In Kudavasal Panchayat there are 49 Gram Panchayats. The basic objectives of the federation are:

1. Location specific peculiar problems can be tackled locally.
2. When Government officials deal with Panchayat Presidents their approach varies from individual to individual. There is no perspective or uniformity in dealing with Panchayats. They give room for caste and political considerations in dealing with Panchayat matters. In order to avoid such variations and discrepancies an association is needed.
3. Information blockade is a major instrument through which Panchayat Presidents are made to tow the line of the officials. To disseminate information to all Panchayat Presidents an association is necessary.
4. In every Gram Panchayat, the weak and meek Panchayat Presidents have to face a volley of local problems. Local issues have to be sorted out at that level. They should not be brought out of the specific Panchayat area. Sometimes Vice-Presidents or at times Ward Members and on a few occasions the traditional Panchayat leaders disturb the Panchayat. On such occasions the federation should interfere and solve the local problem. Since the Federation leader is a local leader having much recognition in that area the problems can be tackled easily.

Capacity Building for EWRs

Training is an essential skill building tool which carves or adds sharpness to every human being to perform extraordinary and excellent management facts. When it is given at the initial stage, the administrators will surely bring creativity and transformation to the entire society. Even though many of them are illiterate, the method of teaching will surely enrich their knowledge of both neo-literates and literates. The teaching, along with role models and risks taken by several models will clearly visualize the real situations and make the trainees interested observers. When the EWRs of the entire state are provided with such type of capacity building they will surely acquire good administrative skills and everyone will shine as role models within a short period of time.

But the government takes steps to provide Panchayat training only long after they become Panchayat leaders. The training materials are not full-fledged but vaguely explain about the Panchayati Raj System. The Acts and Rules are not clearly explained.

On the other hand, the Rajiv Gandhi Chair for Panchayati Raj Studies, Gandhigram Rural Institute organized a series of training programmes of five days duration with the help of The Hunger Project, New Delhi. These training programmes were conducted exclusively for the EWRs of 13 Southern Districts of Tamil Nadu.

Emergence of Issues

The first three days of the training programme specially focused on the principles of Panchayati Raj System, accounts keeping, procedures for Gram Sabha meeting, roles and responsibilities of Panchayat President and Ward Members, retrieval methods of common property resources, various sources for increasing Panchayat financial resources, etc. All these Panchayat administrative techniques were clearly taught by well experienced retired higher officials, with legal inputs, along with examples. These classes clearly visualized the Panchayat management, which made the EWRs realize the opportunity provided to them at an early stage.

The EWRs who have never spoken any words frankly discussed various issues and personally clarified their doubts from the experts. The last two days were scheduled for discussing social development issues which were deeply rooted in their minds, as they have decided to undertake works under sanitation, reproductive health care of mother and children, health of adolescent young girls, economic development of SHGs and youths, planning for sustainable village development through people's participation along with SHGs, etc.

The issues discussed by them were:

- Lack of sufficient economic sources.
- More control due to proxy politics.
- Non-cooperation of government officials.
- Interference of politicians marginalized the scheme benefits in favour of them.
- The most vulnerable poor people were not listed under the BPL list.
- The resolutions passed in Gram Sabha were not carried out due to lack of funds, resulting in less people's participation.
- Destruction of CPRs due to environmental pollution by industrialists.
- No proper information dissemination by government departments.
- Non-cooperation among the Ward Members.
- No sufficient sanitary workers.

> *The MLAs/MPs were also elected by the people, but they lead a luxurious life and do not meet the people frequently. They expect some financial contribution from the people for fulfilling any kind of demands put forth by the people. But in the case of the Presidents, they render services to the people and also face the revenge of the opposing persons and the people's demands were not fulfilled. This affects the morale of Gram Panchayat Presidents who work hard, sincere, transparent and true.*
>
> ***Ms. E. Bhavani, President, Merpanaikadu Panchayat, Pudukottai District.***

Formation of Association

The following paragraph flashed the reality of the situation of the women Panchayat President situations, which was also endorsed by the after Presidents today; who participated in the capacity building programmes organized by GRI. The EWRs who were forced to attend the training programmes, by the officials were accompanied by the male members of the family. This showed that the women have been made totally powerless and have been totally deprived of their rights and resources due to male domination.

> *"In order to function on their own, the opportunity has been provided to women through reservation. Being in power, women have become a fruit bearing tree severely hit by stones, in the form of male dominance, character assassination and threat from mafia. Having faith on us people have elected women as their representatives. Therefore, we should work hard and create a revolutionary change in our villages. We should also join hands to curb the social evils from eroding the society."*
> ***— Ms. Masanam, President, Udayathur Panchayat, Tirunelvelli District***

The EWRs shared that in most of the union level general meetings, the male Gram Panchayat Presidents never allowed them to express their ideas and views and also mocked at them whenever they tried to clarify their doubts. But in the training programme, the women oriented classes motivated them to share their administrative hurdles and realized their worth and roles and responsibilities. The prime problems raised by them are proxy and non-cooperation and bureaucratic control of administrators. Even the union level meetings are attended by the male members of the family on behalf of women leaders, hence they have not seen or familiar among themselves. For future participation in various programmes, they collected the contact numbers of their fellow District EWRs.

At the end of the each training programme the project facilitators explained about the activities of the association, they showed interest to learn about the experience of the federation and extended their willingness for collective bargaining the representatives registered their membership in the prescribed format of the association. Then they themselves selected one District representative and Block level representatives respectively. The EWRs who performed Panchayat activities with the support of SHGs and also those EWRs who are the member of SHGs voluntarily took-up the responsibility for the activities of the association.

Formation of SC/ST Women Block Panchayat Chairpersons Association

The Rajiv Gandhi Chair for Panchayat Raj studies, in association with the State Institute of Rural Development, conducted a 4-day leadership and information workshop for SC/ST Women Panchayat Union Chairpersons from 27th to 30th January, 2003 in Gandhigram. It is a special training programme designed by the government. Since the Rajiv Gandhi Chair is conducting leadership training for Gram Panchayat women leaders with support of The Hunger Project and supporting women's associations exclusively to deal with women's problems, it was accepted as an opportunity. There are totally 33 Union Chairpersons in the state. They felt that they are discriminated on the basis of caste even though they or (their husbands) belong to the AIADMK and the DMK, both belonging to the Dravidian Movement which work for women's liberation and social justice.

> ***Ms. Vasantha, Mayilam Union Chairperson, Villupuram District*** *expressed, women should be economically empowered, attend more number of capacity building programmes, enrich their administrative skills, participate in every activity and perform their duty by themselves. The EWRs should include the women issues in their resolution.*
>
> *The next federation should be formed immediately after the forthcoming election and the district level federation activity should be given more importance, she stated. Familial responsibility and male domination are the hurdles in their functioning. This should be prevented and controlled with the help of the federation.*

Upon hearing about the success story of the Women's Federation, the Union Chairpersons also wanted to do the same for which they sought the help of the Rajiv Gandhi Chair. After obtaining all the details of the federation they formed an association. These Union Women Chairpersons association members participated in several meetings organized by the EWRs and lended their full support for them and raised their voice against the problems encountered by them.

Workshops

The GRI facilitated the EWRs federation in organizing State level and Regional level workshops in their respective Districts and Chennai. In the Regional workshops, the District higher officials, NGOs, press, role models and other pro-Panchayat institution members were invited. The struggles and success encountered by them, the responses by the District officials, etc., was projected by the media for wider dissemination. Many of the local problems like water disputes, sufficient infrastructure facilities, land disputes, fund allocation, non-conventional energy sources, benefits for weaker sections and dalits, implementation of schemes, etc. were solved by the District Administration. The discussed problems which were not considered, were taken up by the District-wise federation representatives to the State level workshop, in which NGO personnel's role models, media, Panchayat supportive institutions participated. Each District-wise representative put forth their demands and a consolidated memorandum was prepared by the President of the EWRs association and were discussed in the interface with Rural Development Secretaries and higher officials. The State higher officials responded the issues along with other concerned department officials and communicate the District administration over phone. These developments were discussed in a press meet for wider dissemination. Thus federation wisely organized the State level workshops, to focus their demands during the legislative assembly, budget sessions and met the leaders of several ruling political parties and opposition party and stressed them to include their issues in their party manifestoes.

Major issues highlighted during the State Higher Officials Meet:

- Reduction of electricity tariff.
- Retrieval of CPR from encroaches.
- District fund for Panchayat.
- Revenue for Panchayats from mines and minerals.
- Proper fund allocation and dissemination of information from the district administration.
- Cooperation of several government departments.
- Formation of a district committee along with Union Council. Chairpersons for rural development.

> ***Ms. Savithri, President, Mahilancheri Panchayat, Thiruvarur District*** *faced a problem created by the traditional Panchayat. The traditional Panchayat sentenced the President to leave the village and ordered the people not to talk to her and excommunicated her from the village. The Gram Sabha meet was not conducted and the officials did not take any step when she made a complaint. The President of the EWRs Federation brought it to the notice of the DRD, District Collector and the Press. The problem was solved; now she leads a normal life and she is also involved in*

The federation has tirelessly highlighted the demands before several higher officials, political party leaders and other Panchayat supportive institutions. They did not seek more funds but asked for their rights to get the sources which are available in their Panchayat areas and expected the cooperation of Government officials during crises.

In one regional workshop, Dr. Suriyakanta Mishra the honorable Minister of Panchayat Raj, Government of West Bengal was the Chief Guest, and shared his West Bengal experiences with EWRs. In this meet, the EWRs discussed on the governance of education, governance of health, governance of environment and governance of weaker sections. These discussions highlighted the role of EWRs in social development issues.

Special Meet with Second Term Presidents

The Reservation of seats in local governance throws a space for the women, to prove their leadership qualities in the public arena. Many EWRs have developed their negotiating skills with the support of various capacity building orientation programmes rendered by pro-Panchayat institutions. Based on their best performance and Panchayat management, with the support of the people, they occupied the position for one more term. They have experienced multitude of obstacles to discharge their responsibilities and met success across the threatened Section 205. Keeping this in view, GRI organized a regional workshop exclusively for these eight years experienced EWRs from various Districts of Tamil Nadu, on 11th and 12th of August, 2005 and decided to study about their eight years administrative experiences.

Sixty-four EWRs from twenty-nine Districts and the District level office-bearers who are in the EWRs Federation for the past six years met and discussed some of their experiences to draw a road map for their federation jointly and individually for themselves. Their success, struggles and their needs were discussed openly and thoroughly. Deep rooted issues, memorable solid achievements historic struggles have been highlighted in their deliberations. Their performance, struggle and achievement brought recognition for them from the community. They learnt about the art of mobilizing people to the Gram Sabha and developing partnership with the officials.

Struggle to Succeed

The EWRs realized the following, as essentials for their success:

- Periodical attendance to any meeting
- Interface with officials
- Efficient Panchayat management
- Realize their worth
- Intensive function and confront any type of disputes
- Continuous crisis management and crowd management equip them with courage

- Well understood the society within the painful administrative process
- Achievements built self-confidence
- Concentration on internal resource mobilization
- Motivated by several role models
- Projection of achievements and struggles by media
- Realized the potentials of collective action
- Opportunity seeker
- Demonstration of innovative potential.

> ***Ms. Pappa, President, Athankaraipatty Panchayat, Madurai District*** *praised GRI for providing training and many exposure visits, and also an opportunity for sharing the State level issues. She again stated that more number of women have participated in the Gram Sabha and have also started to claim their needs without any hesitation. It is a great success for the entire womenfolk. She requested the EWRs to concentrate on issues like women's education, women's health, especially ill health due to breast cancer, anemia, female infanticide, violence against women, etc. — a total fight against every atrocity against women.*

The EWRs also shared the obstacles which blocked their continuous performance, as the government selected the beneficiaries without consulting the EWRs, non-cooperative attitude of the officials, complicated administrative structure, no much importance given to managerial perspective, emergence of corruption, false projection of media, provision of poor training programmes, non-consideration of well performed EWRs, diversion of MLA/MP funds, no exclusive Secretary or Director for Panchayats, officials lending preference for proxy, no proper importance given to MLP, ill-treatment for Dalit leaders and community, no counselling for familial burden/brutality etc.

Even though they were bounded by several severe obstacles, they have performed transparent administration and proved their collective bargaining power. Most of the social development issues were taken up with the support of women SHGs, youths, school students, traditional Panchayat leaders, weaker sections and community based organizations. Most of them aimed to become the members of assemblies or else occupy the positions in grassroots governance, and a few decided to pave the way for the youngsters by lending their support.

Interface/Exposure visit to Model Panchayat

Fifteen Panchayat Presidents visited West Bengal on the invitation of Hon'ble Minister of Panchayat Raj and Rural Development. The interface programme was hosted by State Institute of Panchayat Raj and Rural Development (SIPRD) of West Bengal.

After an initial briefing about the system of Panchayat Raj in West Bengal, the participants were taken to the Sugandha Gram Panchayat in Hoogli District headed by Ms. Shamoli Bhavin. She explained about the functioning of Panchayats. When the participants enquired about the selection of beneficiaries for various schemes, she said that her Gram Panchayat has constituted Beneficiary Committee which looks into the beneficiary.

Next, participants were taken to Hoogli District Panchayat Office to meet its Chairperson Ms. Krishna Banerjee whose protocol is equivalent to Minister of State. She shared a few words with the participants explaining their linkage with the Gram Panchayat and told about her achievements in the following area: Mid-day meal scheme, Sanitation, Health, SHGs and Education. Since she involved herself with the mass movement and maintained close collaboration with the people she has achieved this much.

Next, they were taken to the Panduva Panchayat Samiti situated in Hoogli District and met Ms. Shukla Mukherjee who heads the Panchayat Samiti. She is a leader of grassroots movement and now she works on mid-day meal scheme and SSA. They had a brief discussion. Next, the team went to Jamuna Gram Panchayat which collects more revenue and has a shopping complex on its own which added to their income. They had discussion about the Sanitation, Mid-day meal and IAY houses. Participants were taken to look an IAY house entrusted by the beneficiary himself.

The EWRs were taken to several model Panchayats within the State like Semmipalayam, Odanthurai, Michaelpattinam, Devipattinam, Sakkarakottai and Thamaraikulam. Even though many of the EWRs have served as role models, trainers to other representatives, they wanted to share their experiences with these model Panchayats. Due to the hike in electricity tariff, low fund allocation, the Panchayats were not able to fulfil its financial needs, for the provision of basic facilities to the poor. They were interested in learning the techniques followed for Panchayat management, income from local resources and other negotiating skills from those Panchayats.

The selected model Panchayats received awards from the District administration for the implementation of Total Rural Sanitation Programme and Rainwater Harvesting System with the support of the people and Community Based Organisation. Thamaraikulam Panchayat received Nirmal Gram Puraskar Award from our President of India and Michaelpattinam Panchayat was honoured by Chief Minister of Tamil Nadu and World Bank for cent per cent fulfilment of proper Rainwater Harvesting System. Semmipalayam and Odanthurai Panchayat utilized several non-conventional energy sources, carried out income generating activities for SHGs and several other activities towards sanitation and education. All these Panchayats are implementing the solid waste management and transform the wastes into wealth. Sakkarakottai and Devipattinam Panchayats are examples of communal harmony.

The exposure visit only provided an opportunity for the EWRs to share their experiences and as a result they emerged with a vision for the sustainable development of Panchayats. They realized the following:

- The Panchayat administration should be people centred
- Ensuring quality in all activities
- Proper and systematic account maintenance
- Transparency and honesty
- Having faith and respect of people
- Linkage with SHGs and youths
- Activation of Village Development Committee
- Adopting appropriate technologies
- Gender sensitized

- Importance given to marginalized sector
- Build up rapport with government officials
- Team-ship with Ward Members
- Communal harmony
- Availing all schemes
- Creation of mass awareness
- Special attention to water and sanitation
- Alliances with Community Based Organisation
- Respect the opponents' opinion
- Proper income generating activities to SHGs.

Ms.Kamalam, President, Kullichettipatti Panchayat, Dindigul District *thanked GRI for providing the opportunity of sharing, with the EWRs of various Districts of Tamil Nadu. She shared her experience during the exposure visit to model Panchayats of Coimbatore District, wherein she learnt the administrative techniques followed by the model Panchayat President and that the Panchayat should be people centred, the problematic opponents should be approached initially and the crisis solved directly, maintaining transparency.*

The EWRs Brought out the Changes in Governance

The EWRs are interested in breaking new ground. They are known for their path breaking activities.

Ms. Dhanapackiam, President, Keelmavizhangai Panchayat, Villupuram District requested the EWRs to fulfil the basic amenities of the people. She said that she is an independent leader without any interference by her husband in Panchayat activities. She always approaches the officials with the relevant records during the discussion of any issue. She has collected water charges from every house and systematic water supply has been provided. She has also attended a technical training programme, and been trained in electric pump mechanism. Whenever a mechanical problem arises she herself repairs such defects. When the best Panchayat award was given to her Panchayat, she utilized the amount for community utility purpose. She urged the EWRs to maintain the records with perfection.

Ms. Jesu Mary, President, Michealpattinam Panchayat, Ramanathapuram District. Even before the Government of Tamil Nadu passed an order for 100 per cent rainwater harvesting, she installed 100 per cent rainwater harvesting structures and won appreciation. The Government of Tamil Nadu passed the order only after two years of her completing the work.

Ms. Sahaya Mary, President, Kakkanur Panchayat, Villupuram District. She evolved a Village Based Management System to ensure clean water to all the houses without any difficulty by involving the community and getting their monetary contribution. In the whole of Tamil Nadu no Panchayat was collecting water charges but she collected the same with the active backing of the community. The government considered it a model and made water an affair of the community and passed an order in this regard.

Ms. S. Rani, President, K. Rayapuram Panchayat, Pudukkottai District. She totally abolished the practice of using polythene from the village Panchayat area.

Ms. M. Kala, President, Noothulapuram Panchayat, Dindigul District. She created a citizen's centre where she provided all information related to development and governance and the citizen's centre was made a place to discuss public issues. To create well informed citizens she has created this centre. Informed citizens go through all the documents provided in the centre and render assistance to the needy. Further the centre discusses issues of the public in the interests of the community.

Ms. Veerakalaiarasi, President, Veppankulam Panchayat, Sivagangai District. Providing assistance to the differently abled, destitutes and widows is the priority.

Ms. Chinnammal, President, Orathupatti Panchayat, Sivagangai District, declared that, by providing nail cutter and toilet to the school, a new culture could be created among the kids.

Ms. Eswari, President, Appipalayam Panchayat, Karur District and Ms. M. Rani, President, Vanduvancherry Panchayat, Nagapattinam District. Stopping the sand mining in their Panchayat area is the main target. It is livelihood security and protecting ecology and environment.

Ms. Jamruth Beevi, President, Devipattinam Panchayat, Ramanathapuram District, who fulfilled a long felt need of the pilgrims who visit Rameswaram. An important shrine, a water pond, lies on the other side of a water-logged stretch and the devotees had to cross the water to reach that pond. After a long struggle she constructed a bridge between the road and the shrine. It was appreciated by all the communities. In the same way she created a small tank for a Hindu temple which generated tremendous support from the Hindu families.

Issues of Women to the Forefront

The EWRs, with the support of the SHGs, have brought the issues of women to the forefront. Initially the EWRs formed their own association and they discussed the women's issues in their forum. They used to invite women activists and feminists to their association for interaction. By constantly conscientizing the women leaders the EWRs have grown highly sensitive to women's issues. Women leaders have taken conscious steps to bring the issues of women to the public at the grassroots level. A long list of activities has been identified for the EWRs, including combating domestic violence. The EWRs have started associating themselves with the State Women's Commission to address their problems. Many of the EWRs have started associating themselves with SHGs and, with their support; many of the women's issues have been discussed in the Gram Sabha. While prioritizing the activities in the Gram Panchayat Women have identified a few works for which they had fought against men in the PRA exercise done in model Panchayats. These kinds of activities are getting recognition at the grassroots because of the presence of women leaders and the SHG members.

First Annual Mela

The Elected Women Representatives of Tamil Nadu decided to show their solidarity and raise their voice against the problems they face in the process of governance at the grassroots through their

Association of Elected Women Representatives of Local Bodies in Tamil Nadu with the staunch support of Rajiv Gandhi Chair for Panchayat Raj Studies, Gandhigram Rural Institute. Accordingly the first Annual Mela of the EWRs was organized at Gandhigram Rural Institute on May 15th, 2005. Women Panchayat Presidents from all the districts of Tamil Nadu participated in the programme and raised several issues.

The main objectives of the programme were to discuss the problems in governance at the grassroots, to identify ways and means to solve those problems, to evolve a strategy to get the support of government officials, to increase their collective voice and their negotiating skill and to seek the help of the media to project their trials and triumphs.

The chief guests of the Mela were Shri A.K. Venkata-subra-manian, I.A.S., Dr. Rajaram, I.A.S., Director, Rural Development, Government of Tamil Nadu, Shri Para-meswaran, ADRD, Dr. T. Karuna-karan, Vice-Chancellor, Gandhi-gram Rural Institute, and Ms. Bimla Chandrasekar, Director, EKTA, Madurai. The issues shared by the EWRs were consolidated and responded by the ADRD.

> ***Ms. D. Latha, Chairperson, Thovalai Panchayat Union, Kanyakumari District*** *stated that due to political intervention the local bodies are not able to perform, even though they have the requisite skills to tackle them. The officials do not co-operate with them and they were afraid of the EWRs who might dominate them. After getting capacity training, EWRs are well versed in all Panchayati Raj Institution Rules and Acts, but during the performance, the EWRs are massively intercepted by the political parties. She felt proud of the EWRs who have the chance of realizing the power given to them.*

Removal of encroachment with RDO through District Administration, periodical capacity building exercises for Panchayat Presidents, circulation of brochure from the government with all information related to Panchayats, micro level planning exercise to all Panchayats, activation of Village Development Committee with relevant Department officials, reduction of electricity tariff, necessary steps for the control of pollution and supply of computers for every

Panchayats—these are the suggestions made by the ADRD with the support of DRD. The whole proceedings were observed by Ms. Bimla Chandrasekar, Director of EKTA, an NGO working for women's rights, gave here comments as hereunder:

- More problems for women and Dalit women.
- Even though right to information is here, we are not getting it.
- Access to resources is limited.
- Legitimization of elected body is missing.
- Women have more responsibilities. Strategies should be evolved considering the aspect.

In order to make them perform better we have to help them by

- Motivation
- Training
- Media help
- Reconsidering the Section 205 of Tamil Nadu Panchayat Act
- The trick of working with differences should be given up

*The District Collector of Pudukottai District released special fund to the **K. Rayavaram** Panchayat for the desiltation of the PWD tank and with his help, **Ms. Rani Sathappan** got NOC from PWD to desilt the water tank belonged to PWD. By doing this exercise PWD tank has come to the fold of Panchayat.*

Other crucial issues are:

- Lack of understanding
- Failure to see women as leaders
- Society should also be trained.

Then the Director of Rural Development visualized the present status of local governance and explained the development activities undertaken by the Tamil Nadu Government for the Welfare of Panchayats. The whole programme was covered by the press for wider dissemination.

Second Annual Mela

Every year the Association of Elected Women Representatives organises a Mela for aggregating and articulating the problems they have faced in the Panchayats and they seek remedy for all the problems. The association develops a strong linkage with media and through media they highlight their problems also. This year, the Mela was organized in the Multi-purpose Auditorium of Gandhigram Rural Institute on 25th September, 2005. Thiru S. Murugaiah I.A.S., Collector, Dindigul District, Thiru P. Murugesan, Project Officer, DRDA, Dindigul District, Dr. G. Pankajam, former Vice-Chancellor, Gandhigram Rural University, and Dr. R. Kousalya Devi, Managing Trustee, Gandhigram Trust were the Chief Guests of the programme. A total of 400 Elected Women Representatives from all over Tamil Nadu participated in the Mela. The Programme was framed to discuss the following areas:

- Experience of success and struggle have to be shared by the Elected Women Representatives.
- Discussing the role of Panchayats in Managing Natural Resources.
- Evolving strategies for strengthening the federation of the EWRs.
- Discussing the role of Elected Women Representatives in Women and Child Welfare.
- Finding out ways and means of achieving Millennium Development Goals and Mission 2007.
- Discussing the role of Panchayats in Health Governance.

Dr. G. Palanithurai, when introducing the significance of the Annual Mela of the Federation of Elected Women Representatives of Tamil Nadu informed that among the 30 lakh representatives, even one-third did not get training. But in Tamil Nadu training was properly given to all. Though training alone is not sufficient to work efficiently, the Elected Women Representatives of Tamil Nadu realized the need of the Federation. In the context of a society where one could witness the feudal thought, casteism, religious fundamentalism, class hierarchy, political groupism and even personal vengeance among the villagers, administering the Village Panchayat involving public is a challenging task.

Against this backdrop, achievements gained by the Women Presidents have to be looked into, Dr. G. Palanithurai advocated. It is in this context the members of the Federation meet in Gandhigram Rural Institute to assess themselves their own federation activities so as to discuss how it could be further strengthened to meet the new challenges in course of time, he observed.

> ***Ms. Rajeswari, President, Koppu Panchayat, Trichy District*** *who is a retired teacher, is pride of 33 per cent reservation for women in local self-governance. She requested EWRs to work cooperatively with Police Department during critical situation. Her area is known for communal violence and riots. She explained that the people are not cooperative with Panchayats in the beginning. Many of the common properties encroached by the influential people, recovered from them with the help of Police. EWRs should learn about the women related laws, and they should get a legal support.*

Mr. S. Murugaiah, District Collector, emphasized the importance of leadership qualities especially self-reliance, co-operation, public opinion and self-sensitive. He demanded action, instead of words from the leaders. He informed that there are 106 women Presidents in Dindigul District and with the help of the Gandhigram proper orientation was given to them. He further advised the participants to do innovations as each human being has varied potentials. Mr. Murugesan, the Project Officer, DRDA Dindigul District, advised the participants to make use of the new enactment "Right to information" and make efforts to contact all the line departments to learn the details of the activities, schemes and budget allocation.

The EWRs shared their experiences, hurdles and success stories with other participants regarding the Common Property Resource Management. Mrs. Jesumary, President of Michaelpattinam Panchayat of Ramanathapuram District expressed that she has transformed the wastelands into fertile lands by growing Jetropa plants and due to the proper maintenance by the people, her

Panchayat is now in the stage of getting yields from those plants. She proudly stated that from this yields not only her Panchayat get income but it will also help the people below poverty line to make their status wealthier.

There are successful Village Panchayat Presidents who redeemed valuable prime land from the powerful encroachers; there are successful judicial intervention to arrest the unmindful exploitation of natural resources. The reason for the success of these cases is that the President of the concerned villages had taken a planned and systematic approach. They collected all the details of the concerned encroachments, sensitized the community by referring the value of the land, scope for its utility for common purposes and the income to the Panchayat. The Presidents made use of the mass media in this regard. Further, they had consistent follow up with the officials. Moreover they had a team of youths and SHGs, Volunteers, Village Leaders and dedicated ward members. This unified tasks was always a successful one in redeeming the encroached lands, Mr. Thirunavukkarasu, Field Coordinator, The Hunger Project explained. He further, shared the role of NGOs in facilitating the President of Vanduvancherry Village Panchayat where the silicon sand mining was illegally undertaken. He appealed to the federation representatives to step into the struggle of their members in the protection of village common.

Strengthening the Federation

To ensure periodical meetings, the District level committee members should be encouraged by GRI to meet themselves. It is also necessary to collect membership fee so as the members would come to establish their status – **Representative from Pudukkottai District.**

It is only after receiving training in GRI we had realized the significance of solidarity among the EWRs. At the union level it is picking up. Meetings during "Namathu Gramam" were wisely used to share the issues among the EWRs. The benefit of being a member is realized by many. Hence it would be easy to start the District unit in the District of Madurai. Men Presidents use their political influence. For women, the federation would be a better choice – **Representative from Madurai District.**

At least if one Women President who is a potential organizer is identified, we could strengthen the association —**Representative from Ramanathapuram District.**

In each district there should be a facilitator to speed up the process of federating the EWR – **Representative from Sivagangai District.**

The President of a Special Village Panchayat explained that the concept of "Networking", "Working together" should be understood by the Women Presidents. Further the social environment should encourage Women Presidents. In the context of Male Chauvinism it is very much necessary for EWRs to have a Federation as it is a very strong support base — **Representative from Trichy District.**

Dr. G. Palanithurai remarked that the strength of women is not through power and authority; it is only by moral strength women can come up. Truthfulness and honesty will bring an image to them.

Dr. Kousalya Devi, The Managing Trustee of the Gandhigram Trust delivered the valedictory address. She emphasized the importance of women literacy and women and children health. She appealed to the participants that being the leader in the rural area, women have more opportunity to transform the society to a new way of understanding with regard to health and welfare. Further the social issues like dowry should also be targeted by women leadership. On witnessing the inspired achievements of many Women Presidents, she addressed all the participants to consolidate their efforts and energy so as their voice could be heard.

Dr. G. Pankajam, Former Vice-Chancellor of Gandhigram Rural Institute stressed the EWRs to concentrate on governance of education.

The Association President *Ms. Ponni Kailasam* consolidated the demands put forth by the District-wise representatives and finally, the EWRs who gathered in the Mela pledged for working towards the Millennium Development Goals (MDGs).

Evolutionary Process of the Federation of EWRs

Reservations for women in the institution of local self-governance become the entry point for the women. Being elected and become the representatives, the women's capacity and efficiency in dealing the public issues especially the issues in the areas of Panchayat administration demanded a systematized building up exercise. And through Gandhigram Rural Institute they had orientation and sensitization.

The sensitized women leaders sharpened their vision on social development issues and the issues related to the management of CPR. In this task they came to the realization that to tackle the issues they needed solidarity among themselves as they had to face the challenges of the selfish individuals. Hence the EWRs established their own association through which they started to address their issues collectively to the officials. The EWRs as a collective body were able to influence the officials and their linkage with the higher officials became strengthened.

In this process of collective empowerment it was realized that the active members of the association had to be equipped properly to handle the need of their teams as well as to spread their association activities as a movement so as they could influence the policy-makers to have a gender perspective in decision-making. Hence the phase of federation had come up.

EWRs of different regions had periodically met and shared their experience. Along with this, they had been empowered with the information on women issues especially local specific ones. To comprehend the process of challenges and achievements, interface programme have been carried out within the state and to the nearby State Kerala.

For a wider dissemination of the experience of the federation and its members, the annual conventions have been conducted for which, the ministers, the higher officials, the women activists and the media were invited. The EWRs made use of these opportunities to project their leadership potential as well as the strength of their solidarity in reacting to the policy of the government when it was anti-social. There were occasions of endorsing the good initiatives of the government also. The 15-point programme of GO Tamil Nadu had been analyzed by the EWR during their annual convention and charted out the area on which they could work in collaboration with the government.

By involving boldly in the public arena through PRIs. The EWRs gained the attention of MLAs and MPs. By sharply making criticism when the GO Tamil Nadu introduced the sale of cheap liquor the EWRs declared that they would launch an agitation if the government referred to withdraw. And they won in their attempt.

The seriousness shown by the EWRs on the issue of the protection and management of CPR resulted into the action by the government mechanism against the activities of illegal mining, encroachments, pollution of water sources. These experiences gave them strength to deal with the higher officials of the Government administration.

The activities of the federation enlisted the hidden potential of the women leadership. The fear and non-faith of common men on the women empowerment had been dispelled by the successful leadership of EWR. The society comes forward to accord honour and respect to the EWR. During the time of social collaboration, public functions and during the time of any other public event, the practice of paying undue importance to the men folk had been slowly changed. Among the EWR, there are many, who independently function and bring progress in the life of commoners especially to the weaker section. The federation had such an impact on their mindset.

There are EWRs who realized the immense scope and opportunities in party politics and so some of them were burred by the political leaders. It is a threat as well as opportunity, they felt.

The federation is now a registered institution with a broader vision and objective of working with all those who come forward to extend their support to the process of women empowerment through Panchayats. The federation has become an identity as well as an institution for the cause of EWRs.

In its evolutionary and functionary process, the federation of EWRs has overcome many challenges and obstacles and is moving up towards the next phase of consolidation and self-actualization.

Implications of Federation

1. The association influenced the government to extend the

existing reservation for women for one more period and the request was accepted by the government. This shows the prime success of the united efforts of the federation.

> ***Ms. Chinnammal, President, Orathupatti Panchayat, Sivagangai District,*** *the EWRs has to organize periodical meetings, not only to strengthen the federation but also to flash the crises to the notice of the concerned departments.*

2. In a meeting with the DRD, the office bearers of the federation pleaded the government for an interface between Panchayat Presidents and the District Collector regularly at periodical intervals. The DRD accepted their request and instructed the Collectors to meet the Panchayat Presidents once in a month.
3. The EWRs, use to bring to notice the problems/demands of their area to the officials at the District level. But the District officials could not solve some issues. The EWRs, in turn take those issues to the notice of the State level officials. There are number of cases that were dealt with by the State level officials through telephone instruction to the District officials.
4. The federation has created a cordial relationship with media and become partners for wider information dissemination. During State Level Committee meetings they use to invite the media and share their challenges, hurdles and success stories. They also sought the help of both print and electronic media to focus the issues they face in Panchayat administration. Now the media has taken steps to project the success stories of EWRs.
5. The EWRs visited several sectoral departments for getting the appropriate administrative details based on the issues they have identified. The Government officials motivated and supported these EWRs for their administration. Many government programmes were drafted based on the suggestions referred by the EWRs and many officials of

the State, National and experts were taken to these village Panchayats.

6. The EWRs motivated other EWRs to perform their functions on their own without proxy. They insisted the Government officials for not allowing the male members to attend the official meetings on behalf of EWRs. Whenever they come across any problem while performing their duty, they approach legal advisors to get it solved and also assist their fellow EWRs in this regard.

> ***Ms. Kaliammal, President, Thethupatti Panchayat, Karur District,*** *compared the federation with the joint family, both of which have various roles and responsibilities for the members, especially women, who are the responsible persons for the smooth maintenance of the family. Likewise, women are the principals who can perform unitedly. She recalled the success stories with the support of the federation in eliminating cheap liquor, Section 205 against EWRs, 2 term reservation for women and voicing against the murder of EWRs by the mafia. So the federation has the power to tackle any kind of global issues.*

7. Apart from performing their assigned role they started working towards social development issues like – eradication of Child labour, Liquor, Violence against women, Providing livelihood security for Vulnerable sections, Physically and mentally challenged persons, Old age persons, Widows, Destitutes etc.
8. In the federation meetings the EWRs used to discuss the problems faced by fellow Dalit Panchayat President and after realizing their problems, they have started working for the upliftment of Dalits in their Panchayat. They have also condemned political parties' interference in Dalit Women Panchayat activities.
9. The EWRs concentrated more on the protection of environment from industrial pollution, prevention of the usage of plastic covers, exploitation of mines and quarries,

etc. They have taken up ventures in solid waste management, tree planting, desiltation of ponds to protect the environment etc. Since they are more sensitized and conscientized, now-a-days the EWRs speak more about social and environmental issues in any public forum instead of telling their success.

10. Through SHGs the EWRs mobilise other women to participate in Gram Sabha and also make them to realise the significance of women's participation in all the activities of the Panchayat. They have shown more interest to learn from other state experience in PRIs especially to learn about their financial management. On the request of the federation, the government accepts to provide computers for Panchayats.

EWRs Demands based on Government Orders

- ✓ Quoted GOs with appropriate Sectoral departments and other State GOs
- ✓ People's participation
- ✓ Activation of committees
- ✓ Claim their rights
- ✓ Livelihood security for the marginalized sectors
- ✓ Quality maintenance (Panchayat assets)
- ✓ Protection of environment
- ✓ Proper Information Dissemination by officials
- ✓ Linkage with SHGs.

11. The EWRs federation meets the politicians frequently to incorporate their demands in the legislative and parliament discussions.
12. By seeing their assertiveness and performance now-a-days many institutions from all over the country are inviting these EWRs to deliver lecture regarding their experiences.
13. The experienced EWRs have become role models and also a trainer to other representatives.

- Learning from other role models, they have started mobilizing internal resources for income generation.
- In order to strengthen their action and to gain critical mass, now-a-days, EWRs have started associating and

working with members of women SHGs. They have created communal harmony and motivate women's participation in Panchayat activities.

- In order to gain strength, to solve a particular problem, they seek the assistance of media, NGOs, SHGs, Youth organizations etc.

14. The EWRs motivate the male representatives of PRIs to work for women and other marginalised sections of the society.
15. Many EWRs have received awards for ensuring the sanitation and cleanliness; they have organised medical camps and social awareness campaign to help the rural mass. They take care of their village women, children, teen-age girls, old age women, physically challenged, etc. They visit the PHCs and Anganwadis periodically and advice the staff for proper maintenance.
16. The EWRs visit Anganwadi, Noon-meal centre and schools frequently. This gives a moral boost to the staff of these centres for proper functioning.
17. To implement the concept of bio-village, these EWRs joined hands with the SHGs, e.g. Vermi Compost, Organic farming, Solid Waste Management, Maintenance of Integrated Sanitary Complex, Tree planting etc.
18. Most of the Panchayat lands are occupied by encroachers. The EWRs concentrate more on evicting the encroachments and most of the EWRs removed the encroachment with people's support.

The Present Scenario

1. The members and office-bearers of the federation of EWRs have acquired role clarity by mutual sharing and under-standing and working together. They have gained new knowledge and understanding on the concepts of decentralization, participatory democracy, and sustainable development, the role of CBOs and gender and social justice.

2. With regard to the performance of Dalit Presidents, the support and the assistance of the federation have equipped them to function independently.
3. Women leaders who are in this federating arrangement are highly sensitized on the issues of social development like

   - Increasing school enrollment, maintenance of school and students' hygiene
   - Construction of public and individual toilets, women's sanitary complex and proper drainage
   - Arrangements for Rain Water Harvesting (RWH) to prevent water scarcity
   - RCH administered through Village Health Nurse and Anganwadi Teacher
   - Maintenance of CPRs for enhancing the Panchayat economy
   - Process of solid waste management, tree planting and eradication of plastic items for protecting the environment
   - Most of the Government programmes like SSA, RWH, Watershed Management and Sanitation are planned and initiated by the Presidents.

Out come

✓ Reservation has been maintained for the second time for women and Dalit.

✓ Cheap liquor scheme was stopped from 14th April, 2002.

✓ Funds released in time.

✓ Government assured to release funds as monthly instalments.

✓ The culprits who murdered Ms. Menaka were arrested and the compensation was also increased.

✓ Election was announced for the four reserved Panchayats.

✓ Sand quarrying has been controlled.

✓ Illicit liquor is controlled in several Panchayats.

✓ Prows culture is regulated

✓ Encroachment had been removed in several Panchayats.

4. The federation has sensitized the EWRs on independence in Panchayat Raj activities and offered guidance and facilities for their empowerment in this regard and also criticized openly the practice of proxy.
5. Attitudinal and behavioural changes are visible: several EWRs have ventured upon innovative experiments, struggling to protect CPRs, courageously interacting with the press, facing challenges posed by politicians, making use of political parties for their cause, quickly and clearly joining together in raising issues and reacting, going without accompanying men to far-away places to attend training programmes/meetings.
6. Upholding women's rights and working for the eradication of violence against women. Opposing the authority and system of the traditional Panchayat.
7. Feeling of second class citizens and subordination has been shed by many members of the federation. They have gained recognition and ensured their presence in formal and informal meetings in the villages. It is a success for women's leadership.
8. The federation has found a way for a meaningful relationship with the bureaucracy, which has mitigated the misunderstandings between the EWRs and the officials. An instance of strongly lobbying and success in influencing policy-making is the discontinuation of the cheap liquor policy.
9. The federation has successfully established networks with local NGOs, SHGs and women activists. It has helped to improve their perception and efficiency in administration and delivery of services.
10. The federation has made efficient use of the services of the mass media for projecting the issues related to their activities.
11. The federation has properly represented the Tamil Nadu State in the All India body, the Association of Local Governments of India (ALGI). The President of Tamil Nadu EWRs is now serving as its State organizer.

12. During the first tenure, the EWRs had the backing of their family members to face the elections. In the second elections they projected their performance. Many EWRs have decided to contest for the open seats in the next elections.

The mechanism and procedure to be implemented

Sl. No.	*Mechanism*	*Procedure*
1.	Need district-wise NGOs support structure for the federation for their activities.	Committed NGOs have to be identified and special orientation has to be given to these NGOs.
2.	Equal representation from all districts in the State Executive Committee.	Northern Districts of Tamil Nadu need special focus in the federation activities at the district level.
3.	Monthly meeting at union level, quarterly meeting at district level and biannual meeting at State level.	Annual membership and registration fee have to be collected from the EWRs for a common fund to run the administration of the federation by the President.
4.	Sharing issues and projecting the same for solutions.	Block level conveners and district level Presidents have to be oriented and facilitated.
5.	Consolidation of issues, lobbying and problem solving process to be indicated.	Documentation and information to be disseminated.
6.	Legal and administrative information for empowerment.	Establishing a communication system between union and district and between District and State Levels.
7.	Special concentration on gender, women and child issues.	Facilitation through legal experts and administrative experts.

Sum-up

The critical mass (33.3% of women elected representatives) has come to perform the critical functions (attacking the issues of hunger, poverty, gender and untouchability) despite facing a multitude of problems in the process of their governance and managing the institutions. They have their own record of achievements and story of struggles. But they are determined to move further to occupy the public space. The journey has started and the support structure has been created to push forward the onward march.

Their imprints in governance, management of institutions, negotiating with different partners and stakeholders, attacking issues and managing the crowd are unique and different from those of men and members of other higher level institutions. Their expressions, perceptions, opinions and observations provide an array of policy implications.

Way Forward

Capacity building for EWRs has to be conducted within a month after they assume office. The training should be intensive and residential. It should not be conducted in the Block Development Office. It should be given only in training institutions. Training should be made mandatory and on any account their males should not be allowed to attend the training. In the training programme, Tamil Nadu Panchayati Raj Act, 1994 updated version, Rules, Government Orders and details of Schemes of Rural Development should be given to all Panchayat leaders as a tool kit for Panchayat Management. The training package should include gender and social development components. In each and every training programme a well-experienced Panchayat President should be made as a resource person to share her experience with other participants. The same training should be given to officials also at the same time. Periodical refresher courses say, once a year, can be organised. Once a month, the District Collector must convene a meeting of officials to redress the problems faced by the women leaders in Panchayat administration.

Males of the elected women representatives' families should not be allowed to occupy the chair and to participate in the official meetings. This has to be followed rigorously and religiously. They should not be permitted to sign any document on behalf of the elected women representatives. Periodically an interface has to be arranged for women leaders with other Panchayats, preferably in other states. This opportunity has to be given to the maximum number of people. The women leaders' federation is a registered body and hence it has to be recognized by the government. A support structure has to be created for women and Dalit leaders.

Learnings

Elected women leaders are of different categories. They are educated, uneducated, highly sophisticated, rich, poor, wage earners, Dalits and others. There are leaders with political orientation and party background. They look at issues only from their party perspective. There are leaders without any political background but they are under the clutches of their husbands or the male members of their families. There are leaders who have commitments and values but there is no awareness and information. There are leaders with high political aspirations. It is to be noted that the leaders who are deeply committed to the issues of the people without political background continue to be active members of the Federation. The Federation attracts more number of Gram Panchayat women leaders as the Gram Panchayat is freed from the party fold and the problems focused on in the Federation are mostly the problems faced by the Gram Panchayat women leaders. One layer of elected women representatives is alert and they are oriented and conscientized but the other segments are not so well oriented. When oriented and motivated leaders take up the development issues, they face a volley of problems. To tackle all these problems they require a support structure. They demand periodical sensitization on vital issues affecting women and other marginalized groups. They require periodical update on Government orders and new schemes of the Government. They are in need of periodical interface programmes. Not all the women leaders of rural and urban local bodies have served the federate. Those who have come out despite obstacles and barriers and those who are struggling with determination have joined together. A large number of elected representatives have not come out of their houses and have not even visited their offices. They are asked to remain inside their houses and the males of their families operate their offices. The Federation is slowly moving towards them. One positive aspect is that when the successful women leaders are being appreciated and covered in the media, the males of the families of the elected women representatives develop an aspiration that their women leaders should also get such appreciation. The Federation has created such a mindset. There is a potential danger in that. The potential leaders who can mobilize the masses at the grassroots level are lured by the political leaders. There are women leaders who look at issues from the perspective of the people and want to serve the people at the cost of their own prospects and, hence, they tend to toe the line of the ruling party in the State Government purely with the intention of getting things done for the people.

By their local action significant progress and changes are made in the life of the communities which, in turn, draw the attention of the academics, administrators and the media. After seeing the implications of women's involvement in governance throughout the world, steps have been taken at the grassroots to build their capacity and skill, sharpen their leadership, and forge alliances with varied partners to project the emergence of the alternative governance. Grassroots women deal with everyday survival and livelihood issues from their own perspective and with the most ingenious solutions as they have a knowledge base which is local in character.

They want to achieve something in life when an opportunity is given. They tend to seek a support base for their activities, especially for increasing their efficiency and capability. They improve their skills constantly and their skill is used for managing the Panchayats. Issues of women and development are brought to the public for debate. They are open to learning and patient to listen. They convert challenges into opportunities. They assume responsibilities and attempt innovations. By their actions, they create new contours of decentralization of powers.

They build alliances to get support for their activities and to spread their innovations and achievements. They run the administration transparently and reduce corruption. They develop alternative governance to achieve development with the participation of the people. A new culture is being evolved and a new value profile is being evolved at the grassroots by the women leaders through their handling of powers. They are emerging models to be emulated. They have registered a striking difference in governing the grassroots institutions. Now the women federation leaders are voicing a demand that all Gram Panchayats should be reserved for women since, in Tamil Nadu, the Gram Panchayat is freed from political contest.

Details of Activities – II Phase

Sl. No.	*Name of the Activity*	*Date*	*Details*
1	2	3	4
1.	Interface Programme	11.07.2003	Meeting with DRD, Chennai
2.	Interface Programme	30.07.2003	Meeting with World Bank Officials at Gandhigram Rural Institute
3.	Regional Workshop	21.10.2003	Networking Elected Women Representatives on Gender and Social Development Issues
4.	Regional Workshop	27.12.2003	Networking Elected Women Representatives of Thiruvarur, Tanjore and Nagapattinam Districts.
5.	Network Meeting	27.01.2004 to 31.01.2004	Associating SC/ST Women Panchayat Union Chairperson
6.	Network Meeting	11.02.2004 to 03.03.2004	Associating Elected Women Representatives of Tuticorin District
7.	Interface Programme	16.02.2004	Meeting with DRD, Chennai
8.	Interface Programme	17.02.2004 to 19.02.2004	Interface with SSF, Bangalore
9.	Network Meeting	11.02.2004 to 03.03.2004	Associating Elected Women Representatives of Tuticorin District
10.	Interface Programme	16.02.2004	Meeting with DRD, Chennai
11.	Interface Programme	17.02.2004 to 19.02.2004	Interface with SSF, Bangalore

1	2	3	4
12.	State Level Workshop	14.06.2004 to 18.06.2004	Associating Elected Women Representatives of Cuddalore District
13.	Network Meeting	21.06.2004 to 25.06.2004	Associating Elected Women Representatives of Tirunelvelli District
14.	Interface Programme	20.07.2004 to 21.07.2004	Exposure visit to Semmipalayam and Odan-thurai, Coimabtore District
15.	Interface Programme	29.08.2004 to 30.08.2004	Exposure visit to Semmi-palayam and Odanthurai, Coimabtore District
16.	Interface Programme	27.10.2004 to 28.10.2004	Exposure visit to Semmi-palayam and Odanthurai, Coimbatore District
17.	State Level Workshop	24.11.2004	Networking Elected Women Representatives
18.	Network Meeting	20.12.2004 to 02.12.2004	Associating Elected Women Representatives of Thiruvarur District
19.	Network Meeting	30.12.2004 to 03.01.2004	Associating Elected Women Representatives of Erode District
20.	State Level Workshop	05.03.2005	Networking Elected Women Representatives, Chennai
21.	Interface Programme	21.03.2005	Meeting with DRD, Chennai
22.	Workshop on ST Women Panchayat Presidents of Tamil Nadu on CPRs	28.03.2005 to 29.03.2005	ST Women Panchayat Presidents are federated
23.	Annual Mela	15.05.2005	Annual Mela of Elected Women Representatives of Local Bodies in Tamil Nadu
24.	Regional Workshop	22.05.2005	Elected Women Representatives experience sharing with Minister of West Bengal
25.	Regional Workshop	02.06.2005	Networking of Elected Women Representatives of Cuddalore District
26.	Regional Workshop	18.06.2005	Networking of Elected Women Representatives of Trichy District

1	2	3	4
27.	Interface Programme	02.07.2005 to 09.07.2005	Elected Women Representatives exposure visit to West Bengal
28.	Regional Workshop	11.08.2005 to 12.08.2005	Experience sharing with second term Presidents
29.	Annual Mela	25.09.2005	Annual Mela of Elected Women Representatives of Local Bodies
30.	Interface Programme	24.10.2005 to 25.10.2005	Exposure visit to Ramanathapuram District

11

ARE THEY WITHDRAWING FROM PUBLIC SPACE?

Introduction

Elected Women Representatives have a Federation in Tamil Nadu and it is functioning for the past six years. Sixty-four elected women representatives from twenty-nine districts–district office-bearers who are in the Federation for the past six years—met and discussed some of their experiences in Gandhigram Rural Institute to draw a road map for their Federation jointly and individually for themselves. Their successes, struggles and needs were discussed thoroughly and openly. Deep-rooted issues, memorable solid achievements, historic struggles have been highlighted in their deliberations. They are covered in this brief write up.

Observation

"We have experienced power for eight years to carry out activities for the benefit of the people as seats have been reserved for women in local bodies for two consecutive terms and now the principle of rotation has to be operated and, as a result, the women who have come to local bodies in the past two terms from the same constituency will have either to contest in a general constituency or withdraw from the public space or take another lower or higher level position in the same Panchayat system," observed by Ms. Susila, one of the office-bearers who assembled in Gandhigram on 11th and 12th of August, 2005. The discussion was around the space which they were occupying currently.

Struggle to Come out from Their House

Reservation of seats for women in local bodies pulled and pushed them from the house to the public space. Working as MLA or MP or in any other office by women would not bring this much of pressure on the women as the elected women representatives at the lowest level who confront a multitude of obstacles and problems. Till date many of the elected women representatives are struggling to come out from their houses to the office when they have to discharge responsibilities. They claim that coming out from their houses to the office itself is victory as many of them are not able to come out from their house from the day of election. Such kind of repressive husbands co-opted their wives to retain power with them for which they have used the women. The elected women representatives' Association is working for the release of the house-arrested elected women representatives through Government Orders. The dominant discourse in many of the places is that as soon as the seats were reserved for women, the men who had prepared themselves to contest in the elections adopted a strategy of preparing a woman candidate from the respective families or social groups and saw the women elected to the positions. Behind all women, men were working with high enthusiasm before the election in the belief that if they were elected, the positions would be handled by the men of the respective families. After the election, the scenario changed and many players started acting in the local bodies to build up the capacity and skill of the leaders, passing orders prohibiting men to attend official meetings on behalf of the women leaders. Yet a segment of bureaucracy is not sensitive to the issues of women and, hence, the officials preferred to discuss official matters with the males of the elected women representatives based on the argument that the uneducated family women do not know anything about the administrative system. Under this pretext they ignore the elected women representatives and sometimes they are even being marginalized.

Capacity Building

Many of the EWRs do not attend training programmes not because they are not interested but because they are not allowed by their male family members to attend the training. They lay down a condition to the EWRs that they will also attend the training programme along with the EWRs. When this demand is unmet, the EWRs are not permitted to attend the training. Training is of two types. One is official and government oriented. The other is semi-official and real leadership preparation. In all government training programmes, EWRs are threatened that unless they obey the officials, they cannot run the Panchayats. They are asked to carry out the Panchayat administration as per the direction of the officials. In a sense it is a preparation of slaves to the Government officials. In the other type negotiating skill is built up in the leader. A detailed analysis of devolution and where the Panchayats are now, what is to be done in the Panchayat for the people and what should be done to strengthen the Panchayat are being discussed in a participatory way.

In a residential training a book consisting of the original Act, Government Orders, details of rural development schemes, and rules are being given and training is given to EWRs on how to use all those documents for Panchayat administration. The training is not an one time affair. It is a continuous process. The role of the training institution is not only to offer training but also to guide the Panchayat Presidents while they are on the job. It is almost a support structure. The EWRs attend the programmes without fail in Gandhigram as it is a support structure and it helps EWRs when they are in trouble. Whenever EWRs face problem, they use three phone numbers: 0451-2451775, 2451063, 044-22235659. When EWRs are harassed by officials, even letters are being drafted in Gandhigram and sent to the concerned officials.

Struggle to Succeed

A sizeable section of the women leaders have been drawn from their houses and have been made to attend meetings and interact with officials and made to realize their worth and they have started functioning as leaders in managing the Panchayats. Their vision has been broadened and their understanding of the society has been widened. When they started functioning intensively, they faced a volley of problems and yet the joy they felt was immeasurable. They felt that the stigma of incompetence had gone. The continuous crisis management in the Panchayat and the crowd management in the Gram Sabha have made them courageous. But the process is painful. Just like a student they learn everyday about society, the Panchayat and government. Further achievements made by them in the Panchayat make them develop confidence in themselves and the system.

The achievements made by EWRs are captured through the media. Their struggles are also captured and they are being published, telecast and broadcast because of the efforts of the Hunger Project. When the media brought to light the achievements, the other Panchayat Presidents developed aspirations to follow the models. The continuous sensitization programme conducted for the media helped a lot to capture such success and struggles.

Learning from Struggle

The elected women representatives, by their performance, by their struggle, and by their achievements, got recognition in the society and this recognition made the other womenfolk develop an aspiration to become Panchayat Presidents. In the past eight years, the elected women representatives have learnt the art of mobilising the people for conducting the Gram Sabha meeting, and developing partnership with officials and other social capitals to perform their role and discharge their responsibilities. Further the elected women representatives have become conscious of women issues because of continuous capacity building exercise and periodical interaction with activists. Working on the issues of women needs a specific strategy and before that people have to be conscientized. Unless people are conscientized on the issues of women, the problems of women cannot be addressed. It is also realised by the elected women representatives that the problems in society and specifically the problems of women, children, Dalits and other marginalized groups can be attacked through collectives. Thus they have realised the potential of collective action. They have a deeper understanding of the issues of the marginalized. This is because of the continuous training. The thought process and mindset of the women leaders in the beginning were in no way different from those of men leaders'. But, in the course of training and regular interaction with gender specialists, the attitude, perception, view and understanding of the women leaders on the issues of women have changed.

Women to Women

Yet another serious issue is conscientizing women on their own problems. They need four literacies, namely, word literacy, money literacy, body literacy and civil literacy. It is a tough job to be done. Since the presence of Self Help Groups women is visible and has become a force to reckon with, they can be used for this purpose. To some extent they are now made literate. It has been realised by the elected women representatives that, with the alliance of SHG members, women leaders in the Panchayats can perform several functions in the domain of children and women. Women leaders have come to the stage of developing a vision for their Panchayats, for the children of their village. They have realised the importance of social development. Now it is easy for the government to push through its social development agenda through the elected women representatives. To that level, elected women representatives are sensitized and oriented. Environmental protection, health governance, governance of education, vulnerability reduction and internal resource mobilization are the major subjects on which the women leaders are trained. At the Panchayat level, they are able to manage the issues effectively. But these models have to be spread to other areas. The models are limited in number. Elected women representatives have come to the level of working on millennium development goals. There are leaders who have developed leadership to attract political parties. Now political parties have started luring the elected women representatives who command a greater deal of respect among the people by their excellent performance.

The elected women leaders who have legitimately occupied their space and manage the institutions are concerned about the confinement of the other elected women leaders by their male family members. The EWRs, through their Associations and Federations, have persuaded the officials not to allow the males in any of the official meetings in the place of EWRs. In many places even higher officials allow the males to carry out activities on behalf of the EWRs in the name of achieving targets. Unless this malaise is checked, the formation of a critical mass will be weakened.

EWR and CPR

Common properties are the lifeline of the poor and also another source of income to the Panchayats. Removing the encroachments is not an easy task and yet elected women representatives have taken steps to remove the encroachments. In this process they have to undergo ordeals. Urapakkam Gram Panchayat President Ms. Menaka lost her life when she took steps to remove encroachments in her Panchayat area. Vanduvanchery Gram Panchayat President Ms. Rani Muniyakannu moved the court to protect the silicon soil. Appipalayam Gram Panchayat President Ms. Easwari fought against industrial pollution in her Panchayat area. Now the elected women representatives have learnt the art of struggling for justice. A large number of elected women representatives have taken innovative steps to augment resources from the assets and natural resources of the Panchayats. Many Panchayats have regained their common properties. Series of steps have been taken to improve the conditions of the commons. The elected women representatives have changed the conflict between Panchayats and SHGs and now both are playing complementary roles to each other for the benefit of the people in the rural areas. Elected women representatives have realised the importance of governance and poverty reduction and development at the grassroots. They have internalized the practice of supervision to be done by the Panchayats on the service delivery institutions. They have given utmost importance to health governance, environment governance and educational governance.

Obstacles

It is true that the so-called beneficiaries of the government (really they are not eligible to become beneficiaries but they got their names included by wielding political power) never allow the Gram Sabha to speak the truth. For this they have a strategy of disturbing the Gram Sabha meeting by using unparliamentary words and indulging in character assassination. In the absence of a strong support base many women leaders are in a disturbed mental state.

Officials always exhibit their non-cooperative attitude towards the elected women representatives and, moreover, they want to dominate the women leaders. Women leaders, whenever they go to an office, go with the statistics and the relevant Government orders to convince the officials. On many occasions, the officials are exposed as the elected women representatives bring up real issues and speak with authority whereas the officials do not have authentic documents. This negotiating capacity has been injected into the blood of the EWRs in Gandhigram through training programmes. The Act, Government Orders, Rules, Scheme details are provided in the form of an anthology to everyone of the trainees and they are being oriented on how to use data and how to use the book. Every Panchayat leader should negotiate with officials with self-respect and self-dignity and this has been taught to them by the Gandhigram training team. The officials prefer only the males of the elected women representatives as it is easy for the officials to negotiate with the husbands and other family members. The corrupt system wants to co-opt the women also. But they do not succeed.

The administrative structure is so complicated in our society. Government officials find it very difficult to bring convergence or synergy among the officials working in different departments. Likewise the departments act on the basis of directions from their officials in the line departments and not on the basis of the orders of the government. A Government order passed by the Rural Development Department is not respected by the Health Department. All departments are sectorally divided and they do not have a perspective of serving the people but they have a perspective of keeping the department activities intact and in achieving their target and satisfying their higher officials.

There is a fitting case in Pudukkottai District. When K. Rayawaram Gram Panchayat President Ms. Rani Sathappan approached the District Collector for financial sanction to desilt the tank managed by the PWD the sensitive Collector passed orders immediately and sanctioned money. But, to carry out the work, the President had to get a no objection certificate from the Public Works Department (PWD). To get such a letter she has to visit the office fifteen times. On the fifteenth day the officials took only two minutes to prepare such a letter and she got it. From this, one can imagine how Government offices respond to Panchayat leaders' demands.

As the Panchayat leaders live near to the people, they are always responsive and accountable and they perform their duties perfectly but officials do not have that mentality and people do not have any hold over the officials. Excepting politicians, nobody can control the officials. It is an irony that the leaders who are responsible and responsive do not have the power but the officials who do not respond to the people have power. Panchayat leaders submit petitions to Government offices for which there is no respect. The leaders who have enough influence are respected in the offices and others are fighting against the bureaucracy. There is yet another serious issue, namely, managerial perspective, which is so essential for the administration of the Panchayats. Neither the State Government nor the Panchayat leaders have a managerial perspective to look at the functioning of Panchayats. It is unfortunate that many of the Panchayats, from the perspective of management, are unviable. Such Panchayats have to be merged with a neighbouring Panchayat to make it administratively and managerially viable. As a result Panchayat leaders find it difficult to run the administration and the people are suffering.

Our system is always favourable only to the rich not to the poor. There is a case where the Panchayat is asked to carry out a work and claim the amount later for which the Panchayat President has to invest money from her own purse and then only get the money back from the Departments. Where will a poor woman representative go for money? So she has to rely on money-lenders. Since the system is complicated and corrupt this kind of practice will lead to further corruption. For the elected women representatives, capacity building is the only salvation for their performance. Periodical interface with other leaders and officials will help them a lot. Refresher courses have to be conducted. Visiting other states and interacting with leaders of other states will help them a lot. Here also one has to recognize the role of Gandhigram Rural Institute. Gandhigram Rural Institute arranges for EWRs to visit other Panchayats within the district, within the State and also to visit other states. It is a powerful learning instrument. Elected women representatives have visited Kerala, West Bengal, Karnataka and New Delhi.

There are different strategies adopted by organisations working for women empowerment and devolution of powers and by women leaders to achieve what they ought to achieve in the space created for the elected women representatives. The strategy adopted by Gandhigram Rural Institute is to appeal to many of the elected women representatives as the strategy envisages a smooth transition for EWRs from their houses to the public space without making much noise. It always advocates building alliance with all stakeholders in the process. The assertion of the EWRs is not through oral dialogue but through performance, building capacity, skill and capability and alliance and performing their roles and responsibilities.

In the political and administrative system, one has to understand the level of corruption. Otherwise it is very difficult to manage the Panchayat. Many of them understood the corrupt practices and they moved into the track. But women leaders did not understand the whole process. The reason why officials do not like to interact with women representative is that they are not in a position to understand the nuances of corruption. They not even understood the language of corruption and its dialects. As a result many of them are struggling. In many places, male family members of elected women representatives moved into the corrupt track by co-opting themselves with the officials and as a result there was no problem for those women leaders. In the world of reform through technology, the administrative procedures have to be made simple. Now an ordinary person cannot understand the administrative procedures and, as a result, Panchayat leaders are threatened. The women leaders time and again discuss how effectively women leaders can emerge as role models for others. In this context one has to recognize the struggle of the EWRs. On many occasions Panchayats are badly projected by the media. Of course, the media can highlight negative issues of Panchayats. But there are remarkable achievements made by women leaders and they are also to be captured by the media. But it is not happening. Of course, the scenario is changing as Gandhigram Rural Institute is taking earnest efforts to sensitize the media through its media workshops. Wherein outstanding women representatives are invited to share their experiences with the media. But this kind of effort has to be taken massively throughout the nation.

It is a pity that training programmes are not seriously thought of and conducted by the government. The majority of the women leaders are not trained fully. Elected women representatives who are in the women Federation are well trained as they are trained by The Hunger Project in Gandhigram. The experts who take classes for the women leaders are retired Additional Directors of Rural Development, Government of Tamil Nadu. They are thorough with the Act, Rules, Procedures, Government Orders and Schemes. They have commitment also. Whenever the women leaders have any doubt, they can contact the resource persons over phone. They give directions and advice. Gandhigram Rural Institute acts as a supporting resource centre providing the wherewithal to stand on their own legs. But it is not the case for all. Of course, the government also conducts training programmes. Resource persons are Extension Officers and Block Development Officers and they teach the subject "Follow the officials; otherwise you will be booked under Section 205". They teach what not to do in the Panchayat instead what to do in the Panchayat.

Section 205 is a provision in the Tamil Nadu Panchayat Act, 1994 which gives arbitrary power to the District Collector to remove the elected Gram Panchayat leader. This has been used by all officials in this state to threaten the elected representatives. By using this provision Government officials have made them act as they like. If we take a list of the elected representatives who have been sacked by using Section 205, most of them are either women or Dalits. Weak women leaders are being easily handled by the officials through the Panchayat Clerk. There are wise women leaders who carefully manage to elect another woman as Vice-President and both of them select a woman as clerk. Others, without knowing this strategy, have men Vice-Presidents who tend to dominate. In that context, the elected women representatives' Federation has demanded the State Government to reserve the Vice-President's post along with President's post for women. Whenever the Panchayat leaders do not cooperate with the officials in their misdeeds, the officials threaten the Panchayat leaders by asking them to bring four years' accounts for verification to the Block Development Office. The women leaders who are strong, knowledgeable with needed support are able to stand up to this and they won't budge. Others succumb to the pressure given by the officials.

There are Panchayat Presidents who have done commendable work in the Panchayats but are not recommended for awards and incentives which are being given by the government. But, instead, ruling party oriented Panchayat Presidents have been selected for awards and incentives. This kind of practice developed by the officials is demoralizing others.

A good number of Panchayats draw the attention of the media and outsiders by their commendable performance. They are appreciated by the higher officials. But the same higher officials never help those Panchayat leaders who are in deep trouble because of the lower level officials. It is obvious from the experience of the Panchayat leaders that the lower level officials are not under the control of the higher officials. Unless the officials at the lower level are properly oriented and controlled by the higher officials, the lower level officials will continue to disturb the Panchayats and destabilize them.

There are women representatives who are in need of counselling as they are undergoing torture in the family due to the harassment of their husbands. There are umpteen number of cases and they have several stories to tell. These women leaders are neither in a position to reveal the problems openly nor in a position of to solve them amicably within the family. Women leaders have been asked to sign documents as per the directions of their husbands and all their deeds are totally corrupt deeds for which the elected women leaders are facing charges. They in fact bow their heads in front of others and officials. There are several reports of wife beating by husbands because the women leaders refuse to accept the directions of their husbands. Compared to SHGs, local body institutions are not getting due attention from the State Government. In our state there is no Secretary for Panchayats, there is no Director of Panchayats. As a result all officials at all levels pay attention to reviewing the progress of schemes and programmes but no one cares for the progress of Panchayats. They find fault with Panchayats if they do not carry out their schemes and programmes. They do not have a perspective to look at the Panchayats as institutions of governance. If Panchayats are able to perform certain things it is because of the officials not because of the leaders. Officials look at Panchayats with contempt as competitors or rivals.

For Panchayat activities, the Panchayat leaders cannot get the needed support from the sectoral departments. Panchayats demand certain things based on the demands of the people but the officials do not care about these demands. On many occasions, the officials in their own way develop pet projects. While implementing these projects, they give money only to a few Panchayats whose Presidents are "yes" men or "yes" women to the officials. This kind of patronage demoralizes the other Panchayat Presidents. It is the experience of the leaders that the officials want only "yes" from the Panchayat leaders. They do not want leaders; they want only subordinates. At every level officials feel that they are the superiors. This culture has to be changed. The women leaders are fighting against this culture. Yet it is painful. Corrupt PRI leaders have a perfect alliance with the corrupt officials and nobody bothers about it. Poor women leaders and Dalit leaders are the victims of the procedures as they refuse to form an alliance with the corrupt officials.

MLAs and MPs are having constituency development fund and they spend it without having any consultation with the Gram Panchayat leaders. People project their demands in the Gram Sabha and they are consolidated by the Presidents and they are presented to MLAs and MPs. But they allocate the money to some other works which are not the felt needs of the people. They are the priority work of the party men and the same party men get that benefits and not the villagers. When such a kind of privilege is given to MLAs and MPs what is wrong in demanding such funds for Panchayat Presidents as Panchayat Area Development fund.

Everyone knows money is being wasted by the MPs and MLAs. It is a simple calculation, that an MP will get Rs.10 crore rupees during the five year period. If he or she gets 10 per cent of the total amount from the contractors through whom all activities are carried out by the MP and the MLA, one can manage Rs. one crore for the next election. Likewise one MLA can manage 50 lakh rupees. It is a known fact that MP LAD fund and MLA Constituency fund are meant for development but they are wasting people's money. Even for small facilities Panchayats are starving for money but MLAs and MPs are spending their money on sand, brick and mortar. It is sad to note that these MPs and MLAs are deciding the fate of Panchayats.

MLAs and MPs are looking at Panchayats as parallel bodies to them. A good Panchayat leader by his/her performance gets the whole hearted support of the people and the local Panchayat leader becomes powerful. Some of the wise Panchayat leaders corner the MPs and MLAs with the support of the community. The elected women representatives adopted a strategy by which a resolution was passed in the Gram Sabha by which, for a specific work, they seek funds from their MLA and MP. For the MPs and MLAs, there is no other option except accepting it as it is the decision of the Gram Sabha. If the demands are not met, they cannot go to the village again for votes. A simple devise is enough to make everyone accountable.

Whenever training is being discussed they target only the elected local body leaders but conveniently they leave out officials from top to bottom and MLAs and MPs are also excluded. For the smooth functioning of local bodies, the cooperation of the officials and the support of MLAs and MPs are essential. But these officials and leaders are not sensitive either to decentralized governance or to the crisis of social development. It is necessary to train the officials and MLAs and MPs. MPs and MLAs are having their own domain of activities. But it is unfortunate that they are also competing with the local body leaders in carrying out the activities. Proper training is needed for all, not only for Panchayat leaders. Political parties are also doing lip service to Panchayats. They are doing a number of dharnas and struggles but they are not taking the devolution of powers to local bodies as a serious issue. Their stand on devolution has to be cleared.

It is unequivocally stressed that the elected women representatives should have negotiating skills to negotiate with officials and other representatives to get things done for the people. While analysing many of the successful cases in Panchayats by the women leaders it is demonstrated clearly that wherever the elected women leaders are having negotiating skills, they have succeeded in their attempts. Yet another skill is needed for the elected women representatives, i.e., crowd management. In the Indian context crowd management is essential as it is demonstrated that the public have developed a strategy for getting things done: they pull the crowd and by showing the crowd they get things done. In Panchayats on many occasions managing the Gram Sabha is a tough job for the elected women leaders. Whoever has got the art of managing the crowd has succeeded and others have drowned in it. Hence Panchayat leaders need such a kind of orientation. In the Panchayats, along with the President, the Vice-President's position should also be reserved for women. In most places, the Vice-Presidents (men) have tried their best to sideline the Panchayat Presidents with the help of the clerk and Ward Members. Only strong women Presidents can withstand the pressure from the men Vice-Presidents. If the elected woman representative is a Dalit woman, and the Vice-President is a caste Hindu, the Panchayat administration will be in the hands of the Vice-President. It will be a struggle for the elected woman representative to redeem the Panchayat from the clutches of the Vice-President.

There is yet another issue preventing the elected women representatives from occupying the position for which she was elected. Officials encourage the males of the elected women representatives' family to attend the official meetings, carry out Panchayat activities, claim the cheques etc. The elected women representatives are not oriented in the corrupt practices of the administration and, hence, they want to cultivate only through the males of the family. This practice has to be curbed. The concept of community wellbeing is not working in the minds of the people. It is always individual benefits that work in the minds of the people. In this context it is very difficult to take community oriented decisions. In many Panchayats the elected women representatives have taken tough decisions earning the displeasure of many families and finally, after seeing the implications of such decisions, people have started supporting the Panchayat President. Till the people see the outcome of such tough decisions, the Panchayat Presidents are being disturbed.

There is yet another issue which is significant in the process of decentralization of powers. It is micro level planning. Micro level planning is important since it will alter the existing paradigm of development activities. The supply driven activities can be changed to demand driven activities only through planning at the micro level. People will look at their life, conditions and resources only through this process. The community will take over ownership of development only through a plan. But it is not happening in all the Panchayats. In the absence of the people, officials' plan is being implemented. Many Panchayats headed by women did planning successfully and now they are carrying out the planned activities. Even in implementing the plan, they have to struggle a lot. Wherever honest officials are in position, EWRs are getting the needed support to implement the plans. In other places, officials look for money.

Many of the elected women representatives, especially from the Dalit community, have carried out substantial programmes in their villages for development. They have been facing a volley of problems and this challenging position has made the Dalit women think whether the needed ambience is created for the Dalit women to contest in the elections. The difficult life does not encourage Dalit women to contest again nor attract another woman. Many of them are losing their faith, as they are not able to function independently. The Dalit women leaders who are co-opted have no problem. But they cannot address the problems of the marginalized or the Dalits.

It is also observed in their interaction that in the existing corrupt system of administration women are finding it very difficult to manage the Panchayats. There are several categories of leaders among women. One group are solid achievers. They have demonstrated their capability by which they manage the Panchayat, the people and the officials. They are forerunners. They are pathfinders. There is yet another group of leaders, struggling in the Panchayat with a little capacity and commitment to achieve. One would find more of challenges in their life. The third category are always in the hands of the men folk. Both the Panchayat President and her family male jointly run the administration. The fourth category of elected women representatives have been asked to remain in the house and the entire Panchayat work is carried out by a male of their family. The first two groups joined together to bring the other segments out of the clutches of men. They found it very difficult. That is why the elected women representatives made a plea that the males should not be encouraged to attend the official work and meetings. Women feel that they can contest only in the seats reserved for women. It is necessary to dispel this belief. Seats are limited only for men not for women. They can go beyond 33.3 per cent of seats. For men it is only 67.7 per cent; for women it is 100 per cent.

In a caste ridden and patriarchal society, women on their own provide transparent administration which in fact strengthens their leadership and they are strong in their dealings. They are the pioneers and pathfinders among the elected women representatives. They were trained by a team of experts in Gandhigram Rural Institute and other training institutions. Yet the problems faced by the elected women representatives are innumerable. How to overcome the obstacles and problems is a major question. In many consultative and training workshops they have been in search of an organizational mechanism by which the EWRs will gain collective bargaining power to deal with problems.

Working on Innovative Projects

It is interesting to note that many innovative concepts are being tested in the Panchayats where women are leaders. For instance the concept of bio village was effectively implemented in many Panchayats headed by women as women leaders have already demonstrated their potential in making the village green by planting avenue trees in the streets, planting wood giving trees in the Panchayat lands, and planting fruit bearing trees in poramboke lands. Many of the vital policies and programmes of the State and Central Governments are being reviewed by the elected women representatives. The Government of Tamil Nadu issued a 15-point programme to make Tamil Nadu the number one state in the country and this was reviewed and they made recommendations also. Mostly the programme touched upon social development issues and natural resource management issues. It was reviewed by the elected women representatives, who suggested ways and means to improve the same and they have also pledged their support to this new programme.

There is yet another issue which is being discussed in many fora to have a separate allocation for women development. There should be a separate plan for women development. The women leaders have quoted the extensive practice of such a plan in Kerala. Yet the State Government does not move forward to accept it. Relentlessly they are pursuing the matter with a sense of hope. By following the footprints of the women leaders, Dalit leaders have demanded the same for Dalits. Thus women leaders are trendsetters. There is real participation of people in public activity in the Panchayats headed by women. They allow all individuals who want to speak and the leaders patiently listen to the people. A large number of SHG women are brought to the Gram Sabha for discussion and deliberation. SHG members take keen interest in attending the Gram Sabha meeting as they are allowed to speak freely whereas in other Panchayats they cannot expect this much of freedom as the Gram Sabha has been made leader centric.

There is yet another interesting observation that many of the vital development issues which had not been discussed seriously in any of the public fora are being forwarded to the Gram Sabha by the government for discussion. The women leaders who are already sensitized and trained on social development issues seriously take up and discuss them with the people in the Gram Sabha meeting. In reality progress is made in many villages on social development and in many it does not take place because of the lack of conscientization process on the part of the leaders and the people. The budget and resource flow to Panchayats is still a myth to many. Internal resource mobilization is being done very actively as the Panchayat leaders are aware of the nuances of resource mobilization. But resource mobilization from external sources, though mandated, is scarce. They are not sure whether Panchayats can get such resources. No perspective budget analysis is being done. But the elected women Panchayat leaders are trying their best to understand the Panchayat finance. It is necessary that a budget analysis has to be made for Panchayats and it is to be explained to the Panchayat Presidents.

On many occasions, it is the elected women representatives who have realised the potential of the media and taken steps to use the media to project the issues which are being faced by them and the achievements made by them. A cursory analysis will reveal that a large number of articles have been written on the achievements of women representatives. This media tie up has been created by the women representatives. It is noticed everywhere that in all training programmes, the elected women representatives are attentive and sincere in attending the capacity building exercise. Often they used to lament that they refer to Government Orders and Notifications whenever they meet officials, but officials are not that much familiar with them. Capacity building exercise is viewed seriously by the women leaders.

Federation

> This is the narration of a woman Gram Panchayat Leader from Virudhunagar District. Initially both men and women joined together and formed a Federation. When they organised a meeting with the District Collector, all went into the room of the Collector. All men leaders sat in the first three rows and the last row was given to the women leaders. There was a discussion between the leaders and the District Collector. But the whole discussion was between the men leaders and the District Collector. The women leaders raised their voice, but they were asked to be silent as discussion was in progress. Finally the men leaders said that the discussion was over all could move out of the hall. The women leaders asked them what happened to the demands given by them. The men leaders said that those can be discussed outside the Collector's chamber. When all came out of the room, the women leaders asked them about their demands. The men leaders said that the Collector would consider them in due course. On that day the women leaders felt that the women had to adopt a different strategy and they formed a separate association. They got a separate audience with Collector and sorted out their problems. When they narrated the experience, the idea came to form a Federation. Thus the Federation of elected women representatives (exclusively women Presidents of Gram Panchayats) was born in Tamil Nadu, facilitated by the Gandhigram Rural Institute. In course of time there were a number of Federations at different levels.

Gandhigram took the initiative to form this Federation as it organised series of capacity building exercises to train the Gram Panchayat Women Presidents with the active support of The Hunger Project. They were not only trained to manage the Panchayats and to administer development but also to provide leadership to the people. In our country in fifty years of democratic governance we have seen many rulers in the name of democracy but we have not seen a leader to lead the society after Mahatma Gandhi. So, in all training programmes how to be with the people as a leader and lead them not rule them was emphasised. Thus the relationship started from training and it continued in forming associations and federations for women leaders. The EWR federations periodically organise regional meetings and consolidate the problems faced by the EWRs and conduct periodical interface with officials. Annually they conduct a Mela in which major issues of the leaders are highlighted for policy advocacy and they meet higher officials, political party leaders. During the time of general elections, they review the election manifesto of the political parties and check whether the issues of local bodies and issues of women are included.

Over a period of six years they have become visible and in fact they have become role models for others. Following this EWR Federation, Block Level Federation for Block Panchayat leaders and District Level Federation for District Panchayat leaders have been formed. Even among the Block level leaders, women leaders have formed their own Federation. SC and ST leaders have formed their own Federation. Among Gram Panchayat leaders, Dalit women leaders have formed their own Federation. They negotiate with officials to settle their problems. Of all the Federations, the Gram Panchayat Women Leaders Federation is strong, vibrant and vocal and it sustains its activities. Various issues have been highlighted over a period of time. Eighty meetings have been organised in different places in Tamil Nadu and each time they have focused on one or two issues which are affecting them and the people, especially women, children and Dalits.

Elected women representatives should strengthen their Federation at the District level. Its structure should be flexible. In every district the Federation should have an office. Once in two months the office-bearers should meet and discuss their issues.

One major achievement is that the rotation of reservation has been set for each ten years which is being quoted by many in our country. This is the only state where reservation of seats for women has been made for every ten years. Yet another major breakthrough for the federation is getting an exclusive Government Order to make the Collector convene a meeting of officials to redress the grievances of EWRs whenever they request. By using this Government Order women leaders in seven districts have made the Collector convene the meeting of the officials and got their grievances redressed. The Federation leaders have gone to meet the Prime Minister of India and handed over petitions to him asking for direct financing of local bodies from the Central Government.

At this juncture the Federation office-bearers of all the districts met at Gandhigram and invited the Rural Development Director, Government of Tamil Nadu, to their meeting. From morning till evening they raised a volley of questions before the officials and they were responded to by the Director of Rural Development. Following the interface, they discussed the future course of action for their Federation. Their discussion was centred round their future course of action in their Panchayats. Many of them were in power consecutively for two terms. Now they have decided to contest in the open constituency along with men. It is to be seen only during the elections. They have further decided to stay in the public's space in any of the positions in local bodies whether it is in Gram Panchayats or in Block Panchayats. The acquired skills, capacity and capability could be effectively used by occupying any of the positions in the local bodies.

By creating a support structure of their own, the EWRs have highlighted the problems of the women leaders in administration. The problems are multi-dimensional in nature and character. Further by conducting a series of interfaces with other State Panchayats and Panchayats within the state and with officials they have equipped themselves in attacking social development issues. The leaders have been conscientized on the issues of women, children and livelihood. An army of elected women representatives has come to the public space and decided to stay on. How to stay on in the public space in the question. Almost all have decided to stay in the public space in different forms. In the next elections, women can contest in general constituencies. They can contest for different tiers, either Block Panchayats or District Panchayats. A set of leaders said that they can contest for Ward Members' posts of Gram Panchayats. Being a Gram Sabha member, the experience gained by the Panchayat Presidents could be utilized. There are Panchayat leaders who want to stake a claim to MLA consti-tuencies. They are interested in seeking tickets to contest in the MLA constituencies. The Federation of elected women represen-tatives could be strengthened by associating themselves with such activities.

Sum-up

The critical mass (33.3% of women elected representatives) have come to perform the critical functions (attacking the issues of hunger, poverty, gender and untouchability) despite facing a multitude of problems in the process of their governance and managing the institutions. They have their own record of achievements and story of struggles. But they have determined to move further to occupy the public space. The journey has started and the support structure has been created to push forward the onward march.

Their imprints in governance, management of institutions, negotiating with different partners and stakeholders, attacking issues and managing the crowd are unique and different from those of men and members of other higher level institutions. Their expressions, perceptions, opinions and observations provide an array of policy implications.

Way Forward

Capacity building for elected women representatives has to be conducted within a month after they assume office. The training should be intensive and residential. It should not be conducted in the Block Development Office. It should be given only in training institutions. Training should be made mandatory and on any account their males should not be allowed to attend the training. In the training programme, Tamil Nadu Panchayati Raj Act, 1994, updated version, Rules, Government Orders and details of Schemes of Rural Development should be given to all Panchayat leaders as a tool kit for Panchayat Management. The training package should include gender and social development components. In each and every training programme a well-experienced Panchayat President should be made as a resource person to share her experience with other participants. The same training should be given to officials also at the same time. Periodical refresher courses say, once a year, can be organised. Once a month, the District Collector must convene a meeting of officials to redress the problems faced by the women leaders in Panchayat administration.

Males of the elected women representatives' families should not be allowed to occupy the chair and to participate in the official meetings. This has to be followed rigorously and religiously. They should not be permitted to sign any document on behalf of the elected women representatives. Periodically an interface has to be arranged for women leaders with other Panchayats, preferably in other states. This opportunity has to be given to the maximum number of people. The women leaders Federation is a registered body and, hence, it has to be recognized by the government. A support structure has to be created for women and Dalit leaders.

12

MEDIA AND GRASSROOTS GOVERNANCE

PART-I

Media Engagement for Panchayat and Women Leaders

Introduction

It is obvious that, in a feudal society, democratization is a difficult task and that the human collectivities that are all gaining advantages in the existing form of governance turn against any form of reform in governance, particularly in giving power to the people as the existing order and practices will be challenged. Of these collectivities, the bureaucracy is the first and most important in keeping itself as unmoved and against the participation of people in decision-making and governance. Hence any proposal or any event which breaks the existing system to bring advantage to the people who are in the last rung will be met with resistance. The bureaucracy does not function in isolation. It collaborates with various forces that are working against democratization and social justice. The bureaucracy knowingly or unknowingly spreads the negative implications of the devolution of powers by projecting the argument that the capabilities of the elected leaders are poor and not to the level of the roles and responsibilities to be discharged by them. Further, the information which should reach the public about the implications of the devolution of powers has not reached them. This information has got stuck in the pipeline of the bureaucracy.

Information dissemination is the *sine qua non* for the success of any programme. In establishing a sound grassroots governing institution, information dissemination plays a very important role. It has to be created in a very complex socio-political and economic context. Unfortunately the system of governance that had been in vogue for the past five decades in India had not created positive climate to provide the needed information to the stakeholders. The Government is always strong and officials are always strong, and they act on information. But people do not have the same access as the officials. As long as information is kept with Government officials, it is logical that officials will be empowered and people are made powerless. But, in a decentralized democratic institution, people and their representatives need to have the information relating to governance and people's participation in governance. The system at the lower level is created as per the design and decision of the Central and State Governments. This information has not been disseminated in the society. The leaders have to equip themselves on the information relating to power and responsibilities entrusted to the newly created Panchayat bodies.

Panchayat leaders and the people always complain that the government at the State level does not provide the needed information. When the government gives information it is loose and not integrated with the institution. Sometimes, it provides information which is negative to the Panchayat system. Information which is needed by the representatives of the people in Local Bodies and members of the Gram Sabha is available in the Government offices but it is not properly distributed among the different stakeholders. Even if it is distributed, the distributed material in the raw form. It can be used easily by the Government officials but not by the people. So information in usable form is not available. There are 12,685 Panchayats in Tamil Nadu and a few Panchayat leaders have committed procedural lapses, which have been highlighted in the press based on the reports given by the District Collectors. On the whole, the picture emerging from the press is not positive towards decentralization. On the contrary the higher level officials brought to light some interesting and valuable achievements of the

Panchayats, which they had gathered during their field visits. Even in reporting the success stories of the Panchayat leaders, particularly Dalits and women in the media, their struggle is not projected. The process of achievement is more interesting than the output. On most of the occasions the media has missed the hidden issues and underlying principles. Reports from other activists also support the findings of the higher officials. Thus, the role of the media in Panchayati Raj raises concerns, as it cannot capture the real issues involved in the process of decentralization.

Problem

There are two issues which the media confronts while covering the local body issues. Primarily our media has been oriented to look at issues from the perspective of the Central and the State Governments. All governance issues are visualized from the perspective of the Central and State Governments. Down below the state, a new set of institutions has been created constitutionally for governance. But the media representatives have not been adequately oriented to cover the real issues in the field. Secondly, the information which is needed to strengthen grassroots governance is available at different levels in the State Government machinery. But this information does not reach the grassroots. Despite the development of the media this information is stuck elsewhere. Further, the available information is not packaged for the consumption of the public as it is raw and only the officials can use it. On the other hand there are stakeholders, namely, Panchayat leaders, lower level administrators and the people who are in need of the same information. At one end information is generated but stocked, and at the other end there are unmet needs for information, despite the presence of a strong and vibrant media.

Solution is at Sight

We brought up this issue with some of the leading media persons and scholars. They approached this issue with an open mind and suggested that media representatives should be oriented and sensitized on the issues of decentralized governance and empowering people. Mr. N. Ram, Executive Editor of *The Hindu,* Mr. Maalan of *Sun TV* and Mr. T.G. Nallamuthu, Press Information Bureau, helped us in this process. First a media workshop was organized and leading senior staff reporters were invited to this workshop. Mr. N. Ram inaugurated the workshop and subsequently experts on Panchayat Raj discussed the issues of decentralized governance with the staff reporters. Mr. Maalan and T.G. Nallamuthu explained the possibilities of using academic institutions for getting the required information on the critical issues of governance at the grassroots.

Yet another issue, which focused on the problems of elected women representatives and Dalits, drew the attention of all. It was only an experiment. In this experiment a package for a media workshop emerged. The experts on decentralized governance identified the linkages between the globalization of economy and decentralization of powers. They explained the background of decentralization throughout the world. The focus was on the framework developed by the Central Government for devolution of powers. The gap between the intention of the federal government and the reality in the State was also discussed. The relationship between the state and the local body institutions was also focused on in this discussion. The struggle of the leaders, women and Dalits at the grassroots to overcome the barriers was discussed. To test this proposition, in the media workshop a group of women and Dalit leaders was made available for interaction. Along with the above an array of documents was provided to the representatives of the media, who expressed their willingness to focus on the above issues, provided regular information is available. It was brought to everyone's notice that Gandhigram Rural Institute regularly brings out the required information, which can be used by the media. There was yet another argument brought forward by the journalists that the materials that are prepared by Gandhigram Rural Institute are highly sophisticated and technical and cannot be used without simplification. The information needs further packaging by way of preparing news bulletins for the use of media representatives. One more suggestion was that this kind of discussions and orientations are needed for media representatives in other parts of the State as well. While interacting with media representatives, it was found that in many of the newspapers and magazines there are no experts/ specialists to focus on grassroots democracy and empowerment.

It was agreed to meet the editorial division and the management to bring to their knowledge the need for specialists to cover these issues. There are newspapers and magazines which keep specialists but have not allotted space, as it was not considered essential. Lobbying was required to get space and specialists in the newspapers. Following the above interventions at the capital (Chennai) level, initiatives were taken to replicate the same workshop in different cities and towns. Experts on Panchayat Raj, women's empowerment and media were drawn towards these media workshops. While conducting the media workshop in different centres, local problems were discussed. It was an eye opener for them. It was believed that the Panchayati Raj System in Tamil Nadu is based on the 73rd Amendment to the Constitution of India on the assumption that when a uniform pattern and structure is designed, the functioning of the Panchayati Raj System would be same throughout India. This was the belief that the media persons had before the workshop. Variations among the states become evident only in the workshop and they wanted to know the states which are the best in devolving powers to Panchayats. Another interesting information which they were not aware of was the variations among the districts in terms of functioning of Panchayats. Each district has its own pattern as the officials keep the Panchayats under their control and Panchayats have been oriented to function according to their wishes. This was another surprising information to them.

Media representatives were sensitized and they were all provided with needed information. Newspapers and magazines like *The Hindu, The New Indian Express, Financial Express, Frontline, Dinamalar, Dinamani, Daily Thanthi, Kumudham* and a number of small magazines started focusing on Panchayats. Good numbers of articles were written in all the above-mentioned newspapers and magazines. Qualitatively good articles and increased coverage of news items has been seen in the print media. The electronic media also joined in this process. *Sun TV* played a major role in this endeavour as Mr. Maalan took the lead. In the panel discussion held on *Sun TV*, experts and Panchayat leaders were drawn and the major issues affecting the Panchayat system were discussed. It is a major cry among the Panchayat leaders that Doordarshan telecasts rural development programmes everyday but they are all taken from other states and not from Tamil Nadu. Despite all the hurdles and barriers Gram Panchayat leaders in Tamil Nadu have done path breaking activities in their respective Panchayat areas. These major achievements could be telecasted and it would be an eye opener for the other Panchayat leaders and a moral boost to the achievers to aim for further achievements. When there are several phone-in programmes organized for several things including cinema, why not one for local governance. Millions of leaders are in the dark as they do not have adequate information to manage the Panchayats for achieving economic development and social justice. We have tried to contact Doordarshan for creating a programme for Panchayat leaders but in vain.

Yet another Problem

The above-narrated events helped in spreading the struggles and success stories at grassroots for popular consumption. There is yet another need, namely, the need for information for practitioners and leaders who are in office and manage the affairs of administration to deliver goods to the people. The elected representatives of all the three-tiers were deprived of information relating to administration, as full-fledged training was not imparted in time. Further, people are in need of information to extract work from the local bodies. There are specialized institutions which offer training and give the necessary information but to reach out to the mass an appropriate instrument, namely media, is necessary.

New Initiative of The Hunger Project

Against this background, a study was conducted among the Panchayat Presidents on the newspapers that are read by them. It was found that among the daily newspapers *Dinamalar* stood first and, hence, the Chairperson of The Hunger Project in Tamil Nadu approached the publisher of *Dinamalar* in this regard.

Dinmalar's publisher Dr. R. Lakshmipathy accepted the proposal immediately and based on his suggestion, The Hunger Project team had a discussion with the Director of *Dinamalar*, Mr. L. Ramasubbu. A whole page was designed in such a fashion that it carried the needed information to the public, representatives of the people and the officials. One section in the supplement covers an issue with the opinion of an expert, one section projects a success story, one focuses on the struggle of a Dalit or a women leader, and another section provides questions and answers and development tit bits. Thus a variety of issues and information were packaged in this page.

It is interesting to note that normally any newspaper has value unto 12 noon. After that the newspaper goes to the waste paper rack. But the *Dinamalar* Panchayat supplement titled "Panchayat Malar" goes to the file. It has become a source of reference for officials and Panchayat leaders. There are instances where Panchayat leaders went to the Panchayat Union office with the supplement, the "Panchayat Malar", and argued with the Block Panchayat officials quoting the Government Order published in the "Panchayat Malar". The question and answer section is very useful to Panchayat leaders. In the "Panchayat Malar" some of the successful Panchayat leaders are projected and an analysis is made as to how she or he was able to achieve developments. The question has been raised that when it is possible in a particular Panchayat why is it not possible in other Panchayats in Tamil Nadu. In the same way struggles have also been focused on and analysis made as to how this conflict and struggle arose in this Panchayat and how she/he was able to manage the struggle. On most of the occasions, women Panchayat leaders are given preference in such coverage. Some of the Collectors are quite positive towards Panchayats and they are also focused upon. While giving coverage to the role of the District Collector the emphasis is on how he is helping Panchayats to make strides in rural development activities. This will be an example to other District Collectors also.

There are allegations against Panchayats and they are also published along with feedback from the Panchayat leaders. In many of the Panchayats the "Panchayat Malar" has been preserved as a precious document. The "Panchayat Malar" has completed one year and hence a need was felt to review it and make further improvements. The supplement has several segments, namely, questions and answers on different areas of local administration, stories of struggle mostly of elected women representatives, success stories, other States' experiences, government orders, readers' quick response, and focus on a social development issue. In the whole of one year, nearly 260 questions were answered covering several subjects, namely, powers, functions, finance, encroachment of common properties, common property resource management, details of welfare schemes. Nine struggles, mostly relating to natural resource management, have been covered. Twenty-nine success stories in Panchayat management, especially in managing development, have been published in the "Panchayat Malar". Visits of other States' representatives and practices in other States have been highlighted, which provoked the Panchayat leaders and the public, and enabled the leaders to demand more powers to local bodies. Specific themes were focused on such as capacity building, water management, issues of women, infant mortality, infanticide, foeticide, health and sanitation, primary education, pre and post-natal care, non-conventional energy sources, common property resource management, human rights, solid waste management, public distribution system. Many critical issues were also raised in this supplement. All the items covered in this supplement are issues related to Panchayat Raj, women's empowerment and social development. This is the first initiative of its kind in the whole nation. While analyzing the spread it is found out that, on an average, one copy of the supplement, of the "Panchayat Malar" is read by 12 - 14 individuals. When circulation comes to three lakhs, it works out that 36 lakh people are gaining information. Following the initiative of *Dinamalar*, some other vernacular newspapers have started publishing details about rural development schemes and some of the important Government Orders. In order to highlight and appreciate the role performed by *Dinamalar* in publishing the "Panchayat Malar" as a weekly supplement for the cause of empowering people, especially women and Dalits, a national honour was conferred at New Delhi by giving a medal with a citation. It was appreciated by all dignitaries, especially representatives from embassies. Following this *Dinamalar* model, a few newspapers in other regions have agreed to provide space for Panchayat activities, especially to cover the stories of the women leaders.

Methodology

A team of experts has been constituted for this purpose under the leadership of the Chairperson of The Hunger Project, Tamil Nadu. The team consists of Mr. K. Vallinayagam, N.S. Chidambaram, and S. Subramanian. They are retired Additional Directors of Rural Development, Government of Tamil Nadu. Two project staff, Mr. Alagu Selvam and Ms. Uma, are to gather information from the field. These findings are then written as articles by the Chairperson of The Hunger Project. All the matters are prepared in the computer laboratory of The Hunger Project and every Friday the write-up reaches the office of *Dinamalar*. Experts' opinion on issues are obtained then and there for stories. In order to keep up the authenticity, the *Dinamalar* has decided to print at the bottom of the "Panchayat Malar" page the full address of Dr. G. Palanithurai for contact, queries and clarifications. By giving this address, the newspaper informed the public that the matters printed in the full page are owned by The Hunger Project and no way *Dinamalar* is responsible. In the whole process, *Dinamalar* has emerged as one of the leading and pioneering newspapers in the vernacular as an expert on Panchayat matters. It has got a drawback that it reaches only a few regions not the whole of Tamil Nadu, because the said newspaper has two managements. Of the two The Hunger Project has started working with the management headed by Dr. R. Lakshmipathy of Madurai. There is a great demand for this newspaper in other regions but they are managed by the other group.

Novelty

A gigantic task is achieved very simply by linking an instrument which is powerful, namely, the media with the people through retired officials under the supervision of a University. Through this exercise everyone gains. For all the stakeholders it is a win-win situation.

Implications

It is found that the concentration and focus of the media on local bodies have increased in the past two years. Newspapers allow reporters to carry more news items about local bodies. In the "Panchayat Malar", it has been published that a book containing the updated Act, rules, government orders, details of rural development schemes is available with the publisher. The same book was given free of cost to the Gram Panchayat Presidents who underwent training programme in Gandhigram Rural Institute. About 3000 leaders have received the book. Apart from them others have also benefited from this book and they have started using the book while dealing with officials. For about four years Panchayat leaders have struggled to get the needed information. The Hunger Project in Tamil Nadu, under the leadership of Dr. G. Palanithurai, started collecting all the Government Orders from the respective departments. Some of the government orders are only executive orders not published in gazette. Some of them are passed through notification. Likewise details of rural development schemes are collected from various sectoral departments. Further the Act has been amended continuously. Relevant amendments have been collected and they are edited properly. Thus the new book entitled "New Panchayati Raj System in Tamil Nadu: Updated Act, Rules, Government Schemes of the Centre and State Government" in the vernacular is a compendium meant for Panchayats for ready reference. No other State has such a comprehensive compilation which serves as a reference book not only for the leaders but also for the officials as there is no administrative manual. In the event of any dispute over any issue it will be referred to Gandhigram

Rural Institute. Dr. G. Palanithurai will directly intervene. Otherwise it will be referred to Panchayat legal adviser, Mr. K. Vallinayagam.

Panchayat leaders have now started asserting their position with the information available with them. Further they have moved to confront the erring officials through their federations. Another interesting impact has been that people have started asking questions of Panchayat leaders. The arbitrary fixing of house tax was stopped as the pertinent GO was published and this was taken to Panchayat Presidents. Panchayat Presidents were not aware of the powers relating to control over industries, share in minor minerals and social forestry. After the publication of the GO, the Panchayat Presidents have started writing letters to District Collectors to take steps to get the share from the respective departments and thereby the District Collectors are taking steps to claim the amount and give their share to the Panchayats. Pudukkottai District is the first in distributing the money from minor minerals to the Panchayats. District Collectors have started writing letters to Secretaries to settle this type of problems with the help of other Secretaries. Panchayat leaders after gaining needed information, have started collecting professional tax and property tax from the private colleges which are located in the Panchayat areas. When it was demanded, the authorities of the colleges were not aware of the rules of the Panchayats. They also got the information from the Rajiv Gandhi Chair for Panchayati Raj Studies. As a result Panchayats have increased their revenue.

After reading the success stories from districts, Panchayat leaders have started asking the District administration to extend such support to the innovative works done in Panchayats. In some places the non-implementation of the latest government orders was brought to the notice of the District Collectors after they were published in the "Panchayat Malar".

There is yet another impact one can see in Panchayat reporting after the conduct of the media workshop and the publication of the "Panchayat Malar," namely, publishing of the issues only on the basis of field visits and not on the basis of the press note prepared by the officials. In the dispute over the sand quarrying in Thiruvachi Panchayat in Trichy District, the District Collector gave a statement about the issue, accusing the Panchayat President, Mr. Cheran. But the President invited the press to the field and asked them to write about the field reality. The people openly made a statement that the Panchayat statement is correct and not the statement of the District Collector.

Conclusion

From this limited experience it is found out that the media is a powerful instrument in empowering Panchayats and the people. The media at present does not have experts but they have space. People need appropriate usable information but they do not know how to get the needed information. Information, which is generated from different sources for administration and development, is raw and has to be properly packaged for stakeholders' consumption. Research institutions and other development organizations have packaged information which can be used by Panchayat leaders and the people. A new culture and practice have been developed among the Panchayat leaders that they collect information from the "Panchayat Malar" and keep them as reference material in the Panchayat office which is being used by public. Panchayat leaders who have also changed their attitude. Now they go to any office only with information for authenticated discussion. Likewise the officials have changed their attitude towards Panchayat leaders. Officials carefully listen and positively dispose of the files as Panchayat leaders approach the officials with authentic information. Questions have been asked and answers have been given. They take the answers as direction for their work. If they get stuck anywhere the Panchayat leaders immediately approach the Chairperson of The Hunger Project. It is not mere information providing. It goes beyond that. We have to go along with Panchayat leaders in their struggle. Administrative practices in Panchayats vary from district to district. While publishing information about experiences the variations in Panchayat administration are minimized. While publishing Government Orders and rules explanatory notes are also published. The explanatory notes are drawn from the experts (they are retired Additional Directors of Rural Development) and are highly useful to the Block Development officials and Assistant Directors of Panchayats. When the Panchayat leaders work with proactive officials, one finds tremendous success and these successes are being disseminated. Thus the media has gradually moved from the negative projection of Panchayats to a positive one.

List of Tables

Table 12.1 : Questions asked in Panchayat Malar

S. No.	*Subjects*	*No. of Questions*
1.	Relating to powers	36
2.	Relating to functions	97
3.	Relating to finance	35
4.	Relating to encroachment	19
5.	Relating to commons	15
6.	Relating to scheme and programmes	24
7.	General administration	34
	Total	**260**

Source : Computed from Panchayat Malar.

Note : While giving answers to the questions the relevant Act, rules and Government orders have been cited. Further, wherever available, page numbers are given.

Table 12.2 : Panchayat Leaders in Struggle

S. No.	*Names of the leader*	*Name of the Panchayat*	*Issues*
1.	Chandrika Sarvesan	Siruthodanallur	Encroachment
2.	Eswari	Appipalayam	Environment
3.	Arumugam	Edayathimangalam	Sand quarry
4.	Cheran	Thiruvachi	Sand quarry
5.	Annadurai	Maravamanagalam	Channel encroachment
6.	Chellammal	Melavalavu	Quarry

Source : Computed from Panchayat Malar.

Table 12.3 : Success Stories of Panchayats

S. No.	*Names of the leader*	*Name of the Panchayat*	*Achievements*
1.	Maruthambal	Panchampatti	Water supply
2.	Abdul Waheed	Parambur	Implementing Welfare Schemes
3.	Kala	Noothulapuram	Citizens Centre
4.	Murugesan	Old Butlagundu	Health and Sanitation
5.	Sahayamary	Kakkanur	Village based management system
6.	Jesumary	Michaelpattinam	Rainwater and harvesting
7.	Kaliammal	Thethupatti	Water supply
8.	Thennarasu	Thaiyur	Using youth power
9.	Bhavani	Merpanaikadu	School enrolment
10.	Ramanathan	Nallukkottai	Huts free village
11.	Dhanapal	Thirumanur	Social Justice
12.	Jawahar	Natarajpuram	Income generation
13.	Ilango	Koothambakkam	Appropriate technology
14.	Anusya	Kunnathur	Peoples contribution
15.	Rani	K. Rayavaram	Polythene free Panchayat
16.	Iruthayaraj	Karisalpatti	Model Panchayat award

Source : Computed from Panchayat Malar.

Table 12.4 : Other States' experiences

S. No.	*State*	*Issue*
1.	Karnataka - Pelanthur Panchayat	E-governance
2.	Andhra Pradesh - Alagathapp Panchayat	Referendum
3.	West Bengal Mayor	Novel method of collecting tax
4.	Rajasthan Panchayat Presidents visit to Tamil Nadu	Water management
5.	Visit of Utharanjal District Panchayat Presidents	Power sharing

Source : Computed from Panchayat Malar.

Table 12.5 : Unique Features

S. No.	*Individual institution involved*	*Features*
1.	Rokkaiya a poet turned Panchayat President	Model for women empowerment
2.	DANIDA	Village based management system for water supply and sanitation
3.	Pudukkottai District Collector	Initiative through Panchayat
4.	Pudukkottai District	SHG product marketing model for other Districts
5.	Pudukkottai District	Selection of beneficiaries and operation of schemes by beneficiary themselves model for other Districts

Source : Computed from Panchayat Malar.

Table 12.6 : Development issues focused

S. No.	*Issues*	*No of Boxes*
1.	Employment opportunity creation for youth	1
2.	Building the capacity of youth	1
3.	Water management - unique practices	1
4.	Women and children	9
5.	Infant mortality, infanticide, foeticide	10
6.	Issues of literacy	5
7.	Health and sanitation - different models	12
8.	Unique women's day	1
9.	School - teacher and students	1
10.	Vital statistics on water in Indian states	1
11.	Common property resource management	1
12.	Population statistics in India	1
13.	Non-conventional resource management	1
14.	Abolition of plastics in villages	1
15.	Panchayat library	1
16.	Issues in slaughter house	1
17.	Human rights and Panchayats	1
18.	Social forestry	2
19.	Panchayats and food security	1
20.	Solid waste management	1
21.	PDS and Panchayats	1
22.	Fishery and Panchayat	12
23.	HIV and Women	1
24.	Street light management	1
	Total	**65**

Source : Computed from Panchayat Malar.

PART-II

Report of the Review of Panchayat Malar Meet

Context

A meeting was organised at Gandhigram to review the journey of the past one year of conceptualising and publishing of the "Panchayat Malar" —a supplement published by *Dinamalar* and to seek inputs from the participants to make further improvements in the Panchayat Malar. The meeting was attended by Panchayat Presidents, retired government officials, media persons and academicians from Gandhigram Rural Institute. The objective of the meeting was to gather suggestions which can be incorporated in the Panchayat Malar to make it more useful and reader oriented. Suggestions were solicited from the participants on the content, layout, design and any other issue related to the Panchayat Malar. The workshop began with an account of the inception of the Panchayat Malar by Dr. G. Palanithurai.

Background

In the present status of local governance, powers have been vested with the Panchayats as per the 73rd Amendment to the Constitution of India. Due to the mentality of the bureaucracy the information about the powers and functions of the Panchayats seldom reaches the Panchayat functionaries easily. The bureaucracy has found it very difficult to hand over power to the Panchayats. Due to this dearth of information, the Panchayat members and Presidents face a lot of difficulties in carrying out the responsibilities entrusted to them by the Constitution.

The media plays a very important role in dissemination of information and in raising critical issues that are relevant to the people. But so far the media has not given adequate attention to development news. One weak news item is analysed for five newspapers and that to is relegated to the annexure. From this one can infer how much coverage is given to each and every aspect.

Newspapers are not oriented or sensitised to write about social development issues. Dr. Palanithurai shared the journey of working with the media to encourage them to write more on Panchayats. In the initial stage lots of workshops were organised with the journalists to sensitize them to write more on development issues. Through continuous dialogue with senior media journalists like Mr. N. Ram (*The Hindu*), Mr. Maalan (*Sun TV*), Mr. T.G. Nallamuthu (Press Information Bureau) and others, it was concluded that regular information on Panchayats should be published in the media. The Political Science Department of Gandhigram Rural Institute and The Hunger Project approached the publisher of *Dinamalar*, Dr. Lakshmipathy, with the idea of allotting one page every Monday under the caption "Panchayat Malar" to cover the issues of Panchayats and development, and he immediately agreed to this proposal. Thus the Panchayat Malar was born. Since February 2003 till now every Monday *Dinamalar* has been publishing the Panchayat Malar. Till now 54 issues have been published in the last one year. Due to the Lok Sabha elections it was discontinued. As per the letter of the publisher of *Dinamalar* it is to be resumed after May 13, 2004. It was decided to have a review of the supplement with a view to making the Panchayat Malar more attractive.

The page has been given news reviews by the people. Many Panchayat Presidents have gained from the information given in the Panchayat Malar. Many have stored the paper in their Panchayats as reference material. There are instances where the Panchayat Presidents have gone to the Block office and reiterated their rights after learning about their powers and duties from the Malar. Each page contains success and struggle stories of Panchayat representatives, information on new schemes, Government Orders and questions of the readers and answers to them by an expert. A team of experts has been constituted which comprises of retired Additional Directors of Rural Development and project staff of Gandhigram Rural Institute under the chairmanship of Dr. Palanithurai, The Hunger Project, Tamil Nadu. All the matter is collected and compiled at GRI. The compiled material is sent to *Dinamalar* every week for publishing.

It has been a year of Panchayat Malar and its time to review the page and improve it in all ways possible to benefit the people more.

Suggestions to Upgrade Panchayat Malar

All the participants profusely congratulated and showed their appreciation to DINAMALAR for taking up such an initiative and publishing PANCHAYAT MALAR. All the participants voiced their admiration for DINAMALAR for having taken such a step in this day of globalisation when every newspaper is becoming more and more commercial. DINAMALAR has devoted an entire page to Panchayats. As a result so many Panchayat people have benefited.

The suggestions from the participants were focused on the content, layout and presentation. Some of the highlights of the suggestions are given below. Each suggestion is subsequently explained in detail.

Highlights

1. Include write-ups on urban local bodies.
2. Should we carry on with the same page or change to a special supplement in a book form.
3. Outreach of Panchayat Malar should be all over Tamil Nadu.
4. Competitions can be organised among the Panchayat Presidents and awards given to winners.
5. The Award can be given named, 'The Hunger Project-Dinamalar award for best performing Panchayat on social development issues'.
6. Publish a book annually compiling all issues of Panchayat Malar. It can be titled 'Dinamalar speaks on Panchayats'.
7. Experiences of other States and countries to be shared.
8. Follow-up of articles can be published.
9. Creation of Panchayat Malar readers' circle.

- There is a need to research who are the readers of the Panchayat Malar. Based upon the readership, the page can be re-designed. The challenge is to repackage the page in such a way that it interests a wide section of people.
- The articles should not be very long. The same information can be packaged in a concise and crisp form.
- Small snippets can be added. Even the success stories can be presented in small snippets.
- Experiences from other countries should be written about. Alternative concepts are being experimented with successfully in other areas. These experiments need to be documented and shared in the Panchayat Malar.
- While writing about Panchayats, issues related to stress management, conflict management, time management, leadership skills, how to increase one's working capacity, communal harmony can also be discussed.
- The headings of the articles should be more attractive and eye catching. The headings should not be drab and dull but should attract the attention of the readers.
- Regarding enhancing the presentation of the page, it was suggested that cartoons may be introduced. In all the papers cartoons attract the attention of the readers and also highlight the issue being raised. A cartoon strip can be started in the Panchayat Malar also. Another suggestion was to add coloured pictures, make the page in colour, if the budget permits, present the data with the help of graphs and charts. Maps of Panchayats, some humorous stories of Panchayats, famous quotes, biographies of a few good panchayat leaders, poems may add more flavour to the page. The page should be designed in such a way that people wait for the next supplement to arrive.
- Can also explore presenting the Panchayat Malar in A4 size —booklet form. After the end of the year all the booklets can be compiled and published in the form of a book. The example of *The Hindu* was cited. *The Hindu* publishes a book called *The Hindu Speaks*. Similarly *Dinamalar* can

publish a book called *Dinamalar speaks on Panchayats*.

- The style of interviewing people can also be widened. Instead of only focusing on individual interviews, focus group interviews can also be attempted.
- A section can be added as to what other personalities like politicians, cine stars and other achievers think about Panchayats. That would help in generating more interest. These personalities can be interviewed and even important messages can be conveyed through them.
- Each week a specific issue can be focused upon. For example, there are 29 subjects to be devolved to the Panchayats. Each week one subject can be discussed in great detail. Similarly anyone issue like health, education, watershed management can be fully discussed.
- While documenting the success stories of the Panchayat Presidents, we can also consider at documenting the experiences of the Panchayat Presidents prior to the 73rd Amendment. That would also help in analysing the leadership prior to and after the 73rd Amendment.
- To improve the reportage it was, suggested that some researchers should go and stay in the Panchayats for a few days. While they stay there, they should note down the activities of the people and the Panchayat representatives and record them. Those experiences in a story form would interest the readers much.
- Linkages between the Gram Panchayat, Block Panchayat and District Panchayat should also be discussed.
- It was reiterated that the Malar should continue to share information on powers and functions of the Panchayats, new schemes, Government Orders. There are also some controversial issues in regard to Government Orders *vis-à-vis* the Panchayat Act. More detailing on the same needs to be done and spread to the people. Articles on the importance of the Gram Sabha should also be written. Democratizing Indian society is very important for which Panchayat Malar should focus on the Gram Sabha.

- Regarding write-ups on Panchayat Presidents, it was stressed that while it was very important to write about the success and struggles of Panchayat Presidents, one should also write about the follow-up of the same Panchayat Presidents.
- Articles should be published in the Panchayat Malar stating problems arising in a particular Panchayat (without giving the name of the Panchayats) due to the apathy of officials. These articles need to be followed up to see if any changes have taken place.
- A quiz competition can be organised for Panchayat representatives. Awards can be given to the winners.
- Even small successes and innovations of Panchayats should be written about. Exposure trips of Panchayat representatives should also be mentioned. While taking the elected representatives for exposure visits to various States, media persons can also be invited to accompany them.
- Information on agriculture, bio-fertilizers etc. should also be given, as they would benefit the rural population.
- Story competitions can be conducted to promote more participation from people. The stories should be on Panchayats and this will encourage more and more people to read and also contribute to the page. The competition can be for leaders and for the public. We can ask the public to give opinions on how the Panchayat should function, on how the officials should act.
- Proper statistics on how much funds are allocated to Panchayats and how much has actually been devolved should be found out and written about. Government schemes can be advertised. Even though there is a provision for the Gram Sabha people are not interested. The Malar should be able to generate more interest among the people to attend the Gram Sabha meetings.
- Information on departments related to Panchayats should be given.
- Most of the reporters do not know much about Panchayats. Só an orientation programme can be organised for them.

Workshops for writers can also be organised to sensitize them about Panchayats.

- *Dinamalar* and The Hunger Project can also constitute an award for the best Panchayat and give it annually.
- There should be a separate phone line in the Department (Gandhigram Rural Institute) to answer queries of Panchayat Presidents.
- Information should also focus on help to women representatives.
- A study circle can be formed for the Panchayat Malar. Periodically the study circle can be convened.
- Information can also be given on what a model Panchayat should be like.
- GOs on other issues related to rural development can also be given. At present all the GOs are focused on Panchayats.
- Write-ups on urban local bodies can also be included.
- A great need was voiced that the Panchayat Malar should reach out to the entire State. At present it is going only to limited districts and that was not enough as many Panchayats get left out of receiving important information.
- Need based information should be provided in the Panchayat Malar.
- Should also collaborate with Government departments and cover the schemes of the government and get the views of the officials. Retired officials can be involved in the same.

Summary

1. Include write-ups on urban local bodies.
2. Should we carry on with the same page or change to a special supplement in a book form.
3. Outreach of Panchayat Malar should be all over Tamil Nadu.
4. Competitions can be organized among the Panchayat Presidents and awards given to winners.
5. The award can be given named, 'The Hunger Project-

Dinamalar award for Best Performing Panchayat on Social Development Issues'.

6. Publish a book annually compiling all issues of Panchayat Malar. Can be titled *Dinamalar Speaks on Panchayats.*
7. Experiences of other States and countries to be shared.
8. Follow-up of articles can be published.
9. Creation of Panchayat Malar readers' circle.

ANNEXURE – I

Table 12.7 : Analysis of News Items in Five Newspapers for a Week

Date	Newspaper	Category									
		Election	Development	Cinema	Business	Education	Culture	Other Countries	Sports	Advertisement	Local Body
03.05.2004	Daily Thanthi	55	17	10	8	13	10	7	8	23	1
	Dinamani	36	14	7	5	9	11	6	7	17	-
	Dinamalar	41	6	5	14	4	6	9	4	14	1
	Indian Express	84	72	-	22	12	06	21	47	48	-
	Hindu	105	38	-	29	12	8	23	56	116	-
04.05.2004	Daily Thanthi	50	35	21	18	2	10	6	9	9	1
	Dinamani	46	26	4	5	6	7	5	7	11	-
	Dinamalar	57	33	8	7	6	6	4	13	71	1
	Indian Express	73	112	-	38	4	6	24	44	40	-
	Hindu	133	42	3	23	34	14	45	43	82	-
05.05.2004	Daily Thanthi	45	34	8	11	7	19	5	9	20	-
	Dinamani	38	8	6	3	3	13	5	6	18	-
	Dinamalar	54	17	5	5	7	12	5	6	31	-
	Indian Express	78	44	-	37	6	13	24	40	43	-
	Hindu	122	46	-	36	3	16	21	50	172	-
06.05.2004	Daily Thanthi	36	21	6	24	23	18	9	4	40	-
	Dinamani	49	18	4	6	4	6	4	3	24	-
	Dinamalar	57	29	8	27	10	10	8	6	53	-
	Indian Express	111	34	-	41	7	4	43	42	50	-
	Hindu	144	105	1	39	12	1	33	51	49	-

(Contd.)

(*Contd.*)

Date	Newspaper	Category									
		Elec-tion	Develop-ment	Cinema	Busi-ness	Edu-cation	Culture	Other Countries	Sports	Adver-tisement	Local Body
07.05.2004	Daily Thanthi	64	28	28	7	5	26	5	2	12	-
	Dinamani	31	12	8	12	14	9	4	5	27	-
	Dinamalar	37	17	6	21	29	12	6	6	24	-
	Indian Express	101	60	14	54	17	10	38	52	34	-
	Hindu	110	60	39	45	11	32	37	53	67	-
	Daily Thanthi	46	7	3	7	14	4	3	4	29	-
	Dinamani	45	17	4	11	16	8	3	3	39	-
08.05.2004	Dinamalar	37	7	2	5	3	3	7	6	41	-
	Indian Express	86	13	5	38	5	2	19	48	34	-
	Hindu	107	76	4	36	72	5	35	57	76	-
	Daily Thanthi	61	25	12	31	25	34	2	5	34	1
	Dinamani	59	28	9	9	10	20	4	4	44	1
09.05.2004	Dinamalar	51	23	15	7	11	12	6	7	47	-
	Indian Express	127	93	21	37	42	23	22	40	42	-
	Hindu	115	100	4	15	17	3	37	79	80	-

Source : Computed from the Newspapers.

13

ROLE OF GRAM PANCHAYAT IN TSUNAMI DISASTER RELIEF

December 26, 2004 is a black day to the coastal villages of Tamil Nadu State, especially to the districts of Nagapattinam, Cuddalore and Kanyakumari. The tsunmai has created a major damage to the life and livelihood of the people in the coastal area. To manage the damage created by the tsunami, an organised effort is needed with partnership. The Panchayat is the nearest responsible, responsive and representative institution which has to act swiftly and firmly to save the people, and carry out relief measures jointly with the government to recover the people from trauma. The machinery required for relief and rehabilitation is huge. In Tamil Nadu there was an argument that in the relief and rehabilitation activities Panchayats were not involved and consulted. Even seminars were organised in which Government officials were criticized as they acted upon their own perception and data projected by officials. But, in the same seminar, a few Panchayat Presidents narrated their activities in tsunami relief and rehabilitation work. They made a point that the government officials came to the scene only after two days. Wherever Panchayat Presidents were committed, they started their work immediately with the active involvement of the youth. The officials and NGO volunteers joined them the next day onwards.

First responsibility of the Panchayat is to take a responsible position in managing the crisis for which enormous will power is needed. Wherever the Panchayat expected direction from the government, many players started their own work and kept different kinds of statistics on death and damage to property. Having realised the dispute over the statistics by the people of the respective villages, government officials took a decision that they would have to collect data on their own. Against this background Panchayats were marginalised. Whenever Panchayats took the lead, government officials followed the direction of the Panchayats. In this context, we are interested in knowing the role of Panchayats in tsunami relief and rehabilitation measures. Four case studies have been conducted and they are presented hereunder.

CASE STUDY-I

V. Chandran, President of Kothattai Gram Panchayat of Parangipettai Panchayat Union, Cuddalore District, has been hailed by many as he managed the crisis created by the tsunami in his Panchayat area. Basically a marine engineer (38) hailing from the fisherfolk community he was in the Middle East for some time to earn his livelihood. He was back to his village and contested in the Panchayat election and won. He carried out the Panchayat activities very effectively with the participation of all despite the opposition from some of his own community men since the election. It was purely election fund. When he heard the news of tsunami he was in a bus. Pudukkuppam was the worst affected area. The total death toll came to 126. Only six persons were in the village. Others totally vacated the village after the tsunami hit that area. The six were involved in removing dead bodies. In fact people living in other villages had the courage to visit the seashore and involved themselves in the rescue operation. Fishermen who lived in Pudupattinam who saw the tsunami waves refused to go the village again. They had such a kind of trauma after witnessing the tsunami waves. The rescue team saved twelve persons. He went to village and bodies were removed and identified. The Jammath came to the rescue of the villagers. They provided food and first aid to the affected families.

When all the dead bodies were brought to one place, the villagers refused to bury the dead bodies. Finally, officials requested the Panchayat leaders to accept the dead bodies. People were in an agitative mood and refused to accept the bodies. They refused to either burn or bury the dead bodies. Finally, he convinced the people. Since he took the responsibility to bring more number of people from outside to help the victims, people started believing him. Before the government started the rescue operation, the Panchayat President took the lead and, as a result, government officials followed the President and he was supported by the government in attending to the needs of the people. The Panchayat President, with the help of the youth and the clerk, collected the data. While doing this exercise he consulted the traditional Panchayat leader on every aspect of relief, rescue and rehabilitation. When he received relief material he openly maintained a note book and the entire responsibility was given to the traditional Panchayat leader. In fact the traditional Panchayat leader who was instrumental in opposing him in his Panchayat area right from the days of his election.

When the data pertinent to the loss of life and property was consolidated, the Gram Sabha was asked to approve the same. As such there was no dispute over the data as a pucca record system was maintained. He created an information centre in the Panchayat office to disseminate information relating to relief and rehabilitation works of the government and other donor agencies.

The Panchayat leader identified the location for a temporary shelter. Necessary facilities were provided at the temporary shelter by the Panchayat. Reboring was done by which good drinking water was supplied. Identity cards were prepared and issued to the affected 427 families. The Panchayat never allowed any agency to deal with the affected persons directly and, in the same way, the Panchayat never allowed the government officers to deal with the affected families directly. In all tsunami affected areas, data management became a big issue. In many of the Panchayats everyone was keeping a list of affected families and approached the donors and the government. But, in this Panchayat, there was only one list which was approved by the Gram Sabha and, endorsed by the traditional Panchayat leader. He maintained a very good relationship with the traditional Panchayat leaders and he was always in consultation with the traditional Panchayat leaders.

Collection of material, storing of material and distribution of material for relief were done in a scientific way. He created a transparent system by which he distributed all the materials to the needy. He saw to it that nobody other than the affected families got any relief material. His involvement in all the activities was from day one. He formed many committees for all activities in order to involve more number of people. Every activity was carried out through a committee. Even in the Gram Sabha convened on 10th February, 2005 to approve the beneficiaries list, he allowed the people to examine each and every name included in the list. He invited higher officials including the District Collector. He carried out activities in a transparent way.

He took special care of children and widows affected by the tsunami. Since affected persons were getting huge sums from the government, relatives showed keen interest in those individuals. To settle all the disputes in the best interests of the individuals, a lengthy dialogue was adopted with the involvement of the traditional Panchayat. Safety measures were taken to save the money given by the government to the affected persons, especially widows and children. All the money which the government gave has been deposited safely.

He established a good rapport with the people and won their confidence which enabled him to have a firm contact with the government officials and NGO representatives. NGOs played a key role in clearing the entire village and now they are providing permanent shelter. In his village all are the poor fishermen. He demonstrated his leadership by maintaining his cordiality with the traditional Panchayat leaders and all the other groups including his opponent who contested in the election. Further he proved his transparent administration by constituting a committee for relief and distribution of relief material by incorporating more number of individuals from the traditional Panchayat leaders group. On all occasions he went to the houses of others and never called anyone to his house. He was always responsive to the call of public, NGOs and government officials. He took responsibility in managing the affairs. He has been firm though he has maintained transparency.

CASE STUDY-II

Manickappangu is a coastal village in Kollidam Block of Nagapattinam District. It is a moderate village in size. There are 10 hamlets in Manickappangu, of which four are fisherfolk habitations, namely, Puthupettai, Perumalpettai, Vellakovil and Kutiyandiyur. Mr. Manimaran is the President of Manickappangu Village Panchayat. He is 45 years old, married and has two sons. His wife is a school teacher. Manimaran's family is basically identified with the DMK party. Manimaran from his boyhood had been a fan of MGR. When MGR started the AIADMK party he joined the AIADMK. Now he is in the DMK because he does not like the style of the present AIADMK leadership.

Manimaran's life is different from that of the other youth in the fishermen community. He was motivated by those educated and employed persons who belonged to fishermen community. His parents were economically well off. So they encouraged him to study instead of engaging in fishing. Manimaran's longing for study moved him further even after he completed his post-graduation. He did his M.Phil., B.Ed., Diploma in Labour Laws and another Post Graduate Diploma in Tourism Management from the Distance Education wing of the Annamalai University.

His father was in Singapore where he engaged in some work and had good earnings. Manimaran's brother worked on a ship. Hence there was no poverty in their family. The socio-economic background of his family made him different from other youth in the fishermen community. In reality, Manimaran does not know the nuances of the fishing avocation. Manimaran is now a progressive farmer. Along with his 3 acre own land, he used to get land for lease and did farming. With his wife's salary and earnings from agriculture, Manimaran is economically in a sound position.

His Entry into Village Panchayat Affairs

During 1996, when the first election under the New Panchayati Raj System was held, he contested for the position of Village Panchayat President. But he could not win. As the State Government was in the hands of the DMK party, Manimaran helped the villagers to avail the eligible benefits from the State Government. He waited for his turn. Once again he contested in the 2001 Panchayat election and won by a good margin of 350 votes. There are nine members in the Manickappangu Village Panchayat of which five belong to the fishermen community. There is only one member from the Scheduled Caste. Though the Village Panchayat is a multi-caste one consisting of Padayachis, Parayars and Christian Vanniyars, the fishermen community is numerically a stronger one than the others.

The Significance of Temple in the Fishermen Community

The fisherman has strong faith in God. Moreover the temple celebration enables the community to get together and so there was a change in the mindset of the fishermen community with regard to temple affairs. Earlier the temple was located near the seashore. In course of time the community realized the importance of a pucca and big building structure for the temple. So the fishermen community relocated the temple site from seashore to a place near the main habitation. A big temple, spacious enough to accommodate the community was constructed. In Manickappangu more than forty lakh rupees were spent to complete the construction of the temple for goddess Chintamani Amman at Puthupettai. Moreover it serves as a community shelter during natural calamity. Further individuals suffering from contagious diseases like smallpox used to stay during the period of cure in the temple premises. The temple priest is usually from one of the families of the fishermen community. In Manickappangu village there is also a priest in the Chinthamani Amman temple. But the heirs of the priest's family failed to adhere to the expected norms and procedures in the temple's day to day affairs. Hence the system of engaging priest from the traditional family was discontinued. Now a person from Brahmin community is engaged as priest in the temple, Mr. Manimaran explained. It is learnt that the Sanskritization process is spreading fast among the fishermen community.

From Poverty to Prosperity

Mr. Manimaran shared that the socio-economic status of the fishermen community is undergoing a big change recently, thanks to the modernization and technological innovation in the fishing avocation. Earlier the fishermen did not venture up to long distances in the sea for fishing. They had only kattumarams. Moreover they did not have different sizes and patterns of fish-net to catch different kinds of fishes in different seasons. But the Pattinavar, i.e., fishermen community is in a better position now. Possess different types of boats and fish-nets and so they go to deep sea and catch different varieties of fishes, Mr. Manimaran explained. Sales by auction is the system of marketing of fishes. Even a non-fisherman can participate in the auction, Mr. Manimaran explained. Thanks to the availability of facilities like transport and communication, fish marketing is a profitable business as fishes can be sold in other area markets and even sent to other States like Kerala where they are processed and packed for export, Mr. Manimaran explained.

Being an educated and socially oriented person, Mr. Manimaran shared that he served to the expectation of both groups, fishermen as well as non-fishermen communities. He further said that the community affairs of the fishermen is wholly looked after by the traditional Panchayat. He said that he does not feel anyone against the social recognition accorded to the traditional Panchayat instead of the constitutionally recognized Panchayat. Mr. Manimaran gave emphasis to activities like promotion of health and hygiene, upgradation of schooling, provision of toilets, street lights, drinking water facilities to all hamlets.

The Disaster of Tsunami and the Response of the Village Panchayat Administration under Mr. Manimaran

Ensuring the timely distribution of water supply is one of the important tasks the Village Panchayat administration is expected to do, Mr. Manimaran said. On 26th December, Manimaran woke up early morning and proceeded to switch on the power pump —OHT water supply system. Though there is an operator to do this, Manimaran did not wait for him. Then, as usual, he went to his field. Near the field there was a tea-stall and in front of the tea-stall there was a pond. Passersby crowded round it and saw that the water in the pond rose up and down around 8.45 a.m.

He then returned home. The houses of the fishermen were located within 200 metres of the seashore. When he was returning, there was an alarming sound. He saw waves from the sea rise up to 10 metres and the water was very thick and dark. Thorny bushes, thatches, broken logs, debris of damaged houses and other buildings all rolled on along the flood water. He immediately shouted at his sons and his wife to run away from the house. He got into his house and brought out his bike and drove to the nearby power plant office to contact the District Collectorate. He came to know that the Collector was already out to attend to the call of the public in this regard. Hence he drove back his bike to the habitation against the flood water but could not. He fell down in the speedy flow of water and he was able to hold on to a tree and escaped.

The villagers ran towards the bamboo bridge over the flooded river to escape from the chasing waves. Though the water was up to level of the bamboo bridge, the bridge was fit enough to cross over. It was so fortunate that just four days back, the bamboo bridge had been repaired. Otherwise there would have been no way to escape, Manimaran said.

Manimaran, with the help of other villagers, enabled others to climb over the bridge and to cross over to the other side, one by one. The youth of Anaikoil Village, which is a non-fishermen village, rushed immediately and helped to rescue the children and the old. In the meantime, the thorny bushes and debris struck against the bamboo bridge and it was later found that there were two dead bodies of children. The corpse of the children were removed and then Manimaran, with others, visited the habitation where they found dead bodies of children and adults. The dead bodies were removed by all and kept at the side of the local temple. Till 4 O'clock in the evening the rescue operation and removal of dead bodies was attended to, Manimaran said. After 4.00 p.m., he thought about his sons and wife. Immediately he visited Thirukadaiyur temple where all the people were staying. On his way, he was told that only one of his sons was seen. He is heart beat rose. With the hope that his family members would be alive, he moved towards Anaikulam in Thirukadaiyur, i.e., 7 kms from Manickappangu. He found his two sons and his wife there. Immediately he returned to his habitation in Manickappangu and engaged in burial activities.

During the rescue operation, it was very hard to walk freely. There were thorns and broken logs which struck against feet and fingers. It was a tough. Ordinary persons could not withstand such a struggle, Manimaran said. Only able bodied individuals could engage in relief work like tsunami relief, he said. When they all engaged in identifying dead bodies, they found one woman trapped between a gate and a wall and the wall fell on her and squeezed her to death. To remove the body, the cement gate had to be lifted up. But it was not easy to do so due to its weight. Manimaran and some youths jointly made an attempt and they were able to remove the dead body of that woman. Manimaran felt that it was a horrible scene to recollect. Manimaran shared that the rescue and relief operations initiated by the Government was not to the expected level. The survey and collection of data by the Government officials was not seriously carried out. The relief packages were not properly reached to the real sufferers, he complained.

The members of the fishermen community, though in fear of recurrence of tsunami like disaster, had a lesson and were getting ready to face the challenge, Manimaran explained. Manimaran suggested the following arrangements to be provided in coastal villages to handle the threat of tsunami:

- Construction of a tall tower like building structure within 500 metres of the sea so that villagers can climb up and escape from the chasing waves.
- The construction should be sound enough to withstand the challenges like tsunami/heavy rain etc.
- The habitation layout should be planned so as to have sufficient space between houses, broad streets, so that all can run away at the time of any threat.
- Thorny bushes should be removed from every direction.

Standing trees are not dangerous. On the contrary, they are saviours.

- There should be a big and spacious community centre with all infrastructure facilities. This should not be any type of temporary shelter.
- Guidance and further backward and forward linkages to those who are ready to have a new avocation other than fishing should be provided. As it is a customary practice in the fishermen families to engage anyone of their sons, if there are more than one son in the family, in fishing, it is possible to counsel these families to encourage other young men to go to new avocations.

The tsunami made them realize the concern of humanity towards fellow beings, Manimaran told. There were a large number of relief and rescue activities which were in unexpected quantum. The fishermen had never thought that the world would come to their side at this level. The compensation to the dead was very much a consolation to the concerned family. But there were cases of wasteful expenditure by the family members, Manimaran observed. Due to the availability of money, the habitual drunkards spent lavishly, some others purchased motorbikes, and only poor families deposited it in banks, Manimaran said. The tsunami had a lot of impact on the culture of the fishermen community. There are now occurrences of early marriage and the mindset of the youth has changed and they have come forward to marry with less dowry. After the tsunami, the youth wish to engage in a settled life, Manimaran felt.

Further, as the period of rehabilitation is a long one, the life style and will power of the youth and adults among the fishermen has changed. Due to monthly doles, provision of household articles free of cost, free supply of rice and other necessary commodities to the affected families, a type of laziness has developed in the minds of the fishermen community. They have failed to muster courage to venture into the sea for fishing, Manimaran observed. Though the role of non-governmental organizations in relief and rescue activities was commendable, the standard of works they undertook was poor. Particularly works like food for work schemes were carried out for name's sake, Manimaran complained. Manimaran felt that there was confusion on the side of the government with regard to the drafting of permanent rehabilitation plans. Moreover there was heavy damage to the farmers also. The agricultural land to an extent of one kilometre from the shore had been filled with salt. The reclamation of these degraded lands has not yet been seriously taken up for discussion by the government, Manimaran felt. But, being a farmer as well as a fishermen, Manimaran is serious enough in providing all eligible assistance, both monetary and goods to all families in the villages of Manickappangu Panchayat, irrespective of farmers, fishermen or farm labourers.

He was of the opinion that due to lack of proper coordination among the NGOs and GOs the implementation of relief and rehabilitation activities was not in an orderly manner. He suggested that in every coastal village there should be a standing committee consisting of all stakeholders, i.e., representatives of the government machinery, non-government institutions, traditional Panchayat committees and the Village Panchayat. They should meet periodically or whenever necessary and convey to the higher level authorities the experience of fishermen at sea during various seasons, the speed of wind, the magnitude of waves, the rainfall details, erosion of sand dunes, mangroves and other natural vegetation along the coastal area. This committee will not only be a disaster management committee but also work for the protection and promotion of coastal based socio-economic livelihood of all sections of the coastal area, Mr. Manimaran explained. Special orientation, exposure and training should be given to the members of this standing committee in this regard. The State and the Central Governments should allot a special fund for the execution of the plan drafted by the Village Panchayats through the standing committee for the overall development of the coastal zones, Manimaran opined.

CASE STUDY-III

Selvi Manimegalai is the President of Cauverypoompattinam Village Panchayat of Kallidam Panchayat Union. She belongs to the fishermen community. She is unmarried. Even at the age of 50 years, she moves fast at the call of the public. The interview was interrupted due to the visit of the revenue officials who came over to the village with regard to the complaint of Selvi Manimegalai against an encroacher. She just sat on a two-wheeler behind the driver and urged him to drive quickly to the spot. It was only after half an hour that she returned and resumed to the interview.

Selvi Manimegalai recollected the worst day, December 26, 2004. On that day she was watching the TV around 7.30 a.m. and the news about the tsunami hit in Indonesia was flashed. She immediately rushed outside and ran to Chinakuttai (small pond) to check for consequence in the village. Manimegalai informed that during the Gujarat earthquake, there was a sensation of body movement in Cauverypoompattinam. Hence, on December 26 after viewing the TV news, she went to the pond side and witnessed that the water in the pond had risen up to two feet and there were bubbles. To alert the villagers she ran to the seashore where the habitation of the fishermen community was located. Immediately she telephoned to higher officials from the police station. In the mean time sea water had come to the shore and within fifteen minutes the water rose to neck level. Children were struggling in the flood and were saved by youths. The walls of houses broke down and the flood water forcibly drew away everything around the habitation.

Earlier six huts had been constructed across the area by the community to house the larger families. Just three days earlier, Manimegalai had evicted all the inhabitants of the six huts and removed the thorny bushes/trees and cleared the approaches to all the roads leading to the shore-habitations. When the tsunami wave hit on that day, it was through that passage the community members ran fast and escaped from the attack of the killer waves. But mostly women and children who could not run quickly became victims, Manimegalai shared her experiences with tears in her eyes.

The northern side of Cauverypoompattinam is the Chinna Cauvery Pattinam where about 300 huts are located very near to the sea. Here 87 deaths occurred, Manimegalai said. She telephoned to various government departments and the District Collector. In the meantime, the Block Development Officials came to the villages and facilitated the relief works. The fishermen community handled the removal and burial of dead bodies. Several bodies lay underneath collapsed buildings and constructions. A JCB machine was brought to remove the debris and the bodies were recovered, Manimegalai said. The Village Panchayat administration arranged for refreshments to the community members. Biscuit and milk were provided. Lunch was also given by the Village Panchayat administration.

The non-fishermen community of Manthekarai volunteered for relief activities. The nearby villagers of Mangamadam and the merchants and traders of Sirkali Town came over and distributed food packets, Manimegalai explained.

Manimegalai said that the life of the fishermen community was very peaceful and joyful. They used to lie down on the shore fearlessly and allowed their little children to run and play on the shore. At the age of twelve years, the boys used to accompany their fathers and happily ventured into the sea. Steadily they learned the lifestyle, customs and techniques of life inside the sea. The boys became full time bread winners of their family at the age of seventeen or eighteen and would get one share of the fishes collected at sea. In the fishing trade there is no master-servant relationship. It is mere sharing of catches based on a basic rule. Whatever they get they share it. They enjoy their life with what they have. Their life is always entwined with nature.

Life in the sea is always a struggle. It is always uncertain and yet they enjoy their life. They have witnessed several challenges in their life. Yet this tsunami has created an irremovable fear among the fishermen. Even if there is a small change in the height of the tide, they imagine so many evils from the backdrop of the tsunami. The tsunami taught many lessons to the fishermen. Now one could find a change in the mindset and behaviour of the fishermen.

When a memorial was constructed in Poompukar for Kannaki, fishermen felt that it is only a protection wall for the memorial. But now they felt that because of the protection wall many saved their lives. But everyone in the seashore area felt that a protection arrangement has to be made either by creating natural barriers or an artificial barrier. Over a period of time the natural barriers have been removed by the people and the government for their advantage. Now the time has come to create such a barrier by planting saplings of different varieties of trees as per the advise of experts. People have witnessed that whenever natural barriers were created people had been saved as the velocity of the tide had been reduced. Now the community has realized the importance of natural barriers and this is stated by the people themselves.

To meet any such disaster, Manimegalai proposed a system. A community-cum-relief hall with pucca construction is very much needed, she explained. Further there should be availability of vessels, utensils, bedding and other livelihood facilities inside the proposed construction, she said.

Life in Temporary Shelters

It was after a period of one month, spent at temples/schools, temporary shelters were provided. The role of NGOs in this was noteworthy, Manimegalai said.

The killer waves destroyed everything, they lost their near and dear ones, houses and other properties, it was a total loss, Manimegalai felt. It was only in the past two or three decades that the life of fishermen had taken the path of progress and prosperity owing to science and technology, Manimegalai said. Due to the availability of boats, the availability of varieties of nets, oil engine, consolidation as a sangam, cooperative venture in fishing, the income was high. Hence the comforts and enjoyments increased. But due to the tsunami everything was destroyed.

The life in the temporary shelter was a horrible one and was very pitiable. Hence the Village Panchayat administration took steps to provide protected water supply, build roads, remove debris and clean roads and passages, protect environmental sanitation, health of women, immunize children and persuade thc government to identify a suitable site to relocate the affected houses, Manimegalai explained.

Manimegalai expressed gratitude to the services and assistance rendered by the government and non-governmental organizations. But she felt sorry for their attitude towards the community. Instead of discussing with the community to identify the felt needs among the youths and children and other stakeholders of the community, the NGO staff just provided what they chose. For instance, to a child of a victim family was given four bags from four NGOs, but nobody bothered to find out what could be kept inside the bags. People wanted more interaction from the people who came from outside but people who came here distributed material and took photographs and disappeared. Donors and the government provided material relief but not psychological relief. This is the feeling of the community.

She suggested that there should be a disaster management committee at the village level, Panchayat level and taluk level in the coastal areas. She was of the opinion that farmers and farm labourers should also be compensated from the government relief packages and NGO assistance. It is the whole coastal economy, environment and the sustainable livelihood which was affected. Hence development should be holistic covering all stakeholders, Manimegalai reiterated.

CASE STUDY-IV

Prathamarapuram is a Village Panchayat located near the Velankanni Church. Seruthur is the fishermen community village under the jurisdiction of Prathamarapuram Village Panchayat. The President, Sri R.V. Swaminathan, explained the details of the relief activities undertaken by his Village Panchayat administration.

The Day of Disaster

The President, hearing the news of the tsunami from the local community, informed the Police, Fire station, RDO and the District Collector over the phone. Since he is a well informed person, he had all the phone numbers. He made arrangements to move the affected people to the hospitals. At the same time, all the families from the coastal area came out and fled to safer places. The President helped them to go over to safer places, far away from the coastal area, by making arrangements with private transport companies, lorry and tractor owners. He found it very difficult to bring transport to this village. Most of them were put into the marriage hall and schools located in the village itself. The President arranged for preparing breakfast and lunch with the help of local community volunteers.

In the meantime, he made arrangements for visiting Seruthur Village. A team of youths and other volunteers from the main village Prathamarapuram joined the youth and elders of the fishermen community, started the identification of dead bodies, and removed the same for burial. In the meantime Government officials started to go over the affected area and collected various details and so the President assisted them by providing the necessary details through verification and clarification from the concerned families and the community. The Panchayat President established his control over the entire activities and left no room for Government officials to act on their own. In the beginning he did not wait for the arrival of the officials.

Association with NGOs

The second and third day after the disaster, a number of NGOs came to the site and distributed various items of relief materials. The President helped them to identify the victim families and assisted in proper disposal of relief materials to the concerned families. By then the Government formed a team of various sectoral officials and the relief work was systematized--removal of debris, restoration of electricity, drinking water supply, link road and connectivity to the affected area. The President joined the official team and assisted them. At the camp site, medical check-up and medicines were also provided by the team.

Various NGOs, volunteers and social institutions visited and a lot of activities were undertaken by them like counselling, distribution of provisions, play materials and other essential materials like blankets, buckets, vessels, etc. to the affected families. In general, the NGOs used to meet the President and sought the help of the Panchayat administration to contact the right persons or community leaders. Without any confusion the relief activities were properly carried out. The President informed that some NGOs, when they directly contacted the affected families, faced a lot of problems in distributing the materials. The presence of the Village Panchayat President brought some order, Swaminathan claimed. Further the President helped in identifying and establishing a temporary shelter with necessary facilities like drinking water supply and toilet and electricity connection.

When the Government arranged the dole and other cash benefits to the affected families, the President assisted the Village Administrative Officer in listing the eligible families in this regard. He gave an impression to the officials as well as the members of the community that he is a person with leadership and sense of commitment. He maintained the exact data with regard to death and damage to properties. He did not permit anyone to take advantage of the misery. He demonstrated his leadership in managing the situation very effectively. In many places the communities were divided on caste lines for distribution of relief material. But in his Panchayat he maintained harmony among various segments of the society.

Role in the Drafting of Micro Level Plan

The President assisted the local NGO engaged by The Hunger Project, Gandhigram Rural Institute, to carry out the Micro Planning exercise. He assisted in identifying the local volunteers, farmer groups and SHG groups, helped in the baseline survey, focused group discussion, in conducting PRA exercise, and drafting the developmental plan for the Village Panchayat. Swaminathan explained that generally the fishermen community was very traditional in nature: they used to come to the Village Panchayat to stake their entitlements, namely, drinking water, road, street lights, etc. For other needs, they used to seek the help of the traditional Panchayat leaders. But tsunami created a new atmosphere and interface with all sections of the community, Swaminathan said. It is a normal tendency among the poor, whether they are affected or not, where there is any opportunity to get any assistance from the government, they utilize it by any means. This is being exploited by all from politicians to officials. This, in fact, created a whole lot of problems in the communities. But Panchayat leaders, with their responsible action could avoid many of the unpleasant situations. The elected Panchayat leaders have to act responsively with a sense of commitment.

Conclusion

It is a major complaint that in the tsunami relief and rehabilitation activities, Panchayats were not involved and they were not consulted. The State Government believed only the officials and not the Panchayats. It is further argued that even the government officials established contact with traditional Panchayat leaders and not with the constitutional Panchayats. But the cases analysed in this study have amply established the fact that wherever the Panchayat leaders took responsibility and responded to the situation without expecting direction from the government officials, they established control over the community. They did not allow the external agencies to divide the community. Panchayat leaders have established good rapport with traditional Panchayat leaders. It is not the power and resources that matter it is only the leadership that matters.

14

RECONSTRUCTION OF VILLAGES THROUGH MICRO PLAN AFTER TSUNAMI

Introduction

Villages and communities which are affected and damaged due to tsunami are in the process of reconstruction and rehabilitation for the past one year. Despite the huge commitment by donor agencies and governments towards rehabilitation and reconstruction, activities are slow since the rehabilitation activities are process oriented. Yet achieving the target of completing the committed activities is difficult as social process becomes so complicated. The entire coastal line Panchayats grappled with the division of communities which were dormant became active as relief activities were carried out sectorally and segmentally by the donor agencies and government departments. It is a pity that variety of development activists got involved in relief and rehabilitation activities and yet people are not empowered and they had been reduced to orphans, beneficiaries and petitioners. As a result they are not made as part of the entire relief and rehabilitation activities. Government departments have started looking at the human sufferings from their own specialization. Both government departments and civil society organizations by their sectoral approach, made the people to fight against each other to get relief and rehabilitation activities. Politicians have started looking at the problems from their party backdrop and intensified the conflict among the groups. Specialized research agencies analysed the problems of particular groups and projected the damages and the loses of the groups leaving many groups unattended. There are institutions in the name of analysis of the power of the communities which have done great damage to the constitutionally created Panchayats and they are totally sidelined in relief and rehabilitation activities excepting in a few places when Panchayats took a lead role. Having seen the anarchy and chaos, Rajiv Gandhi Chair of Gandhigram Rural Institute started exploring the possibility of involving the communities in the preparation of micro plan in each and every Gram Panchayat for reconstruction of the tsunami-affected areas. The key assumption is that people are having energy, skill, capacity and capability to participate in the reconstruction process and by which they can establish their self-dignity. By doing this exercise people can participate and empower themselves. Affected people cannot and need not look at themselves with pity. They can claim their rights to get relief and rehabilitation. The aim of this exercise is to reverse the process of powerlessness to empowerment of the people. This task is very difficult and it is process oriented and not target oriented. Yet an action research was planned and mooted this idea with many of the Panchayats. Of the Panchayats, seventeen Gram Panchayats have agreed to conduct this experiment. Gandhigram Rural Institute's Rajiv Gandhi Chair for Panchayati Raj Studies has started working in seventeen Gram Panchayats with the active support of The Hunger Project, New Delhi.

Having got assurance from the seventeen Panchayats to work on preparation of micro plan, Gandhigram looked for non-governmental organizations who are working in these seventeen Gram Panchayats. Finally, three small NGOs had been identified to work closely with the community. They are to be recognized by the community also. Hence the NGOs who are already working in those Panchayats are identified. They are SEVALAYA, SCORD and REFORM Trust. With the help of the three NGOs we have identified the individuals who are so powerful in influencing the community. They are self-help group leaders, traditional Panchayat leaders, youth group leaders, Farmers Association leaders, Ward Members, caste leaders, political party unit representatives, retired employees living in the respective villages and guild leaders. One day workshop was organized at Nagapattinam to get their opinion about the new exercise to be done at the Panchayat level. The whole day was devoted to analyse the powerlessness of the people and the reasons for their powerlessness and how to empower people has also been discussed. How divisions and conflicts in the community help others to manage the people easily has been explained. For a powerful negotiation with government and other agencies communities should be made intact. Finally, in principle they had agreed to mobilize the people to involve in the preparation of micro plan for overall development of the villages. All the leaders agreed to work with Gram Panchayat. Gram Panchayat should be made people centric and not leader centric. Everyone had agreed to work for preparing a perspective micro plan. First condition stipulated was that this exercise should be based on mutual consent and the process should be based on inclusion and gender. In the whole process of relief injustice was done to the disabled, widows, destitute women, labourers, and Dalits. Hence it was reiterated that the problems of all segments have to be incorporated. Based on the concurrence the District administration was approached and the District Collector and Project Officer, DRDA were met and they were informed of this proposal. In fact they were delighted as they also found it very difficult to carry out development works in the midst of conflict among the groups. With great difficulty they carry out rehabilitation activities. District administration has found out a new opportunity for their work. They have agreed to support this endeavour of preparing micro plan. With the assurance of the leaders and opinion makers of the communities, the three non-governmental organizations and the District administration micro plan initiative was undertaken in all the seventeen Gram Panchayats in Nagapattinam District.

Methodology

With the help of the three NGOs, people had been mobilized for the task of preparing the micro plan for the Panchayats. While mobilizing the community for active participation, the leaders of the Panchayats and communities were sensitized and conscientized on the potentials of the Panchayats, issues of social development, economic development and social justice. Further they are oriented in empowerment and right-based development. A four-day capacity building programme was designed and carried out and for which the leaders were mobilized only by District administration. Officials have been instructed to cooperate with Panchayat leaders and the three lead NGOs in the preparation of the micro plan. The Panchayat leaders along with the community leaders were trained. Field staff of the lead NGOs were also trained to be sensitive on the issues of exclusion and marginalization. Panchayat constituted the Statutory Committees including Planning Committee. NGO staff, Panchayat leaders community leaders, Panchayat clerks and officials involved in preparing the data base. Following the data collection needs of the people were assessed. For need assessment and prioritization of the works, PRA exercises were carried out in all the villages. Apart from PRA, focus group discussions were held. As a result, needs are generated, activities are identified, to carry out activities resources are identified. Disparities among the hamlets (villagers) within the jurisdiction of Panchayats are identified, and activities and steps are evolved.

With the help of the staff of the NGOs, Panchayat Presidents prepared the documents. In the first part, description about the damages caused to the village by tsunami, basic objectives of the plan, general information about the Panchayats and the facilities available in the Panchayats has been made. It is almost the profile of a Panchayat. Second part deals with the methodological nuances adopted to generate data and analyse the same. Details have been explained as to how they have identified the priorities of activities for development and social justice. Third part deals with the sectors, namely agriculture, water supply and sanitation, services education, health, economic activities form and non-form activities. In each sector what is available and what is required and how it is going to be met have been explained in this part. In each document a SWOT analysis has been made and incorporated.

Generating data is not a difficult job, identifying the people's needs is not a tough job, prioritizing activities is not a stupendous task, meeting their needs is the most complicated task as resources are with government departments. Government departments have been trained to carry out activities in the rural areas as they have earmarked resources available with them. Whether the activity is needed to the society or not, they carry out the same and submit a report as target has been achieved. Thus all our activities are supply driven. People made complaints that Government departments have spent huge amount of money on various activities. But they are not for the felt needs of the society. Every year four times Gram Sabha is being convened and in all the four times people express their needs. They are bare minimum. But they are not met. Variety of activities are carried out by various departments in the villages. There is no match between the people's need and government activities.

People informed that Government departments need not spend money in the villages without getting the concern of the Gram Sabha. Against this background this micro level plan gets importance as the prioritized needs are matched with Government department activities. There are certain activities which can be matched with Agriculture Department, a few others can be done by Horticulture Department. Likewise all the activities are classified into department activities. There are certain activities which cannot be done by any of the Government department and for which they seek the help of the donor agencies and civil society organizations. There are certain activities which can be done by the community itself.

They have fixed the responsibilities among themselves to carry out the activities. Further the plan document is legitimized with the approval of the District administration. The plan document with the signature of the Gram Sabha members is being submitted to all sectoral departments. When the entire exercise from mobilizing the people for planning exercise, constituting committees for plan preparation, training the groups in micro level planning, conducting PRA exercise in the villages, conducting focus group discussions in the villages, preparing a plan document, getting the approval of Gram Sabha for plan document to getting the approval of District administration have raised hope among the people and raised confidence among the people.

Following are the details of the analysis the people of the respective Panchayats have made and activities prioritized by them:

Gram Panchayats which have developed Micro Plan

1. Pratabaramapuram
2. Vilunthanmavadi
3. Thirupoondi East
4. Pudupalli
5. Vettikaran iruppu
6. Thennampattinam
7. Kaveripoompattinam
8. Perunthottam
9. Vanakiri
10. Maruthapallam
11. Kalamanallur
12. Manickapangu
13. Thandavankulam
14. Vettangudi
15. Thirumullaivasal
16. Pillaiperumalnallur
17. Chandrapadi

Analysis of Conditions

SWOT Analysis

REFORM TRUST (NGO)

Sl. No.	*Name of the Village Panchayat*	*Strength*	*Weakness*	*Opportunity*	*Threat*
1.	Kaveripoompattinam	Knowledgeable leader, dedicated worker, rapport with the traditional leaders and Government officials; SHGs are active	More no. of labourers, migration poverty among SC families, tourist centre	Good Transport facility, Tourist Centre, more infrastructure, organized youth, Ice plant, Dairy centre	Lands are affected, unemployment in Dalit, Casticism among youth, lack of solidarity among fishermen.
2.	Perunthottam	Popular Leader, Positive mindset of the community, Traditional leadership in all communities	Migration due to unemployment; lack of transport utility and infrastructure, continuous droughts/ flood	Educated youth, people are demanding social concern of SHGs	Casticism – deep rooted prawn farming. The disappointed families who have been affected a lot
3.	Thirumullaivasal	Independent Women leadership, Famous Temple, Tourist Centre, Awakened world members, fishermen habitation very near to the marine village	Larger population scattered hamlets lack of basic amenities. The closeness of fishermen habitation	Scope for Tourist spot, A key village to neighbouring villages scope for fish market	Conflict between fishermen and non-fishermen, fishermen habitation – very near to the sea; natural sand dunes were destroyed; sea water will enter into the village

Sl. No.	Name of the Village Panchayat	Strength	Weakness	Opportunity	Threat
4.	Thennampattinam	Popular leader, optimism of the people, Traditional panchayat in all communities	Integration, lack of transport and infrastructure facilities, drought – continuously affected	Educated youth, people are demanding Social concern of SHG	Casticism, Prawn farms, the disappointed mindset of affected people
5.	Vettangudi	Philanthropist leader, support of members, rapport with fishermen, rapport with government, active SHG, rich Muslim community	Depend on Muslim unemployment in SC, Prawn farming, road severely affected by Tsunami, salinity of land	Mindset of big farmers, more no. of employees in construction, educated youth and active youth in fishermen, drainage of flood water, good system	Big size, unemployed youth, casticism, 3 fishermen habitation, lack of infrastructure
6.	Thandavankulam	Politically influential leader, solidarity among farmers	Gap between the President and the community, Drought, more no. of farmers, lack of understanding between two fishermen communities	Coastal area beautiful scope for beach, plenty of palm trees, fishermen panchayat, herbal plants	Lack of rapport between the President and members, lack of transport facility, more women do not get any employment opportunity

SCORD (NGO)

Sl. No.	*Name of the Village Panchayat*	*Strength*	*Weakness*	*Opportunity*	*Threat*
1.	Chandrapadi	Communal Harmony organised SHG peoples participation, Transport, Communication facilities	Large no. of Agricultural Labourers, Lack of Employment opportunities	Scope in Agriculture, Large number of Labourers – can be oriented in new skills	Alcoholism, Encroachment in Common Property Resources, Lack of natural vegetation along the Coastal area
2.	Maruthampallam	Communal Harmony organised SHG peoples participation, Transport, Communication facilities	Percentage of Library is less	Scope in Agriculture, Large number of Labourers – can be oriented in new skills	Alcoholism, Encroachment in Common Property Resources, Lack of natural vegetation along the Coastal area
3.	Kalamanallur		Lack of good rapport between fishermen and other communites	Scope in Agriculture, Large number of Labourers – can be oriented in new skills	Alcoholism, Encroachment in Common Property Resources, Lack of natural vegetation along the Coastal area
4.	Pillai Perumalnallaur			Scope in Agriculture, Large number of Labourers – can be oriented in new skills	Alcoholism, Encroachment in Common Property Resources, Lack of natural vegetation along the Coastal area

Sl. No.	*Name of the Village Panchayat*	*Strength*	*Weakness*	*Opportunity*	*Threat*
5.	Manickapangu			Scope in Agriculture, Large number of Labourers – can be oriented in new skills	Alcoholism, Encroachment in Common Property Resources, Lack of natural vegetation along the Coastal area
6.	Vanagiri			Scope in Agriculture, Large number of Labourers – can be oriented in new skills	Alcoholism, Encroachment in Common Property Resources, Lack of natural vegetation along the Coastal area

SEVALAYA (NGO)

Sl. No.	*Name of the Village Panchayat*	*Strength*	*Weakness*	*Opportunity*	*Threat*
1.	Prathaparamapuram	Dedicated Leadership of Panchayat President, organizes SHG, People's participation, Transport, Communication facilities	More number of Agricultural labourer are in poverty; percentage of literacy is less; lack of orientation in Common Property Resources Management; lack of relationship between fishermen and other communities	Horticulture products are many; scope for Hori-based village industries	Youths are falling into alcoholism; encroachments, destruction of natural sand dunes
2	Thirupoondi East	Communal Harmony organised SHG people's participation, Transport, Communication facility	More number of Agricultural labourer are in poverty; percentage of literacy is less; lack of orientation in Common Property Resources Management; lack of relationship between fishermen and other communities	Horticulture products are many; scope for Hori-based village industries	Youths are falling into alcoholism; encroachments, destruction of natural sand dunes
3.	Puthupalli	Communal Harmony, Peoples participation, Transport facilities	More number of Agricultural labourer are in poverty; percentage of literacy is less; lack of orientation in Common Property Resources Management; lack of relationship between fishermen and other communities	Horticulture products are many; scope for Hori-based village industries	Youths are falling into alcoholism; encroachments, destruction of natural sand dunes

Sl. No.	Name of the Village Panchayat	Strength	Weakness	Opportunity	Threat
4.	Vettaikaran iruppu	Communal Harmony, Peoples participation, Transport facilities	More number of Agricultural labourer are in poverty; percentage of literacy is less; lack of orientation in Common Property Resources Management; lack of relationship between fishermen and other communities	Horticulture products are many; scope for Hori-based village industries	Youths are falling into alcoholism; encroachments, destruction of natural sand dunes
5.	Vizhunthamavadi	Communal Harmony, Peoples participation, Transport facilities	More number of Agricultural labourer are in poverty; percentage of literacy is less; lack of orientation in Common Property Resources Management; lack of relationship between fishermen and other communities	Horticulture products are many; scope for Hori-based village industries	Youths are falling into alcoholism; encroachments, destruction of natural sand dunes

REFORM TRUST

Basic Details of the Gram Panchayat Areas

Sl. No.	Name of the Village Panchayat	Total No. of Hamlets	Total Popu-lation	Total Ward Members and (SC members)	Total No. of Balwadi	School Details				Health Institu-tions	SHG Total Nos.	Vulnerable Section							Human Loss
						Primary	Middle	High	Higher Secondary			Children 0 – 5	Mentally retarded	Handi – capped	Widows	Destitute	Old age	Adolescents	
1.	Kaveripoompattinam	5	8267	13 (4)	4	1	2	1	-	PHC	82 (5)	216	45	78	368	33		547	110
2.	Perunthottam	7	5787	12 (6)	4	3	1	-	-	HSc	32 (7)	210	20	67	273	52		784	48
3.	Thennampattinam	6	5092	9 (3)	3	3	1	-	-	HSc	44 (6)	160	41	74	214	8		573	97
4.	Thirumullaivasal	5	10137	15 (2)	4	5	1	-	1	PHC	63 (6)	2700	26	125	455	41		547	110
5.	Veetangudi	9	7448	9 (2)	3	3	2	-	-	HSc	31 (9)	250	16	74	226	22		547	1
6.	Thandavankulam	6	4738	7 (3)	1	1	2	-	-	HSc	38 (3)	373	15	45	224	23		776	24

SCORD

Sl No.	Name of the Village Panchayat	Total No. of Hamlets	Total Population	Total Ward Members and (SC members)	Total No. of Balwadi	School Details				Health Institutions	SHG Total Nos.	Vulnerable Section							Human Loss
						Primary	Middle	High	Higher Secondary			Children 0 – 5	Mentally retarded	Handi-capped	Widows	Destitute	Old age	Adolescents	
1.	Manickapangu	10	5436	9 (1)	10	2	1	-	-	HSc	53 (-)	774	18	86	196			420	103
2.	Pillaiperumalnallur	5	312	9 (4)	1	1	1	-	-	Danida Health Centre	34 (1)	83	18	31	135			186	
3.	Chandirapadi	2	1993	8	4	2	-	1	-	HSc	25		10	21	60			286	
4.	Vanagiri	6	7292	9 (2)	5	2	1	-	-	HSc	70 (-)	104	23	71	359			673	
5.	Marathapallam	5	4081	9	3	-	2	-	-	HSc	41 (-)	100	14	49	176			593	
6.	Kalamanallur	7	3451	8 (6)	3	1	1	-	-	HSc	34 (-)	259	7	35	156			403	

SEVALAYA

Sl. No.	Name of the Village Panchayat	Total No. of Hamlets	Total Population	Total Ward Members and SC members	Total No. of Balwadi	School Details				Health Institutions	SHG Total Nos.	Vulnerable Section							Human Loss
						Primary	Middle	High	Higher Secondary			Children 0 – 5	Mentally retarded	Handicapped	Widows	Destitute	Old age	Adolescents	
1.	Prathaparamapuram	2	12776	9 (1)	2	1	2	1	1	HSc PHC	80 (30)		32		246			153	153
2.	Thirupoondi East	6	5676	10 (2)	2	4	-	1	-	-	75 (30)	326	46		283	65	60		
3.	Vizhurthamavadi	4	6081	10	3	3	-	-	1	PHC	65 (20)		19		133	15	113		
4.	Puthupalli	2	3250	9 (1)	1	2	-	-	-	-	30 (20)		27		140	6		235	1
5.	Vettaikaran Iruppu	7	4709	7 (1)	2	4	-	1	-	HSc	80 (30)	272	114		262	12	467	380	48

Summary of Needs

1. Drinking Water

- Sustainability of Drinking Water Supply.
- Quality of groundwater is not good.
- Community is not oriented in the concept of village based management system of water supply and sanitation.
- Special attention through sensitization, orientation and capacity building to the community is very much needed.

2. Street Lights

- In several Village Panchayats, hamlets are located in remote area. Street lights are needed to those places.
- There are no solar lights.
- Transformer capacity is inadequate. Hence additional transformers are required in several Panchayats.

3. Roads/Culverts

- Coastal area is generally neglected. It was told that after the introduction of New Panchayati Raj System only, infrastructure development activities are initiated. Link roads to coastal area are demanded.
- In some villages construction of new bridges are demanded.

4. Other Infrastructure Facilities Needed

- Bus shelter, thrashing floor, SHG building, TV unit/room, community hall, play ground to youth, park and infrastructure facilities in the burial/funeral ground are demanded.
- Women sanitary complex, public toilet for men, household latrines are demanded.
- Desilting/maintenance of water resources, removal of encroachment, tree planting and afforestation activities are demanded.

- Health sub-centre, vetenary centre, service of bank, cooperative institutions are demanded.
- Increasing of frequency of public transportation, mini bus services are demanded. Public telephone booth services are demanded.
- Coastal area–a forestation, promotion of tree planting in private farms, reconstruction of sand dunes, construction of stone walls, check dams are demanded.

Women

A. SHG Women

- SHG activities—strengthening.
- Skill orientation.
  - — Tailoring/readymade garments,
  - — Coir production,
  - — Palm products production,
  - — Fruit Processing,
  - — Computer Operation,
  - — Telephone Booth,
  - — Management of PDS,
  - — Entrepreneurship training,
  - — Cottage industrial activities,
  - — Petty trades.
- Socio-political orientation.
- Women empowerment through Panchayati Raj:
  - — Participation involving/contesting,
  - — Gram Sabha participation,
  - — Involving in various standing committees,
  - — Micro Planning implementation—involvement.

B. Adolescent Women

- Motivation to continue their education.
- Health/Personal Hygiene/RCH activities.
- Educational assistance to continue college/technical education.

- Skill orientation to grown up girls.

C. *Widows*

- Linkage with Self-Help Groups.
- Availing of eligible assistance from the government.
- Skill orientation like SHG members.
- Special attention to the dependents of widows, especially their children's welfare.
- Priority in economic assistance.

D. *Destitute*

- Linage with Self-Help Groups.
- Skill orientation/employment generation.
- Availing of government assistance.
- Ensuring community care/confidence building.

E. *Old Age Persons*

- Availing of government scheme assistances.
- Special health care—reference—follow up.
- Day care centre activities/community responsibility.

F. *Disabled Persons*

- Registration/identity card/government assistance.
- Skill orientation/employment generation.
- Special drive to avail employment to them.
- Day care for mentally retarded—community responsibility.

Details of Needs of Target Groups

A. *Pre-School Children*

- In many villages, the Balwadi facility is not available proportionate to strength of pre-school children.

- The facilities in the existing Balwadi are very limited.
- The environment around the Balwadi centre is not an aesthetic one.
- The parents need orientation in maintaining the personal hygiene of children.
- Weight monitoring and sharing the same with mothers is not seriously carried out. It has to be ensured.

B. School

- Infrastructure facilities are needed in schools.
- Employment of additional teachers in proportionate to the children.
- PTA has to be activated.
- School day, sports day celebrations are not organised—Necessary motivation is needed in this regard.
- Special attention to improve the standard in English and mathematics subjects is needed.
- Plan to improve the total personality of the students.
- Vegetable gardening, tree planting activities have to be inculcated among the students.
- Orientation in computer education to higher class students.

C. Youth

- They have to be organised effectively.
- In some Village Panchayats they have organised youths but they need social orientation.
- In some village youths are addicted to alcoholism. They need counselling and awareness.
- Special attention to skill orientation:
  - — two-wheeler mechanism,
  - — motor mechanism,
  - — diesel mechanism,
  - — simple wiring,
  - — computer operation,
  - — cycle shop,

— fruit processing (south of Nagapattinam),
— fish trade,
— cashew nut process,
— nursery raising,
— vending,
— masonry/carpentry,
— organic farming,
— organising sports/cultural events,
— PRI orientation.

Economic Development Activities — Needs

A. Farmers

- Promotion of alternative crops/demonstration.
- Organic farming/land reclamation in affected areas.
- Organising of farmers committee.
- Strengthening of farmers association.
- Herbal farming.
- Improving the services of Primary Agricultural Cooperative Bank.
- Orientation in horticulture, fish culture.
- Agri-based village industrial orientation.
- Improving the service delivery of the government procuring centre.
- Linkage with the financial institutions/research institution.
- Provision of agricultural equipments/tools.
- Tenancy rights for tillers of temple land (North Nagai Area).

B. Farm Labourers

- Employment opportunity through food for work.
- Alternative employment opportunities.
- Inclusion in social security scheme.
- Orientation in brick making.
- Credit assistance for milch animal/goat rearing.
- Need house site, patta distribution.

- Training in extraction of edible oil and non-edible oil.
- Replacing of huts into fire proof houses.
- Land purchase scheme assistance.

C. Fishermen Community

- Boat, pucca, housing, engines.
- Subsidy for diesel.
- Dry fish yard.
- Godown.
- Auction centre.
- Training in production of fish based items for consumers need.
- Tsunami/weaker warning system.
- Orientation on cleanliness, sanitation environmental management.
- Democratizing the traditional Panchayat bodies.
- Economic assistance to vendors.
  — head load vendors,
  — cycle vendors,
  — establishing rapport between elected Village Panchayats administration and fishermen community,
  — common property management activities,
  — awareness on the ills of alcoholism,
  — special focus on the activities of youth and adolescent girls - welfare and development,
  — construction of cyclone/disaster relief centre,
  — community care to those families who lost their members.

The entire process of mobilization and participation the issues of Dalits, women widows, disabled, vulnerable families, farm labourers children, government service delivery institutions have been included in the planning exercise. Hence it is an inclusive plan. While discussing all those problems with the people of the Panchayats they are sensitized and conscientized on the above issues.

While attending all segments demands the conflict among the groups have been reduced. It took near about six months to bring together all the groups. There was intense fight between Gram Panchayat and fishermen Panchayat, fishermen fight against Dalits and *vice versa.* The issues of disabled, widow, destitute, children, for labourers are not highlighted in the relief and rehabilitation process but through planning they are brought together. Even the details of the Panchayati Raj System had not percolated into the society before the tsunami hit. But during the entire process of preparing the micro plan, people came to know the potentials of the Panchayats. They realized the potentials of the collectives also. Many of the development issues are not known to them. Everyone was demanding a hospital for their villages. After the plan everyone started talking about health governance. People are not aware of many of the schemes and offices which are dealing with the schemes. After this exercise they are having grip over the schemes and the Government departments.

Though Panchayat provided opportunity to the poor and the excluded to raise their voice, they could not do so as there was no conducive climate. But now all the excluded have been included and with the help of external agencies, they have raised their voices. Substantial amount of activities are identified for widows, destitute, adolescent girls, disabled, children and vulnerable families. In normal relief and rehabilitation, the above segments are neglected. It is also clear that neither the community nor the leader of the community sensitive towards governance, development and equity. But now they have realized the importance of the inclusion and equity.

15

PARTICIPATORY DEMOCRACY AT GRASSROOTS

Introduction

Representative democracy is a widely accepted form of governance in the world now. Today more than 50 per cent of the people live under democratically elected governments[1]. Movements are still on to democratize governments and society. It is to be noted that wherever representative democracy has been established as a form of government, still activities are on to democratize the institutions, the organizations and the society. Further, movements have gained voice to get services from the governing institutions which are under the democratic mode. At the same time it is to be pondered whether the countries which are under democratic governance have delivered the goods to the public and maintained peace and harmony among the social collectivities and regions. If yes, how are these democratic governments able to evolve to cope with the new demands and the new pressures emerging from the social collectivities in the given context? If no, why have not these democratic governments delivered the goods? Where have these democracies derailed? This has to be analysed.

Analyzing a country which is known for its puzzle and paradox will throw ample light on the problems, issues and trends in the process of democracy and development. India being the best case, such an analysis has to be made on Indian polity and democracy. The analysis of 50 years of democratic governance has brought out the fact that democratic governance has recorded substantial achievements, delivery of goods and services to the privileged, the ruling elites, the middle class and the poor to some extent. But, as for mitigating poverty, maintaining law and order, meeting the basic expectations of the poor, making them participate in the decision-making, the government institutions do not have the adequate capacity[2]. There are many questions unaddressed in the development and democracy discourse. Is the development which the State institutions pursue the right kind of course needed for a society like India and is the type of democracy which has been pursued the right kind of democracy to address the issues of the people? Both the exponents of democracy and of development do not agree with the present trend of achieving development and the present process of democracy. It is unequivocally demonstrated that both are in trouble. Then what is the alternative arrangement in the orbit of governance? How can the emerging discontented groups be accommodated in the economic activities and in the process of decision-making and how are the development activities to be reframed?

Ills in Governance

Generally governments are shaped and oriented by short-term populism, corruption and the self-interest of political elites. Having seen the negative implications of the government actions, international agencies switched over to the market for appropriate solution to the existing problems. Even the market failed to provide adequate solutions in the areas of inclusion, poverty reduction, environmental protection and public services. It is not only in India but also throughout the world, both north and south, that citizens speak of mounting disillusionment with the government, based on concerns about corruption, lack of responsiveness to the needs of the poor and the absence of a sense of connection with elected representatives and bureaucrats. The discontented groups are multiple in number and complex in character and hence a framework should be designed which should have the capability to accommodate the largely varied groups in the system very actively in the economic and political domain. Further, the system should have the capability to mitigate poverty and reduce corruption, which afflict the society and lead to the emergence of discontented and marginalized groups. This syndrome prevails in many of the developing countries which have borrowed representative democracy from the west and have not evolved as vibrant democracies by incorporating indigenous characteristics and thereby addressed the major issues of the society. The whole world is in search of better governance and it becomes a pressing issue for citizens. In many countries people organized public protest movements and they demanded systemic changes in government. A key challenge now is the construction of new relationships between the citizens and governance[3]. It is unequivocally brought out by the World Development Report (2000-2001) that many poor people around the world perceive large institutions, especially those of the state, to be distant, unaccountable and corrupt[4]. It is further validated and confirmed by other studies that, from the perspective of poor people in the world, there is a crisis in governance[5]. A large number of institutions are involved in ameliorating the conditions of the poor. Yet the poor are excluded from participation in governance. Government institutions and departments are neither responsive nor accountable to the poor. The poor are treated with arrogance and disdain. Poor people feel that they are helpless and they see little protection against injustice, crimality, abuse and corruption by institutions. Not surprisingly poor men and women lack confidence in State institutions even though they still express their willingness to partner with them in development activities. People are disillusioned with governments as they are corrupt, non-responsive to the needs of the poor and allow no space for the people to correct them[6]. The above malaise has afflicted all the segments in the world, both developing and developed. Yet another shocking symptom is the weakness or lack of public commitment to local democracy[7].

In Search of Solution

Though the ills of representative democratic systems in societies which have feudal thought process were predicted much earlier, the real picture emerged only at the time of the advent of globalization. In many countries measures to bring the government 'closer to the people' through decentralization and devolution have prompted shifts in approaches to service delivery that have widened spaces for citizens' involvement. At the same time the increasing marketization of service delivery in many countries has introduced new roles for those who were formerly the beneficiaries of government services. Users have come to be seen as 'consumers' or 'clients' and civil society organizations have become significant co-producers of what in the past were largely state functions. It is a dangerous trend that the state is off-loading its larger social responsibilities to private or non-governmental players. It has compounded the problem further. Service institutions are already non-functional service units in the rural areas. But these units are eating away the public purse yet people do not have any hold over them and as a result they rely on private service agencies by paying money. Poverty striken people, instead of coming out from poverty trap, are moving into the poverty trap, because of the fact that they have to pay for the services derived from private agencies whether it is for health or for primary education.

In this context, throughout the world, a uniform solution has been found, that is, devolution of powers and development with a theory of subsidiarity. But the nuances of practicing the decentralization process vary from society to society or region to region. Local conditions determine the nature of decentralization. This new solution is not borrowed from the west like our representative democracy but it is based on the exercise and re-examination of the traditional forms of political representation. While making this exercise it is found that direct democratic mechanisms are increasingly being drawn upon to enable citizens to play a more active role in the decisions which affect their lives. Here also the question unanswered is: how can the weak and meak move into the corridors of power. This is followed by the efforts to deepen democracy through decentralization of powers from the federal government to local institutions through State Governments. Democratic decentralization and participatory governance are in the development discourse due to the growing sense of disillusionment with centralized governance[8].

Governance at present is being performed by different agencies at different levels in a widely spread spectrum[9]. It is strongly believed that in a decentralized process of governance the opportunity is wider for people to participate and it provides a wider representation to hitherto marginalized social segments[10]. It is quite significant that movements are on for the deepening of democracy and the decentralization of powers[11].

The Paradox

Yet another movement is gaining momentum which is called globalization of the economy. Like democratic decentralization, globalization of the economy is also a significant movement in the world[12]. However, this throws up a paradox: while the economy is globalized how can power be decentralized? One should not estimate that globalization will produce positives alone. Globalization and decentralization will bring opportunities as well as threats and how they are handled by the human collectivities will determine the course of development. As aspiration for democracy and development increases among the people of the world, it is presumed that human collectivities will identify the opportunities and work for prosperity and avoid the threats.

India has a remarkable record of achievements in socio-political and economic realms and equally in maintaining a relatively stable and competitive democracy in spite of diverse social and economic groups with variegated interests and conditions. People are dissatisfied with the way our democracy functions. Some even argue that democracy has failed the people. It has come to the stage of declaring that we are incapable of working out democratic institutions. As proof, they point to the growing criminalization of politics, the venality of the political class and the anarchy marking our legislatures. The rich and the middle class make observations and stop there. The poor are deprived of electricity, road, good drinking water, sanitary conditions, social infrastructure and yet they are the people who keep our democratic system surviving by casting their franchise. The rich get all facilities and abstain from performing their earmarked responsibilities.

The Constitution of India, which is the product of the freedom struggle, unequivocally underlines the responsibilities of the State from Article 38 to Article 51 in the following areas: "securing a social order for the promotion of welfare of the people," "ensuring adequate means of livelihood," "ensure the ownership and control of the material resources of the community are so distributed as best to subserve the common good", and "the operation of the economic system does not result in the concentration of wealth and means of production to the determinant." Governance has to be furbished at the grassroots with "units of self-government" in each village. In all the above areas how we have performed is the major question. By subverting self-government at the grassroots by centralizing the governance activities, people's voices are mutilated and development activities are made captives of the administrative machinery. The Commonwealth Foundation, in its study, has brought to light the increasing gap between the people and the government and the ill-treatment meted out to the people at the hands of the government. How to redeem the society from the deep malaise which afflicts it is a big botheration for many[13]. With the introduction of the new economic movement and new formal and legal institutions for governance at the grassroots advantage is a central question to be examined.

Decentralization and Participation

Decentralization is an instrument by which the bases and framework of democracy will be strengthened. Decentralization will be very effective only if people participate in the whole process. So it draws the attention of the whole world. Around eighty countries in the world are moving towards decentralization. Steps are on to strengthen local democracy by increasing the participation of the people in decision-making for achieving development. In the present context, the concepts of decentralization, governance, people's participation and globalization have generated a debate on their meaning and their implications.

Before moving into the discussion, the related concepts have to be defined clearly for a clear better understanding of the discourse on decentralization and participation. Decentralization is a process of devolving powers from higher level authoritative bodies to lowest level institutions in the society for governance. Participation is an act by which the stakeholders involve themselves either on their own or on compulsion in activities right from deciding things to evaluating the same activities which affect their lives directly or indirectly. It is also imperative to understand the backdrop of the decentralization of powers and the participation of people in governance and development.

It is a paradox that for globalization of economy there are protests from all sections of the society and many of such protests are violent also and yet activities are on in a framework developed by the WTO and governments are working vigorously knowing fully the negative implications of globalization. On the contrary though there is open support from all segments and no protest against decentralization of powers yet governments are not so vigorous in devolving powers to the local institutions to act as autonomous institutions. Even the people do not realize the full implications of decentralization of powers. In the domain of decentralization of powers participatory governance is the attractive solution for many problems of many groups and for different aspects of development. Participatory governance is about making government more inclusive and more effective in poverty reduction. Participatory governance will help the poor and marginalized groups to protect their self-respect and self-esteem. It provides scope and space for organized activities of civil society groups. It further provides scope for generating new kinds of leadership at the grassroots committed to development and closer to people. It essentially builds the capacity and capability of the people in managing their affairs with the help of local institutions.

Resilience of Participation

People at the local level organize themselves and protest against the actions of governments. They are being guided by the civil society or the political parties. Affected individuals and groups join together under the guidance of the NGOs or any other civil society organizations. They conduct protest marches and agitate for correcting service delivery systems such as water supply, public distribution. They are micro in nature. Their activities are shortlived. By making *ad hoc* arrangements, government institutions are tackling these micro movements. There are other groups such as organized women under the banner of SHG (self-help groups). They organize themselves for activities and they are proactive and passive but at the same time they also highlight the issues by which they draw the attention of the government. Massive mobilizations are taking place but they are passive. There is yet another group, independent and active in decision-making. They are the temple committees. Temples are owned by the communities. They take independent decisions and one could witness active participation of all segments in this committee which is highly democratic in character. One missing element is women. They are autonomous in every aspect. Yet another group is the traditional community committee managing the commons. They perform the job very well in managing the commons with the active participation of all stakeholders excepting women. Whenever they need any help from the government department, they seek the same also. There is the fishermen's Panchayat. Fishermen have organized themselves for their fishing activities. They collect taxes also. They settle disputes on inter and intra group conflicts. On all occasions they meet and take decisions. Government departments go with the traditional system. But there are no women in the committee.

The above-mentioned cases are the best examples to demonstrate the fact that there is resilience of participation among the people. But their participation is narrow and sectoral and not legitimized. After the emergence of the modern state, many of the activities of the communities have been taken away from them and they have been vested with departments of the government. Government departments have taken over a variety of functions and responsibilities. Many of the services to the community are being delivered by various departments and they are not well regulated and supervised by the participatory management of the people through a system. As a result one can see the poor performance of public institutions.

New Opportunity

The decline of public institutions in terms of their delivery to the poor and the disillusionment of the poor with the public institutions have provided an opportunity to the right wing scholars to raise their voice high on deregulation, reducing public expenditure, reduction of social services and privatization rather than on people's participation in governance, responsiveness of the public institutions to the needs of the poor and more effective forms of democratic state intervention[14]. In this context, the new dispensations, namely, decentralization of power and empowering people have come to occupy the centre stage in the discourse on governance. It is not an exclusively Indian phenomenon. It is a global phenomenon. But the global phenomenon takes shape and root in India also through reforming governance and this reforming governance takes shape through a series of Constitutional Amendments. Of the amendments, the 73rd and the 74th play a significant role in transforming the character of our democracy from representative to participative democracy.

Of the two historic Constitutional Amendments, the 73rd created an opportunity for the people to participate in the process of governance and development. Making the people participate in the process of governance and development is not easy as they have been driven away successfully in the past five decades from the governance and development domain. The bureaucracy has occupied the space vacated by the people but it does not perform the role assigned to it as it has been oriented to act in accordance with the directions of the higher ups. Roughly 40 per cent of the people are always on the periphery and not in the system as participants. They have been branded either as beneficiaries or as petitioners. They are also complacent with the designation as they want to remain in the same space without any responsibility. In a democracy, they are the vibrant voters and their demands cannot be ignored. Their demands are not complicated. Their main demand is to keep their names in the BPL list and be provided with doles. The political climate is such that populism becomes the mainstay in politics for securing votes. Now it is competitive populism. As a result development takes the back seat. But the 73rd Amendment to the Constitution of India brings a totally new paradigm which emphasizes the fact that the beneficiaries have to be transformed into development participants. Economic development is the task of the community for which they have to plan. The Government will facilitate the endeavour and the initiative of the community. To make it happen, it is necessary to create a new mindset.

To perform the above task the participation of the people is an imperative. Before moving into the domain, the meaning of the concept has to be cleared. The concept of participation is perceived differently by different stakeholders and individuals. Participation means a kind of local autonomy in which people discover the possibilities of exercising choice and thereby becoming capable of managing their own development[15]. The UNESCO document defines participation as "collective sustained activity for the purpose of achieving some common objectives, especially a more equitable distribution of the benefits of development"[16]. It happens in the temple festival committee, the committee managing the commons in the villages, self-help groups and other rural traders guild but not in the Panchayat. Participation takes place in Panchayat at a limited level. The real purpose of participation is to develop human capabilities for development, decision-making and action. Parti-cipation should have some key components: (a) it must start from the lowest; (b) participation must take place at all stages; (c) participation must focus on the issues of the poor; (d) participation must be on substance and issues; (e) it alters existing leadership arrangements; (f) it alters the style of leadership; (g) it brings about conflict also in allocating resources.

To operationalize the above points, steps have been taken and ten key ideas have been generated for putting the theory into practice. They are: level of participation, initiation and process, control, power and purpose, role of the practioner, stakeholders and community, partnership, commitment, ownership of ideas and confidence and capacity. At present, generally, participation is conceived as a phenomenon related to rural development. Organi-zations are plenty and they do their functions as they assume. But the predominance of Government institutions has prevented the participation of the people in governance to decide their economic activities. Participation now anchors on the process of decision-making.

After a long gap participation has been made a reality through the 73rd Amendment to the Constitution of India by creating a Gram Sabha in every Gram Panchayat. The Gram Sabha is an assembly of the people who have registered as voters in the Panchayat area. This provision of creating the Gram Sabha has transformed the very character of democracy from representative to direct and participatory democracy. The 73rd Amendment has created the Gram Sabha but activating the Gram Sabha depends on the State Government and the Panchayat leaders. The whole process of development is changed topsy-turvy by which the supply driven development activities have changed into demand driven activities and that too through a planning process with the active involvement and participation of the people. When we talk about the participation of the people in the process of development, it should mean participation of the marginalized, socially excluded categories like Dalits and women. Their participation is more important as socially and politically empowered groups are always participating in governance and share the spoils. The new dispensation provides this new opportunity to these groups hitherto neglected, oppressed and unattended to. Here one has to clearly understand the new meaning of the term and the process. Participation means, it includes the women and Dalits in decision-making and hearing the voices of the above groups for decision-making. But there is always a potential danger in this new opportunity as social groups will organize and reorganize themselves to suit the new requirements as women and Dalits are fielded as candidates on behalf of the husband or family and the higher caste groups.[17] The marginalized groups are present in the power structure but they are not independent as they are under the influence of the backseat drivers. So participation has to start from the Dalits and women that too poor ones. The participation has to be in all stages from the consultative process with the aim of making the poor Dalits and women the owners of development. This has to continue from decision-making to monitoring, evaluation and implementation of all development activities. Participation should be focused more on the issues of the poor. Normally in the whole process one will witness conflict as new groups come to assert themselves and thereby it will alter the leadership–either the leadership style of the present leader would be changed or the leader himself will be changed. Thus participation will bring the government closer to the people or the people will move closer to the government. People will raise their voices collectively through legitimate institutions for substantial issues of the poor people. Such a wonderful opportunity comes through this new dispensation. But it needs concerted effort on two fronts. The Government at the higher level has to create such an ambience and civil society have to mobilize the people for a new dialogue, discourse and discussion on development issues.

But the moot question is to what extent the provisions of the Constitution are translated into action. It is obvious from our experience that many of the vital provisions of the Constitution have not been translated into action[18]. In this context, a new provision in the Constitution creates a new opportunity.

The Question

The question is whether the new opportunity can be utilized by the people. There is an axiom that when power is devolved to a low level institution from a higher level institution with much responsibility and power, social collectivities will organize themselves with different identities to capture the power and so the provision granted by the Constitution will be denied by the community. This new opportunity is to be seen in this light. While reviewing the literature, one finds that interesting trends are emerging from the field. There are forces working silently and subtly against this process of deepening of democracy as a large number of beneficiaries in the present system are going to be affected in this process; wherever the social collectives are already empowered through different identities, they have started asserting themselves in the public space but their assertions are not positively responded to[19]. This creates tension among the collectivities. It gives a sense that this provision creates conflict among the collectivities. It is to be done peacefully.

Whenever Panchayat leaders are from the dominant community, they draw the people for participation but it is not participation but congregation. But whenever the leaders are able to understand the system perfectly, they deliver the services to the level of expectation and, hence, they draw people to the public space for participation at the grassroots. It has to go beyond this stage. Wherever the social collectivities, especially those from the marginalized, are empowered and assertive, they have started asserting themselves and posited a volley of questions in the Gram Sabha to safeguard their interests. Their demands such as continuous drinking water supply to their hamlets to the level of need, effective service delivery from primary health centres, proper distribution of essential commodities from the public distribution systems shops, proper distribution of government benefits to the eligible beneficiaries, making educational institutions of the government function effectively and efficiently as they only cater to the needs of the poor and marginalized. When voices are raised by the marginalized groups, those who hitherto enjoyed power and position felt uncomfortable whether they were people from dominant castes or the bureaucracy. It became evident from the fieldwork that the marginalized groups were not allowed to participate in full as it would destabilize the position of dominant groups which hitherto enjoyed power, status and position. Wherever the marginalized groups have determined to participate there one finds conflict[20]. Because of their numerical strength, they have got the power to alter the leadership. Many have fostered new alliances with Dalits and SHG women to capture power and accordingly the leadership style has been changed[21]. When a new opportunity is being given to the poor and the marginalized, they have started raising their issues pertinent to the issue of piece of land for their shelter, continuous employment opportunity, effective delivery of service to them by the government departments free of cost. Effective and capable leaders will manage the institutions in a transparent way of administration and accommodate the marginalized groups under this fold. Thus a new leadership is emerging because of the participation of the poor and marginalized. There are Panchayat leaders who have converted the Panchayat and Gram Sabha into information centres, discussion centres, guidance centres, and councelling centres by which the poor and marginalized are being helped. But in many places it is seen that efforts are taken to keep the poor and the marginalized away from the corridors of power and the new spaces created for the participation of the poor and marginalized. There are places where intensive conflicts are goings on among the different segments of the committees. One thing is clear that the Constitutional Amendment has created a new avenue and opportunity to the marginalized to go nearer to power and to get things done for them. It is to be noted that what Mahatma Gandhi wanted to achieve through Panchayats by the participation of the people can be achieved by utilizing the new opportunity created through the 73rd Amendment to the Constitution of India, provided the Gandhian scholars and activists contextually conceptualize the Gandhian framework of governance[22]. There is enormous scope for synergy among the informal organizations to work for economic development, social justice and empowerment of people. Through this synergy, the paradigm of governance will be altered. The bottom layers of governance will be strong and thereby the nation will also be strong. The entire strength of the nation will rely on the people and not on institutions.

Conclusion

What is to be done is more important than what has been done as changes are fast in the society. First, to make the people participate, in governance steps have to be taken fast. It is obvious that in a society where people are deeply divided on caste and are under a strong patriarchy one cannot expect that things will be changed fast. It is difficult to remove all the barriers and obstacles at the grassroots for the marginalized to participate in the decision-making process. Mobilizing the poor and marginalized for public action in the context of resistance from above is a stupendous task for which the leaders at the grassroots should have needed skill and capacity. The leaders who are in the process of mobilizing the poor, marginalized and displaced need a strong support base from the civil society to sustain their activities. Likewise the poor and the marginalized need capacity and support for their participation in public discourse as it alters the existing paradigm of governance and development. The present scenario of participation indicates only violence and conflict as the participation of the poor and marginalized has made the people who are at the helm of affairs uncomfortable. Thus powers have to be given to the lowest unit of governance to take vital decisions on issues which affect the people. This will draw more number of people to participate. Normally people are excluded from participation because they are kept away from knowledge consumption, resources and technology. To empower the people, the capability of the people has to be enhanced. But the existing conditions create a gap among the collectivities in terms of knowledge endowment, resource endowment and technology endowment. So the existing gap has to be bridged among the collectivities. For this, policy options have to be sought. Further an innovative and active democratic culture can be created at different levels to allow the excluded to participate in the process of governance and development.

NOTES AND REFERENCES

1. Huntington, S.P., (1991), The Third Wave: *Democratization in the Late Twentieth Century,* London: University of Oklahoma Press.
2. Atul Kohli, "Crisis of Governability" in *Politics in India* (Ed.), Sudipta Kaviraj, (1997), Delhi: Oxford University Press, pp. 383-387.
3. John Gaventa, *"Participatory Local Governance: six propositions for Development",* IDS Paper presented to the Ford Foundation LOGO programme officers' Retreat, June 2001.
4. The World Bank, (2001), *World Development Report 2000-2001, Attacking Poverty,* New York: Oxford University Press.
5. Narayan, D., Chambers, R., Sha, M.K., and Petesch, P., (2000), *Voices of the Poor: Crying Over for Change,* Washington D.C., World Bank, 2000.
6. Common Wealth Foundation, (1999), *Citizens and Governance: Civil Society in the New Millennium,* London: Common Wealth Foundation.
7. Clark, M., and Stewark, J., (1998), *Community Governance, Community Leadership and the New Local Government,* London: Joseph Rowtree Foundation.
8. Manor, J. (1995), *IDS, Bulletin* April.
9. Hooghe, L., and Marks, G., (2003), "Unravelling the Central State, but How? Types of Multi-level Governance", *American Political Science Review,* Vol. 97: No. 2, pp. 233-243.

10. Kripa Ananthapur (2004), *"Interfaces in Local Governance: A Study in Karnataka"* Working Paper No.187, Madras Institute of Development Studies.
11. Manor, J. (1999), *The Political Economy of Democratic Decentralization,* Washington, D.C: The World Bank.
12. Boutros Boutros, Ghali, (2002) *The Interaction between Democracy and Development,* Paris: UNESCO.
13. L.C. Jain, "Liberated: The State, From the Constitution", *Down To Earth,* (January 2005), p. 58.
14. Fung, A., and Wright, E.O., (2001), "Deepening Democracy: Innovations in Empowered Participatory Governance", *Politics and Society,* 29:1, pp. 5-41.
15. Hari Mohan Mathur, (1986), *Administering Development in the Third World Constraints and Choices,* New Delhi: Sage Publications, p.19.
16. UNESCO, (1979), *Meeting of Experts on the Institutional Problems of Participation in the Strategies of Integral Rural Development,* Paris: UNESCO, p.15.
17. G. Palanithurai, *Process and Performance of the Dalits and Women Gram Panchayat Presidents,* New Delhi: Concept Publishing Company, 2005.
18. When a committee was constituted to Review the Constitution, a curious question was raised as when many of the major provisions are operationalised for the benefit of poor and marginalized why a committee to review the Constitution. This was raised by Granvile Austin a Constitutional Pandit who guided many nations in drafting Constitution.
19. G. Palanithurai, *Functional Efficiency of Gram Sabha: A Report to the II State Finance Commission,* Gandhigram: Rajiv Gandhi Chair for Panchayati Raj Studies.
20. G. Palanithurai, *Dalit Leadership in Panchayat* (Monograph), Gandhigram: Rajiv Gandhi Chair for Panchayati Raj Studies, 2003.
21. G. Palanithurai, "Women in Governance for Development at Grassroots", *The Indian Journal of Public Administration,* Vol.L: No.1, (Jan.-Mar. 2004), 347-361.
22. If the Village Swaraj by M.K. Gandhi is reworked in the current context, the 73rd Amendment will fit into the framework of Gandhi. M.K. Gandhi, *Village Swaraj,* Ahmedabad: Navajivan Publishing House, 1962.

16

SECOND GENERATION REFORM IN DECENTRALIZATION

Introduction

The dominant discourse in our country and everywhere in the world in polity and society is 'economic reform'. It is being pursued vigorously in phases. An equally important subject is decentralization of powers, which is also global in character and dynamic in nature. It is also being discussed and deliberated upon throughout the world through not to the extent that globalization was discussed. It is also true that there is strong opposition to globalization by the masses all over the world but activities towards the process of globalization are also fast carried out despite the opposition. All activities are mediated through government by way of policies and decisions. Globalization deepens its roots through state initiated activities and they are being protected and promoted by the state as the state gains resources and many stakeholders in the state will also gain.

It is a paradox that one finds enormous visible support for empowering the people by strengthening Panchayat institutions and yet activities are not carried out speedily. Despite the support, devolution did not take place as it was envisaged, as there are a series of barriers and obstacles. When there are obstacles and barriers in economic reform, the governments, both of the Centre and the State, have taken earnest steps to push the process. But, in the case of devolution of powers, the same Centre and State Governments have not shown much interest. As a result, people have come to understand that the Central Government is also not interested in real devolution. It is a known fact that the majority of the bureaucracy and the majority of the elected representatives of the people to the state legislature and the national parliament are not positive towards devolution of powers and strengthening of the Panchayati Raj System. Further people have been oriented to leave all responsibilities of development to the government and be prepared for enrolling themselves as beneficiaries in the BPL list and, if they are not getting benefits, they have been oriented to write petitions as petitioners. People have lost their participative culture, community perspective and self-dignity. Their aspirations are growing in geometric proportion as competitive populism works through the party system. Against this background, it is necessary to analyse the issues involved in decentralization of powers and to understand the correct position of devolution of powers from the perspective of the State and the Centre. This write up throws light on some of the ongoing activities in pushing the decentralization process and the barriers and stumbling blocks in the process of decentralization of powers.

Background

Economic reform and decentralization of powers are the outcome of the malady-remedy analysis of the then Prime Minister Rajiv Gandhi and they are being pushed vigorously in society, economy and polity. Normally, in any society, there will be resistance to any change in the existing arrangement and system. Particularly, those who are comfortable in the existing order, will resist transformation. People who are going to gain something out of change will not come forward to push the change. It is always through the decision and policy-making machinery that these changes are pursued. For the success of any event or any programme a centralized drive is necessary to prepare the stakeholders to hold their hands on to it. It should be called a descent and ascent process.

Economic reform includes globalization, privatization, liberalization of economy, which has crossed two phases as it is being pursued vigorously by the Central Government and some of the State Governments, despite stiff resistance from the people. Decentralization of powers is a subject of the State Government and, hence, it is also pursued by the centre through its legislation and by making the State Governments to push this decentralization. This decentralization of powers basically shakes the state machinery, as powers have to flow from the state to local bodies and not from the Central Government to the State Government. One Minister from the Government of Tamil Nadu, Mr. Aladi Aruna, in an interview to a magazine, complained that the Central Government refuses to decentralize powers to State Governments but it asks the State Governments to devolve powers to local bodies. The Central Government has taken some of the powers of the State Government. For instance, education was a state subject in the constitution but now it has been shifted to the concurrent list. While evaluating the powers of the State Governments one would say that the Indian State Governments are enjoying the powers of the municipalities of the West. In this context, it is normal that State Governments resist losing powers. The Minister said that decentralization of powers in India has to be visualized against the above backdrop.

While operationalizing the economic reform the government finds only a little impediment or hurdle in the process within the machinery of the government but in the case of decentralization of powers government finds a lot of obstacles and difficulties in the process internally as many in the State Government machinery have to loose power. Externally decentralization has got popular support while for globalization the reception is totally negative. But it is a paradox that still the beneficiaries of the decentralization of powers are not aware of the new dispensation and its implications.

The decentralization of powers is also a centralized drive as it does not take place as per Article 40 of the Constitution at the state level. Right from the Rippon Resolution, till the passage of the 73rd Amendment to the Constitution of India, intentions were good but one would find obstacles and hurdles in the operationalization process.

While pushing these two reforms two types of obstacles are being faced by the Central Government. As for economic reform, people, that too the poor, resist it through the ballot and so it cannot be pursued vigorously as expected. As for decentralization of powers, the hurdles are from the State Government, the bureaucracy and the society itself. The government at the centre takes earnest efforts to tackle the problems in the economy on its own. But, to push decentralization of powers, the Central Government has not ventured as it ventured in the domain of economy. It needs a strong official machinery at the centre to do the exercise, to supervise the devolution process. Moreover the Panchayat is a state subject and it has to be done only through the State Government.

After passing the 73rd and the 74th Amendments to the Constitution of India, it had to be seen whether conformity Acts have been passed in the respective states to implement the decentralization process. The two amendments are the frameworks and basic guidelines, which give direction to State Governments to devolve powers to create institutions at different levels as institutions of self-government. It is to be underlined that the spirit of the amendments is more important than creating a structure to fulfil constitutional obligations. Understanding the spirit of the amendments and the existing constraints in decentralization of powers is the duty of the state leadership and the leader has to act upon the framework with a sense of commitment and political will. It is not a mechanical act to be done by the bureaucrats as they act routinely on the schemes and programmes of the government. It is a process by which institutions have to be created and made functional on a permanent basis for engaging the citizens in a democratic process for effective delivery of services. It needs a new mindset at every level.

The guidelines given by the two constitutional amendments have set a standard at a minimum level of power devolution. They provide enormous scope and potential for expansion and innovation in devolving powers to grassroots institutions. The State Government should prepare itself for a major exercise to share powers and responsibilities with the lower level institutions to carry out activities on the subjects mentioned in the 11th and the 12th schedules. The State Governments have to perform a very deep exercise to evolve a paradigm to transfer powers, functionaries and finance to the grassroots institutions. The deep exercise should end in creating a conformity State Act to confirm the basic principles of the 73rd and the 74th Amendments to the Constitution of India. An opportunity was created to involve all stakeholders to make this exercise broad based for which one year's time was given to all State Governments from the passing of the amendments to passing of the conformity state acts. The seriousness of the State Govern-ments can be easily understood from the very process of enacting the conformity legislation. The conformity legislation should be made after a due process of wide ranging consultation with a variety of stakeholders. The conformity Acts should be evolved through a participatory process wherein the needed environment and ambience would be created in the process of consultation.

After the passing of the conformity Acts for both rural and urban governance at the grassroots, clear cut guidelines have to be evolved as to how this process of transfer of powers, functions, functionaries and finance has to be done in both letter and spirit. Following the above exercise a massive awareness generation programme has to be carried out among the public on how to make use of the new opportunity for their betterment by their participation and involvement. In the same way people have to be mobilised for elections. Elections have to be conducted for all the positions of all the tiers. Once the elections are over, the elected leaders and the officials have to be trained. While training the elected leaders of the local bodies and the functionaries, MLAs, MPs and other officials who are at the helm of affairs have to be sensitized on the potential of the new dispensation.

A careful evaluation and monitoring of the devolution and the functions of the institutions has to be done. In the same way the performance of the Panchayati Raj Institutions has to be assessed. Based on the assessment and evaluation corrective steps have to be taken. All the activities have to be carried out in a movement mode and not in a programme or scheme mode.

During the same period, economic reform initiatives were taken but these activities were monitored and steps were taken to further the initiatives of the reform. But such a kind of initiative was not taken for decentralization of powers. Studies on local body elections, powers, functions, functionaries and finance devolved to local bodies, functioning of the local bodies and service delivery, performance of the institutions, and the obstacles and constraints the local bodies face while performing their role and responsibility, bring forth a great deal of issues to be sorted out by the intervention of the Central Government.

In the context of a coalition government at the centre, exerting pressure on the State Government to devolve powers to local bodies is a difficult task, that too taking a state subject. But there is another argument that, in the context of the states' reluctance to rejuvenate the local body system, the Central Government enacted the 73rd and the 74th Constitutional Amendment Acts. When there was no political will on the part of the state leadership excepting West Bengal and Karnataka, the bill was contemplated and introduced in parliament. Even to implement the present Constitutional Amendment Act, it is necessary to create a political will on the part of the state leadership. In the absence of political will on the part of the state leadership, the centre has to devise a new strategy and mechanism.

While chalking out a strategy the involvement of the State Government has to be ensured as it is the implementing agency and as the Panchayat is the state subject. Regarding the constraints, the previous NDA government did not give adequate attention to them. But the present UPA government has taken a series of steps to initiate action to further the devolution process. This is the second phase of the decentralization of powers. It started from the creation of a separate Ministry for Panchayati Raj and a full-fledged official team at the centre. Previously it was carried out through the Ministry of Rural Development. The Panchayats gave an impression to the public that they are institutions to implement the schemes and programmes of the government. People have never gained an impression that the Panchayats are institutions of local governance as distinct from the functioning of the Centre Government and State Government. Only a few State Governments have created departments for Panchayati Raj. So the creation of the Ministry for Panchayati Raj is a significant step in the right direction.

Following the creation of the Ministry for Panchayati Raj, seven round table conferences have been organised in different parts of the country with the active participation of State Government representatives at the level of Ministers and Secretaries to discuss and decide on different subjects. The details of the round table conferences are given below:

Table 16.1 : Details of the Seven Round Tables of Ministers Incharge of Panchayati Raj (July-December 2004)

Sl. No.	*Date*	*Place and Round Table Number*	*Topics Discussed*
1	2	3	4
1.	24-25 July, 2004	First Round Tables of Ministers incharge of Panchayati Raj - Kolkata	1. Effective Devolution of Functions 2. Effective Devolution of Functionaries 3. Effective Devolution of Finances 4. Gram Sabhas
2.	28-29 August 2004	Second Round Tables of Ministers incharge of Panchayati Raj - Mysore	1. Planning 2. Implementation 3. Parallel Bodies
3.	23-24 September, 2004	Third Round Tables of Ministers incharge of Panchayati Raj - Rajpur	1. The provision of Panchayats (Extension to the Scheduled Areas) Act, 1996 2. Reservation for Women 3. Reservation for Scheduled Castes and Scheduled Tribes
4.	7-8 October, 2004	Fourth Round Tables of Ministers incharge of Panchayati Raj - Chandigarh	1. Panchayati Raj in Union territories 2. Panchayati Raj jurisprudence
5.	28-29 October, 2004	Fifth Round Tables of Ministers incharge of Panchayati Raj - Srinagar	1. Annual reports on the state of the Panchayats (including preparation of a devolution index)

1	2	3	4
6.	27-28 November, 2004	Sixth Round Tables of Ministers incharge of Panchayati Raj - Guwahati	1. Elections 2. Audit
7.	17-18 December, 2004	Seventh Round Tables of Ministers incharge of Panchayati Raj - Jaipur	1. IT enabled E-governance 2. Capacity building and training

Within a short span of 150 days, from the deliberations of the conferences, 150 resolutions on different subjects have been drafted and they are being approved unanimously by the State Governments. These resolutions have to be implemented by all the State Governments as they have agreed to through the resolutions. The resolutions have been circulated to all State Governments. No State Government has ever registered any objection to the resolutions as they are passed unanimously in the round table conferences. Hence it is another set of guidelines and directives which are to be followed by the State Governments. But there is one difference between the position of the Central Government then and now. After the 73rd and the 74th Constitutional Amendments, there was no supervisory and monitoring mechanism but now we have a new monitoring mechanism as we have a full-fledged Ministry at the Centre.

It is necessary to evaluate the resolutions passed in all the seven round table conferences. They are produced below:

Resolutions of Round Tables

Effective Devolution of Functions

1. The Constitution (Article 243G) provides for "devolution", that is, the empowerment of Panchayati Raj Institutions (PRIs) to function as institutions of self-government for the twin purposes of (i) making plans for economic development and social justice for their respective areas, and (ii) implementing programmes of economic development

and social justice in their respective areas, relating to the subjects devolved to the PRIs, including those listed in the Eleventh Schedule, and subject to such conditions as the State may, by law, specify. Therefore, the key objective is to ensure that Panchayati Raj Institutions function as institutions of self-government rather than as mere implementing agencies for other authorities in respect of such functions as may be devolved on them.

2. While devolution must eventually comprise the entire range of subjects provided for in the State legislation in a time-bound manner, States/UTs may prioritize their devolution programme to ensure that for such functions as are prioritized there is full and effective devolution in empowering PRIs as institutions of self-government in respect of these functions.
3. To this end, the essential step is the identification of activities related to the devolved functions with a view to entrusting each of these activities to the appropriate tier of the three-tier system. To the extent possible, there should be no overlapping between tiers in respect of any given activity.
4. In determining the tier of Panchayati Raj System to which any given activity is to be entrusted, the principle of subsidiarity must, to the extent possible, be followed. The principle of subsidiarity states that any activity which can be undertaken at a lower level must be undertaken at the level in preference to being undertaken at any higher level.
5. On the basis of the identification of activities relating to devolved functions, and through the application of the principle of the subsidiarity, States/UTs may review/ undertake time bound activity mapping with a view to completing this exercise within the fiscal year 2004-05.
6. The activity mapping model as evolved in the Ministry of Rural Development in the Report of the Task Force on Devolution of Powers and Functions upon Panchayati Raj Institutions and the information provided about existing State-wise activity mapping in the fact sheets presented to

the Round Table might be drawn upon by State Governments/UT Administrations for preparing their respective activity mapping exercises.

7. The Union Ministry of Panchayati Raj could, on request, furnish technical assistance and expertise to State Governments/UT Administrations to accomplish activity mapping within the time-frame indicated.
8. With a view to promoting a measure of irrevocability of devolved functions, devolution may be routed through legislative measures or, alternatively, by providing a strong legislative framework for devolution through executive orders.

Effective Devolution of Functionaries

9. The devolution of functionaries to the Panchayati Raj Institutions should be patterned on the activity mapping of activities related to devolved functions.
10. Where the devolved activity requires the deputation of State Government officials to assist the elected Panchayati Raj Institutions in planning or implementing the devolved activity, the officials concerned must be primarily responsible to and under the disciplinary supervision and control of the elected authority.
11. With a view to building a cadre of officials and technocrats specialized in the devolved functions of the PRIs, State Governments/UT Administrations may consider instituting a Panchayat Raj Administrative and Technical service, with the State Government discontinuing further recruitment of staff for such devolved functions.
12. (i) Reconceiving the role of District Rural Development Agencies (DRDAs) as an important instrument for Panchayati Raj development through the progressive merger of DRDAs with the District Panchayats. The technical expertise and other facilities of the DRDAs should become available to all tiers of the PRIs under

the overall responsibility and disciplinary control of the elected authority in the PRIs at the appropriate level;

(ii) The activities of the reconceived DRDA with respect to the three-tiers of the Panchayati Raj System should be patterned on the activity map for the devolution of functions, functionaries and funds so that all the three-tiers of PRIs have equitable access to the resources, expertise, facilities and manpower of the DRDAs.

Effective Devolution of Finances

13. The "sound finances" of the Panchayats is a Constitutional obligation enjoined on the States by Article 243-I. In pursuance of this Constitutional obligation, the States and the Centre, in a true spirit of fiscal federalism, should work together to strengthen the finances of the elected local bodies.
14. To this end, the devolution of finances to the three-tiers of the Panchayati Raj System should be patterned on activity mapping for the devolution of functions and functionaries, thus securing effective devolution of powers to the PRIs through the linking of the devolution of finances to the devolution of functions and functionaries.
15. On the basis of the principles adumbrated above, the State Governments might attempt to prepare a road map, to be made effective as soon as possible, and in any case, by the end of the next fiscal year 2005-06, which might include the following components:
    (a) Devolution, tier-wise and based on activity mapping of:
        (i) Planning,
        (ii) Budgeting,
        (iii) Provisioning of finances;
    (b) Inclusion of a Panchayati Raj Institutions component in the budget of each State/Central Government department based on activity mapping;
    (c) Provision of progressively larger untied funds, tier-wise, to the Panchayats by State/Central Governments;

(d) Provision of untied grants from the Planning Commission to the PRIs, tier-wise, based on activity mapping;

(e) Tier-wise allocations, based on activity mapping of the PRIs, of hitherto unallocated grants, if any, made by previous Finance Commissions, and a pre-determined pattern for the tier-wise allocation within a time-bound framework of grants from the 12th and future Finance Commissions;

(f) A schedule, to be determined by each State Government/UT Administration, of the time-frames within which State Finance Commissions should prepare their reports, for the submission of State Finance Commission recommendations, along with Action Taken Reports (ATRs) to the legislature and for the executive to act on recommendations/ATRs endorsed by the State Legislature;

(g) Steps to encourage PRIs to raise their own resources, especially through the provision to "appropriate" revenues raised by them for their own purposes (Article 243-H).

Gram Sabhas

16. Article 243-A of Part IX of the Constitution provides for the establishment of Gram Sabhas to "exercise such a powers and perform such functions at the village level as the Legislature of a State may, by law, provide".

17. A strong system of Gram Sabhas is the indispensable foundation of good governance through Panchayati Raj.

18. Based on the two principles stated above, State Governments may review the extant legislation to determine the legislative and other steps which remain to be taken to ensure that the "Powers" and "Functions" mentioned in Articles 243-A of the Constitution are adequately incorporated in the State Legislation. In particular, the following points may be examined: –

(i) The need for constituting Sabhas below the Gram level (such as Gram Sansad, Upa-Gram Sabha or Ward Sabha, by whatever name called) with the aim of ensuring that the adult population in each ward is given the opportunity of conveying to the Gram Sabha their views on issues coming up for consideration as also holding the elected Ward representative responsible to the adult population in each ward;

(ii) The periodicity of meetings of Gram Sabhas and Ward Sabhas;

(iii) Provision for full and satisfactory consultation with special or disadvantaged categories of the population, such as women, SC/ST, landless labourers etc.;

(iv) Provision for Mahila Sabha meetings, comprising all the adult women of a Ward/Gram Panchayat area, to deliberate upon and decide the modalities of expressing their views in the Gram/Ward Sabhas;

(v) Endowing the Gram/Ward Sabha with meaningful empowerment through such measures as:

   (a) Right/entitlement to all the information required for the Gram/Ward Sabhas to contribute to transparent and good governance, as well as to make the elected Panchayat truly answerable to the Gram/Ward Sabha,

   (b) Approve, before implementation commences, plans and programmes (including budgets) for economic development and social justice prepared by the Gram Panchayat,

   (c) Authorize the issuance of utilization certificates of funds allocated for the plans, projects of programmes of the Panchayats,

   (d) Identification of beneficiaries;

(vi) Such social audit measures may also be appropriately institutionalized at the Block and District level.

Planning

19. There shall be constituted in every State, at the District level, a District Planning Committee (DPC) by the end of the current financial year wherever such DPCs do not already exist.
20. All DPCs should be constituted according to the procedure laid down in the Constitution in Article 243ZD(2).
21. All States must make provision, by law, for the functions relating to District Planning Committees.
22. The District Planning Committee must take into account:
    (i) Resource endowment of the area;
    (ii) Felt needs of the people; and
    (iii) Relative absorptive capacity.
23. As provided for in the Constitution, each tier of the Panchayati Raj System—Village, Intermediate and District—must prepare the perspective Five Year Plan and Annual Plans for their respective jurisdictions. The same exercise should be undertaken in the Municipalities of each district. The DPC should "consolidate" the plans prepared by the Panchayats and Municipalities, as provided for in the Constitution, rather than prepare the District Plan of its own accord or of its own volition.
24. To fine-tune the plans prepared at different levels, as also to undertake the consolidation of plans in the DPC in a technically acceptable sense, State Governments, in accordance with the provisions of Article 243ZD(3)(b), may specify institutions, organisations and individuals, who may assist the Panchayats, Municipalities and DPCs in preparing plans of a technically acceptable nature.
25. To facilitate such planning, the State Government, in accordance with the provision of Article 243ZD, may indicate to each level of the Panchayats and Municipalities, "the extent and type of available resources, whether financial or otherwise".
26. To the extent possible, resources should be made available to the Panchayats and the Municipalities on an untied,

general purpose basis. Where grants are tied to schemes, guidelines should be broad and simple so that they are readily understood by elected representatives at the Panchayat and Municipality level.

27. Recognizing the financial constraints under which most State Governments at present operate, the primary responsibility for providing untied grants and simplified schemes rests with the Union Government and the Planning Commission. The Central Government may, therefore, consider establishing a mechanism at the Centre which will pool together all the Central Government's and Finance Commission's resources with a view to channellising as large proportion of these as possible to the PRIs through the District Rural Development Agencies (DRDAs) which might be renamed District Panchayat Development Agencies (DPDAs) since they will be receiving all the resources of the Central Government rather than just those of the Ministry of Rural Development alone. In any case, wherever State Governments have abolished DRDAs and merged them with Zilla Panchayats, this channel may be used. The proposed DPDA may be so merged with the District Panchayat that its resources, both financial and in terms of technical manpower, are made available to all tiers of the Panchayati Raj System in accordance with the activity maps prepared by the State Governments for each tier of the Panchayati Raj System.

28. Thus, even as in the case of the devolution of functions, functionaries and finances, planning at each level of the PRIs may be undertaken in accordance with activity mapping.

29. The States, depending upon their resource availability, might appropriately strengthen the sound finances of the PRIs so that planning at the District and Sub-District level is based on an indication of the resources available and those that would be made available for the activities devolved on them.

30. In the budgets of State Governments, besides the traditional division between the State Sector, consideration may be given to incorporating a Panchayat Sector in each departmental budget. At the Centre, the Planning Commission, in consultation with the Central Ministers concerned, might work out similar appropriate arrangements.
31. In allotting financial resources to PRIs, the distinction between administrative grants and development grants may be maintained.
32. State Governments may consider incorporating in their State laws provision for the formation of Standing Committees within each Panchayat body to undertake the responsibilities relating to planning and implementation for the subjects allotted to them. These Committees could have an earmarked budget, based on the Panchayats allocating funds to the Standing Committees, depending on their respective responsibilities.
33. In the preparation of District Plans, priority should be given, first, to plans for the provision of basic minimum needs; second, to the provision of services; third, to facilitating Rural Business Hubs; and, fourth, to general economic development.
34. The Planning Commission is requested to ensure that the XI Plan begins with and is founded on District Plans prepared in accordance with the provisions of Part IX and IXA of the Constitution.

Implementation

35. As institutions of local government, Panchayati Raj Institutions are required to not only plan but also to implement such programmes of economic development and social justice as may be "entrusted" to them, including those in relation to the matters listed in the Eleventh Schedule. As such, points relating to implementation parallel those relating to planning. What applied to planning applies *pari passu* to implementation.

36. Article 243G of the Constitution provides for the implementation of schemes to the "entrusted" schemes by PRIs. This means entrusted schemes should be implemented by PRIs and not by line departments.
37. For the effective implementation of entrusted schemes, the chairperson must act as "chairperson-in-council". There must be full activation of subject-related Standing Committees of the Panchayat so that all elected members of the Panchayat participate in managing all aspects of implementation, from conception to approval; from the calling of tenders to the finalization of vendors; and, from conducting supervision of on-going works to the issuing of utilization certificates. Of course, the Gram Sabha needs to be involved in every stage of the process.
38. Effective implementation also requires that the Gram Sabha plays an active role in auditing both the physical and financial performance of the Gram Panchayat's plan, programmes and projects, as also "entrusted" schemes. Three major functions of the Gram Sabha should be incorporated in the legislation of States:—
    (a) Selection of beneficiaries;
    (b) Approval of plans, programmes and projects prepared by the Panchayats;
    (c) Authorization to issue of Utilization Certificates after having verified the progress of a work. It is crucial that the Gram Sabha's social audit functions be written into the law.
39. The adoption of a Citizens' Charter, the Right to Information by law and community-based movements such as *Jan Sunwais* have been found to be greatly effective aids in the exercise of the effective devolution of powers and responsibilities of PRIs. It is, therefore, recommended that a time-bound plan be put in place, along with a built-in system of checks and balances, for ensuring transparency and community participation in the working of the Panchayats.

Parallel Bodies

40. The devolution of functions, functionaries and finances, based on activity mapping, is required by the Constitution (Article 243G) to be devolved to only the Panchayats and not to any parallel body.
41. If, for reasons of institutional constraints, parallel bodies have been set up or are to be set up, these muse be brought into an organic symbiotic relationship with the PRIs at the appropriate level so that PRIs are fully involved with the work of the parallel bodies.
42. To the extent possible, parallel bodies should be established only where indispensable, and invariably in consultation with, and with the collaboration of, the PRIs at the appropriate level.
43. By law, parallel bodies should be required to report periodically to the Gram Sabha(s) so that the community as a whole is kept informed of the activities of parallel bodies.
44. The Central and State Governments may evolve modalities and mechanisms for granting permission to parallel bodies, including those established by foreign and multilateral donor agencies, so that parallel bodies do not undermine the Constitutional authority of PRIs as ''institutions of self-government'' but work together to their mutual benefit and the common benefit of the community.

The Provision of Panchayats (Extension to the Scheduled Areas) Act, 1996 (PESA)

45. The need to consult the tribal communities and their elected representatives in evolving criteria for the constitution of Village Panchayats and Gram Sabhas in Schedule V Areas, to ensure that tribal communities, on the basis of ethnic identities, are constituted into different Gram Sabhas even within a Gram Panchayat area.
46. The need to take steps to implement in a time-bound

framework the provision of PESA in respect of the rights of the Gram Sabhas in Schedule V Areas:

- to identify the beneficiaries of plans, programmes and projects undertaken for economic development and social justice;
- to grant approval to plans/programmes/projects for local development formulated by Village Panchayats;
- to authorize the issue of Certificates of Utilization of Funds for plans, programmes and projects undertaken by Village Panchayats.

47. The need to empower Gram Sabhas and Panchayats in Schedule V Areas:
    - to safeguard community ownership of land and its resources and thus ensure that tribal land is not alienated;
    - to ensure that they are necessarily consulted before any land is acquired for any purpose;
    - to ensure that their right to ownership of Minor Forest Product (MFP) is assured; that they can plan and manage minor water-bodies; and, that they can control and regulate how minor minerals are extracted, used and marketed.
48. To undertake wider consultation with other Government departments in order that the provisions of other legislation not compatible with the provision of PESA are harmonized with the aims and objectives of PESA.

Reservations for Women

49. It is clear that women have been able to enlarge their representation beyond the minimum $33\frac{1}{3}$ per cent prescribed by the Constitution. In Karnataka, 45 per cent of the elected offices are occupied by women and in Uttar Pradesh, 54 per cent of the Zilla Panchayat Presidents are women. Similarly, in Tamil Nadu, 36 per cent seats of chairpersons of Gram Panchayats are occupied by women.

50. In promoting larger social objectives through PRIs, States may be sensitized to issues of gender empowerment so that the unintended consequences of such policies is not to diminish the role of women in Panchayati Raj.
51. The Constitution does provide for the rotation of seats reserved for women but does not prescribe the number of terms for which seats may be reserved before rotation. Seats may be reserved for one term or two terms or more depending upon the provisions made by the State Legislature in the State Law. There are different practices being adopted in the different States and there are different practices under contemplation in several states. This being so, the option to reserve seats for more that one term is open but it is for the State Legislature to decide the number of terms for which seats will remain reserved.
52. The empowerment of women through reservation in the Panchayats is a necessary first step but needs to be reinforced by a number of other measures such as:
    (a) The provision of Women Component Plans in the budgets of the PRIs;
    (b) Linkages with Self-Help Groups (SHGs);
    (c) Adequate training and capacity building;
    (d) Encouragement to political parties to put up women candidates;
    (e) The opportunity to women to serve a full term when they are elected to posts in the PR system;
    (f) Mahila Sabhas (or equivalent) to facilitate women's concerns and priorities being raised in meetings of Gram Sabhas and Ward Sabhas (or equivalent sub-Gram Sabha forums);
    (g) Separate quorum for women's participation in Gram Sabhas and sub-Gram Sabha forums.
53. Reservations to the post of chairpersons in the Panchayati Raj System has been challenged in the courts of law, calling for an appropriate defence of the provisions in the court and jurisprudential clarification of the issues involved.

Reservations for Scheduled Castes and Scheduled Tribes

54. Article 243D provides that seats for SC/ST be reserved on the basis of the SC/ST population in each Panchayat area. While by and large the States are faithfully following the provision of Article 243D, problems arise where the percentage of SC/ST population is very low. The Round Table demonstrated that the cross-State experience of States dealing with this problem was very useful. Such cross-State exchange of practices and experience may be encouraged.

Panchayati Raj in Union Territories

55. As the Union Government has the responsibility for implementing in letter and spirit the provisions of the Constitution relating to Panchayats and Nagarpalikas, every effort might be made towards evolving the Local Self Government Institutions in the Union Territories as a model for the whole country to follow.
56. Recognizing that decided activity mapping is the foundation for the effective devolution of functions, functionaries and finances, the exercise jointly begun between the Union Government and the joint Administration of Daman & Diu and Dadra & Nagar Haveli may be extended to the other Union Territories.
57. With a view to providing a forum for consultation with a representative body of public opinion on issues generally affecting the Union Territories, the Union Ministry of Home Affairs might consider the establishment of an appropriate mechanism to supplement the elected institutions of local self-government.
58. With a view to institutionalizing consultations on matters relating to Panchayati Raj between the Union Government, the administration of the Union Territories and the elected representatives in the Panchayati Raj Institutions (PRIs), the Union Government may consider establishing an

institutional framework within which periodic consultations are held in New Delhi as well as in the Union Territories. The institutional mechanism could meet twice in a year, once in New Delhi and once in each Union Territory by rotation. In establishing this proposed institutional mechanism, the Union Home Ministry may consider co-opting representatives from other Ministries concerned, including the particular Ministry of Panchayati Raj. This institutional mechanism will consider the specifics of the proposal relating to present shortcomings and future work that might emanate from elected representatives on the one hand and Administrators concerned with Panchayati Raj on the other.

59. In respect of Union Territories covered by the Island Development Authority (IDA), the Union Home Ministry may bring to the attention of the Prime Minister's office the need for IDA to review the implementation of Panchayati Raj in the island territories in its biennial meetings.
60. With respect to the implementation of the Forest Conservation Act and Coastal Regulation Zone, the special development problems of the Union Territories may be brought to the attention of the Union Ministry of Environment and Forests by the Union Ministries of Home Affairs and Panchayati Raj with a view to harmonizing the imperatives of the environment with the needs of development to ensure sustainable development.
61. The Union Ministries of Home Affairs and Panchayati Raj may bring to the attention of the Ministry of Finance the special problems with respect to construction material faced by the island Union Territories with a view to seeking how their costs of construction might be reduced.

Panchayati Raj Jurisprudence

62. Given that the 73rd and 74th Amendments are the longest and most detailed amendments made to the Constitution

there is going to be an evolutionary process through case law for establishing a body of jurisprudence relating to Panchayati Raj. Therefore, it is not surprising that there is a large quantum of litigation, some decided by the courts and others pending in the courts, it being understood that there are approximately 74 judgments at the High Court level and other levels of the judicial system. It is estimated that there are approximately 500-600 cases of Panchayati Raj law pending before the courts. At the same time, it is noted that nearly 90 per cent of these cases relate to individual election disputes and, therefore, the number of outstanding basic issues of Panchayati Raj jurisprudence is relatively limited.

63. On the basis of the experience of the 12 years that have lapsed since Parliament passed the legislation relating to Part XI and IX(A) of the Constitution, there is a need to consider uncertainties, ambiguities and inconsistencies in the body of jurisprudence that has evolved since the passage of the PR legislation by Parliament and the States. To this end, it is recommended that the Union Ministry of Panchayati Raj network institutions such as the Bar Association of India, the Indian Law Institute, the Rural Litigation and Entitlement Kendra, the Institute of Social Science, the Society of Indian Law Firms and other expert bodies to review and categorise the available decisions of the courts with a view to preparing a list of jurisprudential points which might be referred, on the one hand, to the authorities concerned in the Union Government, and, subject to the completion of the procedural formalities, to the Law Commission and the Law Commissions which have been set up in some States as appropriate on the other.

64. Annexed is a list of issues of legal and judicial interpretation raised by different participants in the course of the Round Table deliberations. The Union Ministry of Panchayati Raj, in consultation with the appropriate authorities, will attempt to provide clarifications or arrange to provide a forum for further deliberations on these issues.

65. In view of the need to provide State Governments and institutions of local self-government in the PRIs with a well consolidated jurisprudential database, as well as to continuously update the available information on the database, an appropriate institutional mechanism as well as arrangement for dissemination of this information through electronic methods may be prepared by the Union Ministry of Panchayati Raj in consultation with their counterpart departments in the State Governments and Union Territories. Further, keeping in view the need to bring this information to the attention of elected representatives in the PRIs, State Governments may consider making available information on this database in local languages.
66. State Governments may consider appointing legal officers or providing by other means legal assistance to PRIs to enable them to secure jurisprudential clarifications of the existing law and recorded judgments in interpreting and any ambiguity in the law they may experience. It is recognized that a substantial area of jurisprudential ambiguity arises out of subordinate legislation being delayed after the principal legislation is passed. State Governments may make an effort to bridge this gap as rapidly as possible.
67. In terms of Article 243N of the Constitution, it may be desirable for State Legislation to incorporate, as has been the practice earlier, a Memorandum of Local Government so as to harmonize and reconcile legislation relating to the Panchayats with other legislation impinging on the same issue or issues. It might also be desirable to review all extent legislation impinging on the Panchayats to ensure that the authority and powers granted to the Panchayats under Panchayati Raj legislation are not undermined by other contradictory legislation.
68. Bearing in mind initiatives taken by different State Governments to reduce litigation by establishing alternative conciliation and disputes resolution mechanisms relating to PR legislation, State Governments may consider appropriate legislation and administrative measures suited to their

particular conditions to ensure the smooth implementation of legislative provisions.

Annual Reports on the State of the Panchayats (Including Preparation of a Devolution Index)

69. The Round Table was informed that most State Governments have made arrangements for the preparation of annual administrative reports by the Panchayats at each of the three levels and also for these to be consolidated into a single report at the State level. The usual practice is to place such reports on the table of the State Legislature. Further, the format for the preparation of such reports has been standardized by each State and appropriate modifications are carried out from time to time.
70. However, it was generally agreed that there is scope for upgrading these annual administrative reports into a qualitative self-assessment of the progress of Panchayati Raj in each State, allowing for comparisons to be made and lessons to be drawn with respect to:
    (i) Changes effected over time;
    (ii) Changes effected with regard to different components of the Panchayat Raj System;
    (iii) Cross-State comparisons.
71. It was agreed that besides such qualitative assessment, it would be required to put in perspective policy issues that need to be resolved, policy decisions that were taken, and, policy matters that require review. Besides, there needs to be a special emphasis on innovative steps taken. To the extent possible, reports may refer also to innovative steps contemplated or proposed.
72. In order to make the Annual State of the Panchayats Reports comparable across states, it was agreed that such reports should, to the extent possible, include, in addition to existing chapter/section headings, assessments with respect to each of the dimensions of Panchayati Raj on which

consensus has been reached at the seven successive Round Tables of Panchayati Raj Ministers held between July and December 2004. These subject headings include, *inter-alia*:

I. An introductory section with basic statistics about Panchayats.

II. Effective Devolution:
   (a) Devolution of functions.
   (b) Devolution of functionaries.
   (c) Devolution of finances including budget provision for PRIs and the nexus between these three elements of devolution, including, most importantly, activity mapping and any changes therein that might have been affected in the previous year or are proposed for the coming year.

III. Flow of funds to PRIs and tracking thereof.

IV. Gram Sabhas and sub-units of Gram Sabhas.

V. Planning by the Panchayati Raj Institutions, as envisaged in terms of Article 243G read with Article 243ZD of the Constitution.

VI. Implementation of plans, programmes and projects as envisaged in Article 243G of the Constitution.

VII. Rural Business Hubs.

VIII. Three chapters on Reservations: one on reservations for Scheduled Castes, one on reservations for Scheduled Tribes, including implementation of PESA and one on reservations for women.

IX. Elections to the Panchayati Raj Institutions.

X. Action on State Finance Commission Recommendations.

XI. Audit, including formal audit, social audit and audit compliance.

XII. Staffing of Panchayati Raj Institutions.

XIII. IT enabled E-governance for PRIs.

XIV. Capacity building and training.

XV. Parallel Bodies.

XVI. Jurisprudential issues.

XVII. Implementation of Centrally sponsored schemes, State sponsored schemes and Panchayat specific schemes.

XVIII. Constraints faced by PRIs.

The Annual Reports should be concise but comprehensive.

73. It was agreed that a Devolution Index, in the format indicated in the annexe, might be incorporated in the Annual State of the Panchayats Reports. It was emphasized that the Devolution Index will be prepared by the States themselves on the basis of self-assessment but would be available for further evaluation and assessment by academic bodies. In so far as the Union Government or the Planning Commission undertakes any reassessment of any State's Devolution Index, this must be done in consultation with the State concerned. In any system of incentives or rewards which draws upon the Devolution Index, it should be clearly understood that the Index is at best an approximation which cannot, by its nature, capture many of the qualitative aspects of Panchayati Raj. It should also be recognized that any Devolution Index would be more indicative of the institutional environment within which Panchayati Raj is being implemented than capable of capturing outcomes. The Devolution Index should, therefore, be regarded as at best an illustrative guide to be interpreted in terms of the Annual Report as a whole and not as a definitive ranking of either States or performance on specific parameters or for making inter-State comparisons.

74. Drawing upon the Annual State of the Panchayat Reports of the States, or drafts thereof, the Union Ministry of Panchayati Raj will prepare an Annual Report on the State of the Panchayats in the country as a whole and cause this report to be laid on the table of both Houses of Parliament.

Elections

75. The Indian voter is one and indivisible. The principle of parity between parliamentary and assembly elections on the one hand and Panchayat elections on the other must therefore be maintained, especially as it is noticed that people's participation in Panchayat elections is substantial and generally equal to or higher than that in parliamentary / assembly elections. For example, even in States with difficult geographical terrain, 88 per cent of the electorate has participated in Panchayat elections in Himachal Pradesh and 83.5 per cent has participated in Sikkim.
76. While all matters relating to Panchayat elections have been vested by the Constitution in State legislatures/governments, there is a need to work towards commonality, if not uniformity, in election procedures and provisions. To this end, it would be desirable to vest all responsibilities for the election process in State Election Commissions rather than splitting these up, including:
    (i) Preparation of electoral rolls;
    (ii) delimitation of constituencies;
    (iii) reservations and rotations;
    (iv) qualifications of candidates;
    (v) conduct of elections; and
    (vi) functioning as the first stage of adjudication in election disputes.
77. The Union Government might consider the preparation of a model code relating to the supervision, direction and conduct of elections to the Panchayati Raj Institutions (PRIs).
78. With a view to evolving a common electoral roll for all levels of elections, consultations between the Chief Election Commissioner (CEC) and the State Election Commissioners (SECs) might be encouraged with a view to resolving practical problems that might arise in the preparation, maintenance and updating of such electoral

rolls for elections to be held at different times for different levels of Governments. The Panchayat and Nagarpalika wards should be regarded as the building blocks for electoral rolls for all levels of elections.

79. Consideration may be given to incorporating in the laws pertaining to PR elections the same provisions of disclosure as apply to Parliament and State Assembly Elections.
80. The Election Commission of India (ECI) might be approached for establishing a forum for institutional interaction between SECs and ECI on issues such as directives being issued by the State Election Commission, the use of radio broadcasting for disseminating election related information, anomalies arising out of migration, linking delimitation with census operations, uniformity in service conditions of SECs and proposals like sealing the electronic chip in the Electronic Voting Machine (EVM) and not the machine itself, for evidentiary purposes, thereby leaving the machine free for use in Panchayat elections.
81. States may consider according the same salary and emoluments to State Election Commissioners as High Court Judges are entitled to.
82. It is recommended that the Delimitation Commission be regularly in contact with the SECs, who are members of the Commission, to sort out practical difficulties arising out of the delimitation process.
83. To facilitate the use of Electronic Voting Machines (EVMs) in Panchayat elections, the Union Government, in consultation with the Election Commission of India and the SECs, might consider issues relating to the funding of the purchase of EVMs for the use of State Election Commissions.
84. Elections to District Planning Committees provided for in Article 243ZD of the Constitution might also be brought within the purview of State Election Commissions to ensure full conformity with Constitutional provisions, which has not always been the case.

Audit

85. Since local bodies are now institutions of local self-government, it is necessary to upgrade the work of the Director of Local Fund Audit (DLFA) and other similar bodies to the level required by Constitutional imperatives and, to this end, for DLFA and other similar bodies to work in concert with the Comptroller and Auditor General of India (C&AG).
86. In recognition of PRIs being institutions of local self-government, PRIs themselves should be associated with the preparation of standards and norms and the emphasis should be on fund management and fund tracking, rather than simply on fund flow, to ensure greater accountability.
87. In order to ensure that such audit contributes effectively to capping, reducing and eventually eliminating the scope for corruption in Panchayati Raj Institutions (PRIs), it is necessary that audit and accounting standards appropriate to the work of the Panchayats be established and observed. These standards should be elementary, simple and easily comprehensible to the elected representatives and should focus on:
    - when transactions should be looked into;
    - what should be monitored;
    - how the transactions should be documented; and
    - how they should be disclosed.

88. There is a need to establish an internal audit system at every tier of the Panchayati Raj System and to regard the C&AG audit (or audit by bodies certified or technically guided by C&AG) as complementary external audit.
89. Audit, to be effective, might include the establishment of a National Accounting Standards Board (NASB) for local government accounts and be complemented by the establishment of audit commissions or similar regulatory bodies at the State level.

90. Besides, arrangements may be made in State Legislatures for the establishment of Public Accounts Committees (PACs) specifically for PRIs or for the accounts of PRIs to be submitted to PR Committees of the State Legislatures. State level committees, as in Andhra Pradesh, for the settlement of audit paras may also be considered.
91. It may be useful to complement such institutional arrangements by legislating an appropriate Fiscal Responsibility Act for elected local authorities.
92. Outsourcing of accounting by such measures as Village Panchayats being authorized to employ certify Chartered Accountants against standard contracts might be considered.
93. The training of both officials and elected representatives in sound accounting and audit practices is a high priority. To this end, State Governments are invited to make full use of the Regional Training Institutes (RTIs) functioning under the aegis of the C&AG, in particular the RTI at Kolkata which has been declared a centre of excellence, as also of the Institute of Public Auditors of India (IPAI). Substantial additional funding from the Union Government to facilitate training is a high priority.
94. Those State Governments which have not as yet availed of the arrangements for bringing the C&AG into the exercise of accounting and audit, including the C&AG's Technical Guidance and Supervision (TGS) Scheme for the PRIs, are invited to do so and the attention of all concerned is drawn to the publications of the Indian and Audit Accounts Department, in particular:
    (i) Auditing Standards for PRIs and Urban Local Bodies;
    (ii) Guidelines for Certification of Audit of Accounts of PRIs;
    (iii) Training module of Audit of Gram Panchayats.
95. Given the shortage of staff for undertaking formal accounts and audit work in the lakhs of Village Panchayats, thousands of Intermediate Panchayats and hundreds of Zilla Parishads around the country, it is essential that automation and

computerization of accounts be undertaken with all deliberate speed and, to this end, software like the one being prepared by the Xavier Institute of Management, Bhubaneswar, for the Orissa State Government for maintaining day-to-day accounts, which is expected to be ready by early 2004, be deployed as widely as possible.

96. Social audit is an important complement to formal audit and for the sound healthy development of Panchayati Raj, it is essential to establish a symbiotic relationship between social and formal audit.
97. Social audit must necessarily be undertaken at the level of the Gram Sabha but might also be undertaken at higher levels of the Panchayati Raj System, as in West Bengal.
98. For social audit to be effective and based on the best practices available in different States, consideration might be given to the preparation of Social Audit Policies for adoption by State legislatures and governments so as to provide a framework within which social audit is undertaken. Such social audit policies may be targeted at facilitating popular participation in fighting corruption in Panchayats, as also complementing the formal audit process by quality assessment, ascertainment of preferences and the provision of choices. At the same time, Social Audit Policies may provide for institutional measures to prevent needless harassment.
99. To ensure appropriate follow-up to issues raised through social audit, legislative bodies and regulatory authorities might treat social audit resolutions on par with formal audit paras to ensure consideration and disposal within a time bound framework.
100. Given the critical importance of total disclosure of information for effective social audit, States might consider passing Right to Information legislation, taking into account the legislation already on the books in such states as Rajasthan.

IT Enabled E-Governance

101. It is recognized that IT (Information Technology and Communication) is a vital input of capacity for Panchayats so that they can perform their constitutionally and legislatively mandated functions better.
102. IT ought to be primarily positioned as:
    (i) a decision-making support system for Panchayats themselves;
    (ii) a tool for transparency, disclosure of information to citizens social audit;
    (iii) a means for better and convergent delivery of services to citizens;
    (iv) a means of improving internal management and efficiency of Panchayats;
    (v) a means of capacity building of representatives and officials of the Panchayats;
    (vi) an e-Procurement medium.

In this endeavour, the Round Table specifically proposes the following initiatives:

Process Re-engineering

103. All States shall undertake a time bound exercise of process re-engineering in consonance with the activity mapping already being undertaken by them for the functions transferred to the Panchayats with a view to moving the process of decision-making, implementation, disclosure to the public, delivery of services and reporting and dissemination of information to Panchayat representatives to an IT enabled environment.
104. In this exercise regard shall be had to avoid duplication of hardware and software initiatives by different State government departments and agencies.
105. Considering the functional domain of Panchayats that potentially extends to the 29 subject listed in the Eleventh

Schedule, all e-Governance initiatives at the local level have to converge with the appropriate Panchayati Raj Institution as the nodal point.

Data Ownership

106. Such re-engineered processes shall ensure that the ownership of the data collected at the Panchayat level is with that level in the first instance, as the system becomes sustainable when those who use the data feel that they own it.
107. While owning the data, the Panchayat could also operate, outsource or provide space to IT enabled multi-service kiosk centres that provide IT enabled services to the people, including those that fall within the functions of the Panchayats.
108. The Community Service Centres being rolled out by the Ministry of Information Technology at the Centre may be located in the Panchayat offices so that Panchayat services can also be delivered through these Common Services Centres (CSC).

Training

109. There has to be a systematic approach to training of staff and Panchayati Raj members through a cascading mode of use of IT.
110. The opportunities offered by the satellite connectivity provided through the ISRO, including EDUSAT, can be used for undertaking training.
111. While developing training material, regard shall be had to design user friendly approaches that can facilitate training of the illiterate or the neo-literate.

Software

112. Development of common software application packages

with provision for appropriate customization by States is preferred. In this connection, the National Informatics Centre (NIC), which is a government body present in all districts of the country and which has already done considerable software development for Panchayats, may be considered as the primary software provider.

113. It is recommended that NIC strengthen themselves at all levels and provide dedicated staff through creating a Panchayat informatics division, with a time-bound mandate to develop e-Governance solutions to all levels of Panchayats. This will include the strengthening of the District Informatics Office of the NIC to support the District Planning Committee and the Panchayats.
114. The National Panchayat Portal developed by the NIC for the Ministry of Panchayati Raj to become the information hub that links up Panchayats, the State Government and the Central Government for sharing of information, experiences and best practices. As a first step, all State Governments may immediately link and port the contents of their existing Panchayati Raj websites or portals to the National Panchayat Portal and all District, Intermediate and Village Panchayats can be enabled to link up with the portal. The contents can be regularly updated by the respective stakeholders.
115. A repository of software solutions already developed by several States shall be maintained by the Ministry of Panchayati Raj or an institution nominated by it, so that they can be used by other States.
116. Software development shall be primarily undertaken in open source software, with Indian language interface, so as to reduce the cost of replication and licensing.

Hardware

117. States should consider specifying a framework for common standards for hardware and put in place a system for transparent procurement through competitive bidding.

118. Funds for acquisition of hardware could be dovetailed from various sources and could include:
    (i) infrastructure funds available in multilaterally funded projects,
    (ii) Own incomes of Panchayats,
    (iii) Funds recommended by the Finance Commission for the creation and maintenance of databases,
    (iv) Funds sourced from a fund to be created and managed by the Ministry of Panchayati Raj,
    (v) MP and MLA Local Area Development funds,
    (vi) Purchases based on systems of annuity.
119. Considering the present power situation in the country, while procuring hardware, special attention shall be paid to providing reliable and uninterrupted power supply to computer systems. Special emphasis shall be placed on renewable energy devices and systems that consume less energy.

Infrastructure and Connectivity

120. It is recommended that the NIC expand its communication network, NICNET, to link all Panchayats at all levels by using State Wide Area Network funds provided by the Department of Information Technology, Government of India.
121. State Governments can approach ISRO for providing satellite based connectivity in all the States to facilitate connectivity of all Panchayats. The initial infrastructure cost could be considered to be met or supported by an infrastructure fund that could be operated by the Ministry of Panchayati Raj.

Operationalization of the Plan

122. The initiative of empowering Panchayats with IT capacity shall be treated on par with creating national infrastructure such as power, telecom and roads.

123. Formulate a mission mode/empowered committee mode for IT enabled automation of Panchayat institutions with NIC and other solution providers, keeping in view the national e-Governance action plan of the Government of India.

Capacity Building and Training

124. Training and communication ought to reach all PRI functionaries and elected representatives, namely,
   (i) Gram Panchayat Members, Chairpersons and Office bearers,
   (ii) Intermediate Panchayat Members, Chairpersons and Office-bearers,
   (iii) District Panchayat Members, Chairpersons and Office bearers,
   (iv) All officials concerned at National, State, District, Intermediate and Village level, and
   (v) Standing Committee members at all levels.
125. There should be a special effort made towards sensitizing the media, political parties, representatives in the legislatures, civil society organizations and citizens.
126. There must be special campaigns for mobilization of Gram Sabha members.
127. There must be special training for women, SC/ST representatives as well as first time entrants into the Panchayat system within 3 months of their entry.
128. Training for PESA areas should be designed so as to have regard to the cultural traditions and special needs of tribal people.
129. Training and communication should not be viewed as a single one time intervention but should be a continuous, ongoing process leading to enhanced sense of self esteem and confidence. Training should cover both the "before" and "after" election periods. Initial training and communication should reach all elected representatives within one year.

130. For those Panchayat members who need it, a functional literacy training programme should be undertaken immediately after their election.
131. The Panchayats should be encouraged to have a sense of ownership of the training programmes and play a major role in designing the contents and mechanisms of training. To this end, there must be representation for Panchayat members in the governing boards of training institutions that cater to their needs.
132. The contents of the training should press on strategic and technical aspects and should be based on a systematic Training Needs Analysis arrived at through multi-stakeholder consultative workshops, which should precede the design of training modules and materials.
133. There should be a minimum core curriculum that is common across the States adapted to suit local contexts. Core curriculum should include:
    (i) Vision on *purna swaraj* through *Gram swaraj*;
    (ii) Principles of secularism, equality and human rights emanating from the Constitution of India;
    (iii) Gender equity and social justice;
    (iv) Status of human development;
    (v) Poverty alleviation;
    (vi) Participatory planning, implementation and monitoring;
    (vii) Right to information and transparency;
    (viii) Social Audit; and
    (ix) Rules and regulations covering Panchayati Raj.
134. The overall perspective of the training must reinforce issues of social equity, gender sensitivity and justice among all participants in the process of governance through Panchayati Raj, including all levels of the bureaucracy.
135. The thematic curriculum should include:
    (i) Human Resource Management,
    (ii) Natural Resource Management,
    (iii) Disaster Management,
    (iv) Financial management, including own resource management and accounting,

(v) Sectoral approaches into providing basic human needs.

136. The training strategy should be inclusive, participative and interactive and a composite mix of various interventions:
    (i) face-to-face participatory training;
    (ii) exposure visits;
    (iii) peer training/learning;
    (iv) satellite training;
    (v) radio/cassettes/films;
    (vi) Traditional means of communication;
    (vii) Newsletters, updates and digests of replies of Frequently Asked Questions;
    (viii) Resource centres and Help Desks for Panchayats.

137. Training content and processes should be relevant to the ground reality of elected representatives. It should continue to develop and evolve, based on feedback and impact assessment. Training should become a two way process so that feedback can help in reforming the content and process of training, as also result in systematic changes in Panchayat and Government functioning.

138. States should move towards formation of training networks and collectives to share experiences, learn from each other, and access material from each other. States should also institutionalize collaboration with Community Based Organizations at the State, District, and Block level.

139. Training should inspire elected representatives to form federations or collectives and enable them to voice their demands for genuine devolution and development.

140. Trained members should be encouraged to become resource persons for further training of Panchayat representatives in peer to peer learning, both within and outside the State through regional or national tie-ups.

141. Training should include exposure to the best practices through visits to other Panchayats.

142. All open universities may tie-up with IGNOU and build linkages with the SIRDs and other similar institutions engaged in training and capacity building.

143. Training programmes should be designed especially for the secretarial and technical staff working with Panchayats through institutions such as IGNOU. Such training programmes should lead to formal certification on achieving prescribed standards of learning.
144. Education in democracy and the constitutional role of Panchayats as institutions of local self-government should be made part of the school curriculum.
145. It shall be the endeavour of the Central Government to provide in as short a time as possible a Panchayat capacity building fund through the Ministry of Panchayati Raj, which could include a certain percentage of Central transfers specially earmarked for that purpose. Similarly, State Governments should also create a Panchayat Capacity Building Fund for periodic training.
146. There should be a national perspective plan on de-centralized training and capacity building for all PRI functionaries with specific objectives, time frame and resources.
147. States can benefit by the use of pedagogy and training techniques with information accessible to all. The Ministry of Panchayati Raj could develop a repertoire training programmes, including training resources and manuals developed by the Commonwealth. Development of master modules in training in issues of gender, poverty, mass communication etc. could also be developed.
148. Independent training impact assessment studies should be periodically undertaken to assess the outcomes of training and identify emerging needs for follow up.
149. States shall work towards upgradation of training centres such as SIRDs and extension training centres at the district and block level and below.
150. With respect to the training needs of Panchayat members from the Union Territories and States with Sixth Schedule areas, the Government of India should identify a SIRD or a group of institutions that could undertake the training.

Evaluation

Since this new dispensation (decentralization) is centrally driven, everybody expects that the Central Government should take all necessary steps and it is the responsibility of the Central Government to exert pressure on the State Government to devolve powers to local bodies. One has to be realistic and constitutional as the Constitutional Amendment has been passed in the Parliament with two-third majority. It gives a legal connotation that the decision is taken and it is binding on all concerned. Subsequently the State Governments have also agreed to implement the new dispensation. Having committed themselves to devolve powers, the State Governments have to implement the decentralization of powers in letter and spirit. To perform the above exercise the State Governments' leadership should have political will. In the absence of such political will, at least the people should have the will to demand powers legitimately to local bodies. Ultimately powers are to the people. So the demand has to be generated from the people.

Responsibilities are not vested solely with the Ministry of Panchayati Raj. It is only a guiding unit though it has to monitor how effectively the devolution takes place in this country. There are a number of agencies, institutions and organisations involved covertly and overtly in this process of devolving powers to the grassroots institutions and strengthening the institutions to deliver goods and services to the people efficiently and effectively. The major roles are with the Central Government, State Governments, Central Planning Commission, State Planning Commissions, Finance Commission, Election Commission, training institutions, civil society organisations, the media and academic institutions. If these organisations and institutions act and function independently with a sense of commitment and responsibility organically as per the 73rd Constitutional Amendment, activities could have been carried out efficiently. But, unfortunately, all the organisations and institutions which are working in purview of the State Governments, look for guidelines from the State Government instead of acting from the spirit of the Constitutional Amendments. The media and non-government organisations are of course independent and yet they are not oriented towards the perspective of decentralization of powers. So the major responsibility is vested with the State Government.

A lot of efforts have been taken by the UPA Government in strengthening Panchayati Raj. It is to be noted here that a Joint Parliamentary Committee which was constituted by the NDA Government made a thorough analysis of the status of devolution of powers. It indicted both the Central and State Governments for its negligence in taking earnest efforts to devolve powers. The Committee criticized both the Central and State Governments for their lapses. Yet, there was no action. But, after the formation of the UPA Government, a new Ministry was created for Panchayati Raj and its creation has made a point known to all that a new mechanism has been devised to monitor the whole process of decentralization of powers. A Minister was appointed but there was no team. But now it has been created by the Minister by selecting officials sensitive on devolution of powers. It is also known in Indian polity that the Panchayati Raj Minister never gets recognition. Even from the days of S.K. Dey it is history that the Panchayati Raj Minister and the Ministry had to suffer as they always work with the people and for the people. Working in this Ministry, the minister and the officials have to face difficult situations. The Finance Minister who speaks about globalization will get appreciation but the minister who speaks about decentralization will get bricks even though the outward support for decentralization by the public is strong.

By the earnest efforts of the Panchayati Raj Ministry as a follow up to the Round Table Resolutions several steps have been taken. In the resolutions of the Round Table the following points have been reiterated:

1. Panchayats are not implementing agencies,
2. They are institutions of self-government,
3. Power should be given through law,
4. While distributing activities among the three-tiers there should not be any overlapping,

5. Law of subsidiarity has to be maintained,
6. Functionaries have to be fixed corresponding to functions,
7. A Panchayati Raj administrative and technical service cadre has to be created,
8. Merger of DRDA with District Panchayats and change of nomenclature,
9. Finance on the pattern of activity mapping,
10. Financial allocation for Panchayati Raj in State and Central budgets,
11. Larger amount as untied fund for Panchayats,
12. Untied grants to Panchayats from Planning Commission,
13. Gram Sabha has to be strengthened,
14. Ward Sabha can be created,
15. Enabling conditions should be created to ensure women and Dalit participation,
16. Constitution of District Planning Committee in mandatory,
17. Planning exercise has to start from the Panchayat,
18. A women and Dalit component plan could be created,
19. Creation of parallel bodies has to be totally avoided,
20. A strong tie-up between Panchayats and SHGs,
21. Laws contradictory to the 73rd Amendment should be made null and void,
22. Assessment has to be made every year by using Devolution Index,
23. Annual Report on devolution has to be prepared,
24. All complicated issues in elections have to be sorted out by strengthening the Election Commission,
25. Adequate attention has to be given to capacity building,
26. Establishing e-Governance at grassroots,
27. A vibrant accountability has to be established.

The Round Table prevailed upon the Planning Commission that the 12th Finance Commission allocation should be sent to the three-tier Panchayats through the State Government by following the principle of fiscal federalism as per the roles assigned to each tier. The amount transferred to the State Government has to be transferred to the Panchayats within fifteen days failing which the State Government has to pay the interest also to the Panchayats. To transfer funds, Panchayati institutions of all the three-tiers should be in position. Otherwise the State cannot get the allocated money.

Devolution of powers has been resisted by various forces of which the parallel bodies are the major obstacle. The parallel bodies have been designed by the Central Government departments through their schemes and by donor agencies through their projects. The Central Government has created a powerful parallel body called the MPLAD scheme. The State Governments have also followed the same to thwart decentralization by introducing the MLA Constituency Development Fund. The MPLAD has been reviewed and unequivocally it has been stated that it is a colossal waste of money and that the money is misused. Hence the National Advisory Committee has recommended the scheme to be abolished. Once it is done away with the MLA Constituency Development Fund will also be done away with. It has not only recommended the above but also recommended 27 Action Points to the governments. They are:

A. Recommendations for Implementation by the Government of India (GOI)

(i) The additional allocations recommended by the Central Finance Commission to States (and, in particular, the supplementary sources to local governments) should be contingent upon the States fully implementing the suggestions offered by the GOI and also the recommendations of the State Finance Commissions in relation to LSGIs.

(ii) A Devolution Index needs to be prepared for all States and at least one-third of the allocation of Centrally sponsored schemes in the Panchayat functional domain or block grants (when introduced) may be allocated to State Governments on the basis of this Index. The Devolution Index may be prepared by the States based on a framework developed by the GOI.

(iii) PRIs should be the principal agency (instead of District Collectors) for schemes such as MPLADS. The MPLADS funds may be deposited with Zilla Parishads as untied funds and Members of Parliament may indicate their preferences for schemes/programmes to the concerned Zilla Parishad or Block Panchayats/Gram Panchayats, which should be implemented by the Panchayats as part of the overall village/area/district plan.

(iv) Several new schemes, missions and projects such as education mission, health mission, employment guarantee scheme, mid-day meal scheme and universalisation of ICDS programmes are being handled by the Union Government in pursuance of the National Common Minimum Programme. Local self-government institutions should own, manage, monitor and control these new programmes and missions.

(v) Given the Union Government's considerable influence in dealing with States, this can be leveraged to promote State devolution to local governments. The bilateral and multilateral funding agencies may be advised that their support for projects related to the functional domain of local governments as envisaged in the Eleventh and the Twelfth Schedules has to be contingent upon implementation through elected local governments.

(vi) Articles 243N and 243ZF stipulate that all laws inconsistent with Part IX of the Constitution shall lapse upon the expiration of one year from the date on which the 73rd and 74th Amendments came into effect. The Union Government can constitute a task force to identify all such inconsistencies in Union laws as well as in laws in each State for preparing a report within three months. Such inconsistent provisions of law will be deemed to have been repealed, failing which the Union can direct States to ensure conformity with the Constitution and citizens could invoke the writ jurisdiction of the higher judiciary.

(vii) The Eleventh and Twelfth Schedules listed 29 and 18 subjects, which come within the purview of local governments. While the principle of subsidiarity should guide allocation of subjects, the economies of scale, managerial capacity and applicability of services across several Panchayats and other factors will determine a rational division of functions. Such a division will also be State specific, given the diverse historical experiences and different levels/types of evolution of local government tiers. A task force should undertake this activity mapping to be implemented by States. All future allocations and assignment of responsibilities should be based on such distribution of functions.

(viii) The fiscal responsibility and accountability of local governments are the cause of much concern. The Union Government may consider enacting legislation incorporating mandatory measures to promote fiscal prudence and accountability in local governments across the country. Such legislation should also include provisions defining the responsibilities of State and Union Governments in respect of funds flow and personnel matters, so that fairness, predictability and transparency will be institutionalized. The law should encompass non-partisan and fair procedures.

(ix) A national 'IT for Panchayati Raj' programme should be launched immediately with the following three initiatives:

(a) A nationally networked and computerized system, including the treasury system, is a necessary prerequisite to effectively monitor fund flows and utilization and to facilitate devolution. The Union Government will need to launch a fund for this purpose and operationalise the national computerized network within one year.

(b) A series of information outlets like STD/PCO booths for disseminating information and making available various forms, services and transactions to the public can be set up by encouraging local entrepreneurs. A combination of services for the consumption of both the government and the public through these units will make them commercially viable and socially relevant.

(c) Backend support by parallel ICT efforts for computerization of various services can become operational with networking across Gram Panchayats, Taluka Panchayats, Zilla Panchayats and Panchayat departments at the State headquarters.

(x) The concept of district plans/district budgeting should be introduced during the year 2005-06 itself instead of waiting for 2006-07. This should be based on block grants to districts. The basic planning exercise should be undertaken at the Gram Panchayat level. The use of spearhead teams or project facilitation teams should be ensured. The project facilitation teams should be given intensive training through the district capacity building organisation set up with a multi-disciplinary background as part of the Zilla Parishad. The exercise of district planning and district budgeting could be linked to the backward district fund suggested by the Planning Commission but should not be limited to the backward district fund.

(xi) MPs and MLAs ought to periodically declare specific details of the works done under the MPLADS and MLA Fund schemes. Similarly, in Parliament, it is suggested that such details may be shared (with a full discussion with questions raised), which the concerned member may be required to defend.

B. Recommendations for Implementation by State Governments

(i) Concerted efforts towards better accountability and performance of the local bureaucracy need to be pursued. For this purpose, the provisions of the revised Right to Information Bill need to be invoked and implemented particularly with the help of PRIs and other agencies.

(ii) It is necessary to reconsider the current funding system, with added emphasis being placed on Panchayats generating more internal revenues at all the three levels with matching government funds. External funds with no commitment to raise internal resources could make the PRIs irresponsible/corrupt.

(iii) The States have to increase the share of transfers to PRIs from State Governments as untied grants by (a) consoli-dating State schemes with broad rural development objectives into untied grants as Kerala has done; (b) making these grants a share of State revenues; (c) explicitly defining (through state legislation) formulae to allocate grant to Panchayati Raj Institutions; and (d) transferring collection of village taxes, such as land revenue and irrigation tax, to PRIs. The formula of transfer should not only give weightage to population and poverty but also to efficiency in increasing the sources of revenues of PRIs through own and assigned taxes and increasing their capacity to collect.

(iv) The focus of decentralisation should rest on outcome-orientedness rather than just measuring the inputs and evaluating the utilization and percentages thereof. For each tier of LSGI, a Panchayat-metric grid may be evolved, which will become an evaluation framework for any LSGI.

(v) The quality of work done by Panchayats should be closely monitored by teams of media persons, civil society members, such Panchayat leaders from the neighbouring districts as already done excellent work and stakeholders. Based on these reports, the Panchayats should be graded and future funds linked to this grading. Strengthening financial management and audit procedures will also enhance the accountability of local bodies, to their Standing Committees and people's representatives as well to the government.

(vi) Consultations may be held with State Governments to enact and implement PESA uniformly across all the nine States in conformity with the Central Act, with the requisite IEC activities in order to create greater awareness and understanding.

(vii) In the structure of Gram Panchayats, Taluka Panchayats and Zilla Panchayats, there is a disconnect between the Gram Panchayat President and Taluka Panchayat. There ought to be a system of representation of Gram Panchayat Presidents in the Taluka Panchayat with direct election of the Taluka Panchayat President. A similar system ought to be in place for Zilla Panchayats as well.

(viii) Gender empowerment: States may take up measures such as the provision of women component plans in the budgets of PRIs, linkages with self-help groups (SHGs), encouragement to political parties to put up women candidates and opportunity to women to serve a full term (when they are elected to posts in the Panchayati Raj System), Mahila Sabhas (or equivalent) to facilitate women's concerns and priorities being raised in meetings of Gram Sabhas and Ward Sabhas (or equivalent sub-Gram Sabha forums) and shed quorum for womens' participation in Gram Sabhas and Ward sub-Gram Sabha fora.

(ix) The State Governments should put in place and implement a comprehensive training and capacity building programme for elected representatives of local self-government institutions and Panchayati Raj Institutions. Such training programmes should preferably be completed with universal coverage within one year of the holding of elections to these bodies. The Central Government should facilitate and incentivise such programmes through monetary and other support. External expertise should be sought liberally for carrying out these training programmes.

(x) States could be afforded the option of doing away with one of the Panchayat levels after the implications of efficiency, equity and participation have been studied.

(xi) Institutional links between political decentralisation (in the form of PRIs) and administrative decentralisation (in the form of user committees) promoted by external donor projects need to be strengthened.

(xii) Panchayats are often too large: the Kerala Panchayats cover about 23,000 people and the Orissa and West Bengal Panchayats some 15 to 20 villages. Smaller bodies need to be formed for operational purposes. It is suggested that for each function of the Gram Panchayat, the Gram Sabha be a forum where people can volunteer or be selected to be part of the Committee looking after a specific function, e.g. MDM, PDS, FFW, health, Anganwadi, lights, water, etc. A member of the Gram Panchayat can be identified for each of these committees for good-quality service delivery leading to development and excellence.

(C) Recommendations that will Require Legislative Action

(i) Electoral rolls for all elections —local, state and national— should be common. The Constitution provides for separate electoral rolls for local governments. The practice of adopting the Assembly electoral rolls with the Election Commission of India and State Election Commissions functioning in coordination could be universally adopted by consensus and appropriate incentives and assistance provided to facilitate such uniform procedures;

(ii) The State Finance Commission is appointed under Article 243-I and its functions are similar to those envisaged under Article 280 for the Central Finance Commission. Making the two Commissions coterminus will require an Amendment to Article 243-I, facilitating the appointment of a State Finance Commission by the Governor at the expiry of every fifth year, or at such earlier times as the Governor considers necessary;

(iii) Article 243K may be amended to extend the power of reserving constituencies for various sections, and the power of delimitation of constituencies to State Election Commissions, to be exercised in consultation with the State Government.

(iv) The district tier of local government should represent both rural and urban populations. Article 243D needs to be amended facilitating election of a single representative body at the District level for the population, rural or urban. Correspondingly, Article 243ZD (providing for the Committee for District Planning) will become redundant.

Yet another drive at the Centre is that the Departments of the Central Government operating rural development schemes have been made to agree that those schemes have to be implemented through the Panchayats and not through any parallel body and this process has been monitored.

Further the Panchayati Raj Ministry has taken two issues for immediate monitoring: training and District Planning Committee. District Planning Committee activities have been monitored. Under the employment guarantee scheme 50 per cent of the works have to be given to Panchayats, to implement the resolutions and to monitor the activities, periodical meetings of the Ministers of the Panchayati Raj System of the State Governments has been fixed. One meeting was conducted in Kochin.

Before 2007, all Gram Panchayats should be given computer and the administration computerized. The ministry has taken earnest steps to conduct a dialogue with the World Bank on parallel body creation while giving grants to various development projects. In order to strengthen the hands of the Panchayati Raj Ministry, the National Advisory Council has made two sets of recommendations to the Central Government and State Governments.

In order to activate the planning process from below, for the Eleventh Plan period, Panchayati Raj Ministries of all the State Governments will meet during November 2005 to prepare a road map.

Conclusion

The second phase of decentralization started from the creation of a separate Ministry for Panchayati Raj. A person with full understanding of and commitment to decentralization of powers was appointed Minister. The Minister created a full-fledged Ministry and started working on strategies to strengthen the Panchayati Raj System in India. His strategy of convening Round Tables paid rich dividends. As Rajiv Gandhi conducted the DMS meet and came up with the 64th and the 65th Amendments to the Constitution of India, Mani Shankar Aiyar raised the issue of stagnation of power devolution with the State Ministers and Secretaries and arrived at a consensus on the steps to be taken by State Governments, various agencies, organisations and institutions. He got the approval of the State Governments on the resolutions and they are to be implemented with the active intervention of the State Governments. To implement the resolutions pressure has to be built up from the bottom. Civil society organisations, Panchayat leaders and the media have a major role in it. Earnest efforts are made at the level of the Central Government to put the Panchayati Raj Institutions in proper place with the active cooperation of the State Governments. But, to operationalise the efforts, the supporters of Panchayati Raj should be alert and exert pressure on the State Government and on other agencies involved in devolution of powers. More activities have to be generated at the grassroots level. It should be made a people's movement. Women, Dalits and the marginalized have to organise themselves to stake their claim for which civil society organisations have to help each other. In this context the development organisations can form a network and constantly they have to engage themselves on the issues of Panchayati Raj Administration. They can act as support organisations for the Panchayat leaders. The civil society organisations can enable the Panchayati leaders to form their own federation and they can exert pressure on the governments as it is being done in Tamil Nadu. Training institutions have to take keen interest in building the skill, capacity and capability of the Panchayat leaders and change the mindset of the officials through the training programmes. The media has to cover and capture the performance and innovative activities carried out by the Panchayats. Not only that, the media can capture the struggles in the process of empowerment. More focus should be given on the grassroots issues. They can get the support of the academic institutions with regard to Act, rules and procedures relating to Panchayat administration. To make the Panchayat a knowledge centre and a citizens' centre, knowledge institutions have to establish links with Panchayats. Communication institutions have to help Panchayats to be net-worked with the outside world through a set of connectivities. Software companies can design programmes for management of Panchayats and they can be given to Panchayats. Entrepreneur centres can help in creating a business hub in every Village Panchayat. Thus a movement has to be built up from the bottom.

CONCLUSION

Panchayati Raj System has been established in Tamil Nadu as per the 73rd Amendment to the Constitution of India. But there is a substantial gap between the spirit of the 73rd Amendment to the Constitution of India and the content of Tamil Nadu enacted Act, election was conducted, Finance Commission was constituted, Government orders have been passed, the real conception of establishing self- governing institution is faulty as there is no political will on the part of the leader who is in the helm of affairs in the state. It is a paradox in Tamil Nadu that despite poor devolution of powers, functions, functionaries and finance, Panchayat leaders are able to perform very well by overcoming volley of problems and an array of barriers. In this context, leadership matters much in grassroots governance.

While analyzing the Panchayat powers, and finance of Tamil Nadu, one would come to a conclusion that the State Government has demonstrated its intension clear that Panchayats should be put in tight spot without having needed power and resources. The bureaucracy which has to cooperate with Panchayats to carry out the earmarked responsibilities, has started controlling over Panchayats by keeping their administrative control over the Panchayats.

Panchayat leaders have been oriented by the official machinery to carryout the schemes and programmes of the State and Central Governments. As a result the elected representatives have been made as contractors. To carryout the Panchayat Act, Rules, Government Orders, Schemes of both the Centre and State Governments. But these informations are available with government officials and they are not being shared with the Panchayat leaders. As a result Panchayat leaders are depending move on officials not only for resources but also for information.

State Election Commission has been conducting election regularly. But the crux of conduct of election lies in the method in which election is being conducted. In many places community practices have been coupled with constitutional provisions. Panchayat positions are auctioned but no remedial actions. In four Panchayats, communities have challenged the State Government by not allowing the candidates to contest the election.

State Finance Commissions are constituted. The State Finance Commissions have made series of recommendations. Many of the recommendations have not been accepted. But even the accepted recommendations have not been implemented. Hence constitution of Finance Commission is made a ritual rather than a committed act of the State Government.

MPs are spending their schemes in the villages as per the direction of their party men. MLAs are spending their money in the rural areas as per the direction of their party men, District Panchayat divide the entire resources among the members and in carrying out the activities through contractors, Block Panchayat member also follow the path of District Panchayat, sectoral departments have earmarked resources to be spent in the villages and they spend as per their plan. But totally the demands generated by the Panchayats through the participation of people in Gram Sabha. There is no dearth of resources but they are not being spent based on the demands of the people.

Gram Panchayat leaders have to face the people. People have been oriented to receive benefits from the Government. Now people are compelled to pay tax to the Panchayats have high expectations from the Gram Panchayat leaders.

Despite all limitations, barriers and problems many of the Panchayati leaders have done exemplary performance. They are really path finders. They changed the entire environment by their leadership. A few leaders have practically guided the officials and they became role models for MLAs and MPs by their performance and responsiveness.

Media has significant role in the new dispensation. Media have been oriented to cover the governance aspects of the Federal and

State Governments and not local government. Lot of activities are being carried out at the ground. They are not being focused. Micro policies, micro economics, micro politics and micro development are as important as macro development, macro economics and macro politics. The new Panchayati Raj System is not only being prosperity but also establishes social justice and equality. How the new leaders have created new space has to be captured and disseminated. Many of the local problems have been already tackled by these leaders. The methods and strategies are useful to others also. Hence they are to be disseminated.

District Planning Committee was created through the constitution. Every district should have a perspective District Development Plan. It is only in paper in Tamil Nadu. Money is being spent for conducting meeting for District Planning Committee for the past ten years. No district in Tamil Nadu had developed a plan. But many Gram Panchayats have developed plan with the active participation of the people by which Panchayat leaders have tried to reverse the development activities from the mode of supply driven to demand driven. The implement the plan the Panchayat leaders have to wage a revelators battle against bureaucracy.

Elected Women Representatives at the Gram Panchayat level have been trained adequately to manage the Panchayats. The elected leaders have been facilitated to form their own association to discuss about their problems faced by them while discharging their duties and responsibilities. The women leaders have developed their own perception about governance and development. They act on their perceptions.

While discharging their duties and responsibilities, they evolve a new kind of governance which is different from others. They are responsive and they act on alternative paradigm of development. They act for secularism, work for the issues of children and women. They establish partnership with bureaucracy and community based organization. The women leaders who have formed an association have discussed and chalked out future course of action in strengthening the women leadership.

While Tsunami struck the entire coastal area, the role of Panchayati Raj was discussed in terms of relief and rehabilitation works. In many places Panchayat leaders have criticized the State Government for not having consulted them. Started from day one and entire work of relief was done by the Panchayat leaders and the Government has supported the Panchayat for all its activities. Subsequently reconstruction plan was initiated and thereby Panchayats have developed micro plan with the participation of entire communities.

Decentralisation of powers is not a target oriented activity but it is a process oriented activities, but it is a process oriented activity. The main players in the process have to work continuously to further the devolution process as economic reform. Initiatives are on continuously to reform the economy and in the same way decentralisation of power has to be pushed further and in that process the Central Government has a major role in it. The Central Government has taken initiative in the recent years to give a big push to decentralization process.

BIBLIOGRAPHY

Ajit Banerjee, M., and K.A. Chidambaram, (Eds.), *Renewing Governance: Issues and Options,* New Delhi: Tata McGraw Hill Publishing Company, 1996.

Ali Sofi and Anita Rao, "Reinventing Public Administration for 21st Century" *The Indian Journal of Public Administration,* Vol. XLVI: No. 2 April-June 2000.

Aslam, M., *Directory of Panchayati Raj Training Institutions in India,* New Delhi: Rajiv Gandhi Foundation, 2001.

Athreya, V.B. and K.S. Rajeswari, *Women's Participation in Panchayati Raj: A Case Study from Tamil Nadu,* Chennai: M.S. Swaminathan Research Foundation, 1999.

Bandyopadhyay, B., "Administration, Decentralization and Good Governance", *Economic and Political Weekly,* Vol. XXXI: No. 48, (November 30, 1996).

Bandyopadhyay, D. and Amitava Mukerjee (Eds.), *New Issues in Panchayati Raj,* New Delhi: Concept Publishing Company, 2004.

Bandyopadhyay, D., Amitava Mukerjee and Mitali Sen Gavani, *Empowering Panchayats: Handbook for Master Trainers using Participatory Approach,* New Delhi: Concept Publishing Company, 2003.

Bhattacharya, Mohit, "Conceptualizing Good Governance", *The Indian Journal of Public Administration,* Vol. XLIV: No.3, July-September, 1998.

Boutros Boutros, Ghali, *The Interaction between Democracy and Development,* Paris: UNESCO, 2002.

Buch, Nirmala, "Decentralized Governance, Women's Participation and Poverty Eradication", *Women and Political Empowerment* (Eds.) B. Mohanty and S. Haider, New Delhi: Institute of Social Sciences, Devaki Jain, *Panchayati Raj: Women Changing Governance,* New Delhi: UNDP, 1996.

Clark, M., and J. Stewark, *Community Governance, Community Leadership and the New Local Government,* London: Joseph Rowtree Foundation, 1998.

Common Wealth Foundation, *Citizens and Governance: Civil Society in the New Millennium,* London: Commonwealth Foundation, 1999.

Dahlerup, D., "From a Small to a Large Minority: Women in Scandinavism Politics", *Scandinavism Political Studies,* 11:4, 1998.

Dharampal, The Madras Panchayat System Vol-II A General Assessment, New Delhi: Impex India, 1972.

Dwivedi, O.P., "Common Good and Good Governance", *The Indian Journal of Public Administration,* Vol. XLIV: No. 3, July-September, 1998.

Fung, A., and E.O., Wright, (2001), "Deepening Democracy: Innovations in Empowered Participatory Governance", *Politics and Society,* 29:1.

Gaventa, John, "*Participatory Local Governance: Six Propositions for Development*", IDS Paper presented to the Ford Foundation LOGO Programme Officers' Retreat, June 2001.

Ghosh, Jayati, "Development Strategy in India: A Political Economy Perspective" in *Nationalism, Democracy and Development: State and Politics in India* (Eds.), Sugata Bose and Ayesha Jalal, New Delhi: Oxford University Press, 1998.

Gopal Jayal Niraja, "The Governance Agenda: Making Democratic Development Dispensable", *Economic and Political Weekly,* Vol. XXXII: No. 8, (February, 22, 1997), p. 407.

Government of India, *Powers and Functions of Panchayati Raj Institutions A Framework,* New Delhi: Ministry of Rural Development, 1994.

Government of India, *Renewing Local Self-Government in Rural India,* New Delhi: Ministry of Rural Development, 1994.

Government of Tamil Nadu, *Action Taken Report on the Entrustment of Responsibilities to Three-Tier Panchayats,* Chennai: Government of Tamil Nadu, 1999.

Government of Tamil Nadu, *Democratic Decentralization: Powers Entrusted to Panchayati Raj Institutions,* Chennai: Rural Development Department, 1999.

Government of Tamil Nadu, *High Power Committee Report on Entrustment of Powers to three-tier Local Bodies in Tamil Nadu,* Chennai: State Planning Commission, 1998.

Government of Tamil Nadu, *Report on Roles, Responsibilities and Powers Devolved to Panchayats,* Chennai: Government of Tamil Nadu, 1998.

Hari Mohan Mathur, *Administering Development in the Third World Constraints and Choices,* New Delhi: Sage Publications, 1986.

Hooghe, L., and G. Marks "Unraveling the Central State, but How? Types of Multilevel Governance", *American Political Science Review,* Vol. 97: No. 2, 2003.

Huairou Commission, *Advancing Governance Through Peer Learning and Networking - Lessons Learned from Grassroots Women,* 2002.

Huntington, S.P., The Third Wave: *Democratization in the Late Twentieth Century,* London: University of Oklahoma Press, 1991.

Jain, L.C., "Liberated: The State, From the Constitution", *Down To Earth,* January 2005.

Kanter, R.M., "Some Effects of Proportions on Group Life: Skewed Sex Ratios and Responses to Token Women", *American Journal of Sociology,* 82 (1976).

Kohli, Atul, "Crisis of Governability" in *Politics in India* (Ed.), Sudipta Kaviraj, Delhi: Oxford University Press, 1997.

Litvack Jennie, Junaid Ahmed, *Rethinking Decentralization in Developing and Richard Bird Countries,* Washington D.C.: The World Bank, 1998.

Mac Dougal, Linda, *Westminster Women,* London: Vintage, 1998.

Malhotra, Manmohan (Ed.), *New Century: Whose Century,* New Delhi: UBS Publishers and Distributors, 2001.

Manor, James, *The Political Economy of Democratic Decentralization,* Washington DC: The World Bank, 1999.

Minocha, O.P., "Good Governance: New Public Management Perspective", *The Indian Journal of Public Administration,* Vol. XLIV: No. 3, July-September, 1998.

Narayan, D., R. Chambers, M.K. Sha, and P. Petesch, *Voices of the Poor: Crying Over for Change,* Washington D.C., World Bank, 2000.

Norris, Pippa, "Women in European Legislative Elite", *West European Politics,* Vol. 8. No. 4 (1985).

Palanithurai, G., "The Empowerment Process: Women Representatives in Grassroots Institutions in Tamil Nadu", *Indian Social Science Review,* Vol. 6: No.1 (January-June, 2004).

Palanithurai, G., "Women in Governance for Development at Grassroots", *The Indian Journal of Public Administration,* Vol. L: No.1, (Jan-Mar 2004).

Palanithurai, G., *Dalit Leadership in Panchayat* (Monograph), Gandhigram: Rajiv Gandhi Chair for Panchayati Raj Studies, 2003.

Palanithurai, G., *Development Roles Reversed: People's Initiatives and Governments Participation,* (monograph), Gandhigram, Rajiv Gandhi Chair for Panchayati Raj Studies, 2003.

Palanithurai, G., *From Participation to Self-Governance: An Agenda for Restructuring Tamil Nadu Panchayat Act, 1994,* Gandhigram: Department of Political Science and Development Administration, 1998.

Palanithurai, G., *Grassroots Democracy in Indian Society,* New Delhi: Concept Publishing Company, 2000.

Palanithurai, G., *New Panchayat Raj in Tamil Nadu,* New Delhi: Concept Publishing Company, 2003.

Palanithurai, G., *New Panchayat Raj System at Work: An Evaluation,* New Delhi: Concept Publishing Company, 1999.

Palanithurai, G., *Panchayat Raj System in Tamil Nadu: With Original Act,* New Delhi: Concept Publishing Company, 2003.

Palanithurai, G., *Process and Performance of the Dalits and Women Gram Panchayat Presidents,* New Delhi: Concept Publishing Company, 2005.

Palanithurai, G., *Role Perceptions of Legislations: A Case Study of Tamil Nadu,* New Delhi: Konarak Publishers, 1991.

Palanithurai, G., *Tamil Nadu Panchayati Government Act, Rules and Schemes* (in Tamil), Chennai: South Vision, 2002.

Palanithurai, G., "Building Alliances and Capabilities among the elected women representatives of Grassroots institutions", *Womens Link,* Vol. 10, No.1 Jan-Mar. 2004.

Palanithurai, G., "The Genre of Women Leaders in Local Bodies: Experience from Tamil Nadu" *The Indian Journal of Public Administration,* Vol. XLVII: No.1 (January-March 2001).

Palanithurai, G., "Towards Participatory Governance at Grassroots: Synergisation of Rural Communities and Institutions", *South Asian Journal of Socio Political Studies,* Vol. 4, No. 1 Dec 2003.

Palanithurai, G., B.R. Dwaraki and S. Narayanasamy (Eds.), *Major Issues in New Panchayati Raj System,* New Delhi: Kanishka Publications, 1997.

Palanithurai, G., *Capacity Building for Local Body Leaders,* New Delhi: Concept Publishing Company, 2001.

Palanithurai, G., *Empowering People for Prosperity: A Study in New Panchayati Raj System,* New Delhi: Kanishka Publications, 1994.

Palanithurai, G., *Empowerment of Women: Experience of the Elected Women Representatives in Grassroots Institutions,* Gandhigram: Rajiv Gandhi Chair for Panchayati Raj Studies, 2002.

Palanithurai, G., *Evaluation of Performance of Gram Panchayat Presidents in Tamil Nadu,* Vol. I & II, Gandhigram: Rajiv Gandhi Chair for Panchayati Raj Studies, 2004.

Palanithurai, G., *Evaluation of Process and Performance of Gram Panchayat Women and Dalit Presidents in Tamil Nadu,* Gandhigram: Rajiv Gandhi Chair, 2003.

Palanithurai, G., *Grassroots Democracy in Indian Society,* New Delhi: Concept Publishing Company, 1997.

Palanithurai, G., *New Panchayati Raj System: Status and Prospects,* New Delhi: Kaniska Publications, 1996, pp.57-64.

Palanithurai, G., *Panchayats Communities and Social Development,* Gandhigram: Rajiv Gandhi Chair for Panchayati Raj Studies, 2003.

Palanithurai, G. (Ed.), *Empowering People: Issues and Solutions,* New Delhi: Kanishka Publications, 1996.

Ragupathy, V., *Participatory Management of Natural Resources: Irrigation Tanks in Panchayats,* New Delhi: Concept Publishing Company, 2004.

Rajesh Tandon and Ranjita Mohanty, *Civil Society and Governance,* New Delhi: Sanskriti, 2002.

Rajiv Gandhi Foundation, *Charter of Panchayats,* New Delhi: Rajiv Gandhi Foundation, 1998.

Rajiv Gandhi Foundation, *Panchayati Raj in India: Status Report,* New Delhi: Rajiv Gandhi Foundation, 2000.

Rajiv Gandhi Foundation, *Proceedings of the National Seminar on Panchayats,* New Delhi: Rajiv Gandhi Foundation, 1997.

Rajiv Gandhi Foundation, *Revitalization of Panchayati Raj in India,* New Delhi: Rajiv Gandhi Foundation, 1999.

Rajiv Gandhi Foundation, *Voices from Below: Summary Proceedings of Sub-Regional Workshops on Panchayats: Issues and Recommendations,* New Delhi: Rajiv Gandhi Foundation, 2001.

Ray, Sumita, "Women's Struggle in India" *Advocacy Internet,* 5:4, July-August, 2003.

Robert Chambers, *Rural Development: Putting the Last First,* Harlow: Longman Scientific and Technical, 1983.

Rukmani, R., *Panchayati Raj Institutions in Tamil Nadu: A Historical Review,* Chennai: Madras Institute of Development Studies, 1996.

Sarasvathi, *The Madras Panchayat System Vol-I A Historical Survey,* Delhi: Impex India, 1973.

Sharma, Sumedha, 2000, "Women's Ways of Governance", *Participation & Governance*, 7:19 November 2000.

Siddartha, Sivaramakrishnan, *Panchayati Raj Institutions in India — A Society Study for the World Bank,* Washington DC: World Bank, 1999.

Siddartha, Sivaramakrishnan, *Discussion: Challenges and Opportunities for Panchayati Raj,* New Delhi: World Bank, 1999.

Sivaramakrishnan, K.C., *Power to the People: The Politics and Progress of Decentralization*, New Delhi: Konark Publishers Pvt. Ltd., 2000.

Sundaram, K.V., *Decentralized Multi Level Planning,* New Delhi: Concept Publishing Company, 1997.

Suresh Mishra and Rajvir S. Dhaka, *Grassroots Democracy in Action,* New Delhi: Concept Publishing Company, 2004.

The World Bank, *World Development Report 2000-2001, Attacking Poverty,* New York: Oxford University Press, 2001.

The World Bank, *World Development Report, 2004: Making Services Work for Poor People,* Washington DC: The World Bank, 2003.

Thomas Issac T.M., and Richard W. Franke, *Local Democracy and Development,* New Delhi: Left Word, 2000.

Tornquist, Olle, *Politics and Development: A Critical Introduction,* New Delhi: Sage Publications, 1999.

UNESCO, *Meeting of Experts on the Institutional Problems of Participation in the Strategies of Integral Rural Development,* Paris: UNESCO, 1979.

World Bank, *Engendering Development Through Gender Equality in Right, Resources and Voices,* 2001.

World Bank, *Governance: The World Bank's Exercise,* Washington: World Bank, 1994.

INDEX